60

FARRAR
STRAUS
GIROUX

Praise for bitchfest

"Greatest-hits . . . from the pages of *Bitch*, the leading post-postfeminist culture-crit 'zine."   — *The Atlantic*

"*Bitch* begins where . . . other magazines leave off, pointing out the not-so-hidden sexist messages in . . . movies, television shows and other, less enlightened magazines, showing how the media shapes attitudes about women's lives as well as reflecting them . . . While the anthology's title suggests the anger for which feminists have long been known and reviled, it's also funny. Many of the pieces in the book are filled with comic insights, proving that being a feminist is not antithetical to having a sense of humor."   —MALENA WATROUS, *San Francisco Chronicle*

"[*Bitch*] is one of the most consistently engaging and thought-provoking magazines out there, capable of covering serious topics without taking itself too seriously in the process, [and BITCH*fest* is] a sort of greatest hits collection [that will] keep you alternatively amused and outraged . . . There's the occasional and always well-deserved finger-wagging, but BITCH*fest* is above all else a celebration of womanhood [that] will challenge the way you think."
                                    —ANDREW ERVIN, *The Miami Herald*

"With amplitude and spunk, BITCH*fest* provides a provocative study of contemporary culture viewed through a feminist lens . . . Those unfamiliar with *Bitch* may be surprised to discover how much humor exists between its covers. It's refreshing to see that many of these men and women can author serious critiques without taking *themselves* too seriously."
                                    —BETH ANN FENNELLY, *Paste*

"We love *Bitch* and think BITCH*fest* is an essential component of any feminist's library."   —GUERRILLA GIRLS

"*Bitch* is my favorite magazine. It makes feminism fun, relevant, and approachable—it's like the Marlo Thomas of our time."
                                    —JOEL STEIN, *Los Angeles Times*

bitchfest
Edited by Lisa Jervis and Andi Zeisler

LISA JERVIS (right) is the founding editor and publisher of *Bitch*. She lectures regularly about media and feminism on college campuses nationwide and is a founding member of the training and advocacy organization Women in Media & News. Her writing has appeared in *Ms.*, the *San Francisco Chronicle*, *LiP: Informed Revolt*, *Salon*, *Punk Planet*, *The Bust Guide to the New Girl Order* (Penguin), and *Women Who Eat* (Seal Press). ANDI ZEISLER (left) is *Bitch*'s founding editor and current editorial/creative director. Her writing has appeared in *Ms.*, *Mother Jones*, *Bust*, *Utne*, the *San Francisco Chronicle*, the *Women's Review of Books*, and the anthologies *Young Wives' Tales* and *Secrets and Confidences*.

bitchfest

Ten Years of Cultural Criticism
from the Pages of *Bitch* Magazine

Edited by

LISA JERVIS and **ANDI ZEISLER**

Farrar, Straus and Giroux / NEW YORK

Farrar, Straus and Giroux
19 Union Square West, New York 10003

Library of Congress Cataloging-in-Publication Data
BITCHfest : ten years of cultural criticism from the pages of Bitch magazine / edited by
Lisa Jervis and Andi Zeisler.—1st ed.
     p.   cm.
    "All of the essays were previously published, in somewhat different form, in Bitch
Magazine from 1996–2005."
    Includes bibliographical references.
    ISBN-13: 978-0-374-11343-8 (pbk. : alk. paper)
    ISBN-10: 0-374-11343-2 (pbk. : alk. paper)
  1. Feminism—United States. 2. Popular culture—United States.   I. Title: Bitch fest.
II. Miya-Jervis, Lisa.   III. Zeisler, Andi, 1972–   IV. Bitch (San Francisco, Calif.)

   HQ1421.B525 2006
   305.420973'09049—dc22

                      2005036156

Designed by Benjamin Shaykin

www.fsgbooks.com

10 9 8 7 6 5

to our readers

contents

Chapter 3

The *F* Word

Contents

Chapter 7

281 **Confronting the Mainstream**

Chapter 8

328 # Talking Back:
Activism and Pop Culture

Contents

foreword

Margaret Cho

WHENEVER ANYONE HAS CALLED ME A BITCH, I HAVE TAKEN IT as a compliment. To me, a bitch is assertive, unapologetic, demanding, intimidating, intelligent, fiercely protective, in control—all very positive attributes. But it's not supposed to be a compliment, because there's that old, stupid double standard: When men are aggressive and dominant, they are admired, but when a woman possesses those same qualities, she is dismissed and called a bitch.

These days, I strive to be a bitch, because not being one sucks. Not being a bitch means not having your voice heard. Not being a bitch means you agree with all the bullshit. Not being a bitch means you don't appreciate all the other bitches who have come before you. Not being a bitch means since Eve ate that apple, we will forever have to pay for her bitchiness with complacence, obedience, acceptance, closed eyes, and open legs.

There is a dangerous myth going around this country that sexism doesn't exist anymore, that we have gotten past it and that "alarmist" feminists are an outdated nuisance. Warnings like "Oh, watch out—here comes the feminazi!" abound in our culture, as if for a woman, entitling yourself to an opinion puts you on a par with followers of the Third Reich.

Women who are dissatisfied with the status quo are often met with society's ire. They say we are outlaws, we are enemies, we are in need of a "real man" to show us what's what. Here's just one example: When I was seventeen, I went to see a friend's band in a little roadhouse shack about three hours outside of San Francisco. My friend Rebecca and I were almost the only audience members, except for a really drunk guy near the bar. He kept trying to talk to us, and we just ignored him, which just made him try harder to get our attention. We started laughing at him because he was getting madder and madder that we didn't want to have sex with him. After the show, Rebecca and I walked out to my car, which we had parked next to a field. It was very late and very dark and very rural. We got into the car, and as I looked out Rebecca's side, I saw a man's crotch through her window. It belonged to the drunk guy from the bar, a guy now so angry at our independence that he had sobered himself up and was out for revenge. He tried to open the door, but Rebecca had locked it lightning fast. (Feminists have great reflexes.) Screaming, I peeled out of the parking lot as the formerly drunk, now-even-madder mad guy chased after our car with a pair of nunchakus—yes, *nunchakus*—screaming, "BITCH!!! YOU FUCKIN' BITCH!!!!"

Ever since then, I have been proud to be a bitch. Being a bitch meant I could be safe. Being a bitch meant I could take care of myself. Being a bitch has set me free.

That's why I just love *Bitch*. It is essential reading for the modern woman. It never insults my intelligence or my compassion. Its incredible honesty and unflinching critical eye affirm my own suspicions about our unbelievably sexist, racist, homophobic, and hateful world, and make me feel less alone. I believe that a thinking person in today's society can be driven mad by isolation. Everywhere we look we are bombarded with hypocrisy and exploitation, and then monstrous consumerism preying on us while we are weak, constantly threatening to sell us back to ourselves. We need a bitch with a flashlight to guide us through this darkness.

I don't always agree with what's in *Bitch*. It has given me terrible reviews in the past, but that doesn't matter, because it isn't ever afraid to criticize or question anything, and that is rare and admirable. I would like to have some of that quality myself. [For the record, we have also said many nice things about Margaret as well.   —Eds.]

There are women who don't like being called a bitch. There are even women who claim not to be feminists. That just scares me. How can you not be a feminist? How can you allow yourself to be treated like a second-class citizen and not be outraged by it? How can you align yourself with a dominant culture that hates you? It's true that we women are vulnerable to the cultural forces that seek to brainwash us; media, movies, and advertising all conspire to keep women at each other's throats, dreading age and flab and competing for male attention. How can we not buy into it when it seems like everything and everyone is telling us to?

We need clear and rational thinking, some intelligence to cut through the bullshit. *Bitch* is the perfect chaser to the straight-up woman-hate we encounter daily, and there is nothing more refreshing.

introduction

THE AZTECS HAD QUETZALCOATL AND THE UNDERWORLD OF Tlalocan. The Egyptians had Isis and Osiris. The Greeks had Homer. The Elizabethans had Shakespeare. We have *American Idol*, *Us Weekly*, and Angelina Jolie.

Actually, when *Bitch* was born we had *Beverly Hills, 90210*; *Reality Bites*; and *Mademoiselle*. It was 1996, but even then, before the popular advent of the Internet, reality TV, and blogs, pop culture comprised our contemporary oral traditions, shaped our modern myths, and provided us with our gods and goddesses. As freshly minted liberal-arts college graduates with crappy day jobs and a serious media jones, we were prime targets for movies, TV, ads, and glossy magazines, all of which fell over themselves telling us how to dress, what to eat, where to work, where to go after work, whom to lust after, and how to lust, period. More than that, they sought to tell us—as they seek to tell everyone—who we were.

The thing is, we pretty much already knew who we were—or at least who we weren't. We weren't breathy, baby-voiced Kelly, using her bruised-blonde shtick to steal Dylan away from Brenda. We weren't Elizabeth Berkley in *Showgirls*, shtupping Kyle MacLachlan in a pool in hopes of career advancement. We weren't the waifish, expensively clothed girls draped mournfully across the pages of *Vogue* and *Bazaar*. We weren't even Xena, warrior princess. What we were was curious about what those fictional women and their representational peers had to tell us about our cultural take on femininity, "proper" male and female behavior, and women's place in the world.

We were also obsessed with how pop culture treats—and by "treats" we mean ignores, sidelines, and denigrates—feminism. The mid- to late '90s saw the rise of so-called postfeminism. The concept wasn't necessarily new; it was associated with postmodernism and French feminism, and introduced to nonacademics in a 1982 *New York Times Magazine* article titled "Voices From the Post-Feminist Generation." But now, all of a sudden, there were books about postfeminism, references to it in film and literary criticism, even an entire website called the Postfeminist Playground where a group of women wrote about sex, culture, and relationships from a standpoint that assumed a world where the gains of feminism were unequivocal and its goals roundly met.

Postfeminism is, perhaps not surprisingly, very similar to old-fashioned antifeminism; at bottom, it suggests that the culture at large is just fine and that our pervasive, ongoing struggles with, for instance, workplace equality or work/family balance aren't societal problems—they're personal ones. And winking slogans like "Postfeminism: Boys Like It" revealed an image of feminism and feminists that was still loaded down with some very familiar, very unattractive baggage. The term was (and still is) an insult to the legacy of feminism, an eye-rolling suggestion that we need to get over it and move on, already. But postfeminism can exist only in a postsexist world, and we're not there by a long shot.

If we were, feminism wouldn't still have this persistent image problem. A gorgeous woman like Ashley Judd can be loud and proud about being a feminist—even appearing on the cover of *Ms.* in a T-shirt reading "This Is What a Feminist Looks Like"—but when tasked with conjuring up feminism, most of the mainstream media still sees lumpy, frizzy, hairy she-trolls advancing with castrating knives in hand. It's this persistent misconception that sometimes makes our *f* word seem so much more controversial than that other one. Every young feminist has a story about the time she had a run-in with it. Maybe it was chatting with a high-school classmate about an upcoming march for reproductive rights, only to hear her deliver the gentle dis: "Well, I believe in equal rights, but I don't need to march for it." Maybe it was overhearing a male peer complaining in the college dining hall, "I'm here to *learn*, not to hear about women's issues." Maybe it was a new friend responding to an offhand comment about not fitting the girly-girl mold with, "You're not one of those militant feminists, are you?" As twenty-three-year-old women in 1996 (and as thirtysomethings now), we found it ridiculous and enraging that such simple concepts—that women deserve equality, that gender shouldn't determine the course of our lives, and that the world we live in is often arranged in a way that does not serve these goals—freak people out so much. And the sparks of indignation we felt ignited a burning need to correct the record about what both women and feminism can and should be.

That indignation is a big part of why we chose to call the magazine *Bitch*. (If you were wondering about that name, you're not alone.) We'd argue that these days the word "bitch" is as loaded as the term "feminist"— both are lobbed at uppity ladies who dare to speak up and who don't back down. This is not to say that *Bitch* is down with being gratuitously mean or catty; no, we just know that taking a stand is usually more important than being nice. 'Cause here's the thing about "bitch": When it's being used as an insult, the word is most often aimed at women who speak their minds, who have opinions that contradict conventional wisdom, and who don't shy away from expressing them. If being an outspoken woman means being a bitch, we'll take that as a compliment, thanks. And if we do, the word loses its power to hurt us. Furthermore, if we can get people thinking about what they're saying when they use the word, all the better. Last, but certainly not least, "bitch" is efficiently multipurpose—it not only describes who we are when we speak up, it describes the very act of making ourselves heard.

That said, we are aware that the word carries a difficult, complex legacy (though the many people who call the office to berate us about the title may think it's all too simple), as well as the fact that its popularity as an epithet is more sanctioned than ever. And yet we still think, ten years later, that it's the most appropriate title for a magazine that's all about talking back.

And what better to talk back to in this intensely mediated day and age than the boundless source of material that is pop culture? Anyone who protests that a focus on pop culture distracts from "real" feminist issues and lacks a commitment to social change needs to turn on the TV—it's a public gauge of attitudes about everything from abortion (witness all the convenient miscarriages that befall characters torn between keeping and aborting their pregnancies) to poverty (two words: welfare queen) to political power (if *Commander in Chief* is accurate about nothing else, it nails the fact that our first female president will be scrutinized through the lens of gender every day of her working life). Contemporary feminism has always had ties to popular culture and its representation of women: Gloria Steinem's first big break was "I Was a Playboy Bunny," her exposé of the working conditions of the cottontailed waitresses in Hugh Hefner's Playboy Clubs; two of the highest-profile early women's-lib actions were a protest of the Miss America Pageant and a sit-in at *Ladies' Home Journal*.

The notion at the heart of *Bitch* is simply this: If the personal is political, as that famous phrase goes, the pop is even more so. And like that other maxim, its truth doesn't mean that we can ignore the other things that are also political. On the contrary, they all go together—living-wage campaigns with critiques of *Maid in Manhattan*, antiviolence organizing with questions about why the Lifetime channel loves its women so victimized—informing each other to keep this movement vital. The world of pop culture is, in a metaphor that has turned out to be all too close to literal, the marketplace of ideas; if we're not there checking out the wares, we won't be able to respond effectively—or put our own contributions on offer.

At the time we first ventured into the Xerox-and-pasteup world of zine making, we were frustrated readers as much as burgeoning activist writers. We wanted to read something that would put the lie to the cliché of young women the nation over saying, "Well, I'm not a feminist or anything," before voicing their desire for equal treatment. We wanted to read something that would call the news media on its ghettoization of feminist viewpoints and its vicious stone-casting at women like Anita Hill and Patricia Bowman, who stood up to abusive behavior from a future Supreme Court justice and members of the Kennedy family, respectively, and were dragged through the mud for their efforts. We wanted to read something that talked about why all the actresses on the cover of *Vanity Fair* and *Details* and all the female musicians on the cover of *Spin* or *Rolling Stone* were dressed in lingerie with their mouths hanging open. We wanted to read something that talked back to the forces that had been talking to us for years: the ones telling us and countless others that, say, men are useful only for the two-carat diamonds they provide, that without children our lives will be sad and incomplete in spite of dazzling careers and intense friendships, that consumer freedom is just as good as social equality.

We realized that if we wanted to read something like this, we would have to write it ourselves.

As the magazine took shape, we saw in it the potential to be more than a forum to air our complaints—we saw that it could be an agent of real change. If we asked more girls and women to stop and think critically about the pop culture they're encouraged to consume unquestioningly, we figured that maybe in some small way we could contribute to changing its messages. If we could encourage a generation of young women and men to look at the culture around them through a lens that prioritized gender representations, they'd be inspired to protest that culture—and maybe by the time those people became ad executives, TV producers, and studio heads, they'd be creating a pop culture that truly reflects all genders accurately. We wanted to remind people, ourselves included, to ask questions about the messages in their media and to speak up—to each other and to the corporations and culture makers behind those messages.

We still do.

bitchfest

1

. . . .

Hitting Puberty

BEING A GIRL HAS ALWAYS MEANT NAVIGATING A TIDE OF
mixed signals and unexplained directives, and when I was ten, none filled
me with more free-floating dread than the Movies. If you're a woman between the ages of twenty-five and forty-five, you know what I'm talking
about: that fateful day in fifth or sixth grade when the boys and girls were
separated (the boys herded, invariably, into the school gym), sat down, and
told, via filmstrip, all about what makes them different.

Those of us schooled by Judy Blume's *Are You There God? It's Me, Margaret* knew, if only vaguely, that there was something called a period that
happened to girls that made us older, mature, even special. Blume didn't
fully explain the mechanics of menstruation, focusing instead on its importance as a badge of maturity and the fact that it required some cryptic accessories (a belt?) to accommodate; the filmstrip we watched that day didn't
do much better. I don't even recall a mention of blood, much less any step-
by-step explanation of how the monthly process happened and why it was
necessary. All information was disseminated on a need-to-know basis. And
we, as girls, apparently didn't need to know what was happening to our bodies. Nobody told us, for instance, that growing pains are actually more than
a figure of speech (a fact that would have saved me, a few years later, from
being convinced that I had nipple cancer). And there was no mention of the
important by-products of our changing bodies, either—the fact that they

might really bum us out, cause us to be jealous of and mean to each other, or attract unwanted attention.

When the boys and girls were reunited in the afternoon, after the Movies, everything had changed. Neither side knew what had gone on with the other, but we now regarded each other warily, armed with our new (if cloudy) knowledge that though we played kickball together at recess and all trapped bugs on the sidewalks before dinner, we were now defined, irrevocably, against each other. I don't know if the boys got a parting gift, but the girls did: a pastel pamphlet, handed out after the filmstrip, produced by Modess and directively titled "Growing Up and Liking It."

Puberty is a time when girls by anatomy become girls by imperative, socialized into a world where we're supposed to be more excited about a big box of maxipads than about, say, the wonders of the solar system. Tomboys are instructed to be more "ladylike." Boys are transformed from buddies into people we're supposed to either stay away from or develop crushes on. Instead of digging on our own unique qualities—our ability to draw or skateboard or double Dutch—we start focusing our energies on fitting in with everyone else, zooming unhappily in on our perceived shortcomings with the precision of the Hubble telescope.

Since 1992, when Lyn Mikel Brown and Carol Gilligan published *Meeting at the Crossroads*, their landmark study on how girls' self-esteem plunges at puberty, we've slowly become aware that the problem is a universal one, affecting girls of all places and races and classes. Mary Pipher, whose 1994 book *Reviving Ophelia* built on Brown and Gilligan's research and prescribed ways for adults to help the girls in their lives through this time of crisis, identified female puberty in America as an update of Betty Friedan's "problem with no name," writing that "America today limits girls' development, truncates their wholeness, and leaves many of them traumatized."

The problem may have had no name, but in the years since Brown, Gilligan, and Pipher identified it, the subject of puberty and its discontents has yielded some amazingly lucid, bracing, and resonant pop culture. From books (Dorothy Allison's *Bastard Out of Carolina*, Danzy Senna's *Caucasia*, Peggy Orenstein's nonfiction study *Schoolgirls*) to TV (*My So-Called Life*, *Freaks and Geeks*) to movies (*Welcome to the Dollhouse*, *Girls Town*, *Thirteen*), the past decade-plus has given girls a bigger platform than ever before from which to talk about growing up and not liking it one bit.

But at the same time, it's also made puberty and adolescence more visible than ever before. We've always been obsessed with youth, but the age of media consent appears to be dropping ever lower. Adults read books about a pubescent wizard and get obsessed with *The O.C.* Teen starlets, once confined to the pages of *Seventeen* and *YM*, are sprawled all over the covers of *Vogue* and *Elle*, which have in turn spawned their own teen versions. Journalists who wring their hands over the thirteen-year-olds who traipse the streets in hoochie-mama ensembles buy their own ass-enhancing pants at Forever 21. The blurring of boundaries between childhood and adulthood in pop representations is sometimes cute and poignant, as in movies like *Freaky Friday* and its remake or those wacky Gilmore Girls, but more often disturbing—as when frat-house retailer Abercrombie & Fitch began peddling tween-size thong panties printed with cutesy come-ons for the training-bra set.

And ever since published studies of teen girls and relational aggression—Rachel Simmons's *Odd Girl Out*, Lyn Mikel Brown's *Raising Their Voices*, and Rosalind Wiseman's *Queen Bees and Wannabes*, among others—became big media news, the nuances of girls' untamed hostility have been shorthanded to bemoan an epidemic of "mean girls." The result is that media outlets have been quick to broadcast the most sensational examples of this girl trouble—girls who physically hurt each other (or worse, hurt or humiliate boys)—but less inclined to draw attention to the culture that does so much to foster our anger and resentment.

It's a difficult time, puberty, and maybe an acknowledgment of that was exactly what those stupid filmstrips, with their clinical, bloodless diagrams and stilted voice-overs, were trying to get across. But on the upside, puberty is often a time when girls in the process of being socialized into their gender are also politicized by it. They have questions that can't be answered by the pink and blue playbooks we've been using to define girls and boys since forever. They don't see why they should accept the status quo rules and limitations—don't climb trees, don't call boys, don't show your smarts—assigned to them just because they happen to be female. They challenge the lessons of sex, race, manners, mores, and everything else about girlhood that we learn everywhere from MTV to *Tiger Beat* to Toys "R" Us. They offer clear insights on crucial intersections of feminist consciousness and pop product. If the culture at large would just listen, we all might learn something.   —A.Z.

Amazon Women on the Moon

Remembering Femininity in the Video Age

Andi Zeisler / WINTER 1996

LIKE SOME GRIZZLED OLD-TIMER SITTING ON THE PORCH OF
the homestead talking about the good old days, I think back to the first time
I saw MTV and pity the prepubescents of today who didn't have the luck to
see, as I did, the wonder of MTV when it first aired. I was eight years old,
alone in my living room, and somehow I knew that I was witnessing a
tremendous event: a connection with something that just wasn't accessible
through after-school cartoons or *Gilligan's Island* reruns. When I recall what
I saw back then, my perception of those early videos creates the memory
that resonates in my TV-addled mind as the truth. And what I remember
best are the images of women I saw on MTV. I'm aware of those representations in a different way than I was in those first golden days when I sat
glued to the small screen, clutching a handful of Fritos. What I say about
these images now comes from filtering them through a screen of theory
and history and related bullshit, but it still comes from what I saw back
then. The women of MTV were not merely women; rather, they were onscreen archetypes of what a video-age woman could be, and they were indelibly printed on my young brain.

6

The Androgyne

By the time the first little MTV spaceman planted his flag on the screens of cable-blessed homes, androgyny in rock music was old news. This was, after all, the post-glam-rock early 1980s. The New York Dolls, Patti Smith, David Bowie, and many others had been praised up and down not only for their musical achievements but also for their knack for appropriating/mocking the styles of the opposite sex. But the legions of suburban tykes lounging in our beanbag chairs in front of the tube didn't know about that. All we knew was that there was a huge number of girly-looking guys staring out at us from the other side of the TV screen, and we were mesmerized. Through Adam Ant and Duran Duran, I absorbed the concept of androgyny unconsciously as I giggled dreamy-eyed over these grown men with made-up faces, these boys who looked too much like girls to be the "opposite" sex.

But then there were the actual girls: Joan Jett, who wore head-to-toe black leather and reveled in crunchy cock-rock riffs in her video for "I Love Rock 'N' Roll"; and skinny, imperious Chrissie Hynde of the Pretenders. These women's physical images incorporated a litany of bad-boy references, from pre-zirconium Elvis to Marlon Brando to Keith Richards. They were aping the style of men whose blatant sexuality made them "dangerous." Not so much rejecting femininity as cloaking it in the historical acceptibility of male rebellion, these women were insinuating themselves into the badass canon. I didn't consciously think that they looked like boys, but when I saw the video for the Pretenders' "Brass in Pocket," I thought that Chrissie Hynde in a waitress's uniform was all wrong. And the end of the video, when she runs out of the diner and hops on the tough guy's motorcycle—well, that was all wrong, too. Anyone who had seen the video for "Tattooed Love Boys" knew that Chrissie would never let her ass be grabbed by a customer and then go for a ride on his hog. She'd get on her own motorcycle and peel out of the diner parking lot, spraying that loser with a mouthful of gravel.

Perhaps the most memorable androgyne of early MTV was Annie Lennox of the Eurythmics. In their first video, "Sweet Dreams (Are Made of This)," Annie wore a man's black suit and held a riding crop (or maybe it was a pointer), her bright-orange flattop rising out of the ensemble over her placidly menacing, masklike face. The dangerous sexuality of Joan and

Chrissie's leather pants was here replaced by the more dangerous sexuality of total gender unrecognizability. No real precedent for female-to-male cross-dressing had been set on television at this point, although the madcap hilarity of men impersonating women had been proved many times over, from Milton Berle to M*A*S*H. The employment of cross-dressing for noncomedic purposes, and by a woman, was jarring. The whispering among my elementary-school friends about this video yielded only one possible conclusion—that Annie Lennox must be a lesbian.

The Future Freak

The second image that appeared consistently on early MTV can best be described as the Space-Age Future Freak. The SAFF, like the Androgyne, took more than one form. There was the faraway-eyed, operatic Kate Bush, the future-Barbie frontwomen of Missing Persons and Berlin, and the space-age amazon Grace Jones, among others. But unlike the Androgyne, the SAFF had no basis in history other than the collective projection of "the future" that held 1980s media in its thrall. Computers, NASA, and ever-expanding medical and industrial technologies were spurring us on to the future, but what about humanity? The fears of future dehumanization, particularly of women, were given paranoid form in movies like Blade Runner and Liquid Sky, where futuristic females invariably took on the form of alien succubi, preying on the hapless male heroes. The sexual female, given power, mutated into something evil that had to be stopped by the likes of Harrison Ford. The message of these films? Future women are going to be scary, castrating sexual deviants. The video counterparts of these cinematic women presented an alternative to traditional notions of what constitutes femaleness. The SAFF was not soft, not yielding, and seemed entirely her own invention. Her voice was clearly that of a woman, yet it was not a "feminine" voice—it was robotic, as Grace Jones's was, or it was the ethereal, otherworldly siren song of Kate Bush.

But the SAFF's physical image was hyperfeminized, caricatured. In the video for Missing Persons' "Destination Unknown," lead singer Dale Bozzio sported a floor-length white mane, a Mylar-and-bubble-wrap dress, and spike heels, and she sang in a high-frequency baby-doll voice while staring at her own bizarre face in a smoky mirror. This image plays into classic notions of woman as the infantlike, narcissistic other. But despite the contradictions inherent in the SAFF persona, she defined the future—unknowable, cloudy, and scary.

The Bad Girl

This MTV archetype was perhaps the most familiar one. As tough as the Androgyne but less masculine, earthier than the Future Freak, the Bad Girl was like a canny, fun older sister—smart and sexy and cut-the-shit direct. All her songs spoke directly to someone—presumably a guy—who was trying to mess with her, and she wasn't having it. Pat Benatar, Toni Basil, the Flirts, the Waitresses, and Patti Smythe of Scandal all embodied a kind of fishnet-stockinged consciousness that allowed them to seem like slutty girls while harboring a clearheaded intelligence and the occasional subversive agenda. Toni Basil's "Mickey" video exploited the whole good girl/bad girl cheerleader motif, with Toni cartwheeling around, pompoms in hand, while delivering the genderfuck line, "Come on and give it to me, any way you can / Any way you wanna do it, I'll take it like a man." Pat Benatar took the Bad Girl role one step further, using the video format to star in mini-movies in which she took on the personae of other bad girls. In "Shadows of the Night," she portrays a 1940s Rosie the Riveter type who dreams of being a ruthless, glamorous double agent. And in "Love Is a Battlefield," probably the tour de force of her video career, Pat plays a teenage runaway whose foray into the big city leads to her working in a seedy dance parlor with other unlucky women. But Pat mobilizes the women into a line-dance uprising against their evil pimp, and liberation ensues. Go on with your bad self, Pat!

Sadly, these would turn out to be the salad days of the Bad Girl, because once MTV realized that their main audience comprised adolescent boys and their hard-ons, the marketing dynamic took over and these women all but vanished. Pat Benatar and Toni Basil were replaced by nameless inflatobreasted bimbos who writhed in videos by poufy-haired lite-metal bands like Warrant and Poison, portraying groupies, porn actresses, and girlfriends. MTV wanted you to believe that this was what a Bad Girl was, but even those of us just graduating from our training bras knew the vast difference between a player and a plaything.

Little by little, the archetypes of early MTV disappeared from the screen, displaced by the ever-increasing popularity of the channel and its ability to create and crush images and fads with heartless precision. The use of women primarily as cheese-metal video ornaments made it necessary for those women who were actual musicians to protect themselves from winding up as yet another babe spread-eagled on top of a Camaro. So women like Tracy Chapman, Suzanne Vega, and the Indigo Girls ushered in a new era of no-frills videos—no leather pants, no bubble-wrap dresses, no Benataresque role playing. They played solid, admirable music that also happened to make boring-as-hell video viewing. Having experienced the myriad over-the-top moments of MTV's first inception, there was no substitute. Well, there was Madonna, who aimed to amass all the aspects of the Bad Girl, the SAFF, and the Androgyne into one package, but that's a whole other essay.

Those early images and videos were powerful. They were novelty and stereotype and affirmation. They provided young girls with ideas of rebellion, sex, and self-sufficiency that couldn't be found in the pages of *Young Miss*. They allowed us to think critically and find fault with other images of women that we saw not only on MTV but also in other media. They inspired us to rock out. If you turn on MTV today, in between segments of *Beauty and the Beach* and *The Real World*, you might—if you're lucky—see something that reminds you of what MTV once was: that brave new world where the women talked tough and the men looked pretty.

Rubyfruit Jungle Gym

An Annotated Bibliography of the Lesbian Young Adult Novel

Lisa Jervis / WINTER 1998

THE GENRE OF YOUNG-ADULT FICTION (YA TO LIBRARIANS and other bookish folks) has always been kinda pedantic, in the best possible way. YA novels have always provided a sort of educational service, a vehicle for young people to address important issues in their lives through narrative; they're the way the culture at large transmits nuanced information about, say, the death of a family member or a first period. So when YA literature takes on lesbianism, it usually results in one of two things: a force of indoctrination into the cultural codes of compulsory heterosexuality, or a lesson in gay pride.

Lesbian books generally go like so: Girl meets girl, each feels something for the other; they spend some time (separately) examining/feeling guilty about/feeling confused about their feelings; they finally talk to each other; they begin a relationship; someone else finds out; something horrible happens; they break up/stay together/renounce homosexuality. Too often, even well-meaning lesbian YAs dole out shame and punishment to their protagonists: rape or expulsion from school, family, and community.

However, the affirming lesbian teen novel has begun to flower—not surprising, considering the progress that has been made in lesbian, gay, and bisexual rights. Fictional young lovers still get in trouble when they're caught having sex; high-school students still scrawl ugly graffiti about suspected sexual practices. But queer YA characters are beginning to doubt themselves less and love each other more. Slowly but surely, we're reaching a point at which het YA fiction has been for years: Lesbian teens can grab more and more reassurance, advice, and inspiration from the genre. Where and how much? Let's see . . .

Patience and Sarah by Isabel Miller (Fawcett Crest Books, 1969)

Set in 1816 Connecticut and "suggested by the life of" two actual postcolonial women, *P & S* is a historical novel with a twist.

JACKET COPY: "Bold, innocent, and strange . . . that was their love."

THE RELATIONSHIP STARTS . . . Head over heels. Butch Sarah meets femme Patience while stocking her woodpile. Before you know it, the two are smooching.

CAN THEY FESS UP? Well, Sarah's always been conspicuously masculine, and Patience lives in her brother's house, so people suspect plenty. And it all comes to a head when Patience's sister-in-law catches them in bed together.

WHEN SOMEONE FINDS OUT . . . Miscommunication and family disapproval at first keep them from leaving their small community together but later force them out. Does that count as punishment? Yes, in that they can't stay where they are and be accepted; no, in that they'd already hatched plans to leave and start a life together.

IN THE END . . . The two women live as wives in peace.

AND THE SEX? Sensually allusive. "Who can count the times the waves will take her unexpected in the deep of a kiss and throw her teeth against my lip and nick it?"

PRIDE QUOTIENT: Yes, Virginia, there have always been lesbians, even in 1800s New England. But, well, the story doesn't exactly feel immediate.

Ruby by Rosa Guy (Laurel-Leaf Books, 1976)

With its political dialogue and the quasi–teacher/student relationship, *Ruby* is almost as much about post–civil rights politics as it is about lovers Ruby and Daphne.

JACKET COPY: "They fill the aching emptiness in each other, learn from each other, love each other, despite the shared knowledge that their happiness will end as abruptly as it began."

THE RELATIONSHIP STARTS . . . Sudden and weird. Ruby admires Daphne from afar and then shows up at her house unexpectedly one weekend morning. Daphne gives Ruby a political lecture, during which she calls Ruby an Uncle Tom, and then they make out.

CAN THEY FESS UP? Daphne's mother is fine with it as long as the girls aren't too open about their love; Ruby's traditional West Indian father objects strenuously, but no more than he would to a similar relationship with a boy. Ruby's sister takes it all in stride.

WHEN SOMEONE FINDS OUT . . . Ruby's father hits her when he realizes that she deceived him in order to spend a weekend with Daphne. Daphne's mother forbids Ruby to take shelter in their house.

IN THE END . . . Daphne breaks off the affair and says she's "going straight." Ruby is reconsidering plans with an old almost-boyfriend. Capitulation to compulsory heterosexuality, or acknowledgment of the fluidity of sexuality? I have to go with the former, given the melancholy tone and Ruby's still-active feelings for Daphne.

AND THE SEX? Rare and nonspecific. "Holding, touching, fondling, body intertwined with body, racing around the world on brilliant waves of color" is as explicit as it gets.

PRIDE QUOTIENT: Low. How could it be otherwise when they're both gonna date men in the end?

Happy Endings Are All Alike by Sandra Scoppettone (Laurel-Leaf Books, 1978)

Two smart, beautiful suburban white girls find each other and fall in love.

JACKET COPY: "Jaret Tyler has no guilt or shame about her love affair with Peggy Danziger . . . But then a disturbed friend of Jaret's younger brother . . . sets out to teach her a lesson."

THE RELATIONSHIP STARTS . . . They are brought together by a mutual pal and become close friends, then more.

CAN THEY FESS UP? Jaret's mother is fine with it; Peggy's sister Claire is emphatically not. The girls are determined that no one else know, because they're scared, and rightly so, of what residents of their small suburban town would think.

WHEN SOMEONE FINDS OUT . . . Jaret is brutally raped and beaten by a guy wanting to teach her a lesson about thinking she's too good to date men.

IN THE END . . . Peggy ends the relationship after the rape because she can't stand the thought of being outed at the trial. However, with the help of a shrink hired by her father—ironically, to help her get over the queer thing—she realizes she's still in love with Jaret and they reconcile.

AND THE SEX? Nothing explicit, but it's clear that they're having plenty.

PRIDE QUOTIENT: Mixed. Jaret is sure of herself and supported by her family; Peggy, even when the two reconcile at the end, is reluctant to claim a lesbian identity. "I only know that I love you and I want to be with you now," she says. Unlike in *Ruby*, however, this does seem to be an acknowledgment of sexuality's fluidity—perhaps because the young lovers are still together.

Crush by Jane Futcher (AlyCat Books, 1981)

In the mid-'6os, at an exclusive boarding school filled with cruel, manipulative upper-class girls, crushes are more than common, but actual lesbian relationships are forbidden.

JACKET COPY: "Jinx knew she had a serious crush on Lexie, and knew she had to do something to make it go away. But Lexie, who always got her way, had other plans."

THE RELATIONSHIP STARTS . . . Lexie, the fastest, most glamorous golden girl at Huntington Hill, takes Jinx on as a project, which starts their intense friendship.

CAN THEY FESS UP? Jinx believes she must keep the depth of her feelings for Lexie secret not only from everyone at school but also from Lexie herself. She knows she could be kicked out of school for being queer, and she also senses Lexie's underlying unreliability.

WHEN SOMEONE FINDS OUT . . . Both girls end up expelled.

IN THE END . . . Jinx is disillusioned about the relationship, while Lexie seems unchanged.

AND THE SEX? Not quite happenin'. The two kiss and rub up against each other once or twice, but no more.

PRIDE QUOTIENT: Nil. Jinx may survive okay, and even goes to the college of her choice, but there's really nothing but misery connected to lesbianism here.

Annie on My Mind by Nancy Garden
(Farrar, Straus and Giroux, 1982)

Even though some plot elements are similar to those in *Crush, Annie* is a fundamentally optimistic story of friendship and romance.

JACKET COPY: "Liza never knew falling in love could be so wonderful . . . and so confusing."

THE RELATIONSHIP STARTS . . . The two girls meet in a museum and strike up a friendship, which takes them both by surprise with its intensity and slowly becomes romantic.

CAN THEY FESS UP? Nope.

WHEN SOMEONE FINDS OUT . . . Annie and Liza get caught having sex in the house of two teachers for whom they've been house-sitting, and at the same time the lesbianism of the two teachers is uncovered. Liza is suspended from school and almost expelled, and the teachers get fired.

IN THE END . . . The two lovers, after one estranged semester away at college, redeclare their love and plan to spend a holiday together.

AND THE SEX? Cutaway: "A light in the hall . . . made a wonderful faraway glow and touched Annie's soft smooth skin with gold. After the first few minutes, I think the rest of our shyness with each other vanished."

PRIDE QUOTIENT: An explicit lesson: "Don't punish yourselves for people's ignorant reactions to what we all are," says one of the teachers. "Don't let ignorance win. Let love."

EXTRA-SPECIAL INTERTEXTUAL NOTE: Annie buys a copy of *Patience and Sarah* for her and Liza to read.

A Stone Gone Mad by Jacquelyn Holt Park
(Alyson Publications, 1991)

This story spans from 1948 to 1977, which might explain why, in the first chapter, Emily is exiled from her family after her sister discovers her making out with another girl; it might also explain why Emily subsequently tries to be "normal" through relationships with men. What it doesn't explain is why, in 1991, someone would choose to write a novel (for an independent queer publisher, no less) that's so filled with self-hatred and the rhetoric of illness.

JACKET COPY: "When sixteen-year-old Emily Stolle is discovered in the arms of a female schoolmate, she is as appalled as her family."

THE RELATIONSHIP STARTS . . . Which one? Mattie is Emily's older sister's best friend, Lu is a sorority sister, and then there are all those anonymous women from the bars.

CAN THEY FESS UP? Absolutely not; the reaction is invariably disgust and shame.

WHEN SOMEONE FINDS OUT . . . Emily is first sent away and shunned by her family, then later cut off by a close friend who briefly became a love, then made to move out by a bigoted roommate. And, of course, she's plagued with constant shame and the belief that she's sick.

IN THE END . . . After years of denial—and of trying to "cure" herself through relationships with both men and women—Emily sustains a long-term relationship with a woman. She even comes out to some strangers on the subway. But it seems a hollow gesture, since the people who really mattered in her life either never knew about her lesbianism or were unable to accept it.

AND THE SEX? Pretty explicit, in a deadpan kind of way: "Emily's hands dropped to Reena's breasts; the nipples hardened."

PRIDE QUOTIENT: Negative. The fairly happy ending for Emily and her girlfriend Anna can't make up for a story in which, for more than three hundred pages, desire for women is referred to as "that hated curse that was following her," and lesbianism is a "disease [that], surely as any malignancy, ravaged her and ruined those it touched as well."

Dive by Stacey Donovan (Puffin Books, 1994)

A sparely and beautifully written novel that is more about V's father's terminal illness than about her romance with a classmate.

JACKET COPY: "As V falls for Jane, she begins to discover that in love, as in life, there are more questions than answers."

THE RELATIONSHIP STARTS . . . V is drawn to Jane from the very first time she spots her in the hallway, and the two start walking home together every day.

CAN THEY FESS UP? The unreal, almost hallucinatory tone of the book renders the question of to tell or not to tell irrelevant.

WHEN SOMEONE FINDS OUT . . . Doesn't happen.

IN THE END . . . V and Jane are in love.

AND THE SEX? In the same fluid, not-quite-stream-of-consciousness prose as the rest of the book: "Every time I touch her somewhere, and I have to touch her everywhere, she murmurs, the urgency of desire, the surrender to the hands that take us."

PRIDE QUOTIENT: Not clearly articulated but fairly high nonetheless. "I recognize the fact, according to the world, I mean, that two girls having sex together . . . is pretty unusual. What I don't understand is how it got to be that people still think there's something wrong with it. Even I think there's something wrong with it . . . Or I think I thought I did. But I don't."

Good Moon Rising by Nancy Garden
(Farrar, Straus and Giroux, 1996)

High-school seniors Jan and Kerry embark on a typical teen first love: movie dates, kissing in cars, surreptitiously spending the night.

JACKET COPY: "A love story, a portrait of aspiring young actors, and a powerful reminder of cruelty met through intolerance."

THE RELATIONSHIP STARTS . . . New girl Kerry beats Jan out for the lead in the school play. When Jan coaches Kerry on her lines, romance blossoms.

CAN THEY FESS UP? Well, they're worried about it, but they decide fairly early on not to hide the relationship.

WHEN SOMEONE FINDS OUT . . . There's some harassment by schoolmates, which the lovers put a stop to by coming out.

IN THE END . . . The girls are planning how to tell their families.

AND THE SEX? Plenty of making out (with quite sexy descriptions), and Garden doesn't shy away from even more: "Jan traced the sunspots on Kerry's body. 'My golden love,' she whispered . . . 'I never knew hands and mouths could make anyone feel what I've felt today.'"

PRIDE QUOTIENT: Off the scale. "[Jan] faced Kent and, loud enough so everyone would be able to hear, said, 'You were right. The signs were right. I am gay.' With the words came a sense of relief and liberation so great that she felt she never wanted to hide again."

Stormin' Norma

Why I Love the Queen of Teen

Andi Zeisler / WINTER 1998

TWO YOUNG BOYS AND TWO YOUNG GIRLS ARE WATCHING TV. It's cable, it's rated R, a hot tub is involved. Everyone is watching the screen in silence when suddenly one of the boys nudges the other, points to his crotch, and announces, with no small amount of pride, "Look, I've got a boner."

Stock Beavis-and-Butt-Head fare, sure, but it was also the moment when it dawned on me that, when it comes to verbalizing physical feelings about sex, the societal benevolence handed to boys is rarely, if ever, extended to girls. Those of us who grew up in the '70s and '80s entered puberty in the glow of a celluloid world that seemed to have a single raison d'être—to visualize the sexual blossoming of the American boy. Female characters in carbon-copy movies with names like *Losin' It* and *Screwballs* were exhibited as either the facilitators of or hindrances to that all-important loss of male virginity. These movies were supposedly all about girls, but actual girls weren't important enough to figure prominently, except in those moments where attractive body parts were doled out for male satisfaction. We were sluts. We were prudes. If there was any kind of middle ground, we weren't gonna discover it at the multiplex.

Where were we going to find it, then? Most likely at the library, where it was assumed girls outnumbered boys—just as it was assumed we were the moviegoing minority—and could, by default, strut our stuff. But even with

19

whole shelves devoted to telling the stories of girls—historical girls, sporty girls, adventurous girls—there was still one story that too often wasn't getting told: the story of girls and sexuality. And that's where Norma Klein, queenpin of the young-adult boy-girl sex novel, came in to help.

Now, Judy Blume is widely considered the patron saint of teen-girl literature, and not without ample reason. Her oeuvre, which includes *Tiger Eyes*, *Deenie*, and *Are You There God? It's Me, Margaret*, buoyed enough of us through puberty that it should be considered required reading for anyone with ovaries. Tons of us have some variation on the story of sneaking a friend's older sister's copy of *Forever* into our sleeping bag and avidly searching out the much-whispered-about "good parts." But if Judy was the wise older sister nimbly guiding us through the confusing realm of maxipads and training bras, Norma Klein was the wacky, worldly aunt ready to blow our minds with a feminist, intellectual outlook on sex and relationships that would make us look twice at what the movies proclaimed as the Way Things Are. Klein's formidable contribution to the YA canon—fortyplus books—served as proof that even if Hollywood and network TV have boys on the brain and in the billfold, someone was interested in making the sexual coming-of-age of girls equally important. Herewith, nine reasons why Norma K. rocked the young-adult genre.

Her books lived up to the label "young adult."

The paradox of young-adult media—magazines, television, movies—is how, even in the process of trying to make girls feel comfortable with their lives, the messages imparted most often encourage extreme discomfort. Being "yourself," girls are told, is fine, as long as that self concentrates on being thin, pretty, unintimidatingly smart, and boy-friendly. Along this same line, countless authors of novels for girls translated the term "young adult" to mean "shopping-obsessed, boy-crazy bubblehead," and the result was a vast assortment of stories that centered on a female character just dying to be asked to the prom by Joe Hunky Football Fondler. Consider the insanely popular Sweet Valley High series, which focused on a group of walking, talking clichés—the nice girl, the crafty girl, the rich girl, the studious girl—whose apparent sole purpose in life was to gossip and scheme against each other in hopes of scoring a fella.

Unike these books, NK's narratives refused to equate a dance with sublime happiness, or to measure social success with physical looks. Instead, her characters were unspectacular and self-conscious girls and boys, usually in their last year of high school. They've never had a "real" relationship but have developed a substantial battery of expectations and opinions. They meet someone and hit it off, and the story traces the development of the relationship and the myriad changes sex brings to their lives. Where other YA novels would close on the happily-ever-after image of the main character wrapped in her date's beefy arms at the prom, NK's novels asked: What happens after that?

Klein treated her characters as the burgeoning adults they were, addressing the problems that arise when things like sexual jealousy, impotence, and parental envy are introduced into teen relationships. By the end of many of her books, the affair has ended and the characters are ensconced at college, ruminating on what has been learned from this first, complicated relationship, and ready to start another.

She wrote funny, faceted, smart characters.

There's the anxious cellist Robin in *Queen of the What Ifs*, the reluctant starlet Rusty in *Domestic Arrangements*, the misfit lovers Peter and Leslie in *Family Secrets*, the repressed artist Augie in *My Life as a Body*, and the opinionated science whiz Maggie in *Love Is One of the Choices*. They were awkward, lumpy, beautiful, smart, flaky, Jewish, Zen Buddhist, neurotic, outgoing—and most important, they were all of these simultaneously. NK's characters broke the dream-teen mold of most young-adult novels—instead of sucking down Orange Julius at the mall, these kids were more likely to be practicing the bassoon or training their pet chimpanzees. The plotlines themselves were layered and unconventional, focusing on everything from discovering a parent is gay to what happens when twin fourteen-year-olds decide to open a gourmet restaurant to distract themselves from their parents' separation. Klein's young characters, in fact, were almost too cerebral—I mean, how hard would you laugh if you were seventeen and your best friend busted out with a statement like "I believe celibacy sharpens my perceptions of reality"?—but for all their precocity, they displayed enough cluelessness and self-absorption to be believable as actual teens.

She picked up right where Judy Blume left off.

Klein took it for granted that we knew how our bodies functioned and focused instead on the complications that emerge once teenage girls do something with their sex information. If Blume's novels helped girls realize that everything they were feeling and experiencing was normal, Klein took it one step further, emphasizing that not only were the feelings normal, but that girls should never doubt their right and ability to express them.

However, knowing plenty about the insecurities of adolescence, she also threw down a cold, hard reality—teenage girls aren't always applauded by their peers for having an independent, matter-of-fact attitude toward sex. This issue is verbalized in *It's OK If You Don't Love Me* when main girl Jody grapples with the contradictions inherent in her sex ed class's breezy discussions. ("I hate to tell people, even other girls, that I'm on the Pill. I think it's hard to admit that sex is something you want to do or might do. It's one thing to say you believe in it in the abstract, but to come right out and say I guess I'll be sleeping with someone tonight, I might as well be prepared, is hard.")

She put the ladies first.

Not only that, but she posited a world where the gender roles taken for granted by other young-adult novels—even Blume's—were adjusted with so little fanfare that they seemed to always have been that way. Her heroines never stood by their lockers chewing their hair over whether Joe might ask them out; these girls marched right up to Joe without a twinge of indecision.

This female-forward approach was even more explicit when it came to sex. Not only did female characters take the lead, they took it in ways that were widely considered "male"—and curiosity, not capitulation, characterized their experimentation.

She made boys our friends.

Klein gave girls boundless credit for possessing both brains and agency, but never at the expense of her male characters. Many of her books were written from the perspective of teenage boys, and while her male characters—including *No More Saturday Nights'* Tim, a college freshman and single father, and Joel, who flounders his way through a first affair in *Beginners' Love*—weren't what you would call sensitive New Age guys, they were portrayed as thinking, feeling, emotional people. In the YA genre, where boys were regularly depicted as no more than jockish arm trophies who either made girls' lives worthwhile or ruined their reputations, this was, sad to say, more props than were generally given.

Her characters spoke up.

Klein's female characters had a lot to say, especially on the subjects of gender, sex, and feminism. Whether loudmouthed or demure, these girls were each confrontational in their own way, primed and ready to challenge outdated assumptions of gender difference, social conditioning, and more. In *It's OK If You Don't Love Me*, for instance, Jody is outraged to discover how ill informed her younger brother is about sex ("Girls like to do it too, you know"); in *Love Is One of the Choices*, Maggie engages in a passionate argument with her father about whether pornography can appeal to women.

These back-and-forth debates are natural and narrative, rather than pedantic, and they mirror the often frustrating impossibility of schooling one's parents/siblings/peers in viewpoints that buck the status quo. NK's girls and women speak up on behalf of themselves and their gender as a whole, but even when their statements don't illustrate a feminist viewpoint (though they often do), the dialogues that emerge reflect the vital and changing ideas of what girls and women want from society, men, and each other.

She tried to right the wrongs of the information police.

Remember in grade school when boys were informed about erections and wet dreams while girls were told about menstruation in what was essentially a shill for Kotex? That was sex education: Boys learned that their bodies were a source of pleasure; girls were warned that the wrong brand of pad would lead to the ruin of their best white jeans.

Had Norma Klein been in charge, boys and girls would have sat side by side to learn about themselves and about each other, and wouldn't enter puberty with the assumption that sexual attitudes were gender-coded. Klein's books made reference not only to the misguided way boys' and girls' sex education is disseminated, but also to the way the media telegraphs a wealth of wrongheaded moral dogma.

NK worked into her characters' mouths sly commentary on this passage of information and how it causes teenagers to inadvertently participate in their own manipulation; these revelations are an encouragement to look critically at what girls, especially, are told in books that are ostensibly for them. *Beginners' Love*'s Leda, for instance, takes issue with the YA subgenre of the "sexual disaster" novel, in which all teenage nooky invariably leads to misfortune and regret ("God, don't you hate those books for teenagers where they have to get married and she drops out of school and they live over a garage and he works in some used car lot? And there's always some scene where a girl who's had an abortion comes to visit and she's gone insane and becomes a Bowery bum, just in case you didn't get the point"); Maggie of *Love Is One of the Choices*, meanwhile, is relieved that her first sexual experience isn't the bloody horror it's made out to be in books for teens.

She got on the wrong side of book-burning fanatics.

Klein's willingness to point out where society's moral judgments fail teenagers didn't go unnoticed by the people who make those very judgments. Since we all know how well female sexual agency flies in our society—particularly when it involves teenagers—it's no surprise that several of Klein's books have in the past been banned from school libraries, putting them in the company of *To Kill a Mockingbird*, *Lord of the Flies*, and *Brave New World*. But we all know that the books people don't want teenagers to see are the honest ones, and NK's tales, written in the '70s and '80s, remain as relevant and controversial as they were when they were first published.

She changed some lives.

I like to think of Norma Klein as one of my first feminist influences. Not that I didn't log my share of hours mooning over some bowl-cutted junior-high crush when I could have been doing more interesting things. But Klein—along with that proudly erect kid in front of the TV—started me thinking about the inequity that defines the teenage realm: the code of conformity that uses the word "slut" to brand the girl who speaks her mind about sex, the mind-set that not only allows but encourages the devaluation of girls and their sexuality. There was no shortage of girl media to remind us of what we were supposed to want, but Klein proposed an all-important alternative. Her books weren't only fun, smart, and sexy; it's clear to me now that they were also a form of activism—the refusal of one writer to pander to the what-girls-want formulas used by other writers and publishers of young-adult books. Klein died in 1989, but she left a legacy of strong, provocative girl literature that continues to burst the wispy bubble of dyed-to-match pumps and homecoming dances—a gift I know I'll always be grateful for.

Sister Outsider Headbanger

On Being a Black Feminist Metalhead

Keidra Chaney / FALL 2001

I'M NOT SURE EXACTLY WHEN OR HOW IT HAPPENED, BUT AT some point in my childhood I began to think I was a white guy trapped in the body of a black girl. And not just any white guy, either—a guitar player in a heavy-metal band.

Okay, stop laughing. It's no joke. I'm a black female metalhead. Like I said, I can't really tell you how it happened. Maybe it was growing up in the '80s, being fed a steady diet of Ratt videos on Chicago's quasi-MTV UHF station. Or maybe it was coming of age at the same time heavy metal reached public consciousness as the Voice of the Disgruntled Adolescent White Male. Sure, I wasn't white, male, or even particularly angry as a ten-year-old—but I recognized the force of those electric guitars, relentlessly pounding drums, and growling vocals. Even then, I knew that heavy metal was power, and power was irresistible.

Over the next few years, I embraced my heavy-metal destiny. I wasn't ashamed of my love for metal; I just couldn't explain it to most people. Heavy metal has always been and will always be the redheaded stepchild of rock, much maligned and generally misunderstood. Respectable rock fans and critics dismiss it as simplistic and puerile; religious conservatives condemn it as "the devil's music." To a lot of black folks, it's just a bunch of crazy white guys screaming, which is just as bad. Even my older sister, who

26

is almost ridiculously eclectic in her musical tastes (Barry Manilow!), wasn't exactly feeling metal.

Yet in the early '80s, some of us kids in the 'hood did listen to metal. Radio was somewhat less segregated than it is today, but hip hop didn't exist to MTV or radio. We did know about Quiet Riot and Poison, those mainstays of pop-metal. Later, when hip hop came of age and my peers grew out of the Crüe and into Boogie Down Productions and N.W.A., cable television got me intrigued by Megadeth, Anthrax, and Queensryche.

I buried my metal affection at first, not wanting to seem like too much of a freak to my friends, sneaking Metallica songs in between Salt-N-Pepa and Digital Underground on mix tapes. Like decaffeinated coffee, a black female metalhead is something that doesn't make sense to a lot of people; this was especially true at a time when hip hop as a genre was very much linked to the cultural experiences of the black community—"black folks' CNN," as Chuck D once put it. What could I possibly find appealing about heavy metal, seeing as how it didn't reflect my life experience or cultural identity in any tangible way?

Actually, I think that contradiction was what appealed to me in the first place. Heavy metal was so radically different from the music I grew up with that it allowed me to imagine myself as someone radically different from the geeky, awkward preteen I normally was. Even as my burgeoning feminist self felt empowered by seeing Queen Latifah and Monie Love do "Ladies First" on *Yo! MTV Raps* in 1989, another part of me—the one that secretly watched *Headbangers Ball* in my basement every Saturday night—wanted to run away from home and become a roadie for Metallica.

Maintaining the dual identity of regular high-school student by day, hard-rockin' metalhead by night made me feel pretty isolated. Finding other heavy metal–loving black kids in a Lutheran high school in the pre-Internet '90s was no easy task. But by sophomore year, I had encountered some kindred spirits: I met my friend Nicole when she noticed the cover of my *Metal Edge* magazine peeking from my notebook on the way to English class. "You read *Metal Edge*?" she asked in shock. I was ready for another fight—I had already endured more than a semester's worth of ridicule after coming out as a metalhead—but she exclaimed, "So do I!"

It was cool to find girls who read both *Essence* and *Rip*, who could talk about the new Slayer video and the pros and cons of relaxers in the same conversation. I felt validated, even though my mom thought I was suffering the delayed effects of some childhood head injury and classmates accused me of betraying my blackness or flirting with satanism. Instead of trying to change people's minds, I settled for screwing with them. My friends and I wore our metalhead status like badges of honor: We all felt like outsiders for one reason or another, and it was no coincidence that we were all attracted to music that made difference into a source of pride.

It's this sense of self-imposed alienation from "normal" society that's a big part of metal's appeal. In her 1991 examination of the genre, *Heavy Metal: A Cultural Sociology*, Deena Weinstein aptly calls heavy-metal fans "proud pariahs." Metal has never been particularly trendy, even in its heyday, but that outsider element adds much to the music's appeal. "Some people get into music that's not really popular, like heavy metal, to make themselves distinct from their peers," Weinstein told me during a phone interview. "It makes sense that you'd be attracted to it. Teenagers use music to distance themselves from their parents, their upbringing."

There's also the sense of camaraderie and acceptance that is unique to metal fans (well, and Deadheads): a loyalty that borders on obsession. Metalheads are not casual fans. We memorize every word to every song of every album by our favorite bands, we wear tour T-shirts until they literally fall apart, we see our heroes in concert dozens of times, we spend hundreds of dollars on bootlegs and import LPs even if we don't have a turntable to play them on.

But though I was drawn to the outsider appeal of the music in the first place, it was difficult for me to forget my double outsider status at concerts, where guys would gawk and point at me and my metalhead clique as if we were Martians instead of black girls, and we could count the number of black faces on one hand. But once the lights went down and the band came onstage, we were all headbanging and moshing and howling the words to the songs. The music took over, and we could all share that universal bond of loving it, if only for a few hours.

Of course, as in all of rock's subgenres, female metal fans have had to walk that fine line between sighing teen-dream fandom and balls-to-the-wall solidarity. A lot of women embrace and identify with the music and musicians the same way male fans do, while also grafting very girly wants and desires onto metal's aggressive vibes. We want to be tough and emulate our heroes and start our own bands—but, yeah, we also fantasize about hanging out with the guys, dating them, fucking them.

And so female fans found ways to connect with each other: as pen pals, chatting in the women's restrooms during concerts, at record stores, wherever we could. We even had our own magazine, the aforementioned *Metal Edge*, the late-'80s and early-'90s incarnation of which was a strange amalgam of *Kerrang!* and *Tiger Beat*. Glossy pinups and wall-size foldouts sat next to ads for instructional videos like *How to Play Guitar like Yngwie Malmsteen* and classifieds from aspiring musicians trying to start bands. *Metal Edge* never explicitly billed itself as a metal magazine for teen girls, but Gerri Miller, the magazine's longtime editor in chief, had an uncanny knack for appealing to the desires of female metalheads. One of my favorite sections was "When They Were Young," a three-page spread of B-level pop-metal bands' goofy baby photos and high-school yearbook pictures. ("That's how you knew that *Metal Edge* was really for girls," recalls my friend Christina. "No boy cares about what the guys from Slaughter looked like as babies.")

Was *Metal Edge* exploiting our conflicting desires? Maybe. But the magazine was one of the few forums where we female fans could simultaneously indulge our lustful groupie desires and our dreams of being in the band without losing our hard-core credibility.

By the time I entered college, I'd started to reconcile my identity and beliefs with my love for metal, but it was hard to leave my ambivalence behind. If saying that I'm a metalhead and a feminist sounds like a contradiction, then saying that I'm a feminist *because* of heavy metal probably sounds even more so. But metal did empower me. Because the music was so far away from my experience, it didn't place definitions on who I was or could be as a black female. When I listened to Metallica or Corrosion of Conformity, I wasn't a "bitch," a "ho," or some anonymous jiggling booty in a rap video; I wasn't a woman who needed rescuing by some dream-date pop star. I was someone who felt weird in high school, who wanted a place to belong.

Bands like Living Colour and Sepultura took things a step further by bringing a strong antiracist and political tone to their headbanging. Such bands helped me adapt my fandom to my personal ideals, and in turn I examined songs with a critical ear; refused to support bands with racist, sexist, or homophobic lyrics; and wrote angry letters to metal fanzines when they made racist comments. Most important, having the music as an emotional outlet made me feel safe to eventually explore my identity as a black woman and as a feminist, and to find strength in that as well.

Heavy-metal fandom doesn't hold the same place in my life that it did when I was thirteen; I try to keep up with the music, but I'm not deeply immersed in the fan culture. Maybe it's because now that I'm older, I have a greater understanding of my own identity and I don't need the music to help express my feelings or provide a sense of community.

In some ways, music fandom seems a lot more diverse than it was when I was a teen. Thanks at least in part to MTV, kids of different races and ethnicities have more music in common than even a decade ago. It's not uncommon to see a black or brown kid giddily requesting Papa Roach on *Total Request Live*, and hip hop has replaced rock as the soundtrack of adolescent rebellion for kids of every color. Black rockers like Living Colour and Fishbone and newer bands with multiracial lineups like Sevendust and the now-defunct Rage Against the Machine have made strides in crossing rock's color line.

But MTV and radio (including black stations) still don't know what to do with artists who don't fit any preexisting molds, like Me'Shell NdegéOcello or the black-female-fronted rock band Skunk Anansie. So instead of taking on the challenge of exploring black rock, mainstream media largely ignores it. Even now, we sistas who rock don't have a high-profile role model to identify with or emulate. The act of participation in rock music as musicians and as fans is still pretty subversive for black women—for black folks in general, really. I hope at some point the music industry will have the guts and good sense to support black rock, and young black women who want a harder sound than Tracy Chapman will be able to find the emotional connection I did, plus something more—a sense of being represented musically, culturally, and politically. But right now I'll settle for those rare but cherished moments when I spot a girl walking down the street sporting a 'fro and a Korn T-shirt. I'm reminded that we're still out there, challenging the racism and sexism in the industry and in fandom through writing fanzines, making websites, supporting black rock bands—and, if nothing else, messing with images of who the "average" metal fan is supposed to be.

Bloodletting

Female Adolescence in Modern Horror Films

Tammy Oler / SUMMER 2003

AH, MENARCHE. ANY GIRL WHO READ ANYTHING AS A PRETEEN can testify that young-adult novels, teen magazines, and other media specifically directed at teenage girls never fail to depict menstruation as an event that girls anxiously anticipate and celebrate. Yet the most memorable visual representation of a girl's first period tells a very different story. Brian De Palma's 1976 horror classic *Carrie* (adapted from Stephen King's novel) opens with a post–gym class shower-room scene in which high-school pariah Carrie White discovers blood creeping down her legs. She reacts as one might expect a girl oppressively sheltered by a religious-zealot mother to—that is, with utter panic. Her fear and confusion are met with cruelty: The nicer classmates simply wrinkle their noses at her cluelessness, but the bolder ones pelt her with tampons and maxipads, laughing and screaming, "Plug it up! Plug it up!"

It's a moment of excruciating vulnerability and humiliation, but it's also the moment when Carrie discovers the telekinetic power that she will ultimately use to wreak bloody revenge ('scuse the phrase) on her tormentors. The unforgettable opening scene prefigures Carrie's transformation from bullied menstruating girl to menacing, electric horror queen with startling symmetry, for *Carrie* is as much about puberty and menstruation as it is about revenge. The two narratives come to a head at the film's notorious end, and in the ensuing pig's blood–soaked violence, Carrie is not only unable to "plug it up," she does quite the opposite: She opens up completely, unleashing her vast, horrific female power on everyone in her path.

Never mind Judy Blume's Margaret; *Carrie* was my first introduction to the trials of female adolescence. Watching the film at age seven, I was vaguely aware of what it might mean to be a teenage girl, my impression formed by conversations I overheard between my preteen sister and our mother. But nothing prepared me for *Carrie*. My reaction to this set of images linking menstruation, humiliation, and supernatural power was a mixture of fear and fascination: I understood that Carrie's rage had put her firmly in the grip of evil by the end of the movie, but I was nevertheless in awe of her power. And I began to suspect that both rage and power had everything to do with becoming a woman.

Carrie is but one of a whole host of horror films of the '70s and '80s that feature narratives of a "possessed" girl—possessed by spirits or demons, or in possession of otherworldly powers. In *Carrie*, the convergence of possession and puberty takes place most powerfully during the onset of menstruation. Two other films of this period—1977's *Audrey Rose* and 1978's *The Fury*—reference this connection, with female characters whose possession symptoms become extreme with the physical launch of puberty, suggesting an intrinsic link between sexual maturation and susceptibility to the supernatural.

Carrie and her cohorts entered puberty at a time when the horror genre was obsessed with the female curse. The twenty years between 1970 and 1990 produced a multitude of narratives about possessed women, in addition to those about teenage girls, among them *The Visitor* (1979), *Deadly Blessing* (1981), *The Incubus* (1981), *The Entity* (1981), and *Witchboard* (1985). Similarly, horror of this period is full of narratives about satanic/demonic pregnancy, the most famous being *Rosemary's Baby* (1968) and *The Omen* (1976). In these films, possession takes place in women's wombs, and the horror of the film becomes both their literal inhabitation by evil and their capacity to reproduce demonic progeny.

In *Men, Women, and Chain Saws*, Carol Clover's extensive analysis of gender in modern horror, she notes the predominance of these "female portals" in film and notes that "where Satan is, in the world of horror, female genitals are likely to be nearby." According to Clover, to be a portal is to be "open" or susceptible to becoming possessed by satanic or supernatural powers—a reflection of the long-held historical view of women as both cursed and unclean. From the first mythic "open" woman, Eve, Western culture has defined women as more susceptible than men to the temptations of evil, and the language of horror pushes this notion one step further—in these films, women's very bodies become the Pandora's box that unleashes evil into the worldly domain.

For the adolescent girls of this horror-film genre, biology is destiny. Against their wills, their bodies become the site on, in, and through which the films' supernatural battles take place. And while these girls are ostensibly the films' subjects, the narrative action inevitably reduces them to being merely bodies themselves, with their actual experiences rarely investigated or explored. As much as we can identify with Carrie White's painful teenage reality—the bad skin, the social ostracism, the irrationally controlling mother—by the time prom night turns ugly, her humanity is all but gone. She's reduced to the ultimate self-destructive object of horror, and, like her victims, we're asked to react only with fear and terror, not with sympathy or pity.

The girls of supernatural horror suffer from the fact that they are *too* female, which makes them radically different from the subjects of slasher films, the other wildly popular '70s and '80s horror subgenre in which teenage girls figure prominently. The girl survivor of the slasher film is smart, resourceful, and tomboyish—she invariably has a boy's name and avoids the sexual activities that doom her female counterparts. She triumphs, ultimately, because she transcends her gender, a conversion that allows a predominantly male horror audience to identify with her victory over whatever ax-wielding psychopath menaces her. No such identification is prescribed in supernatural horror; instead of objectifying girls for an audience's uneasy sexual pleasure, supernatural and occult movies objectify them exclusively to produce horror and disgust in their viewers.

No film bears this out quite like *The Exorcist*, widely regarded as one of the scariest movies ever. While menstruation is not explicit in the film, the story's preoccupation with blood and bodily fluids, as well as the adolescent anxieties that Linda Blair's Regan MacNeil faces (puberty, divorce, an absentee father, jealousy for her mother's attention), suggests that possession is invoked to mask other forces at work. Throughout the film, Regan's small adolescent body is subjected to as much abuse by her would-be saviors as by her demon possessors. We watch with equal horror the excruciating battery of medical testing Regan endures and the disgusting manipulations of her demon possessors. Regan transforms from girl to female portal so thoroughly that her character's only cry for help is literally written on her body ("help me" spelled out in the raised skin of her stomach). At the end of the film, when an enraged Father Karras, the titular exorcist, physically assaults Regan, the audience barely registers any shock. In no other film context would the act of a grown man punching a teenage girl be acceptable, or even understandable. Yet the action that immediately follows—Karras is himself possessed and subsequently hurled out the window to his death—makes it clear that this is really his story and not that of the young girl left crying in the corner of her room. Regan spends the few remaining moments of the film gaunt and silent, hardly even a witness to her own terrifying trials. No longer "open" (at least not until the sequel) thanks to Karras's sacrifice, she becomes useless as the object of horror—and as the subject of the film.

Growing up on a steady diet of horror movies, I identified something in these images that attracted me in a way that images of girls in nonhorror films never could: As much as becoming a woman in these films is a curse, it is also a source of tremendous power. Made during the height of public discourse about women's liberation and reproductive rights, these films signal a preoccupation with issues raised by feminism. They propose a distinctly feminine source of power that must hide behind a satanic or otherworldly guise, too terrible to recognize and too destructive to respect. In this light, Carrie White's metamorphosis from frightened menstruating girl to force of nature is the ultimate ascendancy to womanhood. Struggling with adolescent insecurities and baffling, embarrassing transformations in their own bodies, these characters unleash the monstrous beginnings of girl power.

I don't mean to suggest that these images are actually positive, but possession has the potential to be a compelling metaphor for female adolescence, with its attendant social anxieties and bodily mysteries. Coupled with slasher films and their grim female survivors, '70s and '80s horror films told dark coming-of-age tales at a time when adolescent girls were virtually invisible elsewhere in celluloid. With a few notable exceptions, like *Fast Times at Ridgemont High* and the Molly Ringwald–ruled realm of John Hughes, films about adolescence during this period—exemplified by *Breaking Away* (1979) and *The Outsiders* (1983)—were dominated by boys.

I'm keenly aware of the limits of such images and our ability to reclaim them; no matter how powerful these girls become or how much they challenge ideas of acceptable behavior, they are never truly agents of their own power. They are able to act only in relation to the greater forces that victimize them. Thrills aside, these films come dangerously close to pressing the conclusion that being female is, in reality, the ultimate horror.

It's this conclusion that's at the center of the 2000 film *Ginger Snaps*, a departure from the clichés of girls in horror and a paradigm shift for the genre. Instead of exploiting puberty as a means to inspire abhorrence in its audience, the film explores it as a complex and isolating part of female adolescence. *Ginger Snaps* reframes puberty within horror's werewolf narrative, shifting the experience of female adolescence away from transformation into portal to transformation into monster.

Curiously, women have historically been all but absent as the subject of werewolf films—a strange oversight, given that the connection between menstrual and lunar cycles seems like an exploitation no-brainer. In *Ginger Snaps*, lycanthropy becomes a means to explore the awkward experience of first menstruation; after title character Ginger suffers a werewolf attack shortly after her first period, the film plays on the double meanings of Ginger's physical changes, from suddenly robust body hair to painful cramps. When her younger sister Brigitte begins to suspect that Ginger is undergoing more than just "the most normal thing in the world," she observes, "Something's wrong—like more than you being just female." Her pointed equation between "female" and "wrong" speaks to the disdain the sisters feel throughout the film toward their female schoolmates and the loathsome condition of being a girl in general. (Ginger and Brigitte, who is fifteen, are—like Carrie White—both years late in starting their periods, a physical manifestation of their desire not to join the contemptible world of adulthood and sexuality.)

The more the film emphasizes the connection between femaleness and horror, however, the more it radically divests the connection of its power. The loathing Ginger and Brigitte feel for their female peers has primarily to do with the world of sexual double standards they encounter among their peers. When discussing her disappointing first sexual experience, Ginger says flatly, "He got laid. I'm just a lay. He's a hero and I'm just a lay—a freak mutant lay." As if to respond to the clichés that express an essential, biological link between femaleness and horror, *Ginger Snaps* entreats us to examine how potentially damaging such links are for young girls. Ginger and Brigitte want out of the preoccupation with "boys, body, and fitting in" that their mother claims is the central experience of young womanhood.

And as if to continue the tradition of revenge in teen horror (and further *Ginger Snaps'* tie to *Carrie*), the film uses Ginger's violent transformation to point out adolescent sexual stereotyping. After she kills one of her many victims, Ginger tells Brigitte with a mixture of pride and despair, "No one ever thinks chicks do shit like this. A girl can only be a slut, a bitch, a tease, or the virgin next door." But despite this self-conscious objection to accepted female behavior, the film refuses to celebrate the mayhem wrought by Ginger, no matter how empowering it may seem to some.

Finally, the film never loses sight of its emotional center—the relationship between the sisters. As Ginger begins to transform beyond recognition, the film makes Brigitte the primary point of identification—she's been left behind, and her conscience concerning Ginger's feral violence is at odds with her need to protect her. We witness Brigitte's struggle to find a cure and save her older sister, yet simultaneously escape from beneath her increasingly menacing shadow.

TAKEN AS A WHOLE, THE PERVASIVE IMAGE OF THE ADOLES-cent girl as portal/monster in the language of horror reflects the power of female puberty to unsettle, disturb, and, at its extreme, horrify. As much as images like those in the likes of *Carrie* and *The Exorcist* offer the possibility of embracing a distinctly feminine source of power, they threaten to reduce girls to mere expressions of their biological essence. The tradition also presents the female body as a contested site: As the girls of these films transform into portal/monster, they move beyond the sexual and into the grotesque, revealing a significant cultural preoccupation with control over the expression of female sexuality by young women themselves.

Yet such metaphors have the capacity to reflect the complexity of adolescence, as in *Ginger Snaps*, where the experience of female puberty itself is varied, exhilarating, and traumatic. Finally, these films reflect the daunting task that real adolescent girls must face: how to forge their identity in relation to their emerging sexuality in a culture that continues to be radically undecided about how to view them.

The, Like, Downfall of the English Language

A Fluffy Word with a Hefty Problem

Gus Andrews / SUMMER 2003

IN A SEPTEMBER 2002 ARTICLE TITLED "COSMO'S CRASH Course in Office Talk," *Cosmopolitan* helpfully guided its readers' anxiety to a part of life they might not yet have agonized about: their speech. "If you're like many young women," the article confided, "you undermine your professional profile by littering your speech with words such as 'um,' 'like,' and 'you know.'"

The article's author trotted out a series of career consultants to reinforce this idea. "Not only does using such words as 'like' and 'you know' make you seem unpolished and inexperienced," explained Kristen M. Gustafson, author of the book *Graduate! Everything You Need to Succeed After College*, who's quoted in the piece, "but it makes people disregard your ideas because you sound as if you don't have confidence in what you are saying."

Slang-bashing is nothing new. Along with rap, heavy metal, television watching, gum chewing, teen sex, and other faves, juvenile speech patterns are periodically written up as a sign of the decline of Western civilization. "Like," in particular, comes in for heavy abuse, thanks in part to the expression's longevity. While slang descriptors such as "groovy," "fresh," and "radical" were quick to fade into peculiar-sounding obsolescence, "like" has retained its currency in youth culture for over forty years.

The beatniks were the first group to be tarred with the "like" brush in the popular imagination. Maynard G. Krebs, the misappropriation of beat cool featured on early-1960s TV show *The Many Loves of Dobie Gillis*, was known to pepper his lazy lines with "like." Whether beatniks actually said "like" or whether it was introduced into mainstream pop culture to exaggerate or mock the differences between beat speech and "normal" speech is unclear. Regardless, the word continued to be associated with youth—and, more specifically, with the fringe elements of youth culture—throughout the '60s and '70s. The 1986 BBC documentary series *The Story of English* linked the origins of "like" to the surf culture that emerged on the Southern California coast in the late 1950s. From there, the documentary hypothesizes, it headed inland to suburban malls, where it eventually fell into the vocabulary of the Valley Girl, that brainless, shopping-obsessed bimbo archetype native to California's San Fernando Valley.

Musician Frank Zappa and his fourteen-year-old daughter, Moon Unit, breathed life into the caricature with 1982's "Valley Girl," wherein Moon Unit parodied her motormouthed peers from Encino in a song that introduced the rest of the world to Val slang like "gag me with a spoon" and "grody." The teensploitation classic *Valley Girl*, which lovingly lampooned its namesake, followed in 1983.

More than a decade later, another teen movie—the *Emma* update *Clueless*, with its Val-speaking, white (or at least whitewashed) Beverly Hills teen socialites—presumed that the Valley dialect's cultural associations had shifted from brainless consumerism to a classier brainless affluence. This is probably why, when I asked a twelve-year-old student of mine in the South Bronx what it means to speak professionally—as opposed to, in her words, "talking ghetto"—she responded, "It means, like, you have to, like, talk like this."

Was she channeling the class implications of "like," or its race implications? It's hard to separate the two. Perhaps she got an earful of Hilary, the spoiled older sister in the African-American family on the early-1990s sitcom *The Fresh Prince of Bel-Air*. Hilary's accent was pure Val, and it certainly signaled upper-class status. Her speech patterns, along with those of her lawyer dad, preppy brother, and snooty butler, provided linguistic contrast to Will Smith's ghetto authenticity.

I grew up near the Valley itself, so "like" has subtly different class implications for me. My prep-school friends and I might well have agreed to meet at, like, the Wet Seal in the Galleria, like, this weekend. But we ignored our own "bad" grammar when conjuring up the stupidest character we could imagine, an airhead whose rapid-fire speech was peppered with "like," "totally bitchin'," and "ohmigawd!" Put bluntly, Valspeak was white trash. We were supposed to abandon mall crawling for more sophisticated pursuits as we got older, and we were supposed to grow out of "like," too. Our parents looked out for our class standing. I got my first drubbing for using the word at age thirteen: A friend and I were in the car, talking excitedly and with abandon, when I realized that my stepmother and father were giggling in the front seat. Eventually, my stepmother turned around to face us and said, "Forty-three."

"Forty-three what?" I asked.

"You've said 'like' forty-three times in the last five minutes." She snickered.

Despite its rich history and subtle sociopolitical meanings, "like" is still just bad English to most adults, an error to be corrected. To linguists, fortunately, the phenomenon is worthy of more thought. In February 2002, the serendipitously named Muffy E. A. Siegel published a paper on "like" in the *Journal of Semantics*. Linguists are generally concerned with describing how words are used rather than with chastising the user, so the article is an assessment of the rules by which the word is deployed, with comments on where "like" challenges established linguistic theories.

Siegel hypothesizes that the use of "like" indicates that the speaker isn't committing to the accuracy of what she or he is saying. This can work in a number of ways. For example, in the phrase "Like, a giant moose knocked our tent over," "like" could be taken to modify the whole phrase, in which case the speaker is giving one example of many things that went wrong on a camping trip. It could be modifying "moose," signaling that the speaker is employing hyperbole (it could have been a small deer that knocked the tent over). Or, more simply, it could mean the speaker wasn't clear on exactly what kind of animal had knocked down the tent. (Granted, this is not a new concept. Even my father, who laughed along with my stepmother's "like" tally, will defend his phrasing "like, five cars at the show" to mean "about" or "approximately.")

Siegel does not address the use of the word "like" in the phrase "was like," where it replaces "said." (For example: "I was like, 'That dog has got to go,' and she was like, 'What? He's such a sweet dog,' and I was like, 'He's peed on the carpet four times this morning.'") But her theory works by extension: "Was like" is a good way for a speaker to indicate that the dialogue she is re-creating should not be taken as the exact words spoken by the participants. This extension also makes a place in English for the phrase "And she's all . . ."

Siegel's understanding of "like" as a modifier places the word among "maybe," "possibly," "you know," and similar phrases known as hedges. So it's not surprising that "like" is associated more with women than with men. Since the 1970s, sociolinguists have noted that women often use hedges to soften the impact of their statements. What would-be grammar police (like the *Cosmopolitan* article's author) don't acknowledge is that hedges say less about an individual woman's lack of confidence than they do about society's expectation that women not be assertive.

Either way, it seems to be a good idea to help young women root "like" out of their speech entirely. But Siegel also offers a more positive perspective on the use of the word. Studying twenty-three tape-recorded interviews of high-school honors students—both boys and girls—from suburban Philadelphia, Siegel found that spontaneity of speech, not insecurity, was most strongly correlated with a flurry of "likes."

While she found that girls did use "like" much more often than boys, she also discovered that speakers of either gender said it less often when they had more time to plan what they were saying. The speaker's comfort level and the informality of the setting also seemed to increase the use of "like." "Happily," Siegel concludes, "if girls use 'like' more than boys, it may indicate as much a gift for intimacy and spontaneity as insecurity."

Alas, fewer young women probably read the *Journal of Semantics* than *Cosmo*, so the results of this survey are unlikely to do much to break the vicious cycle that plagues "like" users: You don't feel confident in what you're saying, so you use "like"; your parents pick on you for saying "like," so you feel less confident in what you're saying; you say "like" more, they pick on you again, and on it goes.

The thrust of popular language use will never sway the gatekeepers of the English language. While "like" and other nonstandard usages spread to their very living rooms, they still cling to the shibboleth that bad English displays the speaker's stupidity. Meanwhile, my twelve-year-old student determines the meaning of "like" from *Clueless*'s Cher and Dionne. What happens when she meets my stepmother, or the *Cosmo* article's author? Will she try to speak Val in an attempt to raise her class standing? How many potential employers will dismiss her as incompetent, either for her adopted Valspeak or for her native South Bronxese?

You can't maintain linguistic purity by sheer force of will, or even through English classes. People don't have to be taught language to learn it. Babies are naturally wired to learn language by example, whether via parents or TV. By now, kids who've never heard of a Valley Girl are surely learning to say "like" from their parents. They may be admonished by those same parents not to use the word; they may learn to code-switch, turning off their use of the word in formal situations—but it's not likely that they'll give it up. Despite attempts to stigmatize it, "like" will live on.

What can *Cosmo*'s job consultants do about it, aside from undermining more women's confidence? According to Siegel, they'll have to deal with it. "The language mavens always say, 'Oh, they're wrecking the language,'" she told *The Philadelphia Inquirer* in 2002. "And it's always girls and working people [who are blamed for it]. But languages change because they need to change. There are so many more girls and working people than there are language mavens."

Teen Mean Fighting Machine

Why Does the Media Love Mean Girls?

Gabrielle Moss / WINTER 2005

LIKE ALMOST ALL FIRST DAYS OF HIGH SCHOOL IN CINEMA history, that of Cady Heron, protagonist of *Mean Girls* (2004), goes poorly. A practical, homeschooled teen raised in Africa by zoologist parents, Cady is mystified by the social customs of American high schoolers and confused by teachers who don't trust her; she ends up eating her lunch alone in the girls' bathroom. Cady, who apparently has never had a negative or hostile thought in her life, is quickly accosted by two very different types of mean girls: the sarcastic "art freak" Janis and the bitchy clique the Plastics. Cady is enlisted in a revenge scheme Janis has hatched against head Plastic Regina George, but soon finds herself enjoying the perks of popularity enough to attempt to unseat Regina and become Queen Bee herself.

Mean Girls spins a fairly pedestrian yarn about the seduction (and subsequent redemption) of an innocent outsider by the posh lifestyles and flexible morals of the popular kids. But while most teen films are based on a potent mix of recalled adolescent fantasies and repressed memories, *Mean Girls* was based on a bestselling self-help book—Rosalind Wiseman's 2002 book *Queen Bees and Wannabes: Helping Your Daughter Survive Cliques, Gossip, Boyfriends, and Other Realities of Adolescence*—that's one of the central texts of a movement that for the past few years has galvanized parents and their daughters against an alleged epidemic of meanness in their midst.

Spearheaded by *Queen Bees*, Rachel Simmons's 2002 book *Odd Girl Out:*

43

The Hidden Culture of Aggression in Girls, and mentoring/workshop programs like the Ophelia Project, the battle against mean girls ostensibly focuses on teaching girls responsibility for their actions and solidarity with their peers. A natural extension of the girl power quasifeminism of the '90s, the fight against mean girls purports to address a problem overlooked by adults and bring it to an audience of youth and their parents.

A closer examination of the assumptions behind the anti-mean-girls movement, however, reveals a far more complicated situation. Though its tenets are beneficial to girls, mean-girls theory also has a dark side, where harmful female stereotypes are given a girl power–savvy spin and spouted by the very people who claim to be working in girls' best interests. The media's reception of the subject raises some disturbing questions about girls, power, and society, and the assumptions inherent in mean-girls rhetoric could leave a powerful and troubling mark on teen culture.

Mean-girls theory dates back to the pioneering 1992 book *Of Mice and Women: Aspects of Female Aggression*, which featured work by (among others) editors Kaj Björkqvist and Pirkko Niemelä, whose studies have been mentioned in almost every article on the girl-bullying phenomenon. In a study of gender and aggression among preteen girls, Björkqvist claimed that women were more likely to display anger "relationally," within the context of their social relationships, rather than in the physical way that's traditionally perceived as "aggressive." Distilling the major forms of relational aggression—gossiping, rumor spreading, socially isolating one's peers—through subsequent study, researchers concluded that when it was given equal weight to physical and more outright verbal expressions of anger, women were just as aggressive as men.

Around the same time, pop psychologists were taking notice of the inner lives of teenage girls. *Reviving Ophelia: Saving the Selves of Adolescent Girls*, Mary Pipher's 1994 bestseller on the dangers of being young, American, and female, described female adolescence as tumultuous, scary, and a "hurricane" from which "no girl escapes." Pipher's work lent teenage girls and their problems a respect they rarely received in popular culture but said little about the possible role of suppressed aggression. This idea was left untouched until Lyn Mikel Brown's 1998 study of teen-girl anger and aggression, *Raising Their Voices*. Brown made explicit her intention to contradict the image, by then well developed, of the teen girl as victim. Advocating "healthy" anger (as opposed to "destructive" aggression) as crucial to girls' self-respect, she linked it to the development of "strong voices" and the ability to "actively resist dominant cultural notions of femininity."

While Brown's book didn't cause quite the sensation of *Ophelia* et al., by the time it was published her topic was more relevant than ever. Taking its cues from the politically aware riot-grrrl culture, the '90s girl power phenomenon—typified by postmodern (and feminism-literate) teen thrillers like *Scream* and *Jawbreaker*, a new national mania for women's soccer, and the Spice Girls—championed a kind of wholesome, boisterous aggression. Though girl power, less a movement than a marketing pitch, stopped short of recognizing the many reasons a girl might have to be angry, it nailed the connection between self-esteem and the ability to display aggression in the dual meaning of one of the era's popular slogans: "Girls Kick Ass."

By the end of the '90s, any truly empowering elements of girl power had been lost in its marketing blitz, and pop psychologists seemed to lose interest in teen girls—until 2002, when "mean girls" became a media buzz phrase. Wedding Björkqvist's theories of relational aggression to *Reviving Ophelia*'s take on girlhood under siege, the mean-girls zeitgeist proclaimed by *Queen Bees and Wannabes*, *Odd Girl Out*, and others transformed teen girls from victims to victimizers. Mean girls made the cover of *Newsweek* and were the subject of hand-wringing everywhere from *The Washington Post* to *Oprah*.

But an examination of the mean-girls coverage reveals a media interested in a few things besides girls' self-esteem.

Much of the coverage focused on *Queen Bees*, with its breezy tone and sound-bite-ready quotes. But its popularity may also stem from Wiseman's dark, not-so-sympathetic depiction of teenage girls. Despite good intentions, *Queen Bees* has some weak points that can be (and have been) interpreted as license to denounce girls as catty and shallow.

Wiseman presents her book as a relatively lighthearted guide to the adolescent heart of darkness she terms "Girl World." But in her reach for humor and hipness, she reinforces much of what she seeks to eliminate. Unlike Simmons, who locates the roots of girls' meanness in the cultural demands of niceness, Wiseman luridly promises to reveal the "nasty things" girls do to one another, but she doesn't take societal expectations regarding female aggression into account in explaining them. Though she rattles off the usual list of harmful media influences—music videos, sexualized advertising, etc.—she narrows her argument by asserting that girls themselves, not the popular culture that feeds them, are the "prime enforcer of these standards."

Furthermore, though Wiseman is genuinely interested in the health, safety, and success of teen girls, those reporting on her work are not. The revelation of the news articles and TV specials that followed the 2002 release of *Queen Bees* and *Odd Girl Out* was not that America had created an emotionally stifling culture for its daughters that sometimes caused them to act out in calculated and hurtful ways, but that girls were, well, mean. The constructive ideas suggested by Wiseman, Simmons, and others for promoting self-esteem and challenging the teen social system were left out of nearly every article on the subject. In a March 2002 article in *The Observer* (U.K.), Tim Field, author of *Bullycide* (and presumably an authority on this sort of thing), declares girls "better" at bullying than boys and is "appalled" by the lengths to which girls go to commit acts of relational aggression. A 2002 episode of *Oprah* on "the hidden culture of girls' aggression" revolved not around the question of why popularity has become paramount to teen girls' existence or how that might be changed, but, as Oprah.com summarized it, "Why are girls so mean?" Questions of cultural and social responsibility for girls' well-being were quickly lost in the sensationalistic and frequently sexist rush to reveal "the truth" about girls. In the ensuing melee, the authors' compelling ideas were spun into stereotypes disguised as social science.

At best, mean-girls theory has been lumped in with the larger field of bully psychology, completely ignoring the gender element except when it provides a little added titillation. At worst, the subject has become a safe cover for hostilities and fears about teenage girls and their power. The media's interest seems to be less about spreading awareness of behavior that hurts girls than about the potential of having real, psychological proof that the only asses girls kick are each other's.

While most of the media dust has settled around this "crisis," mean-girls theory has left its imprint on pop culture. One of the most obvious is the aforementioned film, which alternately embraces and mocks its source material, one moment parodying the idea that "meanness" is something that can be exorcised, the next suggesting that one can be reformed with some well-timed apologics. The film showcases, at its dramatic turn-ing point, a style of consciousness-raising that Wiseman developed for her youth-mentoring program. When hostilities are high and all the film's female students are mad at each other, they must engage in a practice Wise-man calls "owning up," which entails a girls-only group publicly apologiz-ing to each other. (Curiously, the practice was omitted from the curriculum for boys that Wiseman later developed.) *Mean Girls* scoffs at the act's po tential to heal wounds—in fact, it shows the possibly more realistic out-come of dividing the girls further.

However, when Cady does her own "owning up" after being elected prom queen, it achieves the desired forgiveness, and in the end everyone hangs out in one big, nonjudgmental group. But the plot points that take them there are suspect: Innocent Cady doesn't become a Machiavellian power puppeteer because she has anger to vent; she does so just because it's so damn easy. Conversely, the film's end finds former Queen Bee Regina channeling her hostility into a new life as a lacrosse player, suggesting that her anger didn't stem from any specific place, and that her emotional health is simply dependent on "burning it off" in a socially acceptable manner. Likewise, sarcastic Janis is mellowed by the love of mathlete Kevin G. (These are, of course, age-old ideas for how to calm overly aggressive women.) And in the "owning up" scene, a teacher—played by the film's screenwriter, Tina Fey—comments, in response to a question about the girls' self-esteem, that self-esteem is not the issue: "They seem pretty pleased with themselves."

The mean girl has been absorbed as a pop culture figure, while any in-sight regarding how she got that way (or the degree of cultural change nec-essary to eliminate her kind) is forgotten. Self-help has been traded for a more traditional moralizing. Plus, it's supposed to be funny. In boycentric films like *Lord of the Flies*, *Bully*, and the recent *Mean Creek*, teen male anger—which frequently erupts in violence—is given serious moral di-mension; in contrast, Cady does no real soul-searching because her anger is presented as slapstick. (Interestingly, the '80s teen classic *Heathers*, *Mean Girls'* obvious precursor, did involve anger erupting into murder yet was also billed as a comedy.)

Despite all this, the mean-girls craze may have opened the door for a cultural discussion about the importance of female friendship. Talking about what girls will put up with for friendship—pursuing it with a passion previously ascribed only to romantic relationships—can lead to a greater understanding of the crucial role that female friendships play in girls' lives, as important as any romance. And tween/teen media featuring nonmean girls does thrive: The protagonists of popular TV shows like *Lizzie McGuire* and *That's So Raven* value close female friends, and then there's that thriving straight-to-video empire created by Mary-Kate and Ashley Olsen. A T-shirt sold last summer at the tween chain Rave Girl made an even bolder statement: Emblazoned with "Hilary's Best Friend" (referring to Hilary Duff), it's a powerful counterpoint to those "Mrs. Kutcher" and "Mrs. Lachey" Ts that also made the rounds last year. Sure, there must be a lot of competition to be Hilary's best friend, but it would be a joy comparable (or even superior) to wedding a pop idol.

Anti-mean-girls rhetoric sounds feminist because it's nominally about empowering girls; but, once filtered through popular media, it doesn't ask girls to explore their anger or aggression, nor does it address why they're expected to be "nice"—and, more important, how being nice doesn't always leave room for being smart, strong, capable, independent, or adventurous. What could've been a teen feminist movement, touching on some of the great unrecognized truths about life as a girl, ultimately became nothing more than a tired recapitulation of the good girl/bad girl game, with all its attendant moralism. The mean-girls debates could have helped transform the way teenage girls are encouraged to think and act toward each other. But in the end, all we got was another catfight.

2

· · · · · · · · · · ·

Ladies and Gentlemen

FEMININITY, MASCULINITY, AND IDENTITY

IT'S NOT MUCH OF A STRETCH TO MAKE THE CASE THAT MOST of the pop culture landscape, no matter what the ostensible plot or supposed topic at hand, is actually devoted to limning our expectations of men and women, girls and boys, and exploring the tensions therein. Magazines like *Glamour*, *Redbook*, *Men's Health*, and *Maxim* are nothing if not instruction manuals for gender-appropriate behavior. Both *Survivor* and *The Apprentice* saw fit to structure entire seasons around a "battle of the sexes" gimmick. The *Chicago Sun-Times* headlined a July 2005 story "'Guy roles for women' on CBS this fall." (Just what would those "guy roles" be? Why, doctors and lawyers, and, you know, "leaders in charge of large responsibilities and their own complex lives," according to the paper.) Makeover shows from the mild *What Not to Wear* to the surgitastic likes of *Extreme Makeover* often focus on "correcting" gendered traits: On the former, women are forced to trade their baggy shirts and ratty sneakers for, as hostess Stacy put it on at least one occasion, "some clothes that are actually made for women"; on the latter, men with "weak" chins get implants and women with flat chests or, God forbid, facial hair get properly ladyfied. (Putting butch women in prom dresses is also a favorite of daytime talk shows.)

When gender expectations are being reversed, the reversal itself becomes the focus, again demonstrating loud and clear how central gender is to our understanding of the world around us: The pivotal scene of *G.I. Jane*

49

came when Demi Moore kicked her drill instructor in the nuts and said, "Suck my dick." *Commander in Chief* is built around the novelty of a person with tits occupying the Oval Office. Even nature films get in on the act— wasn't *March of the Penguins* as much about the supposed novelty of dad warming the egg for months while mom is off eating as it was about the resourcefulness of adorable flightless birds in the brutal Antarctic winter?

A reliable category of punch lines has always been the transgression and/or maintenance of gender and sexuality's boundaries: Think Ross and Joey's naptime snuggling habit on *Friends*, the 2004 Chevy commercial in which a truck passenger sows discomfort among his friends by singing along to Shania Twain's "Man! I Feel Like a Woman!," *Harold & Kumar Go to White Castle*'s title characters catching each other singing along to Wilson Phillips's "Hold On," 2005 Emmy presenter Conan O'Brien's quip that "every young girl dreams of winning an Emmy—and I am no exception."

There's a lot going on in this little cultural obsession with gender. There's the superficial stuff like the division of multiplex fare into chick flicks and, well, everything else; at the bookstore, it's chick lit versus regular ol' fiction. This is just one of the many cultural hangovers of the age-old notion that the concerns of mankind are universal but stories about women are just, you know, about *women*; the result is a persistent belief among culture makers and marketers that women (and girls) will happily consume stories about men (and boys), but the guys won't do the reverse. Its corollary is the assumption that lack of a Y chromosome means an automatic affection for sappy sisterhoods (think Ya-Ya or Traveling Pants, not Is Powerful). Then there's slightly deeper stuff like the whims of advertisers and the circular arguments of their commercial imperatives. They like our tastes—both in media and in products—divided into pink and blue camps, because it's so much easier to figure out what to advertise where.

But that's far from the end of the story. Gendered identities are more than simply male or female, masculine or feminine. The tomboy and the sensitive guy have been with us as long as the delicate flower and the manly man, and the feminist and queer movements have made room for many more. Title IX brought women onto the playing fields in droves, carving out a female athletic identity far more nuanced and enduring than the tomboy. Organizations as diverse as the Gender Public Advocacy Coalition, whose mission is "to end discrimination and violence caused by gender stereotypes by changing public attitudes, educating elected officials and expanding human rights"; the Hetrick-Martin Institute, which provides services to queer youth; and Camp Trans, the protest-cum–alternative festival that developed in response to the Michigan Womyn's Music Festival's womyn-born-womyn-only policy are loosening the gender binary's stranglehold on our popular imagination. A decade ago, drag queens and high femmes started making it onto the mainstream radar: *Bound*; *Friends*' Carol and Susan; *Priscilla, Queen of the Desert*; RuPaul. These days, a memoir of male-to-female transition can become a modest bestseller, and its author can be treated with respect on *Oprah*. Butch dykes, tranny bois, intersex folks, and the wide range of genderqueers who refuse to check either the M or the F box are moving in—however slowly—from the subcultural fringe: *Hedwig and the Angry Inch*, *Transamerica*, and Jeffrey Eugenides's Pulitzer prize–winning *Middlesex* are only the most mainstream manifestations of a new awareness of gender's infinite complications.

But most of us looking to celluloid for a reflection of ourselves will be sorely disappointed, no matter what our gender (even if we see ourselves as pretty standard males or females—Hollywood archetypes are limited about plenty more than the strict boy/girl thang). When nontraditional identities do make it onscreen, they tend to become confining and one-dimensional. Think *Will & Grace*'s Jack, who was prime time's first out-and-proud flaming fag, or *Sex and the City*'s unabashedly slutty (and always satisfied) Samantha. Both started off as interesting departures for TV but became insufferable caricatures when writers neglected character development in favor of recycled punch lines.

But there's meaning beyond the obvious in our quest to use our pop-culture screens as mirrors. We can't ignore the fact that lack of cultural visibility often translates into political erasure; more important, this gender obsession clues us in to how our culture has dealt with the complex changes and pressure brought by the aforementioned feminist and queer agitation. And it's mostly by playing up clear-cut versions of masculinity and femininity whose boundaries blur only for comic effect, or struggling against change with more and more lad mags, dating rulebooks, and other attempts at keeping us all in our "proper" place.

Bitch has always been concerned with this struggle, arguing loudly for critical examination of how pop culture seeks to define us and for whose purposes—and how we in turn push back to define ourselves. —L.J.

Urinalysis

On Standing Up to Pee

Leigh Shoemaker / FALL 1997

AH . . . URINATION. BIOLOGICAL NECESSITY OR SOCIAL DETER-
minant? And you thought it was just something we all have to do six or
seven times a day in direct proportion to how much and what types of fluid
we consume. However, according to Camille Paglia, urination surpasses its
mundane function of relieving the body of fluid wastes and becomes something entirely different. As she writes in *Sexual Personae*: "Concentration
and projection are remarkably demonstrated by urination, one of male
anatomy's most efficient compartmentalizations . . . Male urination really
is a kind of accomplishment, an arc of transcendance [*sic*]. A woman merely
waters the ground she stands on . . . There is no projection beyond the
boundaries of the self."

Of course, this judgment is based not on the mere act itself, but on the
how of the process, the performance involved in the relief. It's not just what
you have, it's what you do with it that counts. But are men of necessity arc-
shooters and wall-sprayers and women lowly puddle-makers? What are we to
make of all this? Paglia has certainly added a new facet to good ol' penis envy.

Using Paglia's logic, anyone who can shoot a stream of bodily fluid a few
inches or a few feet away from one's corpus is somehow superior, touched by
the hand of God. All you need is a fleshly hose in order to transcend the hor-
rors of embodiment. I am only assuming that she is choosing to ignore lactating women, whose postpregnancy breasts are so laden with milk that one

good squeeze could take out any person in the room. Perhaps superiority should be determined not by the ability to shoot a stream of bodily fluid, but by the type of fluid composing the stream. Personally, I believe the ability to spray milk to be on a higher level than the ability to spray urine. Perhaps this is merely my bias as a woman. However, I think that all those good Catholic artists who depicted the baby Jesus feeding at his mother Mary's breast would agree: None of these pictures showed the holy infant with his mouth greedily slurping at the nipple; rather, he is shown kicked back at a distance, mouth open, a thin stream of white fluid coursing through the air toward the blessed mouth, propelled by the hand of Mary—the first popular documentation of a milk-squirting woman. Arc of transcendence, indeed—you don't see any streams of urine headed toward the mouth of God.

Yet this logic clearly never occurred to Paglia, committed as she is to male superiority. Witness: "The cumbersome, solipsistic character of female physiology is tediously evident at sports events and rock concerts, where fifty women wait in line for admission to the sequestered cells of the toilet. Meanwhile, their male friends zip in and out (in every sense) and stand around looking at their watches and rolling their eyes."

One must wonder: Has this woman never heard of the concept of "potty parity"? It's not that women take that long to pee, though I have stood in line behind some of the slowest—but one must factor in many other variables. Society has urged women to conceal and restrain their physiques in layers of strange undergarments, hose, girdles, etc., which are as difficult to remove as they are to reassemble. Who says that women don't have to concentrate and extend the mind to spatial analysis in order to pee? Also, most women actually wash their hands, even though they don't have to manually direct and position any flesh in order to accomplish the great feat of urination.

On to the matter of toilet type—let's uncover the great mystery of the men's room. Men's rooms typically have two types of urine-receiving vessels: the traditional toilet that you find in your own home, and the urinal, a freestanding porcelain hole in the wall. Some men's rooms expand on the urinal idea to the trough, which, true to its name, can accommodate several excreting fellows shoulder to shoulder. One trough may be the equivalent of ten to twelve traditional toilets. Zip, flip, whiz, shake, tuck, zip, and you're outta there. Superiority based on biology or superior bathroom planning? You make the call.

Of course, the man's ability to zip and flip, coupled with the indiscreet placement of urinals and troughs and rampant societal homophobia, makes the male of the species subject to a much more touchy issue: urinal etiquette. I have been informed by those in the know that talking is out, glancing is out, looking down is out, meticulous shaking is out, bumping is out; in fact, any kind of personal contact or comment is out of the question. Peeing on the cake, however, is accepted and perhaps lauded as an accomplishment—however, since this involves looking down, better do it only when alone or with close friends. Brag about it later. Paying too much attention to your penis or anyone else's while in the bathroom is a sure sign of deviance. Is this the concentration to which Paglia so enviously refers?

While men are ushered into the realm of the public pissoir at young and tender ages (but not too young, because they will look and they will comment: "Yours is so big!" a friend's young nephew was reported to exclaim to a man at a urinal in a public restroom), women are cloistered off into those sequestered cells to do our business discreetly and quietly, with a minimum of muss and fuss. We wait our turn in line for entrance into one of those private cubicles, and upon gaining admittance, turn and lock the door behind us, shutting out all those who would dare to enter and intrude upon our most private moments. Within the stall lies the toilet, the toilet paper dispenser, a hook for hanging loose articles, and another small box, the cell within the cell, for the disposal of that most private of items, the "sanitary" napkin and/or tampon. Bathroom etiquette consists of waiting your turn respectfully, not splashing on the seat, and not taking too much time in the stall. But ah, the freedom that one enjoys in the sweet privacy of the claustrophobic retreat: One's eyes can wander freely, one can smile, chat with one's friends waiting in line, and why, one can even touch oneself without feeling too transgressive.

Compare this sanctimonious confessional with the men's room stall: same basic equipment, but no door, and often, no toilet paper. Imagine the chagrin experienced by the male as he enters the public restroom to take care of business. Suppose he doesn't want to join his comrades at the trough or urinal line—can he attain his dreams of privacy from within the confines of a stall? What if he wants to deny his "natural" superiority by sitting down? Some guys do, you know. The men's bathroom becomes for many a sort of proving ground of machismo, a killing field from which only the most superior may emerge, a site of systematic desensitization through a lack of privacy and forced public urination (and defecation). The message is one that would make Darwin proud: Stand up and piss, or be pissed upon. Could this lack of sensitivity in bathroom design be one factor that is reinforcing stereotypical masculine behavior?

To continue along that stream of thought, what effect does this "camaraderie" at the trough have on the men who experience it continually throughout their lives? What effect does urination in a small sequestered cell have on the women who experience such cloistering in their public and private lives? Are men more comfortable with their body image due to the public parading of their most "private" parts? Or do they learn, again and again, upon entering the men's room, that they must be able to prove themselves physically in order to attain success as a male in society? Do women internalize the message that their excretions are dirty and shameful, something to be hidden from other women and the world? Is the sequestered cell complicit in serving to further the fragmentation of women? Does it, as Paglia states, imply a "solipsistic" women's nature? Do men really gather in public restrooms to create directed streams of urine and contemplate their consequential domination of society? Is it a worthwhile feminist project to create public restrooms that enable women to gather and excrete in the visible presence of one another?

Perhaps Paglia was on the right track, but, as usual, busily engaged in savagely missing the point. Urination as metaphor for natural male superiority? No. Urination as metaphor for the propagation of stereotypes and perceptions of male superiority? Mayyyybe. Urination as concrete example of what we assume about gender and how we reinforce those assumptions—about man's ability to perform under pressure, about man's "transcendence," about woman's unwieldy and inconvenient embodiment? Ah, yes. What might be the implications of an entire generation of men trained to pee sitting down? What might be the implications of a worldwide potty parity law with amendments built in to ensure plenty of good, fresh t.p. and doors for all stalls, men's and women's? Perhaps the revolution must begin not at home, not in the streets, but in the bathrooms of America, for it is there that we learn to deal with some of the most personal interactions we will ever experience. Whether we take it sitting down or standing up is an important issue indeed.

The Collapsible Woman

Cultural Response to Rape and Sexual Abuse

Vanessa Veselka / WINTER 1999

ONE IN THREE. ONE IN FOUR. ONE IN TEN. THAT'S HOW MANY women will be raped in their lifetime, depending on which statistic you believe. As disturbing as the numbers are, almost equally disturbing is the fact that, while each woman is unique, we seem to accept only one response from a rape or abuse victim: total collapse.

The collapsible woman—one model of mental health for an uncountable number of individuals. She is fragile, humorless, and diluted, bearing an uncanny resemblance to the sickly Victorian "angel of the house." Now, like then, when a model of total fragility is held aloft as virtue, women live up to the image out of a lack of alternatives. "Break yourself," we whisper. "We'll be there to catch you." And if you don't, call us when you're ready. Every major media piece on the subject of rape or abuse presents us with the same vision of this collapsible woman. We see the same fight for sanity and purity and the same picture of life after the cathartic process of renewal. This can be seen as support for violated women, or as victim culture—but neither stance offers us much worth striving for. There has to be something better than the toaster prize of being called a survivor, an alternative to the role of the forever-scarred, pain-haunted neurotic.

This deification of fragility offers us nothing but a religion in which the pinnacle of holiness is the ability to break down at any moment, over anything, and call it a return to sanity. I'm not questioning real emotions, nightmares, tears, and pain; they are the inviolable right of every human. How, though, from this, have we come to portray the ideal "recovering" woman as someone who can't go to the grocery store without having her "issues" "triggered"? Sure, there are days, sometimes months, in the life of anybody who has been violated when the need to protect oneself from the callousness of the outside world is absolute. We need, however, to hold up more than a skinless existence as an endpoint. With all the media coverage and attention paid to rape victims in recent years, we still lack models that praise women for getting on with their lives rather than just getting through them.

As a culture, we tell girls from the cradle that rape is the worst thing that can ever happen to them. We say it will destroy their lives and that they will lose their sense of purity. We tell those who were sexually abused that it is natural to feel dirty. We do this because it's true, and we're trying to prepare them so that they don't feel alone when it happens. But aren't we also setting them up to be destroyed, to feel dirty and impure? How much are we training ourselves to crumble? The convenient use of words like "survivor" and "victim" don't really change the messages we are given. While there is no positive side to rape and abuse that could be emphasized, we should tell another, fuller truth. We should say, "This may wreck your life for a while," or "Sometimes you'll feel dirty." But we don't, and we are left with the impression that there is no healthy response other than breakdown. It's as if we see moving beyond the trauma as denying its impact.

A violated woman is expected to fall apart, and not just privately, either; she must disintegrate publicly, in front of friends, in front of professionals, in front of Starbucks. It satiates our craving for arena-style pathos. We want to cheer our gladiators for bravery while they hack themselves to bits in the ring. If a woman chooses not to play, but to find her own private way back, we say she's "in denial." If we don't see her fragment, we say that she's not "dealing with it."

We must question the belief that a cathartic experience is necessary for sanity and healing. I have seen some women push themselves, trying to trigger a dam break, and instead become trapped in neurotic fear. I have seen the release that follows catharsis replaced by a gnawing sense that the revelation wasn't quite deep enough; I have watched as women blame themselves for their inability to fall apart. Instead of being honored for an unwillingness to break, they are dismissed as "not quite ready." It becomes her fault for not being spiritually developed enough to crack. Until she cracks, she can't forgive, and until she forgives, she will never be fully healed. Breaking itself has become the goal.

The way out of this bind is to discover and create new images for woman and the aftermath of rape. But before we can talk about introducing new images, we must first examine how we see the experience itself.

If you have been raped or abused, you're scarred for life. You will never be as you were before the experience. This is also true for falling in love, getting your heart broken, going to war, having a child, or reading a great book. Everything that cuts deeply marks us. We're all scarred for life the second that we intimately relate to the outside world. With rape, the difference is in the nature of the wound.

In recent years, feminists have fought hard to portray rape as an act of violence and not lust. While this has been necessary and difficult, it is somewhat misguided. The real problem is not that we treat rape as sex, but that we treat it as theft. *Merriam-Webster's Collegiate Dictionary* defines rape as forced sex and also plunder—"robbing or despoiling," to be exact. You weren't just violated, we tell a raped woman. You were pillaged. Something of intrinsic value was stolen from you. The fervent belief that this is true is evident on all sides of the issue. From traditional cultures that treat a raped woman as bankrupt to progressive movements that speak in terms of "reclaiming" oneself and "owning" the experience, we tell a woman loudly and clearly that if she was sexually violated she has been robbed, and that the objects stolen were purity and innocence. With the best of motives, we still say to her, "I'm sorry for your loss." We will ask her to "reclaim" her experience, rather than realize its effects. The truth is, if you were raped or abused, nothing was stolen from you. The lowlife who did it threw his soul in the trash, but yours is intact. As long as we cling to the concept of rape or abuse as theft, we are ultimately led back to the belief that a woman's worth and sense of self lie in her sexual purity, and we can speak of her condition only in terms of ownership and loss. To imply that deep within every woman is something essential that can be seen or touched, a vessel containing the real her that can be stolen by someone else, is an absolute objectification of women.

Furthermore, the well-intentioned but limited reframing of rape as vio-

lence, though seemingly intuitive, is difficult and insufficient. When someone is violently, but not sexually, attacked, he or she naturally feels invaded—
but the sense of invasion stems more from the metaphorical than from the
physical. Anyone who is raped, however, *is* invaded. Someone else is inside
of you. It's not metaphor. It's real. Rape is, therefore, forced intimacy as
well as violence. We can't look at it as a sexless crime because it isn't one.
Some rapes are motivated by a desire for power through violence and others are motivated by lust and selfish rationalization. Either way, the act itself
involves sex. When you're raped, it is not a simple attack—it's complete violation of both body and sex along with a very ugly reminder of several
thousand years of female subjugation.

The biggest block to introducing new models of acceptable response to
rape and abuse is our own good intentions. After years of hearing "Get over
it," doctrines that urged us to be as soft as children were a welcome change.
There is a point, however, at which tenderizing oneself can cease to be a release and become a debilitating obsession. Unfortunately, the meanings of
words like "strong" and "weak" have turned to taffy, so that even discussing
a new direction for our response becomes fraught with unintended political bias. Today, in self-help culture, a strong person is someone who shows
her emotional weakness and a weak person is someone who hides behind
a wall of strength. This kind of groupspeak has become its own dogma and
can make debate confusing at best, and at worst, impossible.

At its core, America still dotes on stoics. We romanticize the role of the
tearless hero, even when we know better. In many ways, this is the heart of
our national identity. It defined the ideal American male up until the '50s,
and it affects all of us. We may have tried to kill it in therapy, or squash it
under the heel of the sensitized New Age, but it's bred into us. On the
surface it represents a brutish mentality that stops at nothing and tunes
out emotion like white noise on the radio, and yet we can't shake it off—
because underneath this ode to repression lies something much more powerful. Throughout every formulaic John Wayne story is the message that we
can survive anything. You don't have to compromise, it says; you can get
through without letting them break you. As demented as the packaging is,
the message itself has some value.

The limited imagination of backlash feminists in the '80s brought forth
a model of feminine power that was no more than a mirror image of the '50s

male. It adopted only the bad packaging of the power-hungry aggressor, rather than the quieter message of survival. Unfortunately, sexually abused or raped women, unconvinced by current images of recovery, often fall back on this model of repression and false toughness. The brassy, swaggering bravado of some poor girl who's afraid of her own emotions is a sad statement on what we're offering her as a way out.

There was a scene in a movie, I think it was *Mi Vida Loca*, in which one girl turns to another girl who's been screwed over and tells her to "be a macha" and take care of herself. Instead of "macha" being the feminine twin of "macho," the bullheaded brute, here it is more like the Yiddish mensch: Be a stand-up guy. Be a human. Show some dignity. The command to be a macha could be a call from one woman to another to find her guts and get through whatever is trying to destroy her without losing her pride. Sadly, we have no language in our current dialogue on rape or abuse to convey this to each other. Our history leads us to interpret such a statement as an order to feel nothing and achieve. We automatically assume that vulnerability, compassion, and the need to rely on others have no place in this kind of thinking because we relate it back to the bravado model of feminine strength borrowed from the '50s male.

The question then becomes how to disentangle the powerful call to be a macha from the callous expectation of bravado and repression. In the context of an America that glorifies the iron will of the individual, even introducing a macha model alongside the ravaged image of a sexually abused or raped woman is difficult. We are culturally trained, traditionally, to see these ideals as opposites and interpret the "stronger," stereotypically male model as the preferred one. Paradoxically, in self-help culture, we are trained to throw out the "stronger" model and favor the ravaged, traditionally female one for its emotional demonstration. This polarization is an unnecessary construct; I am suggesting that we widen the range to include something more representative of our true potential.

We need to articulate a new vision that equates feminine strength not with repression and bravado, but with compassion and grit. The single model of recovery from sexual abuse and rape that requires a woman to live in a cocoon of self-obsession and call it a safe environment has the same potential for social isolation as '50s, middle-class suburbs. It also bears an eerie resemblance to the "separate sphere" mentality that early feminists fought so hard to destroy. In the Victorian age, for example, it was popular to be sick. There were even fainting couches, furniture designed to collapse on. The idea was to wane visibly because it was better to be honored for a tragic demise than not honored at all.

Idealizing a state of breakdown, however, rather than the strength it takes to get past one, traps women into believing that moving beyond the trauma is heresy. We need to be able to turn to each other and say, "Be a macha," and know that that means, "I'll cry with you, hold your hand, and give you time. But I won't watch you lie down." Until we can whisper the truth—nothing was stolen from you, that was a lie—and honor women for both their compassion and their guts, we won't stop unraveling. We will always be the collapsible woman.

The Princess and the Prankster

Two Performers Take on Art, Ethnicity, and Sexuality

Karen Eng / FALL 2002

IT'S SUCH A TRUISM, IT'S BORING. TYPE A PHRASE AS INNOCU-
ous as "Asian woman" into a web search engine, and hundreds of sites
featuring undressed Asian cuties to suit every sexual taste materialize; elsewhere, web-based mail-order-bride services tout the benefits of the legendary Asian disposition. Personally, when not making snarky remarks
about it, I prefer to ignore the ubiquity of Asian-lady porn, if not out of exas-
peration then just to stay sane. Artists Kristina Sheryl Wong and Gennifer
Hirano, however, feel differently. Wong's website, Big Bad Chinese Mama
(www.bigbadchinesemama.com), corners web surfers looking for porn and
confronts them instead with hilarious and gross mail-order brides who
bite. Hirano's work, some of which can be seen at www.asianprincess
artifacts.com, explores the dynamics of sexual assault through photography,
writing, and performance. Her Asianprincess character is an Asian cowgirl
in pink braids, bikini top, and thong who often sings "Coal Miner's Daughter" while giving an Asian man a lap dance. Some would call these women's
Venus-flytrap approaches to consciousness-raising politically incorrect, even
potentially destructive. But Hirano and Wong, in choosing to embrace rather
than avoid the exhausted myths of Asian female sexuality, turn the tables
on the oppressor—and on the groupthink of the oppressed.

Though they met only in the last year, the two have led somewhat parallel lives: Both are from Asian-friendly, progressive San Francisco, and both

came of age in a time when the popularity of Margaret Cho, *Giant Robot*, Pokémon, Bollywood, Hong Kong action films, and other Asian products began edging Asian-American subcultures closer to the mainstream. And while neither woman's work could be considered conventional, both take an accessible, pop culture approach to Asian-American politics, as have contemporary entertainers like the comedy troupe 18 Mighty Mountain Warriors and actor/comedian Kate Rigg (of the one-woman show *Kate's Chink-O-Rama*). Using a surefire sales tactic—sex—Hirano's and Wong's alter egos commodify and then topple expectations about Asian women's sexuality, luring in and confronting those who need it most (not just men who fetishize Asian women but also fellow Asian Americans complacent in their ideas of political correctness). Both women explore the possibility of reclaiming porn as a vehicle for probing identity, sexual expression, and self-portraiture, and both dose their politically charged art with unapologetic humor. The results have jangled nerves, provoked arguments, and raised plenty of eyebrows—and they wouldn't have it any other way.

The Prankster: Kristina Sheryl Wong

Go to Big Bad Chinese Mama and you'll be greeted by images of an Asian woman in a long blue Chinese dress inviting you to check out the "demure lotus blossoms . . . the geishas . . . the Oriental sluts"—"whatever you had imagined in your patriarchal, colonialist longings." Click on the angry Hello Kitty icon and you'll come face-to-face with the Big Bad Mama herself, clutching a bag of Chee-tos and mugging as hideously as she can. "Hi there," says the greeting. "I am the Big Bad Chinese Mama. As you can tell, I am a sweet and lovely lotus blossom. This is just like many [mail-order] sites you have seen before but better . . . I have gathered lovely 'Oriental Creatures' from all over the world, who are just as sweet and pretty as me. They will show you just how demure Asian women really are."

The motives behind BBCM are complex. Wong's primary goal is "to catch the oppressor in the act of oppression and use my personal sense of humor as a political force," as the site's manifesto states. "I wanted to subvert the expectations of a nasty guy in search of petite naked Asian bodies by showing him the full ugliness of 'sweet Asian girls.'"

Inside, the Harem of Angst offers a menu of distinctly unappetizing

63

choices. Madame Bootiefly sits on the toilet, trousers around her shins, face obscured. Annie, "an expert in the ancient and delicate art of flower arranging," lolls in a red wig, toting a vacuum cleaner and dragging off a long cigarette. Mikki, a man in drag, is "thirteen, and still in pigtails." She says, "You will also notice my dainty feet, large and unbound, perfect for giving the oriental (back walking) massages. I'm sure you will cry tears of joy with my petite 200 pounds crushing the small of your back."

The site also features such treats as downloadable audio pranks, in which BBCM and her friends crank-call sex-industry companies; the BBCM's Memoirs of an Anti-Geisha ("I have gigantic size $9^{1}/_{2}$ feet, crater zits that break out through my 'silky skin' . . . I have a little pot-belly, I have an ass that needs to go to the gym"); and a Frequently Unasked Questions page that addresses questions commonly asked on mail-order-bride sites.

> Q: Will my bride make an easy adjustment from her Asian Culture to the liberal American lifestyle? A: . . . You may be able to buy yourself a nice little Asian Porno, a buddhist bracelet, or some other object that your capitalistic lifestyle Orientalize[s]—but you cannot buy these women. They are not for sale.

Wong—who lives in Los Angeles and works as an actor, performance artist, and writer, supplementing her income by selling random items (*Iron Chef* promotional fridge magnets, for example) on eBay—explains that her porn/mail-order-bride spoof site was built as a final project for an Asian-American studies class at UCLA and came out of the evolution of her political consciousness. When Wong was introduced to Asian-American studies, she suddenly felt she had a context for "every awkward experience I had growing up." With her newfound sense of political awareness, she says, "I was literally walking on campus and fuming." By her second year, she was exploring ways of expressing herself through performance and art. She had also begun to notice that the political agenda in Asian-American studies classes was annoyingly homogeneous. "A lot of the same issues kept coming up, especially about stereotypes and representation." All anyone wanted to do, it seemed, was tear apart Asian Americans on TV, in media, in literature: Amy Tan emasculates Asian men, Margaret Cho isn't funny, Lucy Liu is a dragon lady, and so on. In her eyes, her peers' attitudes limited Asian-American identity to narrow, fragmented roles. Such attitudes, says Wong, also imply that individual Asian Americans should be held accountable for representing the whole group.

Wong created Big Bad Chinese Mama as much to poke fun at the righteous indignation of her classmates as to put herself on the front lines. She wanted to confront the "nitpicky people"—who she felt were getting too comfortable in their academic bubble—with the reality of racism in the real world. The site's metatags, which juxtapose keywords like "American," "Asia," "feminism," and "ass-kicking anti-geishas" with "mail-order," "Orientals," "cock," "suck," "lesbians," and "teen on teen," bring the two worlds skidding toward each other. Wong expected her peers to be insulted. "I expected [them] to say, 'How can Kristina Wong represent Asians that way?' Then I want them to look at the [negative] responses in my guest book from all the white men, and black men, and Asian people . . . and see [that] *this* is the ignorance out there that we're not experiencing in our highfalutin class where we get to talk about how wrong sweatshops are as we wear sweatshop clothing." Instead, more people than she expected responded positively, posting congratulatory messages indicating that they understand what Wong is up to.

As for the response from the public at large, BBCM's message boards are clogged with white-supremacist rants from people who accidentally stumbled in looking for porn. ("Another clueless lesbian feminist bitch who doesn't know jackshit about the motives of either Western men or East Asian women who use online dating services. Fuck all of you or, better yet, let the BBCMs fuck one another.") Some are lucid; most are just hateful spam. The site receives twenty to thirty messages a day, and they're all there, untouched. Wong doesn't edit them because she doesn't want to take a defensive position, censor, or, as she puts it, "micromanage" people's politics. Wong admits she initially felt extremely nervous about porn-seeking strangers looking at her pictures at all hours of the day and night, but she stood by her conviction to take her project into an "unsafe" space. She now feels her highest intentions are being fulfilled when visitors interact on the boards, and she points out the political empowerment that comes from being unfazed. "Why are we so scared to accept rejection? That in itself is art. I would rather see the hate on my site than on the KKK site . . . I would rather all that racism pour out, and people who live in their own little bubble look at that and be completely shocked and wake up a little."

"There's a little more anger than necessary, and you leave going, Whoa, this is funny, but I feel completely attacked," Wong concedes of BBCM. "Or, This is funny, but I feel misrepresented. I want to leave people with that raw nerve. Our ancestors worked too hard to get here for us to just sit and be comfy."

The Princess: Gennifer Hirano

At 2001's APAture, an Asian youth arts conference, Asianprincess strode onto the stage to the strains of "Coal Miner's Daughter," holding a pink boom box. A rocking horse sat on the stage, and a slide projected the silhouette of a woman on horseback onto the wall behind her, along with the words "Welcome to Asianprincess Ranch." Wearing a wig of pink braids, a cowboy hat, a bikini top, a tiny skirt, a thong, and red platform sandals, Asianprincess wailed into the mic, then wriggled into the audience, where she performed for individual audience members, seductively straddling men's laps. Around her, the audience's faces evinced a mixed reaction: some clearly shocked, some offended, some confused, some amused, and some just having a great time.

The following summer, the photographic counterpart to this cowgirl burlesque act, *Welcome to Asianprincess Ranch*, was installed at Intersection for the Arts, a gallery in San Francisco. The show consisted of four medium-format color images framed by barbed wire with a magic wand stuck in it; in them, a blonde-wigged Asianprincess looks lost by the side of the road, wearing a thong, a pink chemise, and her trademark red platforms, carrying a pink case and a hobbyhorse. In the last of the four frames, she's getting into a truck driven by a strapping white man. He leans toward her, and she smiles coyly over her shoulder at the camera, kicking up a heel.

During a panel discussion at the gallery, artist Gennifer Hirano posed the following questions from a prose piece she wrote as her own commentary on *Asianprincess Ranch*: "This hitchhiker is: A) Asking to be raped dressed like that on the side of the road. B) Asking for the viewer to make a deeper evaluation of the context of fashion photography, reality, and the constructions of sexuality, race, and gender. C) At the Burning Man festival bartering for fuel for her generator for her Asianprincess Ranch karaoke show." Hirano plays the part of Asianprincess vividly, with so much conviction that it's hard to imagine her out of character. She is unrecognizable in her regular outfit of fuzzy sweater, tortoiseshell glasses, and ponytail. She's soft-spoken and articulate, even as she protests that her in-your-face, sexually over-the-top character is actually very close to her own personality.

The first Asianprincess photo series, called *Empire*, features images of Hirano taken at the Japanese Tea Garden in San Francisco's Golden Gate Park. She wears a blonde wig and Chinese minidress, and holds a paper umbrella. The photos are printed on Asian scrolls bearing Chinese calligraphy that says, "The meaning is nothing, nothing is the meaning." Hirano explains that just because her parents happen to be Chinese American and Japanese, her appropriation of Asian iconography and objectification is no more valid than anyone else's. "I used to think when I was in college that I owned my culture. That white people didn't have the right to wear cheongsams or have Asian tattoos. Then I realized, especially after going to China, that I appropriate my culture all the time, every day. I'm pulling what I think is Chinese symbolism and cultural icons from what I think is Chinese-looking, from cigarette ads and 1970s calendar-girl poses and paintings."

If *Empire* depicts an Asian-American woman in yellowface, *Asianprincess Ranch*, created two years later, is an Asian-American woman in whiteface. "It's weird for people to see an Asian girl singing country music. I want them to think about why that's weird, [to] think . . . deeper than, 'I've never seen an Asian cowgirl before. Are you from Texas?' 'No. I'm not from China or Japan either.' Which culture do I belong to, really, and which is fictitious? They're all fictitious."

Asianprincess grew out of Hirano's undergraduate years at the University of California at Berkeley, where she earned a degree in art practice with a minor in Asian-American studies. Like Wong, she became an activist as she gained political awareness, at one point receiving a fellowship to organize a women's-issues conference. She also began using sexuality in her art to express her anger at objectification of Asian women—"I would wear whiteface and chopsticks in a bun, crawl around on the ground, and break mirrors."

Hirano says she has always been interested in exploring her own sexuality as it relates to ethnicity—as far as she's concerned, the two are inseparable. She suffered four separate sexual assaults in her young adulthood,

and coming to terms with these experiences led her to work as a professional stripper for three years. Sex work, Hirano asserts, was an important
part of the healing process because it forced her to learn to maintain sexual
boundaries with men. "I never got to say no on time, in the right way. I
didn't get to speak up in time," she says of the assaults; stripping offered
her a chance to play at being overtly sexual, while learning how to speak up.

Hirano's fascination with sex work and porn served as a catalyst for
Asianprincess. "Asia Carrera was my first Asian sex-positive role model,"
she states on her website. "I didn't even know it was possible to do sex work
and be intelligent *and* Asian until I discovered her and her website back in
my angry-Asian-girl days in college when I thought Asian porn stars were
'bringing my people down.'"

While Hirano continues to develop the Asianprincess character, and
Asianprincess can still be hired as entertainment for parties and events,
she has quit stripping for a living. She now teaches performance art and
photography to kids, which is less grueling, if also less lucrative.

In addition to performance and photography, Hirano creates gallery in-
stallations and sells merchandise (which she calls "artifacts") based on her
own image. For a few dollars you can buy a Rice Rocket calendar, which features Asianprincess perched atop an Acura, eating from a rice cooker; 3-D
postcards from panels of the *Asianprincess Ranch* photos; or a black-and-
white sticker with an erotic image of the cowgirl with text in Old West–style
lettering that reads, "Sexuality is constructed." She sometimes sets up an
Asianprincess Polaroid booth at gatherings and conventions (like pride festivals, Burning Man, and APAture), where for a few dollars, anyone can get
her picture taken with Asianprincess and take home a piece of the act.

The full scope of Hirano's intent is not readily apparent in Asianprincess's act and artifacts, which are meant to be, for the most part, enticing and playful. For her more directly topical work, she relies on prose and
poetry, which she plans to publish, and spoken word performed under her
own name, out of character and often to live jazz bands—which she describes as a little more "castrating." Instead of flattering and seducing
people, as Asianprincess does, in these performances Hirano directly addresses her experiences, trying to promote awareness about sexual assault.
However, Asianprincess is always willing to talk about these serious issues

if people question her. Hirano says that every time she's out performing and selling artifacts at festivals, at least one person will want to talk more about her intent. As for those who utterly misread her act as an invitation to treat her disrespectfully, she takes the opportunity to challenge their assumptions. "I do put myself out there so that I can come into these confrontations and teach people. I get to put a red light on people and say, 'You are violating me.' It's [a very] empowering thing for a woman to be able to say that."

ONE COULD ARGUE THAT WONG'S AND HIRANO'S AGENDAS may be too complex to be effective: Wong's layers of meaning are buried beneath angry humor that hits so forcefully that one's initial reaction, positive or negative, can preclude wanting or needing to look more deeply—which is what Wong would like her audience to do. Hirano's various levels of engagement aren't readily apparent when Asianprincess is out performing without a ready-to-consume political message—but she doesn't care much what conclusions her audience jumps to. Such disconnect can not only lead to misreading but could be interpreted as contributing to the problem. When I first saw Asianprincess perform, for example, Hirano's approach seemed uncomplicated and not well thought out.

Does the fact that their work requires deeper investigation mean it's either no good or ineffective? I don't think so. Even though my first reaction to each artist's work was very different—I got Wong's spoof immediately, while Hirano's live act made me squirm—both women upset my way of thinking about the performance of ethnicity and sexuality, and my responses to it.

What did my discomfort about Asianprincess say about me, for example? Had Hirano been a blonde, blue-eyed burlesque performer, I wouldn't have cared, but I initially found it hard to accept that an Asian woman would perform a hypersexual character, simply because I would never be able to accept myself performing it. Hirano doesn't respond to the phenomenon of Asian fetishization the way I do. In projecting the responsibility for my discomfort onto her, I also illustrated Wong's point that the responsibility for an entire community's representation can't rest with one artist.

Ultimately, I appreciate that fellow Asian-American women made me question my assumptions. Both Wong and Hirano are admirably committed to not preaching to the converted—instead, they put their confrontational personae out in all kinds of spaces to reach a wide cross section of spectators. Their bait-and-switch tactics dauntlessly invoke questions of ethnicity and sexual agency without handing out any pat answers.

What Happens to a Dyke Deferred?

The Trouble with Hasbians and the Phenomenon of Banishment

Athena Douris and Diane Anderson-Minshall / FALL 2002

A LESBIAN WHO SCREWS A MAN IS SUCH A CLICHÉ, IT'S THE plot of a Kevin Smith movie, numerous *Jerry Springer* episodes, and thousands of pornos. For some straight men, it's proof that lesbians just need some good dick. For homophobes, it's a trajectory that follows God's supposed plan for "normal" sexual relations between men and women. For many dykes, it's a scandalous bit of gossip that makes excellent fodder for dinnertime conversation. And in the eyes of the dyke community as a whole, a lesbian who goes to men has committed the ultimate betrayal—a betrayal that can be properly punished only by exile.

We were two dyke friends who regularly chatted about the tragedy of lesbians who went to men. That is, until it happened to one of us. Out, lesbian-feminist activist Athena fell in love with a man. She lost her job. (She was a sex columnist; her boss quickly labeled her "straight" and "replaceable.") Her closest friend, a former lover, stopped speaking to her. In the space of two months—the time it took for her to realize her relationship with this man was more than a sexual fling—she lost her identity. She went from lesbian to hasbian (a term that first appeared in print in a 1990 *San Francisco Chronicle* gossip column, in which lesbians who'd "gone straight" were declared "all the rage these days").

Athena is far from the first hasbian, or the most infamous. That title might belong to JoAnn Loulan, who was the world's leading lesbian sex

71

therapist for twenty years. She authored our greatest tomes of lesbian sexuality, including *Lesbian Passion* and *Lesbian Sex*, and even coined the term "lesbian bed death." When Loulan started a relationship with a man several years ago, her best friend also stopped speaking to her. She lost speaking engagements, book sales, and, she says, her sense of purpose in life.

"I feel like I got a quickie divorce against my will, like my wealthy spouse walked out with everything and I got nothing," she says, speaking of her estrangement from the lesbian community in an interview with Athena earlier this year. "My life looks very empty to me now, compared to how it used to be. I've filled it up—I've made a life for myself—but it's not the same." Loulan says she's been courted by bisexual organizations who'd like her to head their groups. She refuses because she doesn't identify as bisexual. In an essay published in a 1999 issue of *Girlfriends*, Loulan wrote, "During the 20 years of my adult life that I loved and fucked (and was fucked by) women exclusively . . . I was a lesbian. Now a man comes along and his involvement in my life changes my identity? I don't think so."

But for most of the world—lesbian and otherwise—when a man comes along, it does change everything. Anne Heche, you might remember, stopped being queer in the world's eyes the moment she bedded a cameraman. Heche didn't identify as a dyke to begin with (she has said she was as surprised as anyone when she fell in love with Ellen DeGeneres), but then, many women who fuck women speak of their sexual identity in the same terms. Ani DiFranco has always sung and spoken openly about her relationships with both men and women. Yet when she partnered with a man, many of her fans disavowed their former icon, shuttered their fan sites, and moved on. Then, of course, there's Julie Cypher, the woman who left her husband and sidelined her own film-directing career (remember *Theresa's Tattoo?*) for Melissa Etheridge. They had two kids and became America's gay family delegates, turning up at every rally, every benefit, every awards show. Then they split up, and suddenly Cypher was, dykes declared, straight all along.

The reasons behind this kind of rejection—a phenomenon we have termed "dyke banishment"—are many. Loulan believes that it's a result of homophobia—that lesbians feel so overwhelmed and negated by society, we can't see the pain we're creating when we exile another woman. Often, dykes who reject women like Cypher say they're justified because women who love men have easier lives, so they don't deserve the protection, companionship, or support of the lesbian community. In some ways, they're right: Male-female couples enjoy thousands of perks unavailable to queer couples, including the rights to marry, inherit, and share custody—not to mention the ability to walk down a street holding hands and not be bashed.

But in other ways, the matter may not be so simple. An out dyke can be marked for the rest of her life, no matter who she's with. Athena's queer past means that her future in-laws, who are fundamentalist Christians, will not allow her to take her boyfriend's two-year-old niece into the yard to play (the "gays molest children" fallacy). She has been barred from family gatherings that fall on religious holidays (the "God hates fags" myth). One future in-law accused her of satanism. At a time when some lesbians refuse to see her as one of them, she's dealing with the most vitriolic homophobia she's ever faced.

The root cause of dyke banishment may also lie in the queer community's concept of sexual orientation. In today's GLBT culture, there's a belief that sexual orientation has a permanent, biological core. It's a concept frequently expressed by women who say, "I was born a dyke," by most coming-out narratives, and by T-shirt/bumper-sticker slogans like "I can't even think straight." This sentiment can be traced to the late 1800s, when sexologist Magnus Hirschfeld claimed that queers were "born that way" in order to advance gay rights in Germany. The theory found modern expression in the early 1990s, when the GLBT community seized upon the work of Simon LeVay for the same reason. LeVay found a link between hypothalamus size and homosexuality in men. This finding was spun into an argument for civil rights based on the thesis that if being gay isn't our choice, then it isn't our fault—and we deserve all the rights of people born with a larger hypothalamus. As it applies to lesbians, the biology-is-destiny theory is used by the queer community to discredit the lives of dykes who end up in love with men. By this logic, women who were "born gay" (i.e., women whose behavior is consistent) are real, authentic dykes who deserve the support of the lesbian community. Women whose behavior is inconsistent, on the other hand, appear to be shifty, confused liars who dart all over the sexual continuum, not because they were born that way but because of poor choices—which is why they are rejected not only by the lesbian community as a whole but also by their closest friends, who can't reconcile their concept of lesbian pride with their best friend's morphing sexual orientation. And so the questions are: Are dykes who fuck men confused? Have we made poor choices? Were we straight all along—as we've been told by friends, family, and the media? Did we go from licking pussy to sucking cock because we wanted to betray the lesbian community? The answer to all these is no. In fact, dykes who fall in love with men can be seen as acting on the principle that love sees no gender—a long-used catchphrase of the queer community itself. If the GLBT community could begin to accept the idea that a lesbian's sexual orientation may change over the course of her life, dyke banishment might become less severe. But to eradicate the urge to ostracize altogether, the lesbian community would need to address our negative stereotypes of male-female relationships. Although some progressive heterosexual women may find this hard to believe, many lesbians consider any relationship between a man and a woman to be inherently detrimental to the woman. Due to this mischaracterization, a false polarity is created between heterosexual and lesbian relationships, whereby the former are seen as inferior and the latter as superior—not just sexually, but as they reflect female development.

Both stereotypes are false. Being a lesbian does not guarantee relationship bliss—domestic violence, for example, occurs among lesbians just as it does among heterosexuals. Likewise, having a male partner does not doom a woman to a life as the perpetually frustrated housekeeper of Betty Friedan's *The Feminine Mystique*. If we truly care about the lives of dykes, we should care about their lives even after they've partnered with men. We should not assume that their queer identity short-circuits the minute they make love to a man. We should not jump to the easy conclusion that a lesbian who's with a man was "never a real lesbian." We must make an effort to understand how these women identify—as dykes, as bisexuals, as queers, or as women who do not identify at all—and respect their self-determination. Because, ultimately, the question is not, Do these women deserve to be called lesbians? The questions are, rather, Why do we, the queer community, find it necessary to punish dykes who step outside some predetermined boundary of lesbian culture, and how can we stop? What are the queer possibilities in a relationship between a dyke and a man? How can we offer support to a woman who's in the process of being banished?

And, most important, how can we include partnerships between dykes and men in our formal and informal queer communities? The answers to these questions will transform lesbian culture—by broadening its scope and changing its face—and it's a transformation that's been a long time coming.

On Language

You Guys

Audrey Bilger / FALL 2002

OPRAH SAYS IT. MY YOGA INSTRUCTOR SAYS IT. COLLEGE STU-
dents around the country say it. The cast of *Friends* says it, as do my own
friends, over and over again. At least ten to twenty times a day, I hear someone say "you guys" to refer to groups or pairs that include and in some
cases consist entirely of women. I get e-mail all the time asking after my (female) partner and me: "How's everything with you guys?" or "What are you
guys doing for the holidays?" In informal speech and writing, the phrase
has become so common in American English that it's completely invisible
to many who use it. In response to my post on the topic, participants on
WMST-L, a listserv for women's studies teachers and scholars hosted by the
University of Maryland, report that it's not confined to young people, nor is
it an altogether recent development (some of the participants' older relatives used it in the '50s and '60s). Furthermore, the usage is beginning to
spread to Canada, England, and Australia, largely through the influence of
American television.

What's the problem? people ask when I question this usage. The language has evolved, and now "guys" is gender neutral, they say. Even those
who consider themselves feminists—who conscientiously choose "he or
she" over "he"; use "flight attendant," "chairperson," and "restaurant
server"; and avoid gender-specific language as much as possible—seem
quite willing to accept "you guys" as if it were generic. But let's do the math:

One guy is clearly male; two or more guys are males. How does a word become gender neutral just by being plural? And then how do you explain something like Heyyouguys.com, "The Man's Search Engine"? Can the same culture that says "it's a guy thing" to refer to anything that women just don't get about male behavior view a woman as one of the guys?

Current dictionaries, such as *Merriam-Webster's Collegiate Dictionary*, eleventh edition, tell us that "guys" may be "used in plural to refer to the members of a group regardless of sex"; but then, we need to keep in mind that dictionaries are not apolitical. They record the state of language and reflect particular ways of seeing the world. (This same tome offers the word "wicked" as one synonym for "black.") My 1979 ninth edition of *Webster's* includes no reference to gender-free guys, an indication that "you guys" had not yet become a standard form of address.

In "The Ascent of Guy," a 1999 article in *American Speech*, Steven J. Clancy writes, "Contrary to everything we might expect because of the pressures of 'politically correct' putative language reforms, a new generic noun is developing right before our eyes." Although Clancy doesn't take issue with the development (as you could probably guess from his disparaging tone on the whole idea of feminist language reform), his report ought to make us stop and think. During the same decades in which feminist critiques of generic uses of "man" and "he" led to widespread changes in usage—no mean feat—"you guys" became even more widely accepted as an informal and allegedly gender-free phrase. What Clancy concludes is that English contains a "cognitive framework in which strongly masculine words regularly show a development including specifically male meanings (man, he, guy) along with gender nonspecific forms . . . whereas in English, feminine words do not undergo such changes." In practice, that is, terms signifying maleness have been more readily perceived as universal than those signifying femaleness. Or, to put it another way, if you call a group of men "you gals," they're not going to think you're just celebrating our common humanity.

And this should trouble us. After all, haven't we been largely pleased by the way the media has worked to adopt at least a semblance of nonsexist language? Newscasters and other public figures make an effort to avoid obviously gender-biased words, and major publications such as *The New York Times* and *The Wall Street Journal* do the same. In spite of vocal criticism from those who view such shifts as preposterous, genuine feminist language reform has gained some ground. But as is the case with all advances brought about by feminism and other progressive movements, we need to stay on top of things—or else we may wake up one day to find them gone. This seemingly innocent phrase may be operating like a computer virus, worming its way into our memory files and erasing our sense of why we worry about sexism in language to begin with.

Up until a couple of years ago, I used the phrase as much as anyone, and I never gave it a thought. "You guys" sounds casual, friendly, harmless. When two female friends told me one day that it bothered them to be called "you guys," my wounded ego began an internal rant: *I'm* a literature and gender studies professor, *I* know about language, *I* spend much of my time teaching and writing against sexism, and here were people whose opinions I valued telling me that *I* was being patriarchal. Impossible! And then I started listening. I listened first to my own defensive indignation. Clearly, my friends had touched a nerve. Deep down I knew that they were right: Calling women "guys" makes femaleness invisible. It says that man—as in a male person—is still the measure of all things.

Once I copped to being in the wrong, I started hearing the phrase with new ears. Suddenly it seemed bizarre to me when a speaker at an academic conference addressed a room full of women as "you guys"; when a man taking tickets from me and some friends told us all to enjoy the show, "you guys"; and on and on. It was as if these speakers were not really seeing what was before their eyes.

Alice Walker, a vocal opponent of this usage, recounts how she and filmmaker Pratibha Parmar toured the U.S. supporting the film *Warrior Marks* and were discouraged to find that in question-and-answer sessions audience members continually referred to them as "you guys." "Each night, over and over, we told the women greeting us: We are not 'guys.' We are women. Many failed to get it. Others were amused. One woman amused us, she had so much difficulty not saying 'you guys' every two minutes, even after we'd complained" (from "Becoming What We're Called," in 1997's *Anything We Love Can Be Saved*). Because it took me the better part of a year to eradicate this usage from my own speech, and after hearing friends—whom I've encouraged to follow suit—apologize when they slip back into it, I feel like I understand the problem from the inside out. Most of us are familiar with the idea of internalized oppression, the subtle process by which members of disenfranchised groups come to accept their own lesser status. We need to recognize that accepting "guys" as a label for girls and women is a particularly insidious example of that process.

Many people on WMST-L have offered alternatives, ranging from the Southern "y'all" or less regionally marked "you all," to the Midwestern "yoonz" or "you-uns," to the apparently unhip "people," which is associated, it seems, with nerdy high-school teachers and coaches. "Folks" received the most support as a truly gender-free option. Some suggested "gyns" as a playful feminist variant. A more radical solution might be to use a word like "gals" as generic and get men used to hearing themselves included in a female-specific term. Although the majority of those who posted and wrote to me privately viewed the spread of "guys" as something to resist (with many noting how they sometimes regressed), others expressed hope that the phrase would indeed free itself from masculine connotations over time. One professor writes, almost wistfully, "I, for one, have always liked the formulation 'you guys' and wholeheartedly wish it were gender neutral. English could use a gender-neutral term to refer to a group of people (or even to individuals for that matter) . . . I've had students (female) be offended when I've used 'you guys' to them, but I still like it for some reason." I think many feminists who find "you guys" acceptable would similarly like to believe that it is indeed nonsexist. It's a powerful phrase precisely because it seems so warm and cozy. But we ought to ask what we are protecting when we claim that "you guys" is no big deal.

Sherryl Kleinman, professor of sociology at the University of North Carolina in Chapel Hill, has dedicated herself to eliminating the usage. She argues, in "Why Sexist Language Matters" (published in *Center Line*, the newsletter of the Orange County Rape Crisis Center), that male-based generics function as "reinforcers" of a "system in which 'man' in the abstract and men in the flesh are privileged over women." With the help of two former students, Kleinman developed a small card to leave at establishments where "you guys" is spoken (it's available to download at www.youall2.freeservers.com). The card succinctly explains what's at stake in this usage and suggests alternatives. She reports that distributing the card has aroused some anger. After dining with a group of female friends and being called "you guys" several times by the server, Kleinman left the card along with a generous tip. The server followed the women out of the restaurant and berated them for what he perceived to be an insult. Christian Helms, who designed the card's artwork, comments, "It's interesting how something that is supposedly 'no big deal' seems to get people so worked up."

Most of us have probably had the experience of pointing out some type of sexist expression or behavior to acquaintances and being accused of being "too sensitive" or "too PC" and told to "lighten up." It's certainly easier just to go along with things, to avoid making people uncomfortable, to accept what we think will do no harm. If you feel this way about "you guys," you might want to consider Alice Walker's view of the expression: "I see in its use some women's obsequious need to be accepted, at any cost, even at the cost of erasing their own femaleness, and that of other women. Isn't it at least ironic that after so many years of struggle for women's liberation, women should end up calling themselves this?"

So open your ears and your mouth. Tell people that women and girls aren't "guys." Stop saying it yourself. Feminist language reform is an ongoing process that requires a supportive community of speakers. The more we raise our voices, the less likely it is that women and girls will be erased from speech.

Skirt Chasers

Why the Media Dresses the
Trans Revolution in Lipstick and Heels

Julia Serano / FALL 2004

AS A TRANSSEXUAL WOMAN, I AM OFTEN CONFRONTED BY people who insist that I am not, nor can I ever be, a "real woman." One of the more common lines of reasoning goes something like this: There's more to being a woman than simply putting on a dress. I couldn't agree more. That's why it's so frustrating that people often seem confused because, although I have transitioned to female and live as a woman, I rarely wear makeup or dress in a particularly feminine manner. Despite the reality that there are as many types of trans women as there are women in general, most people believe that trans women are all on a quest to make ourselves as pretty, pink, and passive as possible.

Trans people—who transition from male to female or female to male and often live completely unnoticed as the sex "opposite" to that which they were born—have the potential to transform the gender class system as we know it. Our existence challenges the conventional wisdom that the differences between women and men are primarily the product of biology. Trans people can wreak havoc on such taken-for-granted concepts as feminine and masculine, homosexual and heterosexual, because these words are rendered virtually meaningless when a person's biological sex and lived sex are not the same. But because we are a threat to the categories that enable male and heterosexual privilege, the images and experiences of trans people are presented in the media in a way that reaffirms, rather than challenges, gender stereotypes.

Media depictions of trans women, whether they take the form of fictional characters or actual people, usually fall into one of two main categories: the deceptive transsexual or the pathetic transsexual. While both kinds of characters have an interest in achieving an ultrafeminine appearance, they differ in their ability to pull it off. Because deceivers successfully pass as women, they generally serve as unexpected plot twists, or play the role of sexual predators who fool innocent straight guys into falling for "men."

Perhaps the most famous deceiver is Dil, in the 1992 movie *The Crying Game*. The film became a pop culture phenomenon primarily because most moviegoers were unaware that Dil was trans until about halfway through the movie. The revelation comes during a love scene between her and Fergus, the male protagonist: When Dil disrobes, the audience, along with Fergus, learns for the first time that Dil is physically male. When I saw the film, most of the men in the theater groaned at this revelation. On-screen, Fergus has a much more intense reaction: He slaps Dil and runs off to the bathroom to vomit.

The 1994 Jim Carrey vehicle *Ace Ventura: Pet Detective* features a deceptive transsexual as a villain. Police lieutenant Lois Einhorn (Sean Young) is secretly Ray Finkle, an ex–Miami Dolphins kicker who has stolen the team's mascot as part of a scheme to get back at Dolphins quarterback Dan Marino. The bizarre plot ends when Ventura strips Einhorn down to her underwear in front of about twenty police officers and announces, "She is suffering from the worst case of hemorrhoids I have ever seen." He then turns her around so that we can see her penis and testicles tucked behind her legs. All of the police officers proceed to spit as *The Crying Game*'s theme song plays in the background.

Even though deceivers successfully pass as women, and are often played by female actors (with the notable exception of Jaye Davidson as Dil), these characters are never intended to challenge our assumptions about gender itself. On the contrary, they are positioned as "fake" women, and their secret trans status is revealed in a dramatic moment of truth. At the moment of exposure, the deceiver's appearance (her femaleness) is reduced to mere illusion, and her secret (her maleness) becomes her real identity.

In a tactic that emphasizes their "true" maleness, deceivers are often used as pawns to provoke male homophobia. This phenomenon is especially evident on shows such as *Jerry Springer*, which regularly runs episodes with titles like "My Girlfriend's a Guy" and "I'm Really a Man!" that feature trans women coming out to their straight boyfriends. On a recent British reality show called *There's Something About Miriam*, six heterosexual men court an attractive woman who, unbeknownst to them, is transgendered. The broadcast of the show was delayed for several months because the men threatened to sue the show's producers, alleging that they had been the victims of defamation, personal injury, and conspiracy to commit sexual assault. (The affair was eventually settled out of court, with each man coming away with a reported $100,000.)

In contrast to the deceivers, who wield their feminine wiles with success, pathetic transsexual characters aren't deluding anyone. With her masculine mannerisms and five o'clock shadow, the pathetic transsexual will inevitably insist that she is a woman trapped inside a man's body. The intense contradiction between the pathetic character's gender identity and her physical appearance is often played for laughs—as in the transition of musician Mark Shubb (played as a bearded baritone by Harry Shearer) at the conclusion of 2003's *A Mighty Wind*.

Unlike the deceivers, whose ability to pass is a serious threat to our ideas about gender and sexuality, pathetic transsexuals—who barely resemble women at all—are generally considered harmless. Perhaps for this reason, some of the most endearing pop culture portrayals of trans women fall into the pathetic category: John Lithgow's Oscar-nominated portrayal of ex–football player Roberta Muldoon in 1982's *The World According to Garp*, and Terence Stamp's role as aging showgirl Bernadette in 1994's *The Adventures of Priscilla, Queen of the Desert*. More recently, the 1999 indie film *The Adventures of Sebastian Cole* begins with its eponymous teenage protagonist learning that his stepdad, Hank, who looks and acts like a roadie for a '70s rock band, is about to become Henrietta. A sympathetic character and the only stable person in Sebastian's life, Henrietta spends most of the movie wearing floral-print nightgowns and bare-shouldered tops with tons of jewelry and makeup. Yet, despite her extremely femme manner of dress, she continues to exhibit only stereotypical male behaviors, overtly ogling a waitress and punching out a guy who calls her a "faggot" (after which she laments, "I broke a nail").

While a character like Henrietta, who exhibits a combination of extreme masculinity and femininity, has the potential to confront our assumptions about gender, it's fairly obvious that the filmmakers weren't trying to do so. On the contrary, Henrietta's masculine voice and mannerisms are meant to demonstrate that, despite her desire to be female, she cannot change the fact that she is really and truly a man. As with *Garp*'s Roberta and *Priscilla*'s Bernadette, the audience is encouraged to respect Henrietta as a person, but not as a woman. While we're supposed to admire these characters' courage—which presumably comes from the difficulty of living as women who do not appear very female—we're not meant to identify with them or be sexually attracted to them, as we are to deceivers like Dil. Ultimately, both deceptive and pathetic transsexuals are seen as "truly" men.

In virtually all depictions of trans women, whether real or fictional, deceptive or pathetic, the underlying assumption is that the trans woman wants to achieve a stereotypically feminine appearance and gender role. The possibility that trans women are even capable of making a distinction between identifying as female and wanting to cultivate a hyperfeminine image is never raised. In fact, the media often dwells on the specifics of the feminization process. It's telling that TV, film, and news producers tend not to be satisfied with merely showing trans women wearing feminine clothes and makeup. Rather, it is their intent to capture trans women in the act of putting on lipstick, dresses, and high heels, thereby making it clear to the audience that the trans woman's femaleness is a costume.

While mass-media images of biological "males" feminizing themselves have the subversive potential to highlight ways conventionally defined femininity is artificial (a point feminists make all the time), the images rarely function this way. Trans women are both asked to prove their femaleness through superficial means and denied the status of "real" women because of the artifice involved. After all, masculinity is generally defined by how a man behaves, while femininity is judged by how a woman presents herself.

Thus, the media is able to depict trans women donning feminine attire and accessories without ever allowing them to achieve "true" femininity or femaleness. Further, by focusing on the most feminine of artifices, the media encourages the audience to see trans women as living out a sexual fetish. But sexualizing their motives for transitioning not only belittles trans women's female identities; it also encourages the objectification of women as a group.

Two 2003 examples are the HBO movie *Normal* and a two-part *Oprah* special on transsexual women and their wives. While both of these offerings were presented as in-depth, serious, and respectful attempts to tell the stories of trans women—and they deserve some credit for depicting trans women as human beings rather than two-dimensional laughingstocks—both pandered to the audience's fascination with the surface trappings that accompany the feminization of men.

Normal tells the story of a pathetic-type trans woman named Roy (the character's name remains male in the credits) as she comes out to her family and community as transgendered. *Normal* has a fetishistic take on women's apparel and accessories from the opening scene, in which we see bras and underpants hanging from a backyard clothesline. Thus, from the beginning the movie sexualizes the very concept of female identity and reduces all women (trans or otherwise) to mere feminine artifacts. We see Roy bumble her way through her first embarrassing attempts at shaving her armpits and trying on women's clothing, and are shown two separate incidents where she wears perfume and earrings to her blue-collar workplace only to be ridiculed by her macho coworkers. At virtually every turn, the producers of *Normal* transform Roy's transition into a hapless pursuit of feminine objects and artifice.

The *Oprah* special was a little more promising, primarily because it involved actual trans women. The entire first episode featured a one-on-one interview with Jennifer Finney Boylan, author of the recent autobiography *She's Not There: A Life in Two Genders*. Boylan's book attempts to reach out to mainstream audiences: It focuses on the difficulties she faced being transgendered throughout her childhood and marriage, and traces her eventual decision to transition. While Winfrey's conversation with Boylan was respectful and serious, the show nonetheless opened with predictable scenes of women putting on eye makeup, lipstick, and shoes, and the interview itself was interspersed with "before" pictures of Boylan, as if to constantly remind us that she's really a man underneath it all.

What always goes unseen are the great lengths to which producers will go to depict lurid and superficial scenes in which trans women get all dolled up in pretty clothes and cosmetics. Shawna Virago, a San Francisco trans activist, musician, and codirector of the Tranny Fest film festival, was organizing a forum to facilitate communication between police and the trans community. A newspaper reporter approached her and other transgender activists, but was interested not in their politics but in their transitions: "They wanted each of us to include 'before' and 'after' pictures. This pissed me off, and I tried to explain to the writer that the before-and-after stuff had nothing to do with police abuse and other issues, like trans women and HIV, but he didn't get it. So I was cut from the piece." A few years later, someone from another paper contacted Virago and asked to photograph her "getting ready" to go out: "I told him I didn't think having a picture of me rolling out of bed and hustling to catch [the bus] would make for a compelling photo. He said, 'You know, getting pretty, putting on makeup.' I refused, but they did get a trans woman who complied, and there she was, putting on mascara and lipstick and a pretty dress, none of which had anything to do with the article, which was purportedly about political and social challenges the trans community faced."

Requests like these from nontrans news interviewers and film documentarians are common. I had a similar experience back in 2001, just before I began taking hormones. A friend arranged for me to meet with someone who was doing a film about the transgender movement. The filmmaker was noticeably disappointed when I showed up looking like a normal guy, wearing a T-shirt, jeans, and sneakers. She eventually asked me if I would mind putting on lipstick while she filmed me. I told her that wearing lipstick had nothing to do with the fact that I was transgendered or that I identified as female. She shot a small amount of footage anyway and said she would get in touch with me if she decided to use any of it. I never heard back.

Jamison Green, a trans man and transgender activist, has written about his invisibility as a transsexual person because reporters typically look for "the man in a dress." Media makers tend not to notice—or to outright ignore—trans men because they're unable to sensationalize them the way they do trans women without questioning the concept of masculinity itself. And in a world where modern psychology was founded on the teaching that all young girls suffer from penis envy, most people think striving for masculinity seems like a perfectly reasonable goal. Since most people cannot fathom why someone would give up male privilege and power in order to become a relatively disempowered female, they assume that trans women transition primarily as a way of obtaining the one type of power that women are perceived to have in our society: the ability to express femininity and to attract men.

Feminist theory is not immune to the problems that plague representations of trans issues. While many feminists—especially those who came of age in the 1980s and '90s—recognize that trans women can be allies in the fight to eliminate gender stereotypes, others, particularly those who embrace gender essentialism, believe that trans women foster sexism by mimicking patriarchal attitudes about femininity, or that we objectify women by trying to possess female bodies of our own. Many of these latter ideas stem from Janice Raymond's 1979 book *The Transsexual Empire: The Making of the She-male*, which is perhaps the most infamous feminist writing on transsexuals. Like the media makers discussed earlier, Raymond assumes that trans women transition in order to achieve stereotypical femininity, which she believes is an artificial by-product of a patriarchal society. Raymond does acknowledge, reluctantly, the existence of trans women who are not stereotypically feminine, but she reserves her most venomous remarks for those she calls "transsexually constructed lesbian-feminists," describing how they use "deception" in order to "penetrate" women's spaces and minds. She writes, "Although the transsexually constructed lesbian-feminist does not exhibit a feminine identity and role, he [*sic*] does exhibit stereotypical masculine behavior." This puts trans women in a double bind, where if they act feminine they are perceived as being a parody, but if they act masculine it is seen as a sign of their "true" male identity. This damned-if-they-do, damned-if-they-don't tactic is reminiscent of the pop cultural deceptive/pathetic archetypes.

While much of *The Transsexual Empire* no longer needs to be taken seriously—its premise is that "biological woman is in the process of being made obsolete by bio-medicine"—many of Raymond's arguments are echoed in contemporary attempts to justify the exclusion of trans women from women's organizations and spaces. In fact, the world's largest annual women-only event, the Michigan Womyn's Music Festival (MWMF), still enforces a "womyn-born-womyn" policy specifically designed to prevent trans women from attending. (Full disclosure: I am one of the organizers for Camp Trans, the annual protest of MWMF's policy banning trans women.) Many of the excuses used to rationalize trans women's exclusion are not designed to protect the values of women-only space but rather to reinforce the idea that trans women are "real" men and "fake" women. For example, one of the most cited reasons why trans women are not allowed to attend the festival is that we are born with, and many of us still have, penises. (Many trans women either cannot afford or choose not to have sex-reassignment surgery.) It is argued that our penises are dangerous because they are a symbol of male oppression and have the potential to trigger abuse survivors. So penises are banned from the festival, right? Well, not quite: The festival allows dildos, strap-ons, and packing devices, many of which closely resemble penises.

Another reason frequently given for the exclusion of trans women from MWMF is that we would supposedly bring "male energy" into the festival. While this seems to imply that expressions of masculinity are not allowed, nothing could be further from the truth. MWMF allows drag king performers, who dress and act male, and the festival welcomes female-bodied folks like Animal (from the musical duo Bitch and Animal) who identify as transgender and often describe themselves with male pronouns. Presumably, MWMF organizers do this because they believe that no person who is born female is capable of exhibiting authentic masculinity or "male energy." Not only is this an insult to trans men, but it also implies that male energy can be measured in some way independent of whether the person who is expressing it appears female or male. This is clearly not the case. Even though I am a trans woman, I have never been accused of expressing male energy, because people perceive me to be a woman. When I do act in a "masculine" way, people describe me as being a tomboy or butch, and if I get aggressive or argumentative, people call me a bitch. My behaviors are still the same; it is only the context of my body that has changed.

This is the inevitable problem with all attempts to portray trans women as "fake" females: They require one to assign different names, meanings, and values to the same behaviors depending on whether the person in question is perceived to be a woman or a man. In other words, they require one to be sexist. When people insist that there are essential differences (instead of constructed ones) between women and men, they further a line of reasoning that ultimately refutes feminist ideals rather than supporting them.

Women and men are not separated by an insurmountable chasm, as many people seem to believe; most of us are only a hormone prescription away from being perceived as the opposite sex. Personally, I welcome this idea as a testament to just how little difference there really is between women and men. To believe that a woman is a woman because of her sex chromosomes, reproductive organs, or socialization denies the reality that every single day we classify each person we see as either female or male based on a small number of visual cues and a ton of assumptions. As a feminist, I look forward to a time when we finally move beyond the red herring of biology and recognize that the only truly important differences that exist between women and men are the different meanings that we place onto one another's bodies.

Fringe Me Up, Fringe Me Down

On Getting Dressed in Jerusalem

Danya Ruttenberg / WINTER 2005

THE KID WHO WORKS AT MY *MACOLET* (CORNER STORE) HAS stopped talking to me.

Yaakov, who's about seventeen, was totally my buddy when I first moved to Jerusalem for a year of rabbinical study. He helped me remember the Hebrew for words like "shopping basket" and made sure that I knew I was buying cottage cheese instead of, say, one of the nine thousand other possible cheese products available at the Israeli *macolet*. He waved to me when I walked by. It was sweet.

Then one day I forgot myself and went to buy juice straightaway from the language intensive I'd been taking, dressed as I would have been back home in Los Angeles. Suddenly it was all over. He wouldn't even make eye contact with me.

In my normal life as an American rabbinical student, I wear a *kippah* (or yarmulke, a kind of head covering) and *tzitzit* (ritual fringes that are worn on an undergarment but often hang out from under one's clothes). In Numbers 15:37–40, God tells the Israelite people to "put fringes on the corners of their garments . . . and you will see it and remember all of God's commandments." In other words, *tzitzit* are a sort of wearable Torah intended to constantly remind the wearer of the relationship he or she strives to have with the Divine—and to implicitly hold the wearer responsible to that relationship. I notice that a particular part of my heart actually unfolds

90

and opens when I untuck the *tzitzit*, and that kind of openness is crucial when attempting to connect to the Divine in prayer. The *kippah*, on the other hand, is neither commanded in the Torah nor described in the earliest codes of Jewish law, though it's one of the strongest *minhagim* (customs) in our contemporary practice. It's generally understood that covering one's head shows respect for the Divine and an acknowledgment of the fact that God is above greater than us mere humans.

I took on these practices because of my own personal contract with God—because they reflect and strengthen my spiritual life and spiritual commitments. I wear these things because of God, but I feel entitled to do so because of feminism. See, neither item is traditionally worn by women. According to Jewish law, women are "exempt" from having to wear *tzitzit*—it's not a requirement for women, as it is, technically, for men. But it's not forbidden, and there is room in Judaism to take on *mitzvot* (commandments) to which one is not personally obligated. The *kippah*, legally speaking, is less complicated because it's "only" a custom—albeit a strong one. There's nothing "unkosher" about my decision to wear these things, and I believe that anything that helps to foster a connection with the Divine is good and to be encouraged. If ritual garb helps me to be a kinder, more compassionate person who is more connected to the world and those around me, why would I *not* wear it?

Whatever the legal details, in the semiotics of traditional Jewdom, I'm a pretty serious gender transgressor. In my own denomination and seminary, it's not a problem—philosophically and practically, there's plenty of room for me to get my fringe on. But in more traditional circles of Jewish culture (including at my *macolet*), I may be perceived as nothing less than a threat to the natural order of things.

Back in Los Angeles, I wear jeans, a tank top, and my *kippah* with the *tzitzit* flying in the wind, and I feel like me—religious, committed, and also of our contemporary cultural time and place. When I'm out and about in my heavily Jewish, largely Orthodox neighborhood, I typically hear one question or comment a day—ranging from the curious to the snarky—but in general people are nice, respectful, and well trained in American pluralism. In the United States, there are many different denominations and modes of Jewish practice, and the dominant American Jewish culture reflects this mix. Female rabbis, queer synagogue activities, and interdenom-

inational dialogue are increasingly commonplace; it's more or less understood that there are a number of ways that one can be a Jew. Here in Israel,
on the other hand, Judaism is generally understood to be only a traditionally interpreted version of Orthodoxy.

The prospect of a year in Jerusalem was, as such, fraught with hard
questions, not the least of which centered around my wardrobe. I knew that
my understandings of Jewish law on gender issues would not reflect the
dominant culture—and I also knew that a literal hanging-out of my ideas
would be loaded and not always well received.

I decided, therefore, that when I'm just walking around Jerusalem, it's
good both for keeping the peace and for my own self-protection to fall under the radar a little. So I often wear bandannas instead of *kippot* and I keep
the *tzitzit* tucked in. Since Israel is a country of dichotomies and extremes,
this puts me in one of, for me, two possible categories. When I wear pants
and/or a tank top, I signify "secular Jew/Israeli" on the street—pants are
considered by many traditionally religious Jews to be men's clothing, and
revealing the shoulders is not considered modest dress. Unlike the inter-
pretation of Diaspora Jews, who might identify as mostly secular but get a
little spiritual or religious every now and again, in Israel "secular" tends to
connote "completely secular"—of the modern world and wholly disinter-
ested in Judaism. (Secular Jews are sometimes called *hilonim*, or "desecra-
tors," in part because of their willingness to do things like go to the discos
on Friday night, the Sabbath.) So when my dress suggests that I am secular,
people may assume that I have progressive political views, am interested in
new music and nonreligious cultural events, and have a lot of modern ideas
about gender, society, and all sorts of other things. All of this is true—but I
spend my Friday nights in prayer.

By contrast, when I wear a skirt and a T-shirt or long-sleeved shirt, I signify "nice Orthodox girl." People will likely assume that I follow Jewish law,
keep kosher and Shabbat, value Torah study, and spend a lot of time thinking about God. And while I do all of these things, I don't identify as Orthodox and have some very different philosophical and religious perspectives
from those who do.

My sartorial choices telegraph a range of meanings, and wearing the
tzitzit out is often perceived as an invitation for attention: I've had people
ask me very intimate questions about sex a moment after asking me about

my *tzitzit*, two moments after meeting me—it's as though wearing them opens me up to lots of other kinds of bodily scrutiny. At the same time, I've had secular Israelis tell me that I'm a wonderful model of rebellion against the religious establishment—which is funny, because I wear them specifically as an expression of my faith. It's sad, really, that there are so few models here for what Judaism can look like.

That said, I'm ambivalent about navigating these issues in Jewish circles. After all, I have willingly put on long skirts and elbow-covering tops to visit other communities and cultures—while traveling in India and Morocco, and also to attend a friend's church service in my own hometown. Those are not my spaces, and I feel it's just good manners to be respectful and mindful of my role as guest. Certainly, it could be argued that when entering Jewish communities not my own, the same rules apply. And if I go somewhere like the ultra-Orthodox neighborhood of Mea Shearim (an important destination for those of us who want to buy holy books on the cheap), where life is in many ways radically different from my own, I can tolerate dressing in the drag of their cultural norms for limited amounts of time. Because, of course, drag is exactly what my long skirt and elbow-covering top is: an enactment of a certain set of gender ideals in a purely performative way. I don't really mind having to do this from time to time; there's a part of me that enjoys playing dress-up.

I have more trouble pretending to be something I'm not (or pretending not to be something I am) in liberal Modern Orthodox circles or my mixed-denomination neighborhood in Los Angeles, both of which are either literally or metaphorically closer to home for me. Even if women in *kippot* aren't a common sight in either of those spheres, I am a religious woman and I wear a *kippah*. At some point it's only fair for me to stake ownership in that fact: Judaism is my religion too. And it becomes just as problematic for me not to stand up and assert my relationship with and obligations to God, to claim my spiritual life, as it would to provoke with my *tzitzit*. To what extent should the culture of my neighborhood take precedence over my own understanding, grounded in Jewish law, of how this works?

In every religious tradition there is an interplay between issues of ego-nullification and individual identity—there are times when it's appropriate to be reminded that, ultimately, it's not all about you. For women in particular, the spiritual work of what writer Carol Lee Flinders calls "self-naughting" has the potential to run counter to many important feminist principles: Find your voice. Tell the truth as you understand it. Establish your self, your identity. Do not annihilate yourself to please others. Fight cultures in which double standards and sexist dictates make women or their bodies the problem.

A male colleague recently told me that he decided to tuck in his *tzitzit* because he became unsure if he was seeing them for his own spiritual benefit or showing them off to others, and he wanted to err on the side of humility. I sometimes wonder if my own showing off is sufficiently great that it would be wise to put the fringes away. In some respects the answer is yes. But for women, there's another *s* word in play, and it matters: "silencing." The *mitzvah* is about seeing them, and when I tuck my *tzitzit* in, I notice all the men on the street who get to leave theirs swaying, who do not have to shift how they perform one of God's commandments out of concern for personal safety or to put other Jews at ease. If I always kept them tucked in, would I be enacting humility or buying into my culture's suggestions about what a good girl does and doesn't do, placating those who would rather not see women take on these practices at all? Is it ever possible to fully tease out one from the other?

I'd be lying if I said that there was no activist dimension to all of this. I put the *tzitzit* on and keep them on because of their tremendous spiritual power and the benefit I receive from wearing them, but an upside of wearing them untucked is the number of conversations I've had with other Jews—particularly women—about the *mitzvah*. I was recently chatting with a new colleague who had been thinking about wearing *tzitzit*; by the end of the conversation we were planning a workshop/crafts night with half a dozen women so that everyone could learn how to make the undergarment and attach the fringes. I'm thrilled if any of my choices have helped other women and men move closer to taking on practices that strengthen their own connection to and relationship with God. I know women who wear *tzitzit* and always keep them tucked in, and while I respect their decision, when I was first taking on the *mitzvah* I would have loved to know that I wasn't the only one in my community doing so. In fact, I had never thought about doing it until I met another woman who wore her *tzitzit* out. Expanding the range of possibilities for everybody is a feminist value, and bringing people to *mitzvot* is a Jewish one.

From there the answer seems, fleetingly, clear. But even so, the issue is too complex for me to sit pretty with my self-righteousness. At a Sabbath afternoon lunch with a friend I hadn't seen in years, my *tzitzit* wearing somehow came up. (I was wearing a dress that day, so the fringes were hidden and the conversation was theoretical.) My friend is an Orthodox rabbi who teaches radical-feminist theology, has encouraged women to enter the rabbinate, and is a regular at the most feminist Modern Orthodox synagogue in Jerusalem. And he—wholly accustomed to women in prayer shawls and having no philosophical opposition to women in *tzitzit*—actually shuddered as we talked about it. "It's . . . even for me . . . it's just a really visceral thing," he said, somewhat apologetically.

People—even allies—sometimes need time to get used to new things. I'm too old to think that I have to shove my beliefs down the throats of others, and yet I'm also too old to think that it's always my job to keep others from being uncomfortable. As I understand the world, a little discomfort is sometimes a healthy thing. And more to the point, is my choice to wear an article or two of clothing that transgresses traditional norms to be understood as getting in someone's face, or simply living my own life?

I don't think there are any easy answers, and I'm pretty sure my responses will shift both over my year in Jerusalem and over my lifetime. As I write this in a café, there's a do-rag on my head and the fringes are tucked in, and at this moment, it feels okay. What I might need to do in the same café, or at synagogue, or at my school tomorrow or the day after that might be different—and that's also okay.

It's nice to remember that for others, too, things sometimes shift. After several months of concerted effort on my part, Yaakov has come around a little. He now responds to my greetings and doesn't scurry to hide when I come by the store for milk. It's still a little weird when I'm *kippah*-clad, grabbing an iced coffee on my way to school, but on other days when I wave hello, he's begun to wave back. I don't expect him to change everything he believes about Judaism and gender, and that's not my agenda. For other reasons, his recent softening is encouraging—after all, if there's a way for Yaakov and me to live together in our little neighborhood, maybe there's hope for all of us.

Screen Butch Blues

The Celluloid Fate of Female Masculinity

Keely Savoie / BITCHfest 2006

A WHILE AGO, MY GIRLFRIEND, A., GOT A CALL FROM A PRO-
ducer looking for butch women to audition for *Queer Eye for the Straight
Guy*. The Fab Five were looking to transform a butch in an upcoming show.

"Like, transform *how?*" A. asked, imagining, I suppose, how she might
compare to Janet Reno in a skirt.

The producer assured her that her butch identity would not be compromised, and they booked her for an interview later that week. I squealed like
a girl when she told me and immediately pulled out a notepad to start list-
ing proposed improvements to our apartment. We talked about what colors
we would suggest for the living room, how we could replace our cat-
scratched sofa with a spankin'-new sectional, and, of course, where a flat-
screen TV would look really good. But as the interview drew nearer, it hit
me that the show was primarily about *her*, not our co-op. And then the real
excitement dawned: My girlfriend could be one of the only butches seen on
television since *The Facts of Life*'s Jo Polniaczek.

Don't get me wrong—the fact that TV these days is all about queer has
not passed me by. Gays have sprung up everywhere from the obvious *L
Word*, *Will & Grace*, and, of course, *Queer As Folk*, to the not-so-obvious queer
characters on otherwise-straight shows like *The O.C.*, *The Wire*, and *ER*.
Even the straightest shows have occasional gay appearances: *Law and Order:
SVU*, *CSI*, *Wife Swap*, *Survivor*, even *American Idol*. But while television is

teeming with queers, the roles women play seem to have gotten straighter. It seems that prime time has flung the doors open ("ladies first!") to the whole rainbow spectrum of gender-bending men, but women on TV occupy a very narrow band—from kinda femme to ultrafemme. Girl-on-girl sexuality has no doubt evolved—girls have made out with other girls on everything from *Six Feet Under* to *Gilmore Girls*—but our gender expression is stuck in Stepford. Even true lesbian couplings, like those on *The L Word*, *Queer As Folk*, and the dearly departed *Buffy*, are overwhelmingly femme-on-femme.

After A. was interviewed for *Queer Eye*, I set out on a little quest to find butches on TV, just to see where we really stood. I immediately ran into trouble.

In the real world, it's not difficult to suss out how someone identifies. Butchness is an overall presence, a melding of character, presentation, mannerisms, and personal identity. Clothes often offer clues, but they're only part of the story. A. never wears skirts and lip gloss, but if she did, it wouldn't make her any more feminine—it would just look weird. When I asked A. to describe the essence of butchness, she called it a gravitational pull toward typically masculine things. "I was always playing football with my brother instead of doing feminine things with other girls," she said. "Butches are who they are before the environment comes along and screws with them and says, 'You are a woman, you are supposed to do x, y, and z because that's what girls do.'"

But with television being what it is, I was reduced to ferreting out butches by relying on the less-than-scientific "has short hair, wears pants" stereotype. By that definition, even I could be a butch, so I figured I was giving the TV world every benefit where there was a doubt. Even so, I quickly found there wasn't even much to doubt. Shane, *The L Word*'s resident ladykiller, could be seen as butch, given her swagger and voracious libido, but her goth-caliber eyeliner addiction undermines any substantial butchy pretense. Sandy, Dr. Kerry Weaver's firefighting girlfriend on *ER*, has a certain butch appeal, as does lesbian detective Kima Greggs from *The Wire*, but they both have long hair and are pretty in typically feminine ways—not an automatic disqualification for being butch, but I wish they were more obvious.

More blatant butches do exist, but they're easy to miss. There are the "wait, I blinked" butches, who occasionally pop up on the *The L Word*, but they tend to be on and off the set so fast you think they may have just tripped over it on their way to lunch—or they may actually be errant sound dudes. Then we have the straight butches, those poor women who are frequently tricked, cajoled, or corralled into appearing on the ubiquitous makeover shows like *What Not to Wear* that have piled up on TV like poo in the dog run and purport to teach women how to become "real" women for the edification of the audience and their beleaguered (and almost always unattractive) husbands. A recent episode of *Maury Povich* featured women in "manly" jobs—a firefighter, a zookeeper, and a mechanic among them. Povich chided their indifference to typical feminine frills: "Don't you want to feel sexy? Don't you want to feel like a woman?" And after shoehorning them into dresses, blowing out their hair, and slapping on some makeup, he applauded their new look: "You were really women under there!" By the looks of many of them, they were not nearly as happy as Maury to see their feminine sides.

In short, it's pretty sorry pickings out there, butchwise. Oddly, the dearth of butch representation seems to have gotten worse. Characters like the aforementioned Jo, Carla from *Cheers*, even Roseanne challenged gender-typical roles more than almost any character on contemporary shows, where their kind of butch appears only for a minute, to serve as a "before" picture for a newly feminized version waiting to emerge. A. remembers what a revelation it was to see her own aesthetic mirrored on *The Facts of Life*: "It was like seeing a family member." There is one spot of hope on the horizon; perhaps not surprisingly, it comes from *The L Word*. Many of the show's lesbian viewers complained that the show's glossy-haired, Prada-clad waifs, while scoring high on the eye-candy scale, left a lot to be desired in the dyke-versity department, so the show responded: For its third season, *The L Word* promises a new, *improved* butch. I am standing back with cautious hope that Daniela Sea will better the butch benchmark set by Nancy McKeon, with nicer hair and clothes, of course.

Big-screen butches are in a different predicament from their TV counterparts. They manage to score a tad more screen time, but when they do elbow their way through the sea of slender feminine sidekicks, it's only so they can die horribly in the end.

Only two movies in the last three years have featured butches in a leading role. There was Clint Eastwood's *Million Dollar Baby*, in which Hilary Swank plays Maggie Fitzgerald, a boxer who ultimately chooses assisted suicide after an injury leaves her paralyzed from the neck down. And there was *Monster*, the filmic portrait of serial killer Aileen Wuornos that starred Charlize Theron, her extra twenty-five pounds, and the dental prosthetics that miraculously transformed her flawless features into Wuornos's exaggerated grimace of poverty and despair.

Both movies were the subject of unstinting critical acclaim upon release. Swank and Theron, of course, both won Oscars for their "powerful" performances as butch women, but it was undoubtedly more about the daring it took for gorgeous women to debase themselves by gaining weight and looking unforgivably torn up than about any special consideration the Academy gives to breaking down gender barriers. If anything, the subtext is that crossing gender lines is such an enormous feat that accomplishing it at all is worthy of an Oscar: No ordinary woman could do such a thing.

The characters of Maggie and Aileen embody most of our cultural stereotypes about butches: the predatory, man-hating dyke butch (Aileen); the asexual butch (Maggie); the poor white trash butch (both); the emotionally disturbed butch (Aileen); and that all-time favorite, the dead butch (both).

This is where the huge disconnect is: In the real world, butches are everywhere. There are a lot of butches among urban lesbians, yes, and there are the stereotypical butches pumping gas, teaching gym, and running drills in the army. But they're also in suburban malls, in corporate offices, and in SUVs with their broods of children.

The problem is that women who take on masculinity as part of their identity violate two key rules of pop culture: They don't play to the male-friendly aesthetic of sexy, and, in taking on masculine characteristics, they assume more power than our culture is willing to give them. They are not fuckable in either sense of the term. Nelly men, on the other hand, don't violate that standard. They both play to the male eye and, in feminizing themselves, relinquish the social power that they, as men, naturally possess. For men, the punishment for crossing gender lines is inherent in the act of feminization.

I don't pretend that pop culture is a democracy: I don't expect proportional representation. But the total absence of images of butch women—and the erasure of them when they do appear (whether it's in the form of a makeover or a murder)—speaks to a disturbing inability among television and movie producers to deal with women who don't fit neatly into their gender boxes. What does this mean for us as a culture? Sure, we're going through a spasm of social and political regression, but have we actually devolved from the days of Jo?

It may be just a matter of time. TV and film will inevitably grow to reflect the culture as a whole, if a buffer, better-looking version. My hope is that progress made cannot be unmade, even if it's forced underground for a time. As I write this, there are four cable channels exclusively geared toward gay audiences, and although they, too, do their share of stereotyping, they push the gender envelope. A new series called *Transgeneration* on the gay network Logo follows four transgendered college students as they wrestle with the slippery concepts of gender, identity, and biology. I can see some of A.'s struggle as a butch in the faces of the female-to-male transsexuals whose lives have been suspended between cultural expectations and their own inescapable yearnings to break free. It will be a long time before a show like *Transgeneration* crosses over to a mainstream outlet, but it might be a beginning—a place where questions of gender are earnestly asked, and the humanity and drama inherent in them are allowed to unfold.

The producers for *Queer Eye* never did call us back. Maybe they pulled the plug when they saw that A. really would not be made over in some more feminine version of her butch self—or maybe, as she prefers to believe, she was "just too hip" to change. Whatever the case, I'm sure that one day I will see a butch on TV—a butch who is not going to be stuffed into a skirt or stuck in a coffin by the end of the show. Until then, I will continue bravely patrolling pop culture to the upper end of cable channels in search of butch characters. Unfortunately, it won't be from that new flat-screen TV I wanted so badly.

Dead Man Walking

Masculinity's Troubling Persistence

Brendan O'Sullivan / BITCHfest 2006

MASCULINITY IS DEAD. MORIBUND, WITHOUT A PULSE, SEEING the white light. But don't be fooled; it's not gone yet. As the 1989 classic *Weekend at Bernie's* demonstrates, sometimes death doesn't matter—sometimes a carcass suffices.

Sociology and pop culture have taught us that the features we attribute to men are just a rough assemblage of daily rituals. Folks born (or declared by doctors to be) XY are furnished with a slew of cultural prompts on how to dress, act, and interact to best imitate the character of Man. But the traditional construct of masculinity is facing a fatal crisis: Where once there was relative certainty about what it meant to "be a man," there is now an explosion of different—often conflicting—possibilities.

We've got *Queer Eye for the Straight Guy*'s posse of how-to homos showing the straight men of New York how to be men, even spreading the gospel to the most hetero corners of culture with their recent makeovers of both Red Sox and rodeo stars. Then there's Jonathan Antin, the unquestionably straight male hairstylist (don't call him a barber), whose reality show *Blow Out* is propelled by equal parts aggressive posturing (when he doesn't get his way) and emotionally charged weeping (when his new hair product line succeeds). And don't forget those bumbling leading men and beta males populating the television and movie screens, from the drunken antiheroes of *Sideways* to the dim-bulb slobs of prime-time sitcoms like *The King of*

Queens and *According to Jim.* Just what do these guys think they are doing with masculinity? And how did they get on my TV?

Traditionally understood masculinity is still readily identifiable in pop culture, of course. To be a man, you're expected to be a skosh insensitive, especially about things like Valentine's Day and wedding plans. A taste for sports is important. Definitely no crying, you big sissy. Ditto for wearing dresses, barrettes, and mascara. You shouldn't frighten easily. And if at all possible, be the breadwinner in your überhetero relationship—emphasis on the hetero.

This is but a small sampling of the rules—or rather, "instincts," because masculinity is supposed to come naturally. Recall that the rules of *Fight Club* didn't include the requirement of being a dude. It was simply referenced in the fourth and fifth rules: Only two guys to a fight; only one fight at a time, fellas. The club itself was predicated on masculinity—a men-only rule would've been redundant.

But despite this pompous certitude, mainstream rule violations like those mentioned above are exposing the myth behind this rulebook. There's a growing recognition that anyone can perform traditionally male traits; the if-it-looks-smells-walks-and-talks-like test doesn't work for men anymore. We've got butch women, drag kings, genderqueers, and trannies hijacking masculinity, and conversely, men who are far from hitting the target. It seems that we aren't satisfied with what's "natural," and we're stretching the concept to suit our needs.

Witness former baseball star and steroid poster boy José Canseco enthusiastically modeling women's lingerie on VH1's train-wreck reality series *The Surreal Life.* Clinging to relevancy, masculinity has been reduced to caricaturing itself. *He's a Lady*, another recent "reality" catastrophe, was devoted entirely to a fake drag queen competition among a dozen men. Not surprisingly, there was no subversive intent behind the show; it was an analysis-free exercise in reinforcing traditional masculinity by using it as a frame of reference. The show generates a reaction similar to watching a dog open a jar of peanut butter on *America's Funniest Home Videos*: Dogs are dumb! They aren't supposed to open jars! Ha-ha! Our laughter could come from a radical understanding (Dogs aren't dumb! We're silly for thinking they aren't supposed to open jars! Ha-ha!), but most of us, still taking Bob Saget's cue, are laughing because men aren't supposed to shave their legs, not because we're foolish for believing they shouldn't.

There are many different folks encompassed in this "we" and "us," however, and we don't all share the same vision for the dead dude's place in our culture. Some hope to give masculinity its proper eulogy: a complete reorganization of society where the man/woman distinction no longer wields its power. Others recognize masculinity's end but fear the hijinks that would ensue if manliness lost its significance as a societal organizer. You can hear their lamentations: How would people know whom to pick for kickball? Or ask to the prom? What if the only way to tell the boys from the girls was to peek at their private bits (and, geez, even that gets complicated)? Sex before marriage would become the eleventh commandment—just to be sure. If people can't tell boys from girls, our whole society would come to a screeching halt.

Our reaction to this vision of social chaos has not been to stage a proper funeral, but to hold on tighter to the dead concept. Even the "we" who are calling for the funeral are not RSVPing. Masculinity is enjoying a vibrant posthumous influence as we cling to its "necessity." We're setting the table for our dead father, making sure dinner's ready by six. But why are we keeping a place for him?

It could be suggested that, once people believe strongly enough in something, they are inclined to ignore any evidence that contradicts it. The plot of *Weekend at Bernie's* is organized around this level of confusion: Since everyone expects Bernie to be alive, the protagonists' game of reanimating the corpse is never uncovered. But that doesn't quite work because, unlike the duped supporting cast of *Bernie's*, we are already aware of masculinity's ruse.

But there's another explanation: While masculinity is obviously still performed earnestly and dutifully by men every day (even by those who stray from the most well-worn areas along its path), those of us aware of the game are still playing along. We just add a spoonful of irony to make it go down easier. With a wink and a nudge, men can perform their masculine duties, making it clear they are aware it's all an act. Irony allows us to admit, or at least refer to, masculinity's passing and yet sustain the deceased concept (perhaps cryogenically freezing it, like Stallone in *Demolition Man*, in case we need it down the road). A man might open the door for a woman, but with one meaningful glance can communicate, "I know this is silly, but I want to do it anyway." The woman, in turn, can silently reply, "I'm glad you're smart enough to realize what you are doing, but I'm still glad you're doing it." And thus, masculinity is sustained despite, and by the very reference to, its death.

To think about it another way, imagine that a script for a family TV show from the 1970s was produced today. Though it was written with perfect seriousness at the time, it would literally be impossible for the show to be anything but kitsch to us. The father figure could only be seen as ironic, mocking fatherhood. His masculine gestures would be overdone and hilarious because they are perfectly sincere. Expecting a laugh track, we'd hear only silence. One need look no farther than *That '70s Show*, which uses this historical shift for its comedic edge; its best humor emanates from the zealous masculine gestures of patriarch Red Forman—but with the anticipated laugh track accompaniment. We view sincere masculinity as either a sign of earnest youthfulness ("he's so cute") or aged backwardness ("he's so old-fashioned"); both invite condescension. But our ironic assaults on masculinity aren't as clever as they seem. Masculinity still has the last laugh, as we go on structuring our reality around its remains. And so we've resurrected the plot of *Weekend at Bernie's*, toting around a dead guy so that our world doesn't fall apart. Masculinity's symbolic death won't be complete until we've stopped organizing our society around it—until we've closed the casket. But we're still holding up his arms and gesturing for him.

It's obvious that the artistic failure of *Weekend at Bernie's* could've been avoided if the status of masculinity had actually been rendered in the body of Bernie. What a movie it would have been if, instead of pretending that Bernie's limp corpse was alive, the protagonists had simply "pretended" he was dead, cracking jokes about how pallid and subdued he seemed—perhaps even enlisting the other characters in this masquerade. Bernie could "live" on forever—undead—just as masculinity is doing. After all, once everyone is joking about his lack of vitality, who would dare declare it for real? And what would it matter, anyway? Their assertion would just be absorbed by the joke. If everyone is already joking about the emperor's "skimpy" new clothes, the boy who observes that he's wearing nothing no longer matters. If only the cast of *Bernie's* had the refined sense of irony that we do, it would've reached trilogy status.

Our charade is, of course, functioning alongside the continued faithful performances of masculinity's true believers. But masculinity's death is now appearing in the very pop culture that helped build and sustain it for so long. It's not a coincidence that reality TV has been the biggest source of this instability. Without scripts and multiple takes, people's "complexities" (i.e., genders) are bound to break out.

This gives those of us who want to bury the masculine corpse an unprecedented opportunity. And what are we doing with this opportunity we've said we want? We're lounging around cracking jokes, pleased with our command of irony. It makes you wonder if we really desire what we're demanding. It's so much safer to make demands you never expect to be fulfilled.

One problem, it seems, is our failure to recognize that gender is not synonymous with masculinity. Although masculinity couldn't exist without gender—since the first is just one expression of the second—gender itself can survive masculinity's demise. Failing to grasp this, we're left thinking that if masculinity dies, then gender is buried with it. And because gender is leading a rather sprightly existence at this historical moment—gender identities are hatching everywhere—we mistakenly think that masculinity must also be a spring chicken. If we don't want to kill off gender, we resign ourselves to masculinity.

But if masculinity is like Bernie, gender is like *Melrose Place*. Almost the entire cast changed from beginning to end—yet the show kept on running. *Melrose* didn't need any particular character (well, except maybe that evil Michael Mancini guy) to continue year after year. Gender can flourish without Billy or Allison, but masculinity doesn't exist without *Melrose Place*. Conflating the characters with the show stops us from seeing this situation clearly. There can and will be other genders if masculinity is buried. The show will go on. In fact, it is inconceivable that gender, which essentially has its hands in the entire jar of human behaviors, appearances, and preferences, could disappear. But it *can* give way to a multiplicity of gender expressions, to a million ways of being a recognizable human—instead of just two.

Of course, all the same could be said for femininity. But I wouldn't know anything about that . . . being a guy and all.

3

. . . .

The *F* Word

LET'S RUN DOWN THE LIST: FEMINISTS ARE UGLY, HAIRY-legged man-haters. Feminists are women who don't resemble doormats. Feminism is, as Pat Robertson infamously put it, "a socialist, anti-family political movement that encourages women to leave their husbands, kill their children, practice witchcraft, destroy capitalism, and become lesbians." Feminism is the radical notion that women are people. Feminism is dead because women have rejected its tenets. Feminism is dead because it has succeeded in all it set out to do.

Feminism's contentious position in the popular imagination is as old as feminism itself. Commentators both male and female, feminist and not, have tussled over its meanings, goals, intentions, and even its morals since well before the term even entered our lexicon. At the dawn of the woman suffrage movement, in June 1854, a writer for *Harper's New Monthly Magazine* (known to contemporary readers as *Harper's*) gave his assessment of those who wanted to see women become full societal participants: "A woman such as ye would make her—teaching, preaching, voting, judging, commanding a man-of-war, and charging at the head of a battalion—would be simply an amorphorous monster . . . She might be very estimable as a human being, honorable, brave, and generous, but she would not be a woman." (This anonymous man also conjured the hairy-legged man-hater's nineteenth-century foremother: "with horny hands covered with fiery red scars and blackened with tar, her voice hoarse and cracked, her language seasoned with nautical allusions and quarter-deck imagery, and her gait and stop the rollicking roll of a bluff Jack-tar." His inspiration was a Scottish sea captain named Betsy Miller.)

In the early '70s, as the next phase of the movement bloomed, women's liberation garnered national coverage every week, both negative and positive. Opponents pronounced the movement "absurd and destructive" (Midge Decter, author of 1972's *The New Chastity and Other Arguments Against Women's Liberation*) and its adherents "petty . . . and vindictive [women] who cannot solve their own problems and want the govenment to do it for them" (Phyllis Schlafly, leader of the STOP ERA campaign widely credited with torpedoing the Equal Rights Amendment). Major news outlets ran headlines referring to marches as "parades" and declaring, "Women's Movement Is Seen as Leading to 'Self-Hatred.'" They published observations that "the demonstrators were preponderantly attractive young women wearing miniskirts and boots" and articles about how President Nixon's daughter Julie "says leaders of the women's liberation movement are 'alienating a lot of women and most of the men.'" Columnists insisted that although "a sensible case exists that women as a group are subject to certain unjust exploitations," they're not "oppressed" because they're not "slaves toiling hopelessly for Pharaoh with no hope this side of death."

Newspapers also devoted miles of column inches to feminist activities, most notably the fight for the ERA, often noting that the majority of Americans supported it and publishing editorials urging its ratification. *The New York Times* published articles by Susan Brownmiller, Betty Friedan, Robin Morgan, and others. There seemed to be at least a glimmer of understanding that the stereotype of the hirsute harpy was just that—a stereotype. An October 1971 poll conducted by Louis Harris Associates asked three thousand women and one thousand men what came to mind in response to the term "women's liberation." Twenty-five percent answered in the category "Women working for equal rights—opportunities—equality with men" and another fifteen in "Women wanting better jobs—pay—equal jobs—pay with men." Six percent chose "Bunch of frustrated, insecure, ugly, hysterical, masculine type women."

The nonnews media landscape was also transformed by feminism, from Mary Richards's independent career-girl ways (and, less subtly, Maude's abortion) to an Enjoli perfume ad featuring a dressed-for-success babe shedding her work clothes for a slinky ensemble. (The soundtrack was a lyrically re-tooled version of the Peggy Lee classic "I'm a Woman": "I can bring home the bacon / Fry it up in a pan / And never let you forget you're a man.") *Charlie's Angels* may have been a jigglefest featuring glamorous gals taking direction from an invisible and all-powerful father figure, but without feminism, a trio of female undercover detectives would never have made it past the first network meeting.

The '80s are usually what comes to mind when someone says "back-lash," and, as Susan Faludi's landmark work amply demonstrated, that decade was full of breast implants and tales of unhappy professional women whose empty personal lives belied earlier feminist promises of "having it all." But the '90s also saw an explosion of work by a whole slew of backlash feminists, women who felt free to claim the label "feminist" even as their books accused the movement of ruining women's lives and ruining everyone else's fun. Camille Paglia, Katie Roiphe, and Christina Hoff Sommers got tons of press and were anointed as feminist spokes-women, while folks like Peggy Orenstein, bell hooks, Paula Kamen, and Katha Pollitt were writing actual feminist—rather than just feminist-baiting—work on many of the same issues and getting way less attention.

After more than three decades, pop culture continues to suffer from a bad case of simultaneous progress and backlash—and the longer it's been around, the more complicated the symptoms get. Ginia Bellafante's infa-mous June 29, 1998, *Time* cover story, touted by the oh-so-original cover line "Is Feminism Dead?" declared that the movement had abandoned its social change roots to be "wed to the culture of celebrity and self-obsession." Bellafante's tone suggested that she longed for more activism, but had she done any substantive research, she could have reported on a whole lot. To give just a few examples, the Third Wave Foundation had been funding feminist organizing among women under thirty for more than a year when she wrote her article; Sista II Sista's Freedom School began training young women of color in community organizing in 1996. Antisweatshop orga-nizing was gaining momentum on campus, fueled in large part by female students putting their feminist principles into action. But instead, Bella-fante took the mainstream's word for it and anointed Ally McBeal and the Spice Girls as feminism's flailing poster children. (As a *Salon* commentator quipped at the time, "Sure, 'Ally McBeal' is a popular show—but so was

'Three's Company' in the 1970s, and no one ever accused Suzanne Somers of being a feminist icon.")

Bellafante, unfortunately, is far from alone in her severe misunderstanding. The backlash years found feminists defending clinics against anti-choice protesters, staffing rape-crisis centers and domestic violence shelters, marching against U.S. intervention in Central America, flocking to women's studies classes, familiarizing the culture with the term "sexual harassment," agitating for lesbian rights, and much more—while most of the mainstream media was busy reporting that feminism was irrelevant to the average woman. Today, in the face of the oft-repeated cliché that young people aren't interested in feminism, young feminists of all genders have been protesting the IMF, the School of the Americas, and the war on Iraq; they have been working to dismantle the prison-industrial complex and to secure living wages for tomato pickers; they have been organizing against human trafficking and for trans visibility. As Vivien Labaton and Dawn Lundy Martin put it in the introduction to their 2004 anthology, *The Fire This Time: Young Activists and the New Feminism*, "People wonder who is carrying on the legacy of the women's movement, and they look to the same old haunts to find the answers. The problem is, they are looking in the wrong places." Those old haunts may not be entirely empty—folks under twenty-five reportedly made up at least one-third of the million people who marched on Washington for reproductive freedom in April 2004—but they're just a small part of the neighborhood now.

Without widespread recognition of the true scope of feminism's influence on all social justice activism, the notion of feminism as defanged girl-power fluff is inevitable: It comes straight from the way record producers, screenwriters, women's-magazine editors, chick lit publishers, and ad copywriters lift selections from movement rhetoric and use them to dress up their retrogressive pap. That Enjoli ad has more than a few contemporary equivalents: Take mining giant De Beers's invention of the right-hand ring, which the company claims is all about "the strength, success, and independence of women of the twenty-first century." Or check out Stouffer's launch of a new frozen diet pizza, which was marketed with ads that said: "The vote. The stay-at-home dad. The push-up bra. The Lean Cuisine pizza."

The distinction between feminism's vibrancy, nuance, and commitment to social justice and the superficial appropriation of its catchphrases could not be more crucial. The messages of mainstream culture, commercial forces, conservative political trends, and the like all too often combine to make audiences unable to sort feminism's unfinished business from its failures; they make it all too easy to confuse the reality and range of our movement with distortions and misrepresentations of it. The writers in this section are wrestling with the way the mainstream seeks to use, abuse, and misuse feminism—and what we need to do to stop them.   —L.J.

And Now a Word from Our Sponsors

Feminism for Sale

Rita Hao / FALL 1998

AS WE APPROACH THE END OF THE MILLENNIUM, FEMINISM appears to have made significant strides into mainstream culture—we have a surfeit of women's magazines aimed at all permutations of politics, ethnicities, orientations, appearances, lifestyles, interests, and ages (*Ms.*, *Mode*, *Latina*, and *Women and Guns*, to name just a few), we have TV shows targeted specifically at us (leading women Buffy, Ally, Sabrina, Veronica), we have our own cottage industry in music (the Lilith Fair, Missy Elliot, Fiona Apple, the Spice Girls). This is indeed something to celebrate—but before we rest, smug and Katie Roiphe–like, on our laurels of "battle's already won, stop whining already" feminism, it might be interesting to explore the ways the media has constructed its apparently unquestioning acceptance of women and feminism.

Sure, it's great that we have, for once, so many options to choose from. But the main reason the media can support this diversity of voices rests on what the corporate world refers to as . . . well, money. So who's paying for those articles on Courtney Love in *Spin* magazine? Who's supporting the WNBA on ESPN? Who keeps *Jane* afloat? Advertisers. And what are they saying?

I've noticed recently that advertisements have started trying to speak to me in my own voice. Part of this stems from the fact that, as a twenty-five-year-old woman working a corporate day job, I represent that new cash cow, the Generation X slacker/corporate drone. (I "slack." Yet I also save in a 401(k)! I am deeply cynical yet also hopeful in the new economic upswing! I am replete with contradiction. Make colas and candy and clothing for me!) But advertisers have also learned that the best way to sell to women is to make them feel as if they're important. As if they matter. In short, to speak to them as feminists.

Okay, I admit, I fall for this trick every time. Give me a pseudofeminist slogan and I'll go for the product in a second. Strong enough for a man—but made for a woman? I love that shit. This little light of mine? Well, of course I'm gonna let it shine, goddammit. Give me two pairs of Lees, posthaste! Sports gear? I don't even play sports, but you know I'm elevating my self-esteem with those grainy black-and-white shots of women doing something sports-related to inspirational music. And the ad for Clairol where the women all turn down dates with "Steve" to "wash their hair"? I mean, the Beavis and Butt-Head–y turn of phrase ("a totally organic [huh-huh, huh-huh] experience") indicates fairly clearly to me, at least, that this particular ad campaign was penned by some sweaty twenty-six-year-old male, but I must admit I find the implication that Steve is somehow, you know, not a hot tamale in the sack to be hysterically funny. Sisters doing it for themselves is always a good message to send.

So—on the one hand, I guess it's good that advertisers have finally realized that smart women are a viable market at which to aim their pitches. I mean, I'm heartened that *Ms.*'s No Comment page, once chock-full of pictures of women being torn to pieces by dogs or something similarly horrific, has now been reduced to a bare three or four entries, one of which is usually a nude shot from a European magazine and another of which is usually an ad for skateboarding equipment. I'm pleased that those throat-clearingly discomfiting douche commercials have been replaced with up-front and frank (but, interestingly enough, equally discomfiting) yeast infection medication ads. I'm glad that the market now views women in a variety of roles—daughters, schoolgirls, teenagers, sexual beings, mothers, businesswomen, sports figures, activists, everything. Rah, rah and yay for us.

But what makes this particular cultural manifestation of quote-unquote feminism (which, arguably, is nothing more than the advertising industry's realization that "hey! women buy things!") an effective way to move units? And what makes this particular movement one that makes advertisers think you'll spend money to hear its messages? What drives this union of feminism and capitalism? I mean, I have my doubts about *Baffler*-chic cultural punditry ("It's all about the Benjamins, baby," is a particularly wanker way to view culture, I think), but let's explore a little, shall we?

Clearly, the strong, self-actualized woman is an image that sells. It makes sense, right? You see one of these ads, you get that strange sensation of—could it be? Could it actually be? Elevating self-esteem? Identification with an image in the media? Oh, my God! Ideally, advertisers are thinking, you'll associate that good feeling (especially since it's so rare) with their brand and think, "Wow, Nike—they make me feel great!" Then you'll rush out and spend the seventy-five cents that you earn to the male dollar on their product.

It strikes me as hypocritical, though, to push this limited, you-can-do-anything vision of feminism on women when even *Vogue* admits that part of the reason why women have self-esteem low enough to need to hear that we can do anything is that this same industry goes around telling us we're too fat/too dark/too loud/too aggressive in the first place, and thus need retail therapy to make ourselves feel validated again. This little light of mine is supposed to shine in jeans that I swear must be deliberately cut to make me look both hipless and paunchy? I'm supposed to feel better about myself because I run my anorexia-inducing fitness routine in "if you let me play, I won't drop out of school" shoes? I don't care if Calvin Klein is telling me to "be fun. be fearless. just be." I still don't think his company puts forth a particularly helpful vision of womanhood. (And, for God's sake, like I really want to be like Kate fucking Moss. Excuse me, I practice dental hygiene.)

Furthermore, this sort of pro-woman schlock isn't even about feminism at all. It's not like we're all supposed to get together and think about the ways gender roles have created artificial barriers between people, or how sexism keeps us from reaching our goals. Oh, no—we're supposed to race out to the mall and buy things. Yeah, that's going to help women secure their right to choose.

Now, I'm not saying that buying things is automatically antifeminist. I, for one, have been espied at Union Square toting bags from the Gap, Macy's, Virgin, Nine West, and Ann Taylor. All at once, even. I love to shop. (Thus, interestingly, perpetuating the idea in some adman's mind that I'm buying nicely made business casual because "Ann Taylor is about being real." No. Ann Taylor is, in actuality, about an extensively stocked line of petite clothing. You compromise where you have to.) But capitalism is a system that maintains its momentum by encouraging people to think only in terms of me, me, me. Interesting that now it's using rhetoric from a movement that has tried, since its inception, to encourage people to understand the ways that sort of self-centered thinking exists as a cover for the exploitation of the labor of people who, for reasons such as color, class, and gender, have been historically considered somehow inferior to the people who actually count. Capitalist feminism welcomes the woman whose Visa card will be accepted at the door into the ranks of the worthy. But what about everyone else?

Ultimately, these ads put forth a vision of feminism that is increasingly devoid of any sense of community or vitality: I am a strong feminist, thus I deserve new shoes/cute clothes/fattening food/beauty products.

And that I have a problem with—because if feminism is about anything, it's about the hidden power dynamics of entitlement. You don't deserve to make more money than me because you pee standing up. You don't deserve to get into college just because your dad went there before you. To take feminist rhetoric and turn it into just another self-centered Ayn Randian trip (Fuck everyone else! Where do I want to go today?) is dangerous.

That said, I feel slightly guilty trashing these ads because I know they disturb the status quo in a lot of ways. I know this because, you know, the only thing in advertising that irritates me more than faux-feminist ads is the backlash against faux-feminist ads. Nike, for instance, has an ad that says, "Breaking the glass ceiling . . . What do[es that] have to do with shoes?" In other words, "Fuck all that pro-woman shit we told you last year; why don't you just go running instead?" Feminism sells, but backlash sells even better.

Even worse is the way Sprite's "image is nothing, thirst is everything" campaign has taken on the recent rise of the Angry Rock Chick with its parody of Courtney/Alanis/Meredith Brooks, which runs basically to the point of: "I can't write lyrics and I can't sing, but I look really good in tight skirts. I hate men and I can't play guitar, but I sell lots of records because I talk about sex." And they also have a Spice Girls version: "We look cute and we look sharp, and we have to do what Sprite says because next month we won't be famous."

Okay, now. Deep breath, deep breath. Let's think about it this way: I know I'm ambivalent about the recent marketing of girl power. But I'm ambivalent about it in a different way than Sprite is. It's not like Sprite's ads are saying, "Hey, Rita, you are so totally right about this angry-Alanis phenomenon turning riot grrrl rhetoric into the same old I-can't-live-without-a-man shtick. Gosh, Rita, isn't it irritating that the Lilith Fair is turning girl rage inward again? We hear you about how the Spice Girls end up pushing a vision of femininity and feminism that re-creates women as rather dim." Oh, no—Sprite's ads are for that most bizarre of phenomena, the nervous Ben Folds Five/Verve Pipe fan who feels threatened by feminist empowerment ("How come them chicks get their own concert tour and us guys don't?").

These advertisers are ultimately trying to have it both ways—get those Gen XX girls who already feel ambivalent about the marketing of feminism by the media, and those Gen XY boys who just feel ambivalent about feminism. Capitalism isn't about welcoming women into the fold, or using our newfound economic clout to make changes in the way the system works. It's about making money. It's about tapping into what really is a very new and powerful phenomenon—the woman who makes enough to pay the rent and several credit card balances, but is young enough to be free of major money-sucking responsibilities—and channeling her for its own ends. So go on, go buy cute things. Buy cute things you want. But make sure you know why you want them. Retail therapy works only if you know what you're trying to cure.

I Can't Believe
It's Not Feminism!

On the Feminists Who Aren't

Julie Craig / SPRING 2002

THE TITLE OF CHRISTINA HOFF SOMMERS'S FIRST BOOK ASKED, *Who Stole Feminism?* Daphne Patai gave one of her books the provocative subtitle *Cautionary Tales from the Strange World of Women's Studies.* Elizabeth Fox-Genovese paraphrased the women she interviewed in the title of her book, *"Feminism Is Not the Story of My Life."* Yet all of these women call themselves feminists.

What all of them have in common is that while they label themselves feminists—and their books show up in the women's studies section of your local bookstore—their theories are overwhelmingly hostile to feminist goals such as holding men responsible for rape and promoting gender equality in the classroom. More important, these authors' close ties to antifeminist organizations, combined with the potent selling power of all things controversial, have made them into media darlings—and given them access to the kind of publicity that writers with more, well, *feminist* feminist views rarely get.

So who are these women? Are they outspoken feminists or traitors to the cause? Unlike the many social critics who vocally oppose feminism as a concept, these authors loudly and publicly embrace the label, despite the fact that "feminism" is a dirty word within the conservative circles that have nurtured them. They defy feminism to make some serious choices about the future of the movement and who fits into it: Can a conservative woman be a feminist? Has feminism become so radical that mainstream proponents of equal rights are alienated by its rhetoric?

These are all interesting questions, but more relevant ones might be: Do these authors actually contribute to the body of feminist work, or do they merely perpetuate the delusion that feminism is a dangerous force with power disproportionate to the number of its adherents?

Camille Paglia: Grandstanding Contrarian

Camille Paglia is, perhaps, the original antifeminist feminist. She maintains that contemporary feminism is faltering "in a reactionary phase of hysterical moralism and prudery" and delights in baiting other public feminists. (She calls Naomi Wolf "Little Miss Pravda" and quotes approvingly another writer who said of Gloria Steinem, "Once we needed her, now we're stuck with her.") Of course, she purports to be the one true feminist, declaring, "My feminism stresses courage, independence, self-reliance, and pride," and leaving no room for feminism as a more political or communal effort.

Paglia's first book, *Sexual Personae: Art and Decadence from Nefertiti to Emily Dickinson*, was published in 1990; 1992's *Sex, Art, and American Culture* and 1994's *Vamps and Tramps* followed in quick succession (more recently, Paglia has dispensed her wisdom in a regular column for *Salon*). Riddled with forceful proclamations backed by scant evidence (as well as a harping nostalgia for the 1960s that would make even the most die-hard hippie cringe), Paglia's critical essays on everything from music to the sexual peccadilloes of politicians are certainly dramatic, but they rarely hold up to scrutiny. Pop culture, she exclaims, is "an eruption of the never-defeated paganism of the West," which sounds edgy and transgressive but fails to explain how today's mass-media *Touched by an Angel* pap is an eruption of anything other than unadulterated smarm. Her platitudes might hold true for the narrow examples she chooses; everything that contradicts her arguments is ignored.

Femmes fatales (such as Elizabeth Taylor, Jackie Onassis, and Madonna) are the only iconic feminists in her worldview, leaving readers to wonder how feminist political leaders, artists, scientists, and other women whose lives don't read like a B-grade romance novel fit into her theories. She champions male sexuality while deriding female sexuality (which is interesting, given that she is a woman) and is particularly hostile on the subject of lesbianism (which is interesting, given that her partner is a woman). "When women cut themselves off from men," she writes, "they sink backward into psychological and spiritual stagnancy." Similarly, she dismisses women's art, asserting that creativity and innovation are essentially masculine traits.

But Paglia really steps on feminism's dress when it comes to rape, as she makes it clear that the celebration of all things masculine extends to sexual coercion. "Feminism . . . does not see what is for men the eroticism or fun element in rape, especially the wild, infectious delirium of gang rape." (Pardon us if we just can't understand that giddy delight.) Paglia's hardheaded advice style, while appealing for its release from the heavy theorizing of academic feminism, lays the blame on women while adamantly refusing to suggest that men take responsibility for their actions.

Christina Hoff Sommers: The War Against Feminism

In her 1994 book, *Who Stole Feminism? How Women Have Betrayed Women*, Christina Hoff Sommers claims that feminism has split into two competing camps: the equality feminists and the gender feminists. Under her definitions, equality feminists have fought for issues like equal pay (and, earlier in history, suffrage) but have now been effectively marginalized within the movement by more vocal gender feminists. This latter species, according to Sommers, wants a radical reworking of society—from education to economics—eliminating all structures they deem patriarchal, overhauling capitalism, and generally disrupting life as we know it. (This division between so-called equality and gender feminists sounds suspiciously similar to the long-standing split between the liberal and radical branches of feminism—with Sommers's answer to the question "Who stole feminism?" clearly being "radical feminists.")

Though her second book, 2000's *The War Against Boys: How Misguided Feminism Is Harming Our Young Men*, focuses on feminist reform in the elementary classroom, feminist pedagogy in the university setting (especially in the formalized context of women's studies) is a particular bee in Sommers's bonnet. The book makes one or two valid criticisms; for example, she rightly questions female students' need for a sensitive, feelings-based classroom (which, of course, plays into stereotypes of women as emotional rather than rational). But for the most part she paints a myopic portrait of women's studies that dwells exclusively on the discipline's worst excesses. Caricaturing the supposed radicalism of the feminist classroom, Sommers muses that women's studies departments should be required to hand out a letter to parents of prospective students declaring, "We will help your daughter discover the extent to which she has been in complicity with the patriarchy. She may become enraged and chronically offended. She will very likely reject the religious and moral codes you raised her with. She may end up hating you (her father) and pitying you (her mother). After she has completed her re-education with us, you will certainly be out tens of thousands of dollars and very possibly be out one daughter as well." Sommers's shortsighted analysis ignores the diversity of women's studies faculties and the existence of other critics of classroom radicalism, and her generalizations do not paint an accurate picture of feminist education any more than they adhere honestly to the realities of feminist philosophy.

Then there's the right-wing connection to Sommers's pop persona: Her works were financed by some notoriously conservative organizations, such as the Olin Foundation. She purports to be a feminist of the equality variety, but gives no evidence that she has ever participated in feminist activism or academics. (Of course, this brings up another question: Must a feminist engage in activism, or is a simple statement of belief enough?) The media attention given to Sommers's biased and poorly researched books, which are regularly featured in the mainstream press, implies that there is both a market for—and a desire to produce—material that panders to the right wing's most paranoid and misguided ideas about the evils of feminism.

Daphne Patai: Feministphobia

Unlike Paglia or Sommers—whose dedication to feminism has hardly been obvious or exemplary—Daphne Patai hails from inside the movement: Her career maps a transformation from feminist critic to critic of feminism. Patai cut her teeth in the rarefied world of the feminist academy with works like *The Orwell Mystique: A Study in Male Ideology* and *Brazilian Women Speak*, an epic-length ethnography. But her growing discontent with women's studies programs led to 1994's *Professing Feminism: Caution-*

ary Tales from the Strange World of Women's Studies, which she cowrote with Noretta Koertge. *Professing Feminism* airs the proverbial dirty laundry of women's studies departments. Two major issues emerge in Patai's analysis: the development of a feminist orthodoxy that, in her view, stifles debate in the classroom, and the overlap of women's studies with activism— which, she argues, transforms classes into therapy sessions riddled with agenda-driven dogma.

It should come as no surprise that *Professing Feminism* was widely embraced by antifeminists. Despite Patai's frequent assertions that women's studies just needs an overhaul, conservatives of all stripes (particularly the Independent Women's Forum) frequently use her work to argue for the elimination of the discipline from university curricula. Her break with feminism was cemented with 1998's *Heterophobia: Sexual Harassment and the Future of Feminism*, which explores the relationship between feminism and what Patai calls the sexual harassment industry, or SHI. She argues that legislative reform and the network of lawyers, advocates, and consultants that has sprung up around harassment are a threat to civil liberties and academic freedom, as policy has shifted from shielding women from quid pro quo harassment (where superiors demand sexual favors in return for promotions, grades, etc.) to protection from "uncomfortable" situations.

While Patai poses some important questions—such as whether workplaces should be sex-free (when many of us meet partners in that very venue) and whether women really need protection from every off-color joke and fumbled come-on—she presupposes that all it takes to end an uncomfortable or hostile situation is to speak up about it, and that those who do so won't be, say, passed over for promotion in retaliation. Patai's suggestions work only for those who will suffer no consequences from standing up to their would-be harassers—an approach that does nothing to address the legal difficulty of finding a harassment policy that is effective in the broad range of situations that occur in classrooms and workplaces nationwide.

Elizabeth Fox-Genovese: "I'm Not a Feminist, But . . ."

Like Patai, Elizabeth Fox-Genovese writes from within the ivory-tower ranks of the feminist academy, as the former head of the women's studies faculty at Emory University. Her first book, 1991's *Feminism Without Illusions: A Critique of Individualism*, is a dense treatise about modern feminism's reliance on political, economic, and social theories that place individual need above social good. She argues that feminism has unquestioningly adhered to individualist practice—to the detriment of both social communities and women's status—and calls for a reconsideration of priorities.

Fox-Genovese's second book, 1996's *"Feminism Is Not the Story of My Life": How Today's Feminist Elite Has Lost Touch with the Real Concerns of Women*, addresses the question of why so many women qualify their support of equal rights with the phrase "I'm not a feminist, but . . ." She wonders whether feminism's pro-choice stance turns away conservative women who might otherwise join the fight for issues like equal pay, and worries that feminism's emphasis on self-actualization alienates women from cultures where family and community are central values. Fox-Genovese concludes with a proposal for a new "family feminism" that centers on rights for women with children—and sometimes doesn't sound much like feminism at all.

Her contribution to *Women and the Future of the Family*, a slim volume published by the Christian-based Center for Public Justice, goes even farther, actively arguing for a return to the Christian nuclear family and a gendered division of labor. The most striking aspect of this tract is the way Fox-Genovese treats feminism as a mistake rather than an unfinished project, handing down an unoriginal list of the ways that girls have been betrayed by the sexual revolution but never considering how feminism is still struggling to strike a balance between sexual liberation for women and sexual responsibility for men. She ignores all the ways feminism tends toward communal rather than individualistic practices and vastly overestimates the protection offered to women and children by traditional families—as if domestic abuse never occurred until individualism and feminism reared their ugly heads. Moreover, she frequently confuses cases where real feminist activism alienates women with instances where women merely buy into negative portrayals of feminism in the media.

But what's most notable in Fox-Genovese's work is the startling hypocrisy of a childless career professor promoting a division of labor that relegates women to the kitchen and nursery—the day-to-day realization of which would certainly exclude her from the very platform from which she makes her pronouncements.

Katie Roiphe: Not Your Mama's Feminism

The daughter of renowned feminist author Anne Roiphe, Katie Roiphe grew up surrounded by second-wave liberal feminism. But her undergraduate years at Harvard left her shocked at the divergence between her mother's matter-of-fact feminism and what she saw as a radical ideology that carried the feminist movement onto the 1990s campus and contradicts her underlying assumption that equality has long since been achieved and further activity toward that end is superfluous.

In response, she wrote *The Morning After: Sex, Fear, and Feminism on Campus*, which was published in 1993 and got a lot of attention for questioning the veracity of the campus date-rape crisis. She casually compares the widely quoted statistic that one in four college-age women has been sexually assaulted to the total number of assaults that were reported and rumored in her college dorms, noting a discrepancy that numbers in the thousands. She attacks the perception that danger lurks everywhere for women, wondering if this unreasonable fear isn't even reinforced by Take Back the Night marches, which highlight women's vulnerability with endless testimonials about traumatic assault. Roiphe's opinions parallel a point hammered home by Paglia and Patai: that stringent behavior rules, with their Victorian notions of feminine fragility, infantilize women. Also in line with Patai, Roiphe protests the chilling effect of sexual harassment rules that promise to protect women from uncomfortable situations.

She seems to think that if one-quarter of her friends have not told her they were assaulted, the statistic must be wrong. (And it's worth noting that as a vocal critic of the entire notion of a date-rape crisis, she would probably be the last to hear about alleged rapes among friends and acquaintances.)

What she fails to realize is that forums like Take Back the Night serve as places for young women who did not grow up with feminism to discover that they are not alone in their experience, that there can be power in voicing private trauma, and that harassment includes situations that are neither quid pro quo nor simply some negligible discomfort.

In the end, Roiphe is a confident young woman lucky enough to have feminist parents and an Ivy League education; her refusal look beyond her own experience, however, makes for a myopic analysis that overlooks the fact that many of feminism's battles have yet to be won.

Wendy Shalit: Putting Feminism Back in the Closet

Wendy Shalit made waves in conservative and feminist circles alike with the publication of 1999's *A Return to Modesty: Discovering the Lost Virtue*, which asked women to voluntarily climb back into a closet of ankle-length skirts and early curfews. Shalit posits that modern female woes can all be blamed on the lack of modesty allowed to women, claiming that unisex bathrooms, sex education in elementary schools, and free condoms on college campuses are among the phenomena that force girls to give up the natural blushing ways that once protected them from harassment, rape, anorexia, depression, unpleasant dates, and pernicious ogling.

While Camille Paglia uses literary, celebrity, and pop culture figures to study the archetypes of the Western imagination, Shalit does her one better by actually holding up these fictionalized characters as models for the way that humanity (particularly the female half) should conduct itself. She seems peculiarly oblivious to the fact that Cary Grant movies and Jane Austen novels do not represent anybody's reality, and—like Fox-Genovese—she appears to think that *Cosmo* is a realistic barometer of American women's thoughts and opinions. She blows right past the fact that throughout the history of Western civilization, chivalrous courtship rules have only applied to wealthy (and usually white) women, since the sequestering of affluent females was facilitated by the economic contributions of slaves and working-class women. Shalit's version of modesty is available only to the minority upper crust—not coincidentally, the same class that she brags about belonging to.

But Shalit's most egregious move is to set up a startling new blame-the victim paradigm: Not only does a woman deserve individual blame if she's attacked, but, by extension, all women are to blame due to a general lack of modesty that leads to wanton male behavior. Even if her dubious claim that modesty protects against sexual violence were true, she ignores how modesty's complement, shame, has historically served to imprison sexual-assault victims in a mire of guilt and social condemnation. Furthermore, Shalit leaves no room for personal choice: A critical mass of women, she implies, must join the modesty club if men are to be browbeaten into civilized behavior (otherwise, modesty will simply be mocked by men who can still get free sex from loose women).

Shalit shares with Camille Paglia a view of masculinity as violent and ruthless, especially when it comes to sex. But here Shalit parts ways with both feminism and her fellow antifeminists by advocating an extreme version of the infantilizing behavioral prescriptions that both Paglia and Roiphe rail against; indeed, she specifically rejects both women as too dismissive of the campus date-rape crisis, but turns around to berate mainstream feminists for failing to recognize how women's immodest behavior contributes to their eventual rape. Mostly, though, Shalit's views fall narrowly in line with those of Fox-Genovese: Both see sexual liberation as a victory of men over women, and both call for women to move backward to reclaim lost ground—a plan that leaves many feminists cold. Shalit wants to be protected from the unseemly parts of life without giving up the rights and privileges that have accompanied women's emergence from the confines of modesty—a have-my-cake-and-eat-it-too whine that few realistic feminists have the time or patience to indulge.

EACH OF THESE WOMEN ADDS A UNIQUE (IF WRONGHEADED, misinformed, or just plain grating) voice to the debate over women's roles both past and future. If nothing else, these authors force feminists to take a serious look at how we identify ourselves and how we define participation in the feminist movement. They stretch the limits of whom we include under the rubric of feminism, and their criticisms expose areas where feminist work is incomplete, pointing the way to important questions that remain unanswered: What's the best way to balance the reality of modern workplace interpersonal relations with an adequate sexual harassment policy? How can we ensure that girls and boys are treated equally in the classroom? Isn't it more crucial to challenge ideas of "natural" male aggression than it is to teach females to restrict their lives in order to avoid it?

Unfortunately, their faux-feminist rhetoric makes it easy for readers to encounter "feminism" without ever encountering actual feminist views and activism. As such, their presence will serve only to take attention away from women whose goals transcend the endless disparagement of feminism itself and create a distraction from the real questions of equality.

Celebrity Jeopardy

The Perils of Feminist Fame

Rachel Fudge / WINTER 2003

ANY CASUAL READER OF THE POPULAR PRESS WILL HAVE NO-
ticed the recent avalanche of books boldly declaring that (are you ready for
this?) women are not always nice to one another. In case you were laboring
under a misconception, it isn't all hearts and roses and sisterhood—women
can be, like, rilly mean to each other. Not only that, what is rarely acknowledged is how badly allegedly liberated women can behave toward one another in the service of feminism. Feminists have long tried to keep their
own bad behavior safely behind closed doors, relegating their infighting to
the pages of movement-only journals or snarky comments made during
group meetings. But the truth is, we feminists seem to have a particular
taste for devouring our own. We have such high hopes for one another and
for the mythical sisterhood that it's especially distressing when a sister mis-
behaves or doesn't live up to her potential.

Nowhere is this complicated dynamic as apparent as in the anointing,
revering, and trashing of feminists who achieve a modicum of celebrity.
Woe to the woman who becomes singled out by the media, portrayed as a
star or spokesperson or symbol—for she has to answer not only to a public
that is at best wary of (and often downright hostile to) feminism but also to
the community of feminists who nurtured her. Second-wave feminists'
memoirs are rife with bitter tales of "star feminists" being told by their sisters not to shine, yet the pattern repeats itself with each new resurgence of

activism. Although they are by no means the only representations of these conflicts, the parallel careers of über–women's libber Gloria Steinem and queen of the riot grrrls Kathleen Hanna demonstrate that one is not born but rather made a famous feminist.

Women have long been conditioned to shun the spotlight and instead seek gratification from motherhood or from nurturing menfolk. For a very long time, there were few places for women in the public sphere at all, let alone venues for women to seize the stage. A key tenet of feminism, from the nineteenth century onward, has been the simple but radical notion that women should have equal access to the public realm, to the world of work, money, power, politics, and influence. Yet at the same time, feminism has advocated for a kinder, gentler, less masculinist conception of that realm, in essence arguing that women are (or should be) less interested in success and power as they've traditionally been defined.

But by claiming that women should eschew success or power, we've done ourselves a disservice. Vilifying leadership and fame results only in our icons being chosen for us—not by us—and so we end up either with overtaxed activists like Steinem and Hanna as the lone voices of a movement or, as is more common these days, with pseudofeminists like Elizabeth Wurtzel or Katie Roiphe as our media-anointed leaders. It also ensures that the public representation of feminism will continue to be created by a scandal-hungry, nuance-rejecting media that has a hard time perceiving women as three-dimensional creatures.

Feminism Abhors a Leader

From its inception, second-wave feminism, aka the women's liberation movement, or WLM, was painstakingly egalitarian in both theory and in attempted practice. Activist and consciousness-raising groups swore by the decision-by-consensus paradigm that's now a caricature of feminist organizing. At its best, the "structureless" approach (so dubbed in 1972 by feminist author Joreen, otherwise known as Jo Freeman) prevented aggressive personalities from dominating groups and allowed everyone to be heard and, of course, validated. The movement's lot system, which aimed to ensure that each woman would have a turn at each task, from running meetings to making public appearances, was also a way for women to tap into undiscovered skills and talents.

This antistructure, antileader stance was a deliberate reaction against the charismatic leadership of the male-dominated civil rights and antiwar movements. It was also an earnest attempt to make literal a central feminist principle: that instances of sexism, whether institutionalized in laws and employment or embedded in interpersonal relationships, are not the complaints of individual women but rather injustices suffered by all women. Appointing one woman as a spokesperson would not only disrupt the committee approach but, more fundamentally, obscure the ingrained, systemic nature of sexism.

However, as it quickly became apparent to many in the movement, the problem with this utopian vision was that some women were better public speakers than others, had more contacts within the media, or quite simply were more ambitious. In the early days of the WLM, few women were bold enough to declare their own desire to be in command or in the public eye, yet the dreaded charismatic figures nonetheless emerged. Women like Shulamith Firestone, Ellen Willis, Susan Brownmiller, Ti-Grace Atkinson, Flo Kennedy, and Betty Friedan were smart, articulate, passionate feminists who were particularly adept at communicating both with the media and with other feminists. But other, equally hardworking women resented their "star power" and argued that these individual women were elitists who had no right to speak for the movement as a whole.

As Susan Brownmiller relates in *In Our Time: Memoir of a Revolution*, "getting your name in the paper was 'personal publicity' that made you a 'star,' guilty of the sin of personal ambition." Flo Kennedy dubbed it "horizontal hostility"—"misdirected anger that rightly should be focused on the external causes of oppression," not on the few women who managed to work with the media. These supposed stars were swiftly ostracized by their sisters for breaking one of the cardinal unspoken rules of the WLM. The art of "trashing"—knocking down emerging stars—was widespread: Women in Brownmiller's consciousness-raising group, for example, circulated a petition against her, claiming that she had sought personal fame by writing about the movement in the mainstream press. Others, like Shulamith Firestone, drifted away of their own accord, disenchanted with the so-called sisterhood for quashing her personal ambitions. Alice Echols's comprehensive history of second-wave radical feminism, *Daring to Be Bad*, is littered with stories of women who left the movement or were forced out because they were unwilling to subsume their career trajectories or drives for personal achievement into the collective good.

Further complicating the matter, most of the members of the WLM distrusted the mainstream media (even the ones who worked for it), and most groups had policies of not cooperating with the establishment press, or doing so only on their own very narrow terms. This stance of noncooperation, however principled, ultimately sabotaged the radical wing of second-wave feminism, as its silence allowed more palatable, media-friendly liberal feminists to become the face of feminism. Writing in 1972, Joreen pointed this out with great precision: "Because the movement did not put [the 'stars'] in the role of spokesperson, the movement cannot remove them. The press put them there and only the press can choose not to listen. The press will continue to look to 'stars' as spokeswomen as long as it has no official alternatives. The movement has no control in the selection of its representatives to the public as long as it believes that it should have no representatives at all."

Sic Transit Gloria Mundi: The "Unlikely Guru of Women's Lib"

The real turning point in the feminist fame game was a 1971 *Newsweek* cover story that declared the long-legged, short-skirted writer/activist Gloria Steinem "the unlikely guru" of the women's movement. Despite the fact that the article was a whole lot of hype—Betty Friedan had been the formal leader of NOW since cofounding it in 1966; Kate Millett, Shulamith Firestone, and Robin Morgan had recently published extremely influential books; and hundreds of other women had started consciousness-raising groups and action collectives—it was self-fulfilling. After the piece was published, Steinem did become the public face of feminism—and the object of bitter jealousy and resentment. In *In Our Time*, Brownmiller describes how she and many of the other radicals were outraged by the hype and by seeing "hard-won, original insights developed by others in near total anonymity be turned by the media into Gloria Steinem pronouncements, Gloria Steinem ideas, and Gloria Steinem visions."

But Steinem—and her glamorous U.K. counterpart, Germaine Greer— served a critical function, as Brownmiller also recognizes in hindsight: "While the radicals were insisting, 'We don't need a leader,' mainstream women needed to have Gloria up there—a golden achiever who wore the armament of perfect beauty, was wildly attractive to men, and spoke uncompromising truths in calm, measured tones that seldom betrayed her anger. And Gloria, for all the complex reasons a person seeks heroism and stardom, needed to become what people wished her to be." Roxanne Dunbar-Ortiz, in her recent memoir of the '60s and '70s, *Outlaw Woman,* is less forgiving, painting Steinem's ascension as a ploy to shift the movement away from radicalism: "Gloria Steinem was being promoted by the New York liberal media establishment as the model for the women's liberation movement."

Whether or not she sought out or desired her stardom, Steinem managed to parlay her fifteen minutes of fame into a lifelong career in public feminism. As she said in a 2000 interview in *Bust,* "I think the challenge is to figure out how to use public recognition to convey some message." She also tried, in both concrete and abstract ways, to deflect the star label. In the early days, she took a cue from the radical feminist cadres and insisted upon speaking only with female reporters, or participating only in articles that would feature several women's voices and not just hers. Current media outlets continue to ask for Steinem's presence, and she always attempts to share the spotlight with other women—especially, of late, the younger generation of feminists.

Backstabbing, Grrrl-Style Now

Alas, the art of trashing was not isolated to the second wave. Sadly, the criticisms of selling out or seeking undue fame resurface with every rekindled interest in feminism. The rise and fall of the riot grrrl movement in the early '90s, in particular, makes for a compelling parallel with the heady days of the second wave.

Even before Naomi Wolf and Susan Faludi—arguably the two most prominent feminists of the early 1990s—rocketed to the top of the bestseller lists, a younger generation of activists had coalesced into a vital, messy new feminist force. Like the radical feminists of the second wave, these women were staunchly antiestablishment, operating outside the mainstream and embracing indie- and punk-rock culture—and they too were inspired to action by the sexism of the men in their supposedly alternative communities. The term "riot grrrl," first invoked as the name of a feminist zine and a gathering of hundreds of angry young women, was interpreted by the mainstream media as the name of the movement. Before this nascent movement had a chance to define itself, it seemed, it was plastered across the headlines of *Time*, *Newsweek*, and *Sassy*, leading girls across the country to start "chapters" and declare themselves "riot grrrls," much to the bemusement of the originators of the term. In a tale that may be apocryphal, Bikini Kill frontwoman Kathleen Hanna purportedly convinced a "mainstream reporter" that there were riot grrrl chapters in cities across the country when there really weren't; in response to the story, girls went looking for the chapters, and when they couldn't find them, they decided to start their own.

In search of a public face for this new movement, reporters latched onto the outspoken Hanna, who was—not at all coincidentally, at least for the media's purposes—a onetime neighbor of rock star Kurt Cobain. Hanna's sudden high visibility soon affected her ability to participate in the very culture she was supposedly leading. In a 2001 interview in *index* magazine, Hanna said, "I went to a couple of Riot Grrrl meetings, but then I faded out of it, because I got sort of famous. I mean, at least famous in my own little scene, I got all this attention." Like Brownmiller, Firestone, and Steinem, she was perceived by some as a traitor.

But from the start, Hanna was, she told *Bust*, "really embarrassed and humiliated by being singled out" and tried to resist being characterized as the leader of riot grrrl—even going so far as to resist being called a riot grrrl at all. In the liner notes to a CD release of Bikini Kill's first two records, the band insists it is not "the definitive 'riot girl band'" and that its members are "not 'leaders of' or authorities on the 'Riot Grrrl' movement." And furthermore, they write, "Tho we totally respect those who still feel that label is important and meaningful to them, we have never used that term to describe ourselves as a band." These mixed feelings about being publicly allied with such a diffuse movement were shared by many of the original participants in riot grrrl, including zine authors and Bratmobile members Allison Wolfe and Molly Neuman and British band Huggy Bear, all of whom ended up declaring a sort of media blackout. Frustrated by their misrepresentation in the press and anxious to maintain control over their images, riot grrrls refused to participate in interviews or be photographed for stories. As a result, as with the radical wing of second-wave feminism, their message was co-opted by the mainstream press and diluted into a slogan of anything-goes girl power.

In the meantime, Hanna struggled with her newfound celebrity, trying to balance her own integrity with the potential to reach a broader audience. Like Steinem before her, Hanna has developed a great awareness of fame's potential, and its pitfalls. In a dialogue with Steinem in *Bust*, Hanna said, "I need to know how, as an FF—Famous Feminist—to deal with these things [backbiting, horizontal hostility disguised as valid criticism]. I need to see the graceful ways that other women have dealt with that."

The Media Abhors a Leaderless Vacuum

Much of the anger directed toward feminist stars stems from a deep-rooted frustration with the way the media treats the movement. Women rise to fame not because they are lauded as leaders by other feminists (even though, like Steinem and Hanna, they might already be seen as role models), but because the mainstream media sees in them a marketable image— a newsworthy persona upon whom can be projected all sorts of anxieties, hopes, and responsibilities. A feminist's fame is often aided by something tangential to her politics—and that something is frequently related to her looks. Gloria Steinem and Naomi Wolf, for instance, rode to fame on the "she's a feminist, but she's sexy!" angle, while Kathleen Hanna was titillating because she was a feminist, a budding rock star, and a stripper. Meanwhile, contrarians like Camille Paglia and Rene Denfeld made news by being feminists who hate other feminists. You get the idea: It's rarely original thought or sharp intellect alone that gets a woman noticed.

These days, the feminist fame machine operates almost entirely outside the realm of feminist activism, organizing, or journalism. More often than not, the women who are held up as icons have little to do with, well, actual feminism. In fact, it takes very little feminist activity to become anointed a feminist icon. Jennifer Baumgardner and Amy Richards, coauthors of *Manifesta: Young Women, Feminism, and the Future*, are among those who have pointed out that feminism's shift away from its activist roots has had serious negative consequences—one of which is that, because feminism is so far removed from grassroots, hands-on action, it is possible for a person like Elizabeth Wurtzel or Katie Roiphe to declare herself a feminist and, with no clearly articulated politics or ideals, become someone people in the media call on when they need a feminist perspective on an issue of the day. As Baumgardner and Richards put it, "[People] have begun conflating celebrity with expertise. She who gets the most attention is presumed to be the 'leader,' regardless of the content of her message or her character."

Moreover, as our culture grows ever more obsessed with celebrity, it has become harder and harder to find examples of living, breathing feminists in the media. The infamous 1998 *Time* cover story that traced the history of feminism from Susan B. Anthony to Betty Friedan to a TV character who never identifies herself as feminist (Ally McBeal, played by Calista Flockhart) is the most well-known example, but it's far from unique. (In fact, the article hardly referenced a single breathing person, instead relying on media images of imaginary women like McBeal and Bridget Jones to speak for women. The few real-life women who were mentioned—Courtney Love, Debbie Stoller, Lisa Palac—were media creators themselves, not activists.) When they aren't fictional characters standing in for real women, public feminists tend to be either only marginally identified with feminist politics (as with the aforementioned Wurtzel) or in fact ideologically opposed to many of the tenets of feminism, as is the case with the current crop of antifeminist feminists. (Formal leaders of mainstream feminist organizations—like Patricia Ireland of NOW and Ellie Smeal of the Feminist Majority Foundation—have been recognized as experts when it comes to commenting on specific public policy issues relating to reproductive rights, but not much more.)

The current scarcity of feminist stars is a curious thing. It could be read as a step forward—a reflection of feminism's evolution, a renewed interest in local activism, and the growing realization that feminism is not a monolithic ideology. It could be a sign of waning public interest in feminism or another backlash, the belief that feminism is over and our work done. It could be that, as a reflection of these conservative times, the most recognizable feminist icons are not actually feminists.

The truth is, feminism is in many ways a victim of its own successes. On the one hand, an awareness of feminism—or at least its basic principles—is increasingly interwoven into American mass culture. But on the other hand, it is rarely explicitly discussed in the mainstream media, except for the occasional pronouncement that it's "dead," or in reports stating that a majority of women do not call themselves feminists.

Looking back on the lesbian-feminist movement of the 1970s, artist Terry Wolverton asks, "In letting go of our worldly ambitions . . . were we truly forging a female model, one that assumed our influence would be psychic, cellular, would work its way through an underground network of women's wisdom? Or were we unwittingly participating in our own marginalization, ensuring our efforts would be lost to history? Were we redefining power or giving up on it?" Wolverton could just as easily be describing the riot grrrls or the third-wavers. It happens again and again—the radicals refuse to be co-opted by the mass culture, and so their history, too, remains obscure.

The proliferation of micromedia—independent websites, underground zines, and info-sharing networks—has infused new blood into feminist activism, as the popularity of Ladyfest and other locally based skill-sharing workshops attest. But without famous faces, or at least provocative new visages, attached to it, this kind of grassroots activism is invisible to nonfeminist media. (And with the rocky state of national feminist media these days, we can't afford to isolate ourselves in a pro-grrrl media ghetto.) To remain vital and relevant to a larger group of women, feminism also needs a public face—or better yet, public faces.

We shoot ourselves in the foot when we punish or ostracize leaders. The lesson of Gloria and Kathleen is this: People aren't right or authoritative simply because they're famous, nor are they bad or bent on screwing over their colleagues. And if we don't select our own leaders, the media will do it for us—much to the detriment of the feminist movement. Feminists have to let go of the notion that to be a public figure is to seek personal glory and personal glory alone, and realize that the desire to take feminism to the public realm comes out of a desire to help craft our own collective image.

Unnatural Selection

Questioning Science's Gender Bias

Keely Savoie / SPRING 2004

SOMEWHERE IN THE MOUNTAINS OUTSIDE OF KYOTO, JAPAN, a group of Japanese macaques are doing something they have no evolutionary right to do: having lots of hot, homo monkey sex. Every mating season, the females couple up with each other. Some of the consortships last only an hour, others more than a week. During the time they are together, these female couples mount each other tens or even hundreds of times, defend each other from male aggressors, groom each other, forage together, sleep together, and choose each other over interested males. According to Dr. Paul Vasey, assistant professor at the University of Lethbridge in Alberta, Canada, among these particular Japanese macaques, the girls get it on with each other more than they do with the boys. And they get off, too: The mounter rubs her clitoris against the mountee's back, while the mountee rubs her own clitoris with her tail, and together they enjoy wanton lezzie action with no reproductive value whatsoever.

Meanwhile, in a lab at the University of Georgia, Dr. Patricia Adair Gowaty, distinguished research professor at the Institute of Ecology, is studying fruit flies that also break the evolutionary mold. Instead of buzzing around frantically trying to mate with any available female while the females sit back and pick the cream of the crop ("Not you. Nope, not you, either . . . Ahhh, what nice complex eyes you have. Yes—you"), Gowaty's males are just as choosy as females, sometimes more so—even though everyone from Charles Darwin to Dr. Phil knows that the evolutionary mandate of males is to mate, mate, mate.

As I furiously scribbled notes during Vasey's and Gowaty's talks at the convention of the American Association for the Advancement of Science (AAAS), all I could think was, Finally, this week of proteomics lectures and career workshops is coming through with the ultimate payoff—sex. But while I reveled in the salacious details of monkeys' erotic lives, Vasey, Gowaty, and other scientists at the seminar had a bone to pick with their discipline.

For all the emphasis on advancement in the field, most biologists still tend to view animal behavior through the socially conservative lens of the field's Victorian forefathers: Sex is strictly for reproduction, and males and females have prescribed roles—a formula that conveniently reflects social values but renders Gowaty's finicky males and Vasey's lusty females the orphans of evolutionary theory. Biologists have known about the lesbian macaques for over forty years—and there is documented homosexuality in over four hundred species—but no one has come up with a satisfying theoretical framework for their nonreproductive sex. And Gowaty's fruit flies are not alone in their defiance of parental investment theory, a branch of evolutionary theory asserting that females are "coy" and males "indiscriminate" due to the respective size of eggs and sperm (hence, the amount of energy each gender invests in its progeny). Yet the theory still stands as the default explanation for differences between the sexes.

Dr. Joan Roughgarden—the tireless feminist, gay, and transgender activist and eminent theoretical ecologist at Stanford University who organized the Evolutionary Aspects of Gender and Sexuality seminar that was the occasion for Gowaty's and Vasey's talks—says research that eschews those archaic assumptions about gender and sexuality is routinely marginalized, swept under the rug, ignored, avoided, and ridiculed. Passive and active sexism in scientific research, she says, have resulted in a skewed and incomplete picture of the world that only a feminist overhaul of existing and future research can correct. Happily, there are scientists like Gowaty and Vasey doing the work, but they face a long, hard slog, not just against die-hard scientific tenets like parental investment theory but also against the recalcitrant professional and academic institutions of science itself.

The organizers of the AAAS conference had unwittingly underscored Roughgarden's point: The seminar was held at 8:30 a.m. Monday, the last day of the convention. Few of the attendees of America's biggest and most venerable science conference had managed to drag themselves to the seminar—most were already on planes home, and those who remained had the difficult choice of sleeping off last night's cocktails or getting up at the crack of dawn on the promise of having some weak coffee and hearing the voices of dissent.

Sexism in science takes many guises, some more subtle than others. My favorite example of blatant "scientification" of sexism comes courtesy of some Greek scientists who purported to solve the age-old question, Can you spot a superlong schlong by scoping a guy's shoe size? Thanks to those gumptious Greeks, we now know that shoe size has nothing to do with the ol' pajama python—but in case anyone really cares, the index finger is a more reliable measure of the man.

I find these studies humorous for their poignantly desperate attempts to validate male power and female subordination. But at a certain point, they take a sinister turn. When pseudoscientific studies claim to reveal the "natural basis" of double standards, they justify abhorrent sexist ideas and behavior by calling them biological destiny. It's one thing to put your pecker under the microscope and tell everyone you've seen the world's biggest prick—it's another to co-opt the tools of science to justify barbaric behavior, claiming culture and consciousness can't hold their own against the genetic writ of male dominance.

Biology is particularly amenable to sexist narratives. Gendered explanations and expectations of animal behavior are so prevalent that challenging them seems to be a Sisyphean undertaking. Perhaps they're so ingrained because they so satisfyingly reflect prevailing social mores: Females are passive and males are aggressive; mothers raise the offspring and fathers' contributions end at ejaculation; sex is for reproduction, so, by definition, anything else is unnatural. Gowaty calls these "just-so stories" that "buttress status quo notions about sex roles that . . . confine women to their 'natural' roles as mothers and subordinates to men."

In evolutionary psychology, evolutionary biology's human cousin, these just-so stories are applied to men and women, especially to their sexual dynamics. Each new study seems to bristle with controversy and bad intentions. They often come out in obscure journals, are filtered through the popular press, and enter public consciousness with such headlines as "Semen Makes Women Happy" and "Male Sweat Brightens Women's Moods." According to these studies, anything secreted from men's pores or penises can make the world a better place.

Whenever a new study comes out claiming to demonstrate the evolutionary justification for the latest topic in the battle between the sexes, everyone from CNN to *Maxim* jumps at the chance to promulgate the same old sexist schlock: Women want love, not sex. Men only want sex. Girl babies break up marriages. Men can't help cheating; it's in their genes. Men can't help raping; it's in their genes. Dr. David Schmitt, an evolutionary psychologist from Bradley University in Peoria, Illinois, recently trumpeted "the most comprehensive test yet conducted on whether the sexes differ in their desire for sexual variety." The media reported that a survey of sixteen thousand people had proved that male promiscuity is hardwired, based on the results of questionnaires Schmitt had college students fill out describing their sexual practices and attitudes.

To be fair, it's not a crime to attempt a broad study of human sexuality. Attempting to illuminate cultural similarities and differences in sexuality and gender roles is certainly an interesting undertaking. But claiming to demonstrate that "hardwired" gender disparities evolved over millions of years on the basis of the questionnaire responses of teenagers in 2003 is stretching the limits of credibility and science. The scientists behind these studies may not intend to promote the macho ideal, but their preconceived notions—combined with a media eager for the buzz of such stories—make for an embrace of the sexist status quo.

Dr. Terri Fisher, a psychologist at Ohio State University, challenges the validity of research like Schmitt's, even while she defends him as a colleague. Although research that relies on self-reporting dominates the field, Fisher believes that asking people to answer intimate questions about their sex lives in a classroom setting is inherently unreliable. She wonders whether, if the subjects are answering questions in a public setting, they are expressing their actual feelings and experiences or responding to a perceived social pressure to abide by certain gender-specific behaviors.

Fisher and her colleague Michele Alexander have designed their own studies to guard against this sort of self-reporting bias. In one recent study,

Fisher controlled the level and type of social pressure her subjects felt as they responded to the questions. Some of her subjects were assured that their answers were anonymous, others thought that they had to hand their questionnaires to another student, and still others had to answer while hooked up to what they believed was a lie-detector machine. By manipulating the pressure students felt to either perform under the scrutiny of their peers or "pass" the fake lie-detector test, Fisher got markedly different results. Like Schmitt's students, when Fisher's respondents answered the questions in the company of their peers, their answers fit social stereotypes. But when students thought they were hooked up to a lie detector, the story changed. The men admitted to having fewer partners, and the women copped to more—a lot more. And both men and women, at the end of the day, had roughly the same amount of sex—which is the only thing that really makes sense, considering that all those straight males had to be finding their multiple female partners somewhere.

In light of Fisher's study, Schmitt's appears to be measuring not the genetic mandate for profligate men and coy women but the amount of social pressure each gender feels to adhere to cultural ideals. Fisher's research is a powerful rebuttal to scientists whose work fails to dig below the surface and instead uncritically reflects and reinforces social stereotypes. Perhaps predictably, Fisher's study also received press attention, but the media managed to twist her findings to fit yet another gendered stereotype: "Fake Lie-Detector Reveals Women's Sex Lies," squawked NewScientist.com. The article opened with what read like a warning to guileless men: "Women are more likely than men to lie about their sex lives, reveals a new study."

It's no surprise that the media tends to overreport and underanalyze results like Schmitt's while ignoring or distorting studies like Fisher's, but—sensationalistic reporting aside—the problem of sexism in biological research still remains a scientific, not a media, issue.

Advances in feminist research can go only so far when the very structure of academia works against the full inclusion of alternative ideas. Despite the scientific conceit of "objectivity," the scientific community is made up of people, and each and every scientist has his or her own belief system, ingrained cultural biases, and blind spots. The scientific method may be the best way we have of achieving an objective view of the world, but it can be only as objective as the questions asked. If one group is doing most of the asking, unseen biases—or, as Gowaty calls them, "assumptions so deep they tend to be invisible"—can creep in without anyone noticing.

Three decades after second-wave feminists began making inroads into academia, and pioneers like primatologist Sarah Blaffer Hrdy began using feminist critiques to improve scientific theories, there is still palpable resistance to feminist perspectives in science. But contemporary biologists who cut their teeth on the scientific critiques of second-wave feminists are putting forth testable theories that are proving to be more accurate and powerful in their ability to explain the intricacies of animal (and human) behavior than much of the gender-based Darwinian dogma that preceded them.

Gowaty's fruit flies are the perfect example. The females have huge eggs and the males have tiny sperm—which, according to parental investment theory, should mean that the females should be extremely choosy, and the males should mate indiscriminately whenever possible. But it turns out that her fruit flies, regardless of sex, employed flexible mating strategies dependent on environment—not gender. In her first trial, Gowaty found that males seemed to be slightly pickier than females when it came to approaching sex partners. In the second test, they were about the same. It might not sound so radical to a feminist, but to Darwin and his descendants, Gowaty's conclusion would be downright shocking: In the end, "There was nothing so like a male as a female, and nothing so like a female as a male." After more than a century of biological theory grounded strictly in gender determinism, it's a statement that could cause a revolution—if it could be heard.

But Gowaty's research has not been cited as often as it could have been. She believes her feminist politics, not the quality of her work, have marginalized her in the scientific community. "My willingness to speak out against things that don't make sense has cost me," she says. A book she published in 1997, *Feminism and Evolutionary Biology*, is already out of print, and she now believes that labeling any scientific work as feminist "is the kiss of death."

"If you don't name something feminist," she says, "it stands a much greater chance of being accepted." She spends a good deal of time and energy defending her work against the arguments of colleagues who dismiss it out of hand because of her politics. There's a twisted logic at play here:

Science is supposed to be objective and therefore beyond politics—so any scientist who is openly political and challenges the idea of hegemonic objectivity is, by definition, unscientific.

Regardless of the political and professional price she has paid for it, however, Gowaty believes her feminism has made her a better scientist—and that her research and others' feminist studies will contribute new and better theories to biology as a discipline. It was, in fact, Gowaty's feminism that led her to review the scientific literature, to check what scientific "proof" lay behind the doctrine of rigid sex roles, and to look for alternative theories to explain observed behavior. What she found was a whole lot of nothing.

"The 'facts' of choosy females and profligate males have organized studies of social behavior evolution, but few ever asked if the 'facts' were correct," she says. In the rare cases where someone did, the papers that proposed alternative theories were all but ignored by the rest of the scientific community.

It is also her feminist bias, Gowaty says, that allows her to see what others have not. Her research subtly turns age-old biological questions on their heads. For instance, in designing her experiments investigating mate choice, Gowaty created a gender-blind trial that makes no assumptions about how males and females are supposed to act—instead of assuming that males are profligate and females are coy. Rather than pairing females with a set of males and asking which males the females prefer, she randomly pairs males and females and watches who approaches whom.

The paradigm shift is simple, subtle, and scientifically unassailable. Gowaty explains, "Being self-conscious about my politics has helped to make my experiments better than they might otherwise be, because I institute a variety of controls that others might also use . . . if they were more aware of their own biases."

One of her favorite tactics is to collaborate with colleagues who do not share her political views, which brings to light assumptions on both sides that might otherwise go unnoticed. And then, she says, she likes to "exploit the goodwill and energy of undergraduates" who do not know her hypotheses or predictions and can therefore make unbiased observations because they don't know what they're looking for. It was with those careful controls that she conducted her fruit-fly experiment. Gowaty's approach to exposing and correcting bias in her science has made her a leader in what might not be a feminist revolution in science so much as a feminist evolution.

Roughgarden agrees that biological research may yet be salvaged from the mire of ingrained sexism on the merit of strong, careful studies. Her book *Evolution's Rainbow* began as a celebration of the diversity of the invisible, forgotten, or ignored multitudes of genders and sexual expressions in the natural world—things that she says are too often overlooked by mainstream biologists. But as she wrote and researched the book, she recognized that while it was a celebration, it was also a rebuke, "an indictment of academia for suppressing and denying diversity in their own teachings."

Roughgarden had a twenty-five-year career in ecology as a man before she transitioned to being a woman, giving her unique insight into the world of sexism in academia. She sees the prevailing theories in biology as a way to "naturalize male prowess" and believes that in a field dominated by straight white men, research has become a self-reinforcing cycle of sexism. "The purpose of their theories is often to buy them prestige, and prestige is found in agreement from other straight white men," she says. "All the other straight white men are in on the racket. [For women] there's no entrée, there's no avenue to make the truth count."

Roughgarden has focused on devising alternative theories designed to encompass the diversity found in the natural world, where, despite popular belief, there are more than two genders, certain organisms (like fish) can change gender throughout their lives, and homosexuality is rampant. Roughgarden wants to send the whole discipline of biology back to school to study the facts of the world through a lens that doesn't filter out inconvenient data that doesn't match social mores.

She has offered her own hypotheses about the evolutionary forces that have shaped gender and behavior—theories that allow diversity in both gender and sexuality while maintaining the power to explain behavior. Instead of sexual selection—Darwin's staid theory that relies on a strict gender binary and consigns females and males across all organisms to specific roles—Roughgarden proffers a replacement theory she calls social selection, which describes behavior in terms of not only its reproductive value but its social value as well. For example, she recasts the famous peacock's tail in light of its ability to communicate social status to other peafowl, both male and female, not just its desirability to peahens. The change is slight, but it allows for a more holistic examination of all behaviors in light of their value in a variety of situations.

Roughgarden's theories, even beyond social selection, are solid and testable, and they bear the hallmarks of careful thinking. They are designed to be tried by field biologists, to be poked and prodded by researchers, and to be revised, refined, or rejected if they prove inadequate. They are designed to invite more questions, provoke more thought, and spur more research into the very areas that have been cordoned off from critical thought for so long.

To Roughgarden, freeing science from the shackles of sexism is as much a political and social task as it is a scientific one. For feminist research to have an impact on the mainstream biology taught in classrooms, it will take confronting those in power—the deans, the awards committees, the granting agencies, "if we have to picket them and attack them and embarrass them at cocktail parties," she says—and demanding that women, gays and lesbians, and people of color be included in the highly political processes that play such an important role in determining what questions are asked in science, and therefore what ultimately becomes public knowledge. Diversifying the practitioners of science is a matter not just of principle but also of scientific integrity.

"Knowledge is only as diverse as the members of the intellectual elite," says Vasey, whose lesbian monkeys are also left out in the cold by biology. "When I look out into the audience [at scientific conferences], I don't see much diversity. It just makes me wonder how much knowledge is being left out."

There are small signs of improvement. There are now more women in science than ever before, though the number remains a pittance. And with much public fanfare, the National Academies of Science inducted seventeen women into its 2003 class, 24 percent of the total. Women now comprise 7.7 percent of the National Academies' members—up from 6.2 percent a year ago. At this rate, we can expect parity in another thirty years or so—around the time Jenna Bush will be running for president.

In the meantime, Vasey's monkeys and Gowaty's fruit flies will continue to do their thing, mindless of the political and academic battles being waged over their unconventional couplings. There is precedent for the hope of feminist scientists prevailing, however. Darwin himself faced considerable opposition from both the religious and scientific communities of his time. But eventually the rigorous science of his ideas proved to be more durable than the rigid politics of his era. Thirty years ago, Stephen Jay Gould and Niles Eldredge proposed the theory of punctuated equilibrium—

whereby evolution occurs in abrupt shifts after periods of relative stasis, instead of gradually, over long periods of time. The theory appears to describe the evolution of science itself, and maybe, just maybe, Gowaty, Roughgarden, and Vasey are poised to punctuate the long-standing equilibrium of evolutionary biology.

On Language

Choice

Summer Wood / SPRING 2004

"YOU CAN BAKE YOUR CAKE AND EAT IT, TOO!" DECLARES
Julia Roberts, playing bohemian Wellesley art-history professor Katherine
Watson in the period chick flick *Mona Lisa Smile*. She eagerly proffers an
armful of law-school applications, standing on the doorstep of the impos-
ingly tony house where Joan (played by Julia Stiles), one of her best students, resides. But it's too late, Joan replies. She has eloped, and now that
she has her MRS, she won't be getting that law degree after all. "This is my
choice," she says earnestly, but her character, like most of the others in the
film, is written so flatly that it's impossible to tell whether we're supposed
to believe her. The filmmakers clearly meant for women in the audience to
breathe a sigh as we watched Roberts's signature grin crumble on hearing
the news—a sigh of pity for those poor, repressed Wellesley girls, and a sigh
of relief that women today are free of such antiquated dilemmas as having
to choose between work and family.

Fast-forward fifty years, however, and the media is full of stories of real-
life Joans: intelligent, ambitious women, educated at the country's top
schools, trading in their MBAs and PhDs for SUVs with car seats. Sylvia
Ann Hewlett claimed to have revealed an epidemic of "creeping nonchoice"
in her much-publicized 2002 book, *Creating a Life: Professional Women and
the Quest for Children*, while Lisa Belkin last year tagged a related trend "The
Opt-Out Revolution" in a *New York Times Magazine* cover story. While

Hewlett profiles high-powered women who "chose" to put their careers first and postpone childbearing, only to find out their ovaries hadn't gotten the memo, Belkin focuses on impeccably credentialed younger women preempting the challenges of balancing career and family by dropping out of the rat race soon after it begins. Neither writer bothers to examine the ways decisions to work or stay home are rarely made solely as a function of free will, but rather are swayed by underlying socioeconomic forces. But both Hewlett's book and Belkin's article do illustrate something crucial—namely, the deep, complex, and uneasy relationship between the ideology of feminism and the word "choice."

The significance of "choice" in the feminist lexicon has fluctuated over time and with the various priorities of feminist movements, but for the past thirty years, it has been most strongly associated with abortion rights. Indeed, since the mid-'80s, "choice" has all but eclipsed "abortion" in the ongoing discourse about reproductive rights. In *Beggars and Choosers: How the Politics of Choice Shapes Adoption, Abortion, and Welfare in the United States*, the historian Rickie Solinger traces the evolution of "choice" in the context of reproductive rights back to Mother's Day, 1969, when the National Abortion Rights Action League (recently renamed NARAL Pro-Choice America) held its first national action, calling it Children by Choice. These rallies gave NARAL an opportunity to market-test "choice" as the movement's new watchword. After Justice Harry Blackmun repeatedly referred to abortion as "this choice" in his majority opinion in *Roe v. Wade*, writes Solinger, choice was cemented as "the way liberal and mainstream feminists could talk about abortion without mentioning the 'A-word.'" Wary of alienating moderate supporters by claiming that women had an absolute right to abortion, movement leaders adopted a more pragmatic rhetorical strategy: "Many people believed that 'choice'—a term that evoked women shoppers selecting among options in the marketplace—would be an easier sell," writes Solinger.

Substituting "choice" for "rights" as both a legal framework and a common language indeed proved successful in attracting some libertarians and conservatives to vote for the "pro-choice" position in numerous state-level abortion contests during the '80s. Because "choice" is, in essence, an empty word, people with vastly divergent political viewpoints can be united under its banner. In retrospect, this is both the word's greatest strength and its ultimate weakness. As various constituencies brought their own political prerogatives and definitions of "choice" to the negotiating table, parents, physicians, husbands, boyfriends, and religious leaders all came to be included as rightful participants in making the abortion choice, significantly weakening the idea that women have a right to make this decision on their own. Solinger identifies the linguistic shift from abortion rights to "the individualistic, marketplace term 'choice'" as deeply problematic, on both a philosophical and a practical level.

The word's primacy in the arena of reproductive rights has slowly caused the phrase "It's my choice" to become synonymous with "It's a feminist thing to do"—or, perhaps more precisely, "It is antifeminist to criticize my decision." The result has been a rapid depoliticizing of the term and an often misguided application of feminist ideology to consumer imperatives, invoked not only for the right to decide whether to terminate a pregnancy but also for the right to buy all manner of products marketed to women, from cigarettes to antidepressants to frozen diet pizzas.

When *Sex and the City*'s Charlotte decided to quit her job, she summoned feminism in her defense: "The women's movement is supposed to be all about choice, and if I choose to quit my job, that is my choice," she tells a disgruntled Miranda, who's busy getting ready for work. After suggesting that Charlotte's "choice" to drop out of the workforce has been unduly influenced by her then-husband, Trey, Miranda hangs up on Charlotte, leaving her shouting, "I choose my choice, I choose my choice," over and over, as if to convince herself that she really does.

Elsewhere in American culture, one of the newest, and arguably most controversial, intersections between "choice," consumer culture, and feminism is the argument that undergoing cosmetic surgery can be a feminist exercise. The leading proponent of this theory is Kathy Davis, a women's studies lecturer at the University of Utrecht in the Netherlands. In *Embodied Practices: Feminist Perspectives on the Body*, Davis decries feminist critiques of plastic surgery, contending that "the paternalistic argument against choice rests on the assumption that women who want cosmetic surgery need to be protected—from themselves (their narcissistic desire for beauty) or from undue influence from others."

For many young feminists, "choice" has become the very definition of feminism itself—illustrated by the standard-bearing right to choose abortion and supported by the ever-advertised notion that they have choice in everything else in life as well. The cult of choice consumerism wills us to believe that women can get everything we want out of life, as long as we make the right choices along the way—from the cereal we eat in the morning to the moisturizer we use at night, and the universe of daily decisions, mundane and profound, that confront us in between.

However, at a time when the language of choice is at an all-time popular high, when it comes to abortion, young women may have the least choice of all, especially if they are minors residing in one of the thirty-three states requiring the consent of at least one parent in order to undergo the procedure. Some reproductive-rights activists have suggested that third-wavers don't turn out in large numbers at the polls—only 52 percent voted in the 2000 presidential election—because they've become complacent about the right to choose that their foremothers worked so hard to win.

Though NARAL Pro-Choice America is now courting young women with a web-based "Generation Pro-Choice" campaign featuring the specter of an overturned *Roe* if Bush is elected for a second term, the current administration's opponents have paid little attention to issues affecting women's other life choices, from the wage gap, health care, and education access to the dearth of quality, affordable child care or federal policies designed to ease the burdens often faced by working parents of any sex. While paying lip service to "choice" in its narrowest definition—i.e., preserving *Roe*—politicians donning the pro-choice mantle continue to neglect the full significance of choice in women's lives and the underlying social and economic conditions that constrain or empower us to do much more than choose whether to bake a cake, eat it, or both.

Such an uncritical language of choice doesn't even work in the movies: At the end of *Mona Lisa Smile*, Katherine Watson has little to show for the choices she makes—no tenure-track job at Wellesley, and no guy, either (assuming, as this is Hollywood, that she was supposed to desire both). The fact that Katherine chooses to leave Wellesley—whether motivated by her pedagogical clashes with older female faculty, her reluctance to become part of the elite academic establishment, or having her heart bruised by the swarthy Italian professor who turns out to be from New Jersey—plays like a pretty unhappy ending for a character who has spent the past two hours trying to convince her students that, at last, women really can have it all.

Laugh Riot

Feminism and the Problem of
Women's Comedy

Andi Zeisler / BITCHfest 2006

SEVERAL YEARS AGO, I SET OUT TO WRITE A PIECE ON WHY THE
potential of feminist humor has never been fully realized in modern pop
culture. I considered the history of comedy as an "outsider" format, discussed the enduring legacy of the humorless-feminist stereotype, and went
off on a tangent about the importance of fart jokes. Pages and pages of notes
and half-finished drafts later, I gave up and stuffed it all in a folder. It would
have all stayed there safely were it not for the fact that I went and watched,
just the other night, Comedy Central's *Roast of Pamela Anderson.*

Pamela Anderson? I know. She's not a comedian. I don't think you
could even pay her the backhanded compliment of calling her an inadver-
tent comedian. There are people who consider *Baywatch*, *Barb Wire*, and especially Anderson's late-'90s series *V.I.P.* to be camp brilliance, it's true.
But there's little evidence that she's ever been the generator of a joke rather
than just the butt of them. (Her two "fiction" books? They don't count.)

I'm no roast expert, but from what I've seen of the Friars Club roasts
broadcast on TV over the years, they honor comedy greats like Milton Berle
and Lucille Ball, and they involve friends and colleagues of the roastee trading naughty humor and inside jokes as part of a shared collegial bond; at
the end, the roastee gets to counter-roast the people involved. It's sort of
like high-school debate club, but with no stopwatch and more penis jokes.

For Pam, there was no shared bond. (There were penis jokes, though,

148

most of them directed at Anderson's ex-husband Tommy Lee.) In fact, with the exception of Lee and a hopped-up, splay-legged Courtney Love, none of Anderson's roasters seemed to know her as anything more than the image she projects to the rest of the world—namely, a walking, talking blow-up doll. And every witticism aimed at her couldn't help but point that out.

So what do the hours I spent gawking at a raunchy tribute to a plasticky sex icon have to do with the problem of feminist comedy? I suppose it's this: Despite all we know about the rich history of women's humor, women's place in the comedy world is still, almost always, as the subject of the joke. And—as if it needed saying—the joke is almost always at her expense.

SO, TO DRAW ON ALL THOSE HALF-FINISHED DRAFTS AND START over: Being an outsider is not automatically a negative thing in the realm of comedy. Much of the most celebrated American wit has its roots in the realm of marginalized and oppressed folks—most notably Jews and African Americans—whose traditions of identity-based humor helped to temper the racism and ostracism they historically faced. Over time, it has been assimilated into the larger lexicon of funny. Think of Richard Pryor, Eddie Murphy, and Dave Chappelle, ecstatically embraced by the very white folks they lampoon. The Marx Brothers, whose physical antics and caricatures of immigrant confusion became black-and-white classics. The observational shtick of Borscht Belt stand-ups Sid Caesar, Mel Brooks, and Shecky Green, which evolved into the comedy-of-nothing aesthetic of Jerry Seinfeld and Larry David. Woody Allen and Albert Brooks, who parlayed Jewish stereotypes of passive aggression and sexual neurosis into big, mordant yuks.

With long associations of social/cultural otherness and potent, often politically relevant humor, women have the potential to be the life of this party. From Jane Austen and Dorothy Parker, Fanny Brice and Lucille Ball, Elaine May and Carol Burnett, Lily Tomlin and Fran Lebowitz, Gilda Radner and Whoopi Goldberg, Sandra Bernhard and Margaret Cho, Kathy Griffin and Wanda Sykes, Kate Clinton and Lea DeLaria, Amy Poehler and Maya Rudolph, the Guerrilla Girls and Amy Sedaris, there's plenty, and I'm even leaving out a whole slew of them just for lack of space. Feminist humorists are also a well-anthologized bunch, appearing in such collections as 1980's *Pulling Our Own Strings: Feminist Humor and Satire*, edited by Mary Kay

Blakely and Gloria Kaufman (which excerpts sources from *The Autobiography of Mother Jones* to *Rubyfruit Jungle*), and Roz Warren's collections *Women's Glib, Women's Glibber* and *Revolutionary Laughter*. Simply put, women's humor does not lack a canon. It's the recognition of the canon as such that's the problem—and the problem behind that is the lack of recognition of women as funny in the first place.

Just as radio DJs refused for years to play female artists back-to-back for fear that their target audience of males would switch the dial, so do comedy-club owners, TV bookers, and magazine editors structure their offerings to woo a primarily male audience. Out of fifty-four humor writers featured in 2000's *Mirth of a Nation: The Best Contemporary Humor*, a whopping nine were women. And as authors Jennifer Baumgardner and Amy Richards point out in their book *Manifesta*, *The New Yorker*'s celebrated humor column "Shouts & Murmurs" went almost a year without featuring the writing of a woman. So the challenge for women is to gain acknowledgment and respect, and avoid simply existing in the chick-humor ghetto of menstrual-cramp jokes, boyfriend complaints, and refrains of "Am I right, ladies?"

Even when it doesn't have to be, humor is understood to be an inherently gendered communication—and one that privileges a male worldview. If a woman doesn't laugh at a man's joke, it surely isn't because the joke itself isn't pants-peeingly funny; it's that the woman isn't equipped with enough of a sense of humor to appreciate it. And while women have always used humor as a means of bonding with each other—whether out of a conscious shared oppression or just because it's fun—this humor has generally been regarded as too narrow to register within a male definition of comedy. Dick jokes are universal; childbearing jokes are not.

The zen koan of humor and gender—If a woman makes a joke and a man fails to laugh, is the joke still funny?—has persisted in the world of professional comedy, and the gender assumptions in humor are still taken as a given even as female comedians abound. "All the women comics I know work and are as successful, if not more successful, than our male counterparts," said Margaret Cho in a 2000 issue of *Bust*. "Yet we'll never get the respect from the boys, ever. None of us do—not me, not Ellen, not Roseanne or anybody. Never, no matter how famous you are, it just doesn't register with them. They don't give it up to you; they don't validate you as being anything . . . They don't want women to be their peers." (This point was amply illustrated by legendary schnook Jerry Lewis at 2000's Aspen U.S. Comedy Arts Festival: When asked by Martin Short what female comedians he admired, Lewis answered, "I don't like any female comedians. A woman doing comedy . . . sets me back a bit. I, as a viewer, have trouble with it. I think of her as a producing machine that brings babies in the world.")

The most acceptable role for women in performed comedy has historically been as part of a predominantly male sketch or improv-comedy troupe—like Elaine May, who with Mike Nichols and Alan Arkin, among others, founded Chicago's now-legendary Second City; Goldie Hawn and Lily Tomlin, featured performers on the '60s free-form TV show *Laugh-In*; and Gilda Radner, Julia Sweeney, Ellen Cleghorne, and the many subsequent female cast members of sketch-comedy standard-bearer *Saturday Night Live*. More recently, indie-comedy ensemble shows—including Fox's long-defunct *Ben Stiller Show* and former MTV offerings *The State* and *The Upright Citizens Brigade*—have exemplified the "Smurfette" model, in which there's one woman in a group of men, often as the reactor to, rather than the instigator of, the humor.

The problem with this setup is that it allows for the perpetuation of the idea that every funny woman is simply an anomaly, an exception to the "women aren't funny" rule. Indeed, even with women as a crucial part of the comedy-troupe structure, their contributions have often been perceived as less central than that of their male counterparts (John Belushi, for one, was notoriously averse to performing with female castmates on *Saturday Night Live*), or even assumed to be tokenism, a nod to political correctness in casting. Even after infiltrating comedy's long-running sausage party, women are still left telling their jokes mostly to each other.

BACK TO PAM. YOU CAN IMAGINE THE JOKES THAT WERE TOLD at her expense at this roast: Pam has big tits. She's a dumb blonde. She's had Tommy Lee's huge penis inside her, so she must have a big giant vagina. Oh, the hilarity! And Pam just sat there and smiled, but not in an "Oh, you got me, Jimmy Kimmel! That twenty-seventh big-boob joke was a real zinger!" kind of way. More in kind of a pained, just-keep-smiling way. And she did not zing back.

I don't know what I wanted from Pamela Anderson. But her very presence up on that dais was a succinct illustration of what Gloria Kaufman, in her introduction to *Pulling Our Own Strings*, posited as the difference between female humor and feminist humor. The former "may ridicule a person or a system from an accepting point of view ('that's life')," while the latter demands a "nonacceptance of oppression." (Handy example: *Bridget Jones's Diary*, in detailing the comedic trials of a woman to control her appetites, both physical and emotional, in service of achieving a stereotypical ideal womanhood = female humor. Gloria Steinem's 1978 essay "If Men Could Menstruate: A Political Fantasy," in which she reasoned that menstruation as a male activity would be a point of pride and a means of power = feminist humor.)

Female humor, in its que-sera-sera acquiescence, may offer plenty of male ridicule, but it also depends on a vision of gender that's limiting to all of us. Female humor tropes are, like Pam Anderson jokes, circumscribed by prepackaged ideas of what supposedly makes a woman both attractive and open to ridicule: big breasts, small skirts, limited intelligence.

Feminist humor, on the other hand, has as its goal a revisioning of gender roles that acknowledges stereotypes but ultimately rejects them. These reactive vs. proactive definitions are often confused, as we know from the people out there who consider mass e-mails like "50 Reasons Why Cats Are Better Than Men" to be examples of shrewd feminist analysis. But ultimately, feminist humor posits that women see themselves not as the butt of the joke but as its instigator—and doesn't see the broad category of men as the butt of the joke, either. Defined as an outsider humor the same way African-American or Jewish-American humor has been, feminist humor demands both an identification of outsiderness and a vision of transcending it.

To tell a joke is to flex power—the power to make someone laugh, the power to make someone feel exposed, the power to hurt. This goes some way toward explaining why it's so easy to deny women the ability to be funny—by dint of gender socialization, we're not supposed to be. With the acquisition of their first doll baby or stuffed animal, young girls are encouraged to play nice, be nurturing, and not hurt anyone's feelings. A pattern emerges: Discouraged from training their wit on others, girls grow up to aim it at themselves, building up a repertoire of stories of their social failures, physical shortcomings, and general inadequacies and inviting others to relate, to laugh with, but also, maybe, to laugh *at*. That's why Pamela Anderson was just sitting there in her see-through shirt at the Comedy Central roast, smiling away. She was embodying female humor: laughing at herself, because, given that everyone was already laughing at her, it was the right response. Like Janeane Garofalo, who in her stand-up days undermined her burgeoning political fervor with descriptions of her less-than-Hollywood figure ("I have the physique of a melting candle"), or Phyllis Diller, who once commented that her Living Bra "died of starvation," Anderson was employing the classic anticipatory retaliation of the female in comedy. Of course, self-deprecation itself has never been strictly girls' territory—right, Woody?—but women make it the crux of their act for different, more indelibly socialized reasons than men.

It's not that self-deprecation can't be funny, but it rarely translates well into political subversion. We can laugh at female comedians' riffs about their weight—say, those of Anderson roaster Lisa Lampanelli—but also feel a twinge of disappointment that the riffs seem so inevitable, reactive instead of proactive. The thing about outsider humor is that while it has that much-needed capacity to unite any given group of oppressed people, another thing it provides is a way for an individual or group to exert power or superiority over another—coincidentally, something that women are socialized not to want or need.

"We are expected, somehow, not to offend anyone on our way to liberation," wrote Mary Kay Blakely in her introduction to *Pulling Our Own Strings*. "There's an absurd expectation that the women's movement must be the first revolution in history to accomplish its goals without hurting anyone's feelings." Humor offered by men, in all its varieties and permutations, shares one commonality—an entitlement to piss off, gross out, and instigate. And at least one, maybe all three, of these things is necessary if feminism is to truly achieve any of its goals for equity, laughter being but one.

Feminism has slowly, incrementally widened the cultural lens through which society views women—their ideals, their accomplishments, and even (though admittedly, not often enough) their appearance. That lens needs a lot more broadening, especially when it comes to humor. Indeed, the road to feminist consciousness is for many women paved with multiple instances of other people whining, "Can't you take a joke?" when we refuse to laugh at the many references to women—smart women, dumb women, sexually stereotyped women, fat women, nagging women, strong women, and odd women—that have always peppered our pop culture as comic relief. If only we crazy, wild-eyed buzzkillers would just let people have their jollies without getting all whiny about it, all would be well, right?

I don't think so. And you don't really think so. And I'd be willing to bet that even Pamela Anderson doesn't, deep down, think so. In a world that continues to posit women's bodies and minds as punch lines, and that judges women's humor by standards that weren't drafted with us in mind (but hey, you're pretty funny for a girl . . .), it's clear that feminist humor's assimilation from outsider aberration into just plain American humor is still a long time coming. But when it does, we'll be the ones asking, just so blithely, "Can't you take a joke?"

Girl, Unreconstructed

Why Girl Power Is Bad for Feminism

Rachel Fudge / BITCHfest 2006

ON THE LONG LIST OF THINGS THAT ARE BAD FOR FEMINISM—
Phyllis Schlafly, *Girls Gone Wild*, pharmacists who refuse to fill birth-control
prescriptions, to name but a few—girl power would hardly seem to be the
most pernicious. And yet as one of the most visible contemporary manifestations of the vague idea of feminism, it earns a special place of loathing in
this feminist's heart. Why? Well, let me count the ways: Girl power reduces
the theoretical complexity of feminism to a cheery slogan ("GIRLS KICK
ASS!"); it represents the ultimate commodification of empowerment; it reinforces the simplistic conception of feminism as being, at heart, "all about
choices." But most of all, it grabbed the rhetoric from one of the most potentially powerful, yet woefully misunderstood, feminist uprisings of my
generation, discarded every ounce of political heft, and reduced it to cheap
iron-on letters on a baby T.

I am talking, of course, about the short-lived explosion of feminist activism and creative culture known as riot grrrl—that early-'90s movement
born out of young women's frustrations with the male-dominated punk-
rock scenes of Washington, D.C.; Olympia, Washington; London, England;
and later, cities all across the United States and Europe. Much like the
founders of the women's liberation movement two decades earlier, who
grew tired of fighting shoulder to shoulder with their male comrades for
peace and justice only to be relegated to coffee-making and free-love-

155

satisfyin' duties, these girls realized that the only way to be taken seriously in their scenes was to make a ruckus of their own.

It's an old story, the co-optation of a subculture, political movement, or underground scene, but in our accelerated, mediated world, it's almost breathtaking how quickly it can happen. One day, you're stenciling "Riot, Don't Diet" on an old T-shirt so you can wear it to a show that night; the next, you can choose from among a dozen premade shirts emblazoned with slogans like "Boys Are Stupid, Throw Rocks at Them." That's the legacy of girl power: To paraphrase Kathleen Hanna, it took the bomp from riot grrrl's bomp-a-lomp-a-lomp; it stole the ram from the rama-lama-ding-dong.

Girl power is difficult to define—let alone attack—because it's not a movement; no one identifies herself as an adherent of girl power or issues manifestos calling for Girl Power Now! (Well, except for the U.S. Department of Health and Human Services, whose Girl Power campaign, launched oh-so-hopefully and just as vaguely in 1997 "to help encourage and moti-vate 9- to 13-year-old girls to make the most of their lives," seems dead in the water, though Girlpower.gov is still online.) The term first gained cur-rency in the mid-'90s, in the wake of well-meaning books like *Reviving Ophelia* and *Schoolgirls*, which declared that if we didn't do something soon to reverse the plummeting decline in girls' confidence, we'd have a national female emergency on our hands. Riot grrrls had already been loudly pro-claiming the revolutionary power of girlhood, so when the prefabricated, plasticized Spice Girls hit the scene and sold millions of records while prat-tling about girl power—which was never really defined, but seemed to sum up as "Be yourself (and wear a Wonderbra if you wanna)!"—many journalists, educators, advertisers, and other concerned girl-watchers seized upon this ephemeral declaration of strength. Unlike the women's libera-tion movement—whose pluralized name immediately conveyed the idea of collective action—and the galvanizing group force of riot grrrls, girl power is sadly, feebly singular: A girl might be able to kick some undefined ass under its auspices, but she won't be organizing any self-defense classes or antiviolence workshops for her peers.

And while the phenomenon of girl power has itself faded from the limelight—along with, thankfully, the Spice Girls—its ethos continues to dominate popular discourse about girls, gender, and equality. As a market-ing tool, it has so thoroughly saturated the worlds of advertising and popular culture that it's become a cliché. It underlies supposedly go-girl teen movies like *Ice Princess*, *Mean Girls*, and *What a Girl Wants*. It allows totally manufactured pop stars like Ashlee Simpson and Avril Lavigne to claim to be edgy, powerful role models. Worst of all, it lulls us into thinking that all of feminism's battles are won, that females in America don't have anything to fight for anymore.

It seems hopelessly idealistic to say this now, but those extra *r*'s in riot grrrl weren't just wacky wordplay: They quite literally put the *grrr* into being a girl. That bold, no-holds-barred expression of anger, aggression, and assertiveness was the linchpin of riot grrrl. The cries for revolution woven throughout the lyrics, slogans, and zines were in part a youthful flirtation with extreme rhetoric, but riot grrrls were also dead serious about changing the world, starting with the circumstances of their own lives. When the U.K. band Huggy Bear sang "Boredom, rage, fierce intention, this is the sound of revolution . . . Her jazz signals our time NOW" over grinding, spiraling ill-tuned guitars and manic, out-of-sync drums, it *did* sound like a revolution was right around the corner.

Riot grrrl expressed its mission lyrically and stylistically but also politically: Like the consciouness-raising groups of '70s feminism, ad hoc riot grrrl groups popped up around the country as young women got together to deconstruct gender, sexism, and patriarchy. They shared their experiences of rape, incest, and the lesser but relentlessly persistent abuses of growing up female in a sexist culture—and then they rose up, picked up pens or guitars or paintbrushes, and made noise about it. Like their foremothers, they saw that the personal was political, but they also made the political deeply personal. They created their own culture of music, fashion, art, and zines as a kind of haven for self-expression, but they also looked outward, challenging their local scenes to make room for female expression. And although riot grrrl was, and still is, often characterized as focusing mostly on personal politics, there was in fact a strong activist component: Individual riot grrrls joined local and national protests such as the 1992 march on Washington for reproductive rights, while bands such as L7 organized massive pro-choice benefit concerts. Taking a cue from the defiantly in-your-face AIDS action group ACT UP, women and grrrls outraged by the treatment of Anita Hill at Clarence Thomas's confirmation hearings took to the streets as the witty, media-savvy Women's Action Coalition. Grrrls formed support networks for rape and incest survivors in their communities, and, in the wake of the brutal rape and murder of Seattle musician Mia Zapata in 1993, local women organized Home Alive, a nonprofit self-defense education and awareness organization that's still going strong today. In short, they recognized that sexism was pervasive and systemic—and that collective action was needed to battle it.

And then the Spice Girls came prancing in. Oh, it's not that easy, of course. A lot happened in between. First of all, there was a self-imposed media blackout: The mainstream press was getting a taste for those exotic grrrls, but many of the bands, zine makers, and activists profiled felt misunderstood and mischaracterized; they decided that the media would never get it and refused to be interviewed or give quotes. (The last straw was a landmark 1992 *Newsweek* article asserting that "Riot Girl is feminism with a loud happy face dotting the 'i.'") Then there was the election of a liberal Democrat with an avowedly feminist wife after twelve years of Reagan/Bush horror, making certain political gains seem safe from erosion; the skyrocketing popularity of "angry girl singers" Alanis Morissette and Fiona Apple, who aired their almost-feminist grievances to stadium crowds; and the ever-complicated Courtney Love, whose transformation from messy, outrageous riot grrrl icon to temporarily less messy, outrageous Versace model nicely captures the confused messages conveyed by girl power. There was also growing momentum to the self-dubbed third-wave feminist movement—which could be described as the better-funded, better-organized, liberal agenda–driven counterpart to riot grrrls' diffused radicalism. (A full discussion of the third wave is beyond the scope of this essay.)

Riot grrrl never really had the chance to coalesce into a coherent movement, to work out its internal conflicts and develop a proper identity, before it was thrust into the media spotlight. And because riot grrrl focused on do-it-yourself creative culture, local action, and freewheeling manifestos that were as much about provocation as developing an ideology, it was much easier for observers to focus on its visual elements, especially its sartorial expression. The classic outfit of baby-doll dress paired with dirty combat boots, accompanied by a smear of red lipstick and Hello Kitty barrettes, was conceived as a visual expression of this girlhood-gone-angry. Media outlets from *Sassy* to *Spin* to *Newsweek* seized on the fashion, but had a hard time seeing beyond the cute to the analysis that underlay it. But rather than preserve and protect the fledgling movement, riot grrrls' impulsive decision to stop talking to the media hastened its demise by leaving the terms of the discussion to the very people who had already proved they'd never get it; not surprisingly, those folks continued to focus on the superficial elements and went on to label any and every manifestation of spunky femaleness "girl power."

An excellent artifact of this time is a 1997 issue of *Spin* devoted to cataloging the achievements of "girl culture," ranging from riot grrrl bands like Bikini Kill to the cheesy TV show *Sabrina, the Teenage Witch* to the Delia's catalog to gritty nail polish to "the midriff" to, aw shucks, *Bitch*. The slippery slope of this compendium perfectly illustrates the confusing superficiality of girl power—and it's no accident that of the over fifty representations of girl culture enumerated by *Spin*, the only overtly, traditionally political one is a pro choice march. In an essay anchoring the issue, Ann Powers perfectly summed up the appeal and the danger of girl power: "Unlike conventional feminism, which focused on women's socially imposed weaknesses, Girl Culture assumes that women are free agents in the world, that they start out strong, and that the odds are in their favor."

And that, my friends, is the lasting legacy of girl power. Of course, it's hard to argue that this is a bad way for girls to grow up, that they shouldn't be assumed to have confidence, agency, and strength. But if girl power provides their primary understanding of gender, when the going gets rough and those girls come face-to-face with sexism, they don't have the tools with which to formulate a critique—nor do they have an awareness of the power inherent in collective activism. In other words, they don't have feminism.

Nowadays, "girl power" is used by the media to mean "females: doin' somethin' unexpected"—that is, girls deviating from the norm of girliness, which, despite girl power's pretense that girls can do anything, often means doing perfectly ordinary things like starting bands, playing sports, or starring in CBS dramas. It's not that these achievements shouldn't be celebrated; it's the underlying implication that when boys or men do these things, it's just life—but for girls, these are extraordinary efforts by extraordinary females. Newspaper articles about female racecar drivers, female boxers, one-armed female triathletes, even—I kid you not—a local female-run gardening conservancy are headlined "girl power." It's no accident that these are all nonthreatening activities—you rarely see girl power used to describe anything that is culturally oppositional or seeks social change (you know, anything feminist), unless the phrase is being used to declaw a potentially sharp critique. A prime example is "Girl Power Rules at New Habitat Project," an August 2005 article in the New Orleans *Times-Picayune* about an all-female Habitat for Humanity team that, while declaring "it's a girl thing," misses a prime opportunity to talk about the feminization of poverty or why it's important that poor women be included in redevelopment efforts in their own communities.

Girl power erases the hard work done by generations of women (and men) to eliminate obstacles, raise consciousness, and level that annoying metaphorical playing field. It shifts the focus from collective action to individual achievement: promoting math-and-science-enrichment programs for middle-school girls, for example, while overlooking the generally abysmal state of public schools. In attempting to empower girls, it reinforces a gender binary by not examining the many ways sexism and gender stereotypes hurt boys too.

It's frequently noted in the media—most recently, by Kristin Rowe-Finkbeiner in her book *The F-Word: Feminism in Jeopardy*—that girls and young women are, apparently, reluctant to embrace the word "feminism." They don't want to think about the reasons behind a feminist movement; they don't want to be allied with anything that implies they are weak, or victimized, or unequal. Girl power sounds like it elevates the ladies, but in actuality it does the exact opposite of what riot grrrl tried to do: It turns the struggle inward, depoliticizes and decontextualizes the cultural messages about gender and behavior. Like the misguided idea that feminism is really only about giving women choices, it turns a collective struggle into a personal decision.

Girl power tricks us all into believing that girls are naturally powerful and therefore ignores the many ways their power is contingent on adhering to cultural expectations of female behavior. If, as Ann Powers wrote so hopefully nearly a decade ago, girls are seen as "free agents," they have only themselves to blame for their failures. The corporate glass ceiling? Well, women just don't want success as much as men do. Domestic violence? If they choose to stick around, battered wives really can't complain—besides, they can murder their husbands and get away with it! Women's athletics are institutionally underfunded? Oh, if there was really a demand for girls to play sports, they'd form their own teams. Women still earn just seventy-seven cents to a man's dollar? That's because they don't want the jobs that pay more.

For generations, feminism has given shape and structure to individual women's obstacles—it turns one woman's lament into a collective yell. Riot grrrl not only gave a new generation of young women a voice and encouraged them to wield it in service of feminism, it also galvanized them into group action. Girl power slaps them on the back and says, "You go, girl," even if it's not at all clear where or why they should be going, and it certainly doesn't say that they might face significant obstacles along the way. Watered-down feminism may be enough to sell baby Ts and thigh-high fishnets; it may even be enough to celebrate the baby-step accomplishments of a few lucky women. But it won't give girls what they need to demand real power.

4
· · · · · · · · · ·

Desire
LOVE, SEX, AND MARKETING

FOR A MAGAZINE THAT ADDRESSES THE INTERSECTION OF feminism and pop culture, could there be a more obvious topic than desire? After all, feminism has been engaged with what women want—sexually and otherwise—since the beginning of the modern movement, and pop culture, of course, is built on carnality and powered by desire's corollary, consumption. Our struggle is to free our desires from the bonds of old-fashioned sexism and double standards as well as unreasonable post–sexual revolution expectations—plus the stirring up of our insecurities to make us buy things that will render us more attractive.

Questions of desire are also a way into feminism for many of us. My own discovery of feminism was a gradual one, powered by several things. The most obvious was an emerging awareness of the gender dynamics in the classrooms in which I was growing up, where boys of privilege whined about being made to read Adrienne Rich ("Can't we read something *everyone* can relate to—like Dostoyevsky?") and having to share the glory of calculus with girls ("Okay, so some of you may be getting A's—but do you really *understand*?"). Another, luckily more positive, was the subtle training I got from my parents: that my sister and I were entitled to our smarts and could do whatever we wanted with them, and that since my mother cooked all of our meals, it was only fair that my father be in charge of kitchen cleanup. And then there was the vague, early-adolescent unease I had about my budding sexuality. Instinctively I knew that what I was feeling was perfectly natural—but I still had to wonder: Am I a deviant because I want to have sex, and I don't particularly care if I'm in love? Because my crushes are powered by lust rather than affection? I knew—from Judy Blume's *Then Again, Maybe I Won't*, from the matter-of-fact way we'd learned about wet dreams in sex ed, from *Porky's*—that boys were supposed to feel that way, popping boners at the slightest provocation. But girls, I'd been led to understand, were different. Desire was supposed to be about something deeper. It was years before I even began to pick apart the tangle of cultural pressures, physiology, and my own unique threads of confidence and insecurity in order to craft some kind of analysis of what was going on. Furthermore, I'm still working on it: Is it ever possible to separate real feelings from cultural pressures or the effects of struggling against them?

These questions haunt people of all genders, and pop culture's reliance on sex to sell, along with today's increasing encroachment of advertising into every last square inch of public space, combine to make them more confusing than ever. The fact that advertisers use women's bodies to hawk everything from beer to bathroom tile is so well known that it hardly bears mentioning—but it *is* worth noting that the habit shows no sign of breaking. (In a stark demonstration of how entrenched the boobs = sales formula is, a July 2005 ad for the industry-promotion event Advertising Week featured a cleavage shot above the words "Advertising: We All Do It." Though a majority of respondents to an online *Advertising Age* poll found the ad to be sexist and insulting, many industry pros shrugged off the criticism. One of the event's sponsors said, "I don't think it's that big a deal," and his colleague opined, "Let's face it, women have always been portrayed as sexual entities in advertising, primarily for the sake of titillating men, and they always will be . . . Just as boob jokes in advertising are tiresome to many, so are mistakenly outdated, lame attempts to engage today's strains of feminists and conscious consumers.")

Even more important is the incomplete transformation of the unwritten cultural rules governing female desire. Feminism has struggled to transform those rules, but it has also been riven by internal debate, judgments, and assumptions about good desires vs. bad ones, healthy desires vs. "male-identified" ones—and about sexuality's importance in the first place. Our culture at large is also of many minds on the topic. As a result, girls' pleasure, though no longer forbidden or denied, is still primarily about display rather than subjectivity. Though the wildly popular *American Pie* franchise was certainly no one-note *Porky's*—its female cast included the requisite on-display sexy exchange student, but also a band geek who knew how to get herself off and a wholesome girl next door who benefited from her boyfriend's newfound oral expertise—1999's *Coming Soon*, a chronicle of three teen girls in pursuit of their own orgasms, was initially tagged with an NC-17 rating even though no flesh at all was bared in the film. It eventually got an R but, unlike its characters, achieved only a limited release. Tween fashion, Britney-style pop tartage, *Sex and the City*, slutty-blonde jokes, and the documentary *Inside Deep Throat* round out the landscape.

Forthright assertions of our own desires are tricky, especially when they're so easily misinterpreted by mainstream culture: For instance, so-called do-me feminism—an instant cliché introduced to the world by *Esquire* in February 1994—recast the thoughtful, nuanced, and far from uncritical work of women like Susie Bright and Lisa Palac as mere invitations to frolic. In its trademark "I'm sophisticated . . . but horny" wishful-thinking, beyond-oversimplified way, the magazine played off feminism's long-standing antisex reputation and said, essentially, Here are some feminists you don't have to be scared of, because they'd like you to fuck them. Many intelligent commentators instantly recognized it as a crock, but those who didn't know any better picked right up on the "trend"—and paved the way for retrofitted romance plots like Amy Sohn's *Run Catch Kiss* to be branded as empowering.

Fact is, it's a hard line to walk: All the talk of porno reclamation by Palac, Bright, and others; books like *Jane Sexes It Up: True Confessions of Feminist Desire*; women-owned sex-toy stores; and, yes, articles in *Bitch* can come off like prescriptive new guidelines for modern sexuality rather than attempts to build a culture in which we can all be in charge of our own desire. Here's a little something that graced our pages in the fall of 1996: "Repeat after us, boys: The male-female detachment-commitment dichotomy is culturally overdetermined. This fallacy is the spawn of an outdated, moralistic double standard from its rutting under a rock with self-help authors and glossy magazine editors. Now say it again. Again. Good. Now fuck us and get the hell out of our apartments." In my own writing life, I've felt a responsibility to be open about my experiences in the hopes that my sharing might ease other folks' acceptance of their culturally unapproved behavior, and maybe help shift the stereotypes of gender and sex just a little bit. But it doesn't always work that way.

It's our very own feminist version of the virgin/whore complex. Anything we say risks reaffirming one of the many stereotypes out there: Feminism leads to [fill in the blank with promiscuity, frigidity, lesbianism, abortion]. Women's sexuality [doesn't exist, is out of control, depends on emotion, is about being looked at, is the polar opposite of some stereotypical visually driven male sexuality]. And with pop culture's ad-driven, shopping-happy nature seeking to channel every person's every last desire into the most profitable avenues possible, well, that just makes it all the more difficult to sort through.

Throughout its history, *Bitch* has consistently strived to examine how pop culture constructs our desires and their ramifications—and the "our" here refers to people of all genders. The results, far broader than sexuality or romance, document the struggle for self-definition in arenas that are at once the most personal and the most influenced by   and influential over— our cultural landscape.   —L.J.

In Re-Mission

Why Does *Redbook* Want to Keep Us on Our Backs?

Amy Harter / SPRING 1997

REDBOOK IS NOT THE HIPPEST MAGAZINE AROUND. IT CATERS to a married-with-children lifestyle, tackling such cutting-edge topics as entrepreneurial housewives and marital relationships. The representation of the '90s woman as a '50s retrofit is what *Redbook* thrives on. But last February, *Redbook* took a step beyond that in a seeming attempt to bring our liberal-leaning American women back to the '50s wholesome in a big way. Lynn Peters's "The Best Position for Making Love (hint: you don't have to be on top)" encourages women to stick with the missionary position.

Even if we ignore—as we must, given *Redbook*'s relentlessly heterosexual, mostly married demographic—the persistent equation of "sexual partner" with "husband," Peters's paean to the missionary position is disturbing. With a bizarre blend of modern ideas and outdated stereotypes (women like sex and seek pleasure, but they're generally passive, romantically motivated, and overwhelmingly concerned with their looks during the act), she's oddly insistent that sex in the missionary position is best for all women, all the time. And why is that? Because the missionary position is "feminine" and "alluring."

This is supposed to be a good thing?

Familiarity Breeds . . . Ecstasy?

Peters calls the missionary position "a Quarter Pounder with cheese," saying, "you know how it's going to look, how it's going to taste and how long it will take to eat." Her picture of an ideal sexual experience is one of familiarity and passivity to the point of boredom: "Lying on your back with nothing on your mind other than, say, how that stain got on the ceiling, you're in the ideal position to unwind and enjoy yourself."

Perhaps I'm biased against articles that compare sex to a greasy fast-food offering in the first paragraph, but the antiquated implication that women are bored by sex sticks in my craw. Granted, most of us have zoned out on those fuzzy dice hanging from the rearview mirror at least once, but we can attribute our disinterest to bad sex. Ideally, shouldn't your own and your partner's pleasure be on your mind instead of the ceiling stain?

All You Have Going for You Is Your Looks. Don't Blow It.

Peters also praises the missionary position because a woman supposedly appears more attractive when she's "reclining with . . . face turned up, lips parted expectantly [and her] hair arranged over a bank of snowy white pillows [than] leaning over [her] husband with . . . stretch marks glistening and everything drooping and jiggling."

True, it's hard to concentrate on pleasure at all if you're worried about jiggling body parts. But why offer the solution of disguise instead of celebration? Instead of encouraging women to increase their fun by not worrying about what their bods look like to their hubbies, Peters validates and even promotes insecurity by scrutinizing and persecuting the postchildbirth female body. By encouraging women to feel ashamed of their sweat, shape, and size—all natural, and as far as sweat and jiggle go, often signs of a good time in bed—Peters plays into the interminable cycle of body hatred that all too often reflects women's experience.

Sex = Romance

Not only does Peters consistently refer to sex as "making love" (which, okay, it sometimes is—but let's face it, that's not always what it is), she writes longingly of pre–sexual revolution television portrayals of "the man on the top, the woman looking up at him adoringly." This adoration or awe during sex is caused by what, his oh-so-breadwinning worldly masculinity above her? Hmm. Experiencing awe during sex should probably derive from a different source, don't you think? She elaborates on this romantic theme by declaring that missionary sex is the most "loving and affectionate, and close to your partner" kind of sex, and it's "the most comforting to finish in— you're cuddling already, for heaven's sake." (Peters likes to plan ahead. But how is man-lying-on-top-of-woman any more cuddle-ready than woman-lying-on-top-of-man? Just a question of physics, really.)

Missionary Sex Really Is Cool!

Peters argues that most women abandoned missionary-style sex in the '70s because it was hip to explore other positions. She depicts a trend for women to be "cool and empowered" by being on top and notes that "overnight, being on the bottom was OUT." She argues that as women gained power and esteem in the '70s, climbing on top became "compulsory," and suggests that women who choose to travel down the path of sexual exploration do so not of their own volition but because it's fashionable or "in." With one comment, she's discounting women's desires and disparaging the gains of '70s feminism—so all we got was the experience of sex on top, which we're ready to give up now anyway? I don't think so. And she's justifying the very logic she's trying to criticize—'cause after all, what she's really trying to do is convince us that the missionary position is cool again.

Mission Accomplished?

Why does *Redbook* care so much about salvaging the missionary position and selling it to its readers? What does it have invested in the piece? A few thoughts: With Peters's article, *Redbook* encourages its readers (straight, married women, mostly) not to think that they may be missing out on some crazy adventurous single sex life (after all, if the missionary position is as good as it gets, why even bother to wonder); it plays on women's insecurities, which is helpful in spurring the readership to buy the products plugged in its pages, which of course keeps the advertisers happy and the magazine in business.

The fact is, women can and do have sex just for sex's sake. Good sex is about knowing what you want and being assertive enough to get it. Sex can be kinky, erotic, loving, sensual, hysterical, all of the above, or just plain fun—whether it's a hit-and-quit situation or a long-term relationship. Sex isn't about being on top or being on the bottom. It's about being anywhere you want to be.

Hot and Bothered

Unmasking Male Lust

Lisa Jervis / FALL 1997

SEX, SEX, SEX—THAT'S ALL MEN EVER THINK ABOUT. RIGHT? If you're a girl, you've always gotta be ready to fend off an unwanted advance, and if you're a boy, you've always gotta be plotting a move. I mean, isn't that what we've all been told since the moment we emerged from the womb and were identified as having one set of genitalia or another? We hear it from other people, we see it in the movies and on TV, we read it in glossy magazines and pop psychology books. Men always want sex, and women rarely do. Women become sexually attracted to the men they love; men fall in love with the women they find sexually attractive. Women want commitment; men run screaming from it. Women are naturally monogamous; men not only crave variety but are evolutionarily programmed to seek it out.

Recent feminist thought has given much attention to destroying the stereotype of women as sexually passive and emotionally needy. Get down: I'll be first in line to take a whack at the image of the marriage-minded, no-sex-'til-I-get-what-someone-told-me-I'm-supposed-to-want, *Rules*-readin', John Gray–worshippin' gal. The thing is, though, that this dichotomous gender construction also makes men out to be nothing more than lying, cheating, uncaring, sex-obsessed louts—and that side of the coin hasn't gotten a whole lot of attention. Traditional heterosexual masculinity—and let me make it very clear that by this I do not mean actual men; I mean the perception of what it means to be a straight man in our current cultural/

popular imagination—has not yet been examined with an eye toward dismantling stale notions of unceasingly high libido and disregard for emotion.

Superhet men's lifestyle magazines, with their instruction-manual tone and we-have-the-secrets-of-the-good-life manner, quite literally teach masculinity: They tell men how to act, what to look like, and what to buy in order to be men. And their focus on sex is uncomplicated and unstinting. Any guy who is any less—or more to the point, any *more*—than a rote sex machine will feel like less of a man after reading one of these things. According to *Esquire*, men are "unfeeling brutes" because of their serotonin levels; *GQ* proclaims, "Sex. That's what [men] want and we'll do anything we have to do to get it," and advises a guy with a lower libido than his girlfriend to see a shrink.

And then there are the implications of cluelessness and infantility. That's what we get in *Men's Health*'s "Tonight's the Night: A moment-by-moment guide to getting it right the first time." Do men really need to be told, "8:05: Offer snacks. Finger food is good," or "9:24: Close ranks. Move your chair closer to hers"? The fact that some magazine editor thinks—even in an oh-look-how-self-deprecating-we-are-doesn't-that-make-us-charmingly-funny way—that men can't figure out for themselves to "be nice" and "not ask her to wash up while you catch the fourth quarter" (those are at 7:33 and 9:22, by the way) is pretty insulting.

What else have popular narratives given us lately? The neo–morality tale *Fatal Attraction* featured a man who couldn't keep it in his pants no matter how much he loved his wife and kid. And just look where indulging his "natural" compulsion got him   the terrorized owner of a boiled bunny. (Not coincidentally, the strong, sexual woman in this film is not cool and independent, as she first seems, but rather incredibly needy and, it turns out, psychotic.) The television show *Men Behaving Badly* (well, the name says it all) features commitment-terrified men with sex drives that override even such basic human qualities as tact and coherent speech. Jokes circulate on e-mail painting men as perpetual children with only one thing on their minds ("Age and favorite sport—17: sex; 25: sex; 35: sex; 48: sex; 66: napping. Age and ideal age to get married—17: 25; 25: 35; 35: 48; 48: 66; 66: 17"). Oh, excuse me, I guess that would be two things: mindless pursuit of sex *and* blind refusal of commitment. The proliferation of brutal and gratuitous rape scenes on film paints male sexuality as rapacious and violent. That we're often meant to see the rapists in, say, *Showgirls* and *Leaving Las Vegas* as disgusting, amoral, and corrupt doesn't really matter. There's a sense of plodding inevitability about these scenes: This is the way men are, they suggest, and this is just what happens.

And then there's mainstream pornography—soft-core airbrushed fluff such as *Penthouse* and *Playboy*. The folks makin' this stuff do men and their range of desires a disservice; their implication is that anything outside the "big hair, fake tits, tiny waist, no pores, limited body hair" aesthetic is deviant, weird, not normal—and not something that a red-blooded American man would be interested in. The common boys-will-be-boys explanation for porn—that men get turned on visually (in contrast to a "feminine" mode of arousal, which is mental and emotional)—is nothing more than an insult, making men out to be Pavlovian dogs who salivate uncontrollably and strain at their trousers upon contact with nudie pictures.

Antiporn arguments, however well-meaning, are no better. Folks like Catharine MacKinnon also believe that men are inherently drawn to porn. And to them, porn is by definition violent, suggesting that it's somehow in men's nature to be aroused by hurting others. Furthermore, antipornography activists think that porn leads men to commit violence—as if men have no self-control or capacity to separate fantasy from reality, as if an erection is a driving force that can't be stopped once it's started. (I'm not gonna bother pointing out that most porn is about mutual pleasure and not violence, and suggesting that sexual representation is inherently harmful to women is infantilizing and wrongheaded . . . Oh, I guess I just did.) Actually, the antiporn conception of the rabidly sexual man is suspiciously close to the hormonal overdrive lionized in magazines like *Esquire* and *GQ*. The only difference is one of perspective: Antiporn folk believe that male sexuality is always threatening, while men's-magazine editors think it's always fabulous.

What all these examples have in common is the severing of male sexuality from any sort of reflection at all: To be a man who is emotional about sex or even one with thoughts more complex than "Yeah! More!" on the subject is not to be a man at all; that's female territory.

My friends and I have seen the havoc this wreaks in our sex lives. Let's see, there was the guy who thought I was needy and unstable because I wanted to have sex with him as often as possible and was kinda disappointed when he turned me down (which would be a perfectly acceptable male reaction to being rebuffed by a woman). Because of this guy's commitment to rigidly gendered sexual behavior, he didn't believe me when I assured him that my desire wasn't tied to some big emotional thang. And, adding even more trouble, if he could've gotten past his disbelief, he would've had to come to terms with the fact that there are women with higher sex drives than his—thus threatening his manly-man status as an all-sex-all-the-time kind of guy.

Then there was the one who was disturbed by my simple request. One morning after—ahem—my needs had not been met, I tried to initiate sex. "I can't," he kept saying. "I have to study." When pressed, he admitted that it wasn't lack of time that was the issue. "I'm not used to women being so aggressive," he told me. When I forced him to be honest, instead of letting him make excuses, I ruined the nice little arrangement we had going: him as someone who wanted sex, me as someone who graciously accommodated him. He was angry that I expected to be forthright about my desire; I left and never went back.

After being told (one way or another) all their lives that they will always be the aggressor in a sexual situation, and they will always want more sex than their partners (assuming, as always, that their partners are female), it's no surprise that men freak out when they are confronted with a woman who wants sex as much as or more than they do. They've been taught that female sexuality is weak—so if a woman's desire matches their own, that must mean that they're (oh, no!) weak, too.

We need to open up definitions of masculinity to acknowledge the reality that we are all sexual, some of us are more sexual than others, and just how sexual we are has about as much to do with gender as it does with breakfast cereal. Instead of being taught that boys have only one thing on their minds, men need to learn that their sex drives, whether raging or trickling, are just fine the way they are—and that they're still men, regardless. This is certainly a feminist project: In order to achieve both gender *and* sexual equality, we need to acknowledge the ways men are stifled by the equation of masculinity with constant desire for and pursuit of sex. Men are no more hyperactive skirt chasers always looking for a quick roll in the hay than women are passive, sexually resistant creatures who use their genitals only as sticky traps in which to catch wedding rings. Until we turn as critical an eye toward stereotypical voracious masculine sexuality as we have toward sanitized, emotional female sexuality, no one of any gender will be truly free to act on genuine desires—in or out of the bedroom.

I Heard It Through the Loveline

And Misinformation Just Might
Make Me Lose My Mind

Heather Seggel / SPRING 1998

CHANNEL SURFERS AND THOSE CRAVING SOUND SEXUAL IN-formation alike, beware: There's a sexually repressive, ignorant, irresponsible advice show in town, and *Loveline* is its name. The televised offspring of a call-in show on the Los Angeles radio station KROQ, *Loveline* appears nightly on MTV with the warning that only "mature audiences" should be watching. Too bad they don't ask the same maturity of their hosts.

Said hosts, twentysomething dude Adam Carolla and "Dr. Drew" Pinsky (identified as "a board-certified physician and addiction medicine specialist"), display all the sexual maturity of a horny third-grader and a neighborhood priest, respectively. Adam's credentials are in stand-up comedy, so he provides the clunky one-liners and penis jokes, and also talks to the celebrity guests (one person or band per show, there to plug a new movie, CD, fragrance, hairdo . . . oh, and to help dish out advice). He's a man of the people, that Adam. The male people, anyway, whom he encourages to be as manly as possible every chance he gets. All this crotch scratching and talking to famous people leaves Drew with the real work of the show—listening to callers and answering their questions about love, sex, relationships, and sometimes drugs. To be fair, he handles the illegal substance stuff quite well. It's those darn sex questions, which are the whole point of the program and make up its bulk, that show him to be a judgmental dimwit who cares more about appearing smart than dispensing accurate information. Want to call in? It's like a trip back in time to the '50s. Just check your brain at the door and come with me.

The show fails us all—female, male, queer, het—but some failures are worse than others. In the spirit of chivalry, let's let the men go first. Straight male callers seem to know better than to risk their sexual self-esteem by calling in with anything serious or seriously embarrassing. If they do, Adam gets first crack at them, squeezing their experience for any jokes that might shake loose before Drew sums them up in a tidy parcel of medical jargon. Woe betide the young man with one testicle larger than the other who calls this show for reassurance that he's normal. Even if the hosts eventually allow that abnormality isn't cause for alarm, the information is couched in so much condescension and teasing that the message gets buried. Carolla's humor is sometimes aimed at male stereotypes (he tells a woman whose boyfriend loses his voice after cunnilingus, "This is just another excuse for not talking after sex"), but there's not enough useful information imparted—or thought involved—to justify all this jiving. Then there's the case of a young man who was concerned that his (male) partner was sleepwalking and might be endangering himself. Not a sexual or a relationship question per se—a medical question, and an interesting one. Our hosts were initially confused as to how the caller was related to his "friend." When they realized it was his boyfriend he was concerned about, an embarrassing silence followed. Drew then dealt out some recommendations, such as going to a sleep disorder specialist. Adam speculated on the types of harm that could befall a sleepwalker (the caller lived near train tracks) and appeared nervous when the idea of tying the sleepwalker to the bed was mentioned. More inappropriate jokes followed; the hosts' obvious discomfort with the caller's sexuality gave the whole episode a mean feel.

Moving on to the distaff side, a recent episode found a twenty-five-year-old woman in the audience, let's call her Betty, standing to ask her question. Betty was in a stable relationship with a man, but she was confused about fantasies she'd been having about making love to a woman. She and her boyfriend elected to explore this further by pursuing a foursome with two other women. Her question: What steps should she take to prevent the spread of STDs between partners and any toys they might use? A reasonable and responsible question for a grown woman to ask, or so I thought. The boys at the helm took a different view.

The most glaring problem was this: Neither Adam nor Drew ever answered Betty's question. (A simple formula for safe-sex success in this situation: Use condoms/dental dams and lube on all toys and partners. Anytime you change partners or orifices, exchange the old latex for a new wrap.) Drew's immediate comment, "Yes, sharing those devices can spread disease," had nothing to do with anything but putting Betty in her place— that special lower deck in hell reserved for device users. He continued by telling Betty, who made it clear that she and her beau were serious about each other and equally excited about the foursome idea, that she wasn't ready for a committed relationship. All the more reason to get that safe sex information out on the table, right? Well, maybe not, because they went to a commercial right after that and never mentioned it again.

In addition to consigning entire activities to the "not for regular, normal folks" pile, Dr. Drew misuses medical jargon to avoid discussing sexual realities—which is a genuine loss for the viewing audience. A caller who sounded excited, confused, and curious about what I instantly recognized as her first G-spot orgasm could have used some reassurance, some cheering on, perhaps an FTD bouquet, and her very own crystal wand so she could explore further. The *Loveline* prescription? Size her up with a diagnosis of "female orgasmic incontinence" and move on. Now, let's leave aside the dubious medical accuracy of that language—what's important is that it's demeaning and certainly not useful to the caller. And funny how Drew and Adam are willing to throw medical science to the wind when it comes to things they do understand, but when faced with something as mysterious as the G-spot, even their senses of humor fail them. Just label it and back away quickly, before anyone notices.

Another area ripe for some honest exploration and discussion, but fumbled on *Loveline*, is the much-maligned rape fantasy. A young female caller, worried because she was having rape fantasies, was brusquely advised to "get counseling." End of discussion. Here's what Adam and Drew forgot to say: Rape fantasies are unsettling but common. If they interfere with your daily life, counseling might help. If they turn you on and don't upset you otherwise . . . hey, go with it. No harm in that. Most important, they're fantasies—not real. Just as thinking about clowns doesn't automatically qualify you to fit in those tiny cars, rape fantasies don't make you a rapist or a victim. It would take about forty-five seconds to tell someone this, but just labeling the caller a nut job and moving on frees up more advertising time (Oh look, a condom ad! What are those for again?) and saves us viewers from actually having to think about our own sexuality, fantasies, orientation, beliefs, or bodies.

Drew and Adam are terribly irresponsible in their work, but it's MTV that really deserves criticism for airing this show. They love to play up sex at every opportunity—I know more about Jenny McCarthy's breasts than my own, at this point—and then turn around and chastise us for enjoying it. MTV is a network with real reach and power where younger viewers are concerned. And not everyone has the luxury of alternate sources with which to discover that, in spite of *Loveline*'s supposed function of providing information, you could get a more accurate sex education from the Pope. My advice to the real mature audience out there—those who are taking charge of their sexuality with research and some trial and error, and taking careful notes—is to skip *Loveline* and start your own show. Don't wait for friends to ask—start conversations about sex and listen to them as you would want to be listened to. Then expand the dialogue. Rather than adopting the locker-room tone of *Loveline*, create a slumber party where everyone tells the truth and learns from each other. And look for me—I'll be handing out the s'mores.

The New Sexual Deviant

Mapping Virgin Territory

Carson Brown / WINTER 2000

I SAT IN THE WAITING ROOM OF THE STD CLINIC, WONDERING if my fellow patients knew my secret. As I pored over pamphlets, I felt terrified that I was giving off some virgin pheromone that nonvirgins could smell a mile away. Was it written all over my face that I was an imposter and trespasser?

The week before, my can-I-call-him-my-boyfriend-yet boyfriend had reported some burning when he pissed, and when his results came back positive but curable, I was told to get checked out, just in case, even though we had never actually done the deed. So there I was, nineteen years old, far from home, trying to see my foray into gonorrhea's grotto as a learning experience. My beau had assumed I was deflowered, and I let him. The moment of my maidenhood that separated ripening from rotting had passed. I was too old to be both a virgin and cool.

A nurse called my number, and I followed her into a small room for questioning. I breezed through the early rounds: Travel in Africa? Blood transfusions? Intravenous drugs? Innocent on all counts. I was on a roll. But then: "Date of last intercourse?"

This woman had heard it all before: hundreds of partners, multiple abortions, religious beliefs disallowing condoms, everything. But when I peeped, "Never," and she looked up from her clipboard for the first time, I could tell this was a new one. Mine was the right answer for church or grandparents, but here, I was wasting time and tax dollars.

She stared, waiting for me to revise my answer. Finally she repeated, "Never?" I shook my head sheepishly. After a pause she asked, "Oral contact?" I nodded emphatically. She went on: "Mutual masturbation?" I nodded again, having never actually heard that term before but getting the idea and wanting to please her. She led me into an examination room and instructed me to strip from the waist down and wait. When the doctor entered— a woman, to my relief—she offered, "So I hear this is probably your first examination?" and I cringed, imagining the chuckles she'd shared with the nurse. "Not to worry." She sat on a stool at the end of the table, told me to relax (yeah, right), and ducked below the V-shaped horizon of my thighs, peeking up momentarily to add, "Lovely sweater."

As I tried to breathe in through my nose and out through my mouth, the doctor proclaimed, "My, what a large hymen you have!" "Thank you," I squeaked out, realizing quickly that it wasn't really a compliment.

"Can you get a tampon in there?" she marveled, taking a close, incredulous look where no man had gone before. "I would offer to give it a little, you know, clip, but I would worry you would never go to the gynecologist again! Ha-ha!"

"Ha-ha!" Translation: It would hurt like a bitch! Meaning it was going to hurt like a bitch when . . .

"It's really up to you, sweetheart," she continued, suddenly maternal. "Maybe it would just be easier to do it now?" No telltale blood, I thought. No pain to hide. But here? Now? This woman? And Jesus, was she really asking me what she was asking me? "Shall I?"

MEANWHILE, MY FRIEND ANNA WAS STUDYING IN PARIS AND had found a Frenchman willing to cash in her V card, which had apparently been her intention all along. I didn't know Anna that well at the time, but I certainly hadn't figured her for hymenically intact: Her drama major, twenty-something age, perpetually tousled hair, exotic looks, older ex-boyfriends, and unconventional lifestyle all pointed to experience. But when it was discovered that Jacques was also servicing a woman down the hall, she seemed disproportionately devastated (if naïvely surprised). Her reaction made more sense when she told me, in a heartbroken e-mail, that he'd been her first.

But recover she did, and started talking constantly about diversifying her sexual portfolio, aiming to boost the count onto two hands. Over a year's time, the club's ranks swelled to four members—"three men and one woman," she would footnote. I consulted my sources and discovered that she had been seeing a woman before she departed for France. I thought it through: She's only ever been involved with one woman, she's slept with one woman, she was seeing this woman before she left, yet she lost her virginity across the pond. The upshot? Anna counted this woman among her partners, but though she came chronologically before the lecherous monsieur, she didn't claim Anna's virginity.

Anna's mathematical maneuvering brings up a number of issues: Why should virginity loss be based on the presence of a penis, automatically relegating same-sex activity to a lower status? For the sake of argument, I'd almost say that maybe, technically, the hymen defines the event. But if that were true, then some random gynecologist holds the key to my chastity belt. Not very romantic. I wanted to choose my own moment as the end of my maidenhood, and Anna should get to do the same. (However, she can't have it both ways: If she can't deal with the fact that she lost it to a woman, then she can't use that woman to pad her numbers.) Most important, though, what is it that makes virginity so uncool these days?

The stereotype is that virgins are timid, old-fashioned, meek, boring, cautious, unattractive, repressed, narrow-minded, and naïve. They have low self-esteem or bad body image. They can't participate in fun conversations about sex. Basically, they aren't rebels. Most products and experiences are marketed to us by equating the hip with the subversive: This is the antiestablishment car to drive, the alternative soft drink to drink, the anticelebrity celebrity to copy. In the end, rebellion is transformed into conformity, and so it goes with sex. How are companies supposed to market their stuff if people aren't actively pursuing sex? How are they supposed to sell cars, clothes, beers, breakfast cereal, perfume, makeup, or travel on the premise that their products will get you laid if people are content to not get laid? So the market pulls out all the stops to ensure that we will remain sex obsessed, so that we'll buy things. Businesses want virgins to feel horrible about themselves, because if virgins were happy being virgins, they would be horrible consumers. As long as they are virgins desperately trying to ditch their virginity, fine. But abstinence undermines economics.

Virginity bias tacks a confusing corollary onto historical social opinion about the sexual behavior of women. Not so long ago, a woman had only to hold a nickel between her knees to avoid slut status. Easy enough. But since the sexual revolution, she can also be slapped with the equally damning "prude" label. We've strayed from the original intent of women's liberation and limited women again, trading in the old prescription (sex will ruin a woman) for one that seems more modern (lack of sex will curdle her). We can't seem to shake the need for a formula, constructing a narrow six-month window around a girl's seventeenth birthday (if that's early enough) as the approved defloration moment. We've led a woman I know to plan, one drunken night, to seduce her twenty-six-year-old cousin rather than go to boarding school a virgin at age sixteen.

While virgins are by no means an actively persecuted group, the prejudice our culture perpetuates against them is insidious. Signaling the near-complete shift from the old-fashioned "men want virgins" mentality, the 1970s bestseller *The Sensuous Man*, written by "M" during the heyday of the sexual revolution, includes a section titled "Hints on Sacrificing Virgins." The author calls virginity "one of woman's most hideous afflictions" and confesses a "general prejudice against women who have managed to keep their virtue intact." He wishes that virgins were forced to wear badges to prevent men from accidentally seducing them, stating that "the term 'virgin' has almost become a gross insult to a woman's sexual attractiveness."

I WAS RECENTLY A BRIDESMAID IN A HIGH-SCHOOL FRIEND'S wedding. She's twenty-three and Christian, and was a virgin on her wedding day—a dying breed—as was her fiancé. In fact, her first kiss was the night of their engagement, and they didn't lock lips again until the altar. And it showed. Truly, it was the most atrocious "You may kiss the bride" moment I have ever witnessed: He went in for the smooch, she leaned in unexpectedly, they bumped mouths. He pulled back, startled; she swayed in for a little more, but it was over. I covered my mouth, horrified that these two thought they were going to do the nasty that very night.

Of the people onstage during the ceremony, I was one of three who knew carnal pleasure. My sexually active compatriots were the bride's partnered lesbian Christian sister and the married pastor. Unmarried and not virginal, I was the only one living in sin (well, except for the sister's minor gay issue).

The pastor's talk that day centered on a line from my friend's self-written vows that said, "I know you [my husband] will never fully satisfy me, that I must look to God alone to complete me." Now, I had thought her comment was not really in the spirit of the day. But the pastor said that she was onto something—they both had to realize that God is the most important person in their marriage. To illuminate this nuanced point further, the pastor offered an image: "Marriage is like a God sandwich." I blushed: This kinky talk from a pastor! But as I looked out into the audience, I saw all the Christian couples nodding. My friend one piece of bread, her husband the other, and God as the meat, always there in the middle. A veritable ménage à God.

Suddenly everything the pastor said took on a sexual meaning to me, all the years of suppressed desire coming out in religious doublespeak. It was all merging, joining, intersecting, and satisfaction, and God was always there in the thick of it. The Holy Trinity had become the holy threesome. It was as if they didn't really love each other, but they both loved God, and that was the ticket. And, in fact, it cast a weird light over the loss of virginity in general because they weren't really making love to each other directly, but rather through God. Even within the union of marriage, when the whole abstinence bet was supposed to be called up at long last, sex was still dirty, base, or empty unless it was mediated by God.

When I tell people this story, it solicits unanimous outrage. Most recently, a woman responded, "What if the bride was allergic to her husband's sperm and didn't even know it?!" The sex-positive brigade thinks my friend is doomed to a lifetime of unsatisfying sex, she'll never have an orgasm, she's ashamed of her body, she's repressed, she's scarred, she's guilt ridden, she'll never masturbate, she needs to see a shrink, she wants attention, she's a lesbian, her husband's gay, it's my responsibility to educate her, her father or priest molested her, she's been brainwashed by evil forces. Hmm. Sounds to me like she's pretty deviant—these are the sorts of comments usually reserved for queers, trannies, prostitutes, porn aficionados, S&M enthusiasts, and the rest of the freaks. Sounds like a Christian good girl just became "alternative." And where does that leave all the formulas?

IF CAPITALISM AND ADVERTISING ARE TELLING PEOPLE THEY have to want sex, Christianity is telling them the opposite. For every woman trying to jettison her cumbersome chastity, there's another who desperately wishes she hadn't given it up. And for every Christian young person who walked the pure walk all the way to her or his wedding day, there are ten who gave in to temptation along the way. To serve them, the secondary-virginity movement was officially launched in 1993 by the Christian abstinence organization True Love Waits, which invites teens to pledge celibacy until their wedding nights, often announcing their new path at ceremonies where parents place pledge rings on their child. Parallel efforts sprang up, such as Sex Respect, which coined the snappy slogan "Control your urgin'—be a virgin."

The secondary-virginity folk are going for a few good things here: first of all, the idea that people have the right to choose their own moment of defloration, that the label of "virgin" is actually arbitrary. If you did the deed but feel horrible about it, you should be able to call a do-over. Revirginizing allows you to define your own existence based on your current behaviors, saying, in effect, "I am who I conceive myself to be." This is a very powerful—and potentially very feminist—notion. Of course, unlike True Love Waits, I would also encourage the flip side: If you've been very physically intimate but haven't technically had intercourse, you should be encouraged to define yourself as a nonvirgin if you want to.

Also, the secondary-virginity model is more gender fair than other sexual rule systems. Here, sex is a no-no for both sexes—zero room is allowed for statements like "boys will be boys." And proponents don't buy the whole "teenagers have such strong sex drives that they just can't control themselves" thing. They respect young people enough to know that they have brains, they can be responsible for their actions, and they can stick to decisions they really want to make. They ride the fine line of accepting and repairing mistakes while setting high standards for behavior, which is, in theory, what Christianity in general does. But the problem with the secondary-virginity movement is that it still says, as loud and clear as any advertising campaign, that there are right and wrong ways and times to have sex, and asks people who do it wrong to deny that part of their lives.

Is sexual terrain really so treacherous that we need strict instructions from the church or the secular gods that are movie stars and models? If we must have a formula, why can't it be that you "pass the test" by doing whatever it is that makes you ultimately happiest? Of course, it's not easy to differentiate what makes me happy from the perks that society awards me for conforming. And it's much simpler to rely on prepackaged identities—whether people are virgins or not, whether they are gay or straight, whether they're loose or frigid by reputation—than to figure out if they're satisfied with their lives. So how can we create a culture free of virginity obsession and outdated dichotomies? It may be time for a third term, a social creature even more unlikely and elusive than virgins: ourselves as individuals.

Envy, a Love Story

Queering Female Jealousy

Anna Mills / SUMMER 2001

HAVE YOU EVER WONDERED WHY HETEROSEXUAL WOMEN ARE consistently drawn to images of other women? Mainstream female America can't get enough of half-naked, conventionally gorgeous women sulking or smiling out from magazine covers, TV sets, and movie screens. Look at the magazine rack in your local drugstore or supermarket—without the words, can you tell *Maxim* from *Cosmopolitan*? Can you tell if the "luscious" women on the covers are supposed to entice a man or a woman? I can't. As feminists, we charge the media with using female bodies to sell everything from soap to beer to Palm Pilots. As often as not, though, these campaigns target women, not men. How do we explain straight women's susceptibility to these images?

Here's the traditional feminist explanation: In a patriarchal society, women's worth is based on attractiveness to men. Women are drawn to images of women who fit the "beautiful and sexy" mold because we want to fantasize about the desire, love, attention, and respect we would get from men if we looked like them. "Land that man, ace your job, and look your sexiest ever!" screams a typical women's-magazine cover line. Sexiness is all about status. Fascination with other women is all about admiration, competition, and envy. Right?

It follows that mainstream American culture expects women to be riveted by each other's beauty. Straight women are often acutely aware of and affected by each other's clothes, jewelry, makeup, and body size. Women are notoriously—stereotypically—competitive and jealous of each other's looks. The cliché that women don't dress for men, they dress for other women, passes without comment. But no one bothers to ask if sexual attraction has anything to do with it—not even feminists. We should. How can the sensual, the erotic, and the sexual not be woven into those complex and intense emotions that women feel when they compare themselves to each other? How can women's intense interest in other women be totally divorced from sexuality?

It's time to queer our views of women's fascination with other women, to free them from assumptions of heterosexuality, and to look at the ways their meanings escape and wreak havoc with heterosexual, sexist norms—and the ways this fascination gets played out in envy, self-hate, female friendships, and women's preoccupation with eating and body image.

An article in the sex section of Women.com—an umbrella site that hosts, among other things, *Cosmo*'s web presence—describes a woman's relationship with her ex-husband's new wife: "One afternoon, I breezed over early for the designated pick-up [of my children]. There, sitting in [my ex-husband's] living room, was a young woman in shorts with the most beautiful legs I had ever seen. Legs are a big deal for me; I'm convinced mine look like storm-uprooted tree trunks. I was glad I was wearing a long skirt."

Read the passage again, this time imagining that the narrator is bisexual. Might one wonder if she was attracted to her supposed rival? The encounter can be read as erotically charged until the narrator turns her reaction into an attack on her own body.

Women are expected to admire, comment on, and gush over each other's appearances. Straight women regularly do so with warmth, enthusiasm, and sensual appreciation. Imagine two women, let's call them Jane and Mary, greeting each other after a separation. "Oh, it's good to see you!" says Jane, giving Mary a warm hug. "You look so beautiful!" Mary exclaims as she leans back to smile at Jane, hands still on her friend's waist. She touches Jane's blouse to feel the material and looks up and down her body. "That skirt makes your butt look so cute!" she adds. Are these women friends, lovers, or flirting? Imagine how shocked you might be if you saw two straight men behaving this way. Once the question of sexual orientation is raised, the scene becomes much more difficult—and interesting—to read.

For many of us, thinness is one of the major qualifications for sexiness. Feminists have documented many of the deeper meanings of women's obsession with body size and eating, including messages about self, desire, entitlement, nurturing, and rage; one of the ways these obsessions function is as a point of intense connection, pain, and envy between women. Obsession with weight makes women hyperaware of each other's bodies—always measuring and comparing, coveting and judging. Is your lunch partner eating a burger or a salad? Did your closest friend gain a few pounds? Many women are similarly obsessed with the various diets and exercise regimens employed by weight-conscious celebrities—thus we have Monica Lewinsky's Jenny Craig diet and Sarah Ferguson's tenure as a spokeswoman for Weight Watchers.

On Oprah Winfrey's video about her own dieting process, *Make the Connection*, she rhapsodizes about Goldie Hawn's butt and announces, "I'm now working out with Goldie's behind in my mind." Later, when Cindy Crawford appears in a skimpy leotard, there's an awkward moment when Oprah openly looks Crawford up and down, taking in her figure with intense admiration. She leans back and announces, "There's a body!"

How far am I going with this? Is all envy really attraction? Are all female friendships chock-full of repressed sexuality? Do women with body-image issues just need to come out? For sociopolitical shock value, it would be delicious to make these claims. For the sake of true and useful theory, though, I want to question just that type of absolutism. My point is not that we're all big dykes, but that the distinctions among sensuality, sexual attraction, and platonic love are not always stable or easy to determine. The erotic is an integral part of the wide range of affection between women. Under a system where women are not encouraged to acknowledge attraction to women— even to themselves—that attraction has to hide somewhere. Where better than in the socially sanctioned obsession with other women's appearance? Where better than in the supposedly "pure" model of platonic friendship?

I know from my own experience that it's possible to completely confuse envy and attraction, and that this confusion can go totally unnoticed by both the woman in question and those around her. It was easy for me to use the concept of envy to spend twenty-two years as a straight girl, never realizing that I was attracted to women.

My mother explained to me when I was eight that gay people weren't bad, just unfortunate. I understood that gay people were different, and that I would never be like them. It never occurred to me I might be one of them. When my friends and I entered puberty, I became acutely aware of other girls' bodies. As I hit fourteen or fifteen, this awareness developed into intense envy and competition with other girls. I remember feeling a jolt when I saw a really attractive girl—a feeling that made my insides twist in despair, believing that I could never look like her. I fantasized about the attention, status, and love she got from men. I thought about how much they must want her. This misery led me to focus more and more on my weight as the source of all my problems. If only my body would change, I reasoned, I could be just like that other girl. And so began a cycle of compulsive eating, hating my body, and dieting that lasted for years.

In college, as I joined feminist groups and read analyses of overeating and dieting, heterosexual feminist interpretations seemed to fit my experience to a T. The books I read explained that I was jealous of other women because my attractiveness to men determined my self-worth. I was socialized to attend to men's desires, not my own. I was focused on keeping my own body attractive and therefore out of touch with what I wanted for myself. Yes, yes, yes.

In my journal, though, I expressed confusion. "It's not just a body, it's a horror. My weight means something else about having a shameful body . . . It started when I started dating. It must have something to do with my sexuality. I always wanted to lose so he would be more attracted to me. I think there's something going on here I don't understand."

No one—not my friends, not the women in my feminist groups, not the theorists writing about body image—mentioned that attraction to women, and ambivalence about my feelings, might be part of the picture. No one suggested that questioning my sexuality might be an option, much less a good idea.

By the end of my junior year of college, I was not eating compulsively, not restricting myself so much, and not beating myself up over what I ate. I was moving toward healthy relationships with men, as well as more body- and self-acceptance. I had read all about lesbian feminism, and I was primed to reinvent heterosexuality in empowering, feminist ways.

And then a strange and wondrous thing happened: A close friend told me she was a lesbian, and I realized I had a crush on her. Over the next few weeks, I surprised myself again and again by noticing that I was, in fact, physically attracted to women. I felt it in the dining hall, walking down the street, sitting in class. Where I used to feel pangs of envy—followed by self-criticism and despair—I now felt attraction. Girls were pretty, cute, sexy. Looking at them made me hug myself, grin, gossip voraciously, blush, and feel goofy. I acted fourteen. I was incredulous at my good luck.

When I had begun to get my bearings as a queer woman, I rushed to the library to read about body image, envy, and sexual orientation. I found feminist-penned theories linking homophobia and male competition, which cited the homoerotic aspects of the military, athletics, the business world, and power relations among men in general. But I found no parallel analysis of women's relationships.

Women's own stories testify that madness, self-hatred, and rage are a few responses to life in a sexist society. The gap between what we feel and what we are supposed to feel is often too difficult or risky to acknowledge; compulsive eating and dieting, starvation, cutting, and abusing our own bodies are all ways women both express and control unnameable feelings. But what feminist theory has not fully explored is the possibility that neuroses, self-hatred, and hostility to other women are responses not only to sexism but also to compulsory heterosexuality (identified and defined by Adrienne Rich in her classic 1980 essay "Compulsory Heterosexuality and Lesbian Existence" as the system privileging heterosexuality as universal, natural, inevitable, and moral, and denying, minimizing, and shaming the existence of queer desires). Women who have no way to acknowledge queer desires may turn the uncertainty, anxiety, and confusion in on themselves, as I did. The violent denial of queerness may be one origin of the self-directed misery and violence that feed jealousy, negative body image, and eating disorders.

How can something so insidious be uprooted? What would women's sense of self, body image, and perceptions of the media look like without it? I can offer only provocative guesses. I have argued that shots of half-dressed models are a secret, unconscious way for women to desire women. Those images might lose some of their power if women were able to acknowledge queer attraction and fully integrate it into their lives. If women admitted openly the possibility of loving women, they might be able to let go of the ambivalent, insecure fascination that sells so many magazines. *Cosmo*'s screaming would begin to fall on deaf ears.

The questioning process allows women to name feelings that span the lesbian continuum Rich describes—the spectrum of sexual attraction, sensuality, affection, and platonic love. Confronting the fear of being a lesbian might open women up for more kinds of closeness with each other, whether or not they choose to be sexual. I know that my own perceptions of women changed after I came out, even with women to whom I'm not sexually attracted. I am warmer, more appreciative, and more affectionate than I was; I enjoy women more. In an openly queer culture, women might let go of some of the critical, insecure awareness of the bodies of women around them. They would likely still enjoy looking at images of other women, but without the edge of fear, self-doubt, and insecurity that denial brings.

The shift to a queer-positive, woman-identified viewpoint would make unnecessary a lot of self-hatred, envy, and self-directed violence. Women might begin to define what they want to look like from within. Women who are used to wishing they could be skinny, clean-shaven, fashionable, and femme might start to ask, "If I were attracted to a woman, whom would I be attracted to?" We might begin to rethink what we find attractive in our own bodies and come to appreciate a round stomach, extra fuzz, or the deep-brown moles on a shoulder blade. Discussions of diets, exercise, and fetish foods could give way to an exploration of what is compelling, attractive, moving, or exemplary in each other. The model's rigidly sculpted posing might still hold occasional attraction, but it would be just one kind of beauty among many.

Living in a culture that embraces the insidious systems of sexism and compulsory heterosexuality, women will not be living lives of our own choosing until we ask a few questions: Whom do you want? Whom do you want to be sexy for? It will be a queer, happy world when the model's hungry gaze loses its pull. Women will let go of old obsessions to revel in a dizzying diversity of beauty. We will find joy in each other through a hundred types of sexual, sensual, and friendly connections. Are we ready?

Fan/Tastic Voyage

Rewriting Gender in the Wide, Wild World of Slash Fiction

Noy Thrupkaew / SPRING 2003

The kiss was not at all like Kirk had expected . . .

"Spock, wait . . . wait," he whispered desperately . . . "I can't . . . we can't . . . you . . . God, Spock . . . I want you. Don't you understand? I want you so much!" Kirk still couldn't believe that the Vulcan knew what he was getting himself into. But Spock was pressed tightly against him and Kirk could feel the hardness. Spock's cock was pushing into his hip, hard as rock and insistent . . . Spock smiled then, only a short, ghostly smile, but it was there.

"Jim."

"Yes?"

"You talk excessively."

—from "Christmas Gifts . . . or Blue Seduction" by kira-nerys

DON'T WORRY, *STAR TREK* FANS, YOU DIDN'T MISS AN EPISODE. But if you haven't been poring over fanzines or trolling the web, you might not have come across the juicy encounters, gender play, and fiercely feminist theorizing found in the world of slash fiction.

Named after the punctuation mark between the names of its lover-heroes (e.g., Kirk/Spock), slash fan fiction was born at the end of the '60s, when inventive viewers started penning steamy rendezvous between Captain Kirk and Mr. Spock in fanzines. But it wasn't until the '90s that slash fiction truly flourished, with the advent of the Internet and its discussion groups, where a growing subculture of writers, editors, and readers could share and critique one another's work. As the number of stories increased, so too did the range of potential pairings. Intrepid slash writers—primarily women—gleefully found the love that dare not speak its name between just about everyone: Starsky and Hutch, Luke Skywalker and Han Solo, even Harry Potter and Draco Malfoy. (HP/DM authors hasten to assure readers that their stories feature the characters in their late teens.)

The relationship dynamics in slash have become just as varied as the couples. Initially steeped in first-time male love between two comrades-in-arms, slash has developed into a free-for-all, exploring S&M complexities, male pregnancy, and other flights of writerly fancy. Slash also attracts critical attention from social theorists, many of whom ponder one of the more interesting questions about the genre: Why do slash writers, who are predominantly straight women writing for other women, focus so much (though far from exclusively) on male/male romantic relationships? Although theories abound—male relationships are truly egalitarian, female characters are too boring to write about—slash has become so diverse that it easily thwarts anyone trying to find one generalizing principle.

With slash's steamy combination of gender-bending plots and playful raunch, it's no surprise that cultural theorists, feminists, and everyday pop culture mavens have found it so intriguing. Like all fan fiction, slash turns pop culture consumers into creators and thrives on a sort of dialogue between fan and character. But it goes one step further than most fanfic by openly interrogating static pop culture notions of masculine and feminine—experimenting with, discarding, or reinventing ideas about gender.

Slash enables its writers to subvert TV's tired male/female relationships while interacting with and showing mastery over the original raw material of a show (key for all fanfic). Writing male characters as lovers allows a richer sense of possibility than duplicating the well-worn boy/girl romances coughed up by most TV shows.

In addition, slash is steeped in a community that amplifies the feminist qualities of much of the genre. While not all slash is self-consciously political, many slash writers identify as feminists and engage one another in vigorous dialogues about gender. In writing about men and discussing the process, many women are taking that room of one's own to another level. They're not only laying claim to images of men but also reconfiguring male behavior—a powerful way to make men their own.

When they're not experimenting with the genre, slash authors—a very self-aware, self-analyzing community—are discussing gender, queerness, and feminism in all their different forms. Add this to a lively academic debate on slash, and you have a rich mélange that makes the idea of a grand unified theory of slash seem laughable. One critic may posit that slash is a space where female writers can create the "ideal" human in a misogynistic world: male body, male power, female ways of relating. Another will argue that slash provides a space for women to work out their gender issues, a place where they can dump the unwanted restrictions of "femininity." Slash is gay. Slash isn't gay. Slash is neither, or a little of both. Slash lets women assert power over men the way the patriarchy asserts power over women. Slash lets women humanize and redraft masculinity. Slash is about nooky. Slash isn't about sex at all. Slash allows women ways of writing (collaborative, participatory) that subvert male ways of writing (copyrighted, absolute, and closed).

Evolutionary psychologists Catherine Salmon and Donald Symons, coauthors of *Warrior Lovers: Erotic Fiction, Evolution and Female Sexuality*, argue that the predominantly female-written genre speaks to differences in mating behavior between men and women. According to Darwinian psychology, our hunter-gatherer forebears had different needs—the men to impregnate as many women as possible; the women to find a nice, stable, dependable man to provide for them. Porn reflects the male desire, say Salmon and Symons, and romance novels reflect the female. As for slash, perhaps the erotic fanfic gives modern women a way to have their cake and eat it too. The genre illustrates how "some women prefer the fantasy of being a cowarrior to that of being a Mrs. Warrior," say Salmon and Symons, but the relationships' emphasis on friendship, loyalty, and fidelity also reflects Darwinian desires for a responsible guy who will stick around.

To a feminist reader, this analysis has some clear flaws, especially the way it strains to explain the gender unconventionality of slash in such retrograde, traditional terms. It's frustrating that Salmon and Symons try to reduce the work of female slash writers down to an essentialist baby-making vs. gender-equality conflict, ignoring examples of fanfic that don't fit into that mold.

More promising is the scholarship of Constance Penley, who argues that female slash authors focus on male/male relationships because they're the most egalitarian. Basing her theories on Kirk/Spock (K/S) slash, Penley critiques the flat characterization of female TV characters and the limitations of what TV and media culture depict as male/female relationships. But in real life, she also argues, women's bodies are too often layered with negative meanings—and therefore become the site for political, social, and moral struggle. K/S slash is a rejection of those problematic bodies and of TV's flat female characters, serving instead as a subversive rewriting of the script in which lovers can share love and work and still be equal. Penley's analysis does have its limitations, however, in that it doesn't cover slash other than K/S.

The more slash—and slash theory—I read, the more convinced I became that no one analysis could explain the varieties of slash, the bent of all slash writers, the political leanings, the gender fuckings, the story rogerings that happen daily on the Internet. All my reading—and attempts at writing—suggests to me that the relationships between male characters allow a writer to strike a harmonious balance between working within the framework of a show and spinning a tale of her own imagination. The best slash I've read captures the rhythm of the characters' speech, probes their psychology, and shows a mastery of complicated plots, all while taking the characters in new directions. And although a similar sense of possibility could await a writer delving into unexpected male/female pairings (Scully and Skinner, for instance) or trysts between two female characters (say, Buffy and Willow on *Buffy the Vampire Slayer*), male/male pairings add an extra dimension—the opportunity to recraft masculinity itself. And for women—straight or queer—who write slash fiction, this certainly seems to add an extra-enticing challenge, a sense of going where no woman has gone before.

It is precisely that quality of ordered freedom that explains why science fiction has become such fertile ground for slash. Science fiction is deeply concerned with utopias, dystopias, possibilities, alternatives, and fantasies, but it is also deeply bound to the order and logic of science (however fancifully constructed it may be). For all its whimsy and strangeness, science fiction also mirrors our own reality. And slash seems to reflect that combination.

Many slash writers are compelled to make male characters a bit more communicative and tender—qualities stereotypically associated with women. But there are pitfalls if one goes too far. Some slash stories have lantern-jawed guys coming home with flowers every day, tying on pink aprons, weeping over lost football games. These stereotypes, "feminine" or no, are boring despite the genders involved. But more than that, these tales are not sexy. There is just too much sameness to the characters—both men so soft and squishy—that one has no sense of how their differences could be complementary, or how they are different characters at all.

And there's another reason not to push a masculine character to unbelievable heights of femininity—it violates that delicate balance in fanfic between precedent and imagination. A writer who frills up a butch male character may earn the wrath of someone like Jane at the website Citizens Against Bad Slash, who writes: "There seems to be an overwhelming tendency in the slash community to make masculine characters so feminine that you could change one of the names to 'Mary' and it wouldn't make a difference . . . Even if we're writing stories about an alternate universe, it's always more interesting when the dialogue and actions of the character are somewhat true to life. The neat thing about slash is that you get to see characters act out what you don't see onscreen, but it loses its appeal when the character is so 'feminized' that you can't recognize him."

While Jane does seem to buy into static masculine and feminine codes of behavior, in the world of stereotypical TV gender roles, her critique makes sense. For this reason, exaggerated feminine characteristics stick out just as much as masculine ones. Sometimes slash writers err in the other direction, writing reams about stoic, uncommunicative men having hot sex. And while that can be fun for a while, the stories that have received the most acclaim in the slash world are ones that show why these men are with each other and what's behind the sex. They also flesh out their heroes with qualities that are a combination of traditionally male behaviors (assertive, confident) and female characteristics (nurturing, communicative). In other words, the best pieces feature players who are more like real people than the characters you find on TV.

Interestingly, unexplored female/female TV relationships seem to hold a similar sense of possibility and limitation. The acknowledged lesbian relationship of *Buffy*'s Willow and Tara, like the overt and obvious male/female relationships, did nothing for me, and indeed there doesn't seem to be as much slash about that couple as there is about other pairings left sub-textual by the show (like Buffy/Willow). With a relationship that airs in real TV time, there's just not enough negative space for a writer's imagination to fill in. The tension between two women who aren't already in a relation-ship is much more promising, however—*Star Trek Voyager*'s Seven of Nine and Captain Janeway, for example, have proved quite enticing to many slash writers.

For many, slash has become a potent way to personalize interactions with a show, to lay claim to it by infusing it with sexual fantasy, gendered role-play, and power dynamics. And for those who are politically inclined, writing slash is a creative endeavor with feminist overtones—one that al-lows people to ponder gender issues in a creative, supportive environment. The world of slash, after all, is populated predominantly by women who are not mere consumers of culture but who have become producers in their own right. Slash writers, along with authors of other fanfic, have changed TV and movie watching from a passive act into a participatory one, allow-ing for the deciphering and creation of meaning. That a slash writer can grapple with gender and power issues adds extra richness to the already subversive practice of writing fanfic.

Luckily, there's no shortage of material. Television leaves a lot to be desired—which means more room for slash writers to fill with their imag-inations. Even if TV changes dramatically for the better—with more pro-grams that highlight deep, complex characters and show a broader range of social issues, loves, and sexual orientations—I'm sure that slash writers will find their space. They're too ornery, too independent, and too ingen-ious to let even the best TV prevent them from finding ways to improve it.

Hot for Teacher

On the Erotics of Pedagogy

Jennifer Maher / SPRING 2004

WHEN I WAS SEVENTEEN, MY ENGLISH TEACHER ASSIGNED THE class a poem by Theodore Roethke titled "Elegy for Jane." In the poem, Roethke mourns the death of Jane, "[his] student, thrown by a horse," eulogizing her "neckcurls" and "pickerel smile." The randy Roethke (who, in fact, had numerous affairs with his students) ends his poem with this lament:

> If only I could nudge you from this sleep,
> My maimed darling, my skittery pigeon.
> Over this damp grave I speak the words of my love:
> I, with no rights in this matter,
> Neither father nor lover.

I read "Elegy for Jane" then as a romantic idealization of the relationship between me and my own randy high-school teacher, Mr. Miller, with whom I was in love. I thought the poem spoke to the desperate desire between us that couldn't find its form, since, like Roethke to Jane, he was neither father nor lover to me.

Coming across this poem years later, I'm more than a little troubled by its representation of the not-quite-fatherly father figure who transmits his admiration and lust via the metaphor of female student as dead bird. At the same time, though, part of me is still touched by "Elegy for Jane," with a nostalgia based on a remembrance of my young student self. Thoroughly male-identified, I was as happy, to quote from the poem, as a "wren [with its] tail into the wind" to imagine myself "trembling the twigs and small branches" while my handsome teacher in his Levi's and tie whispered words of love over my damp grave. Obviously, being female (and, well, dead), these were words that I could only inspire, not write. For a disaffected smart girl like me, poetry by men like Roethke was pure pornography.

Young girls in English class are consistently taught poems like these, poems written by men and inspired by/directed at women. And even the smartest, most ambitious girls are not immune to responding by imagining themselves as the muse and not the iambic musician. Hence, the schoolgirl crush. The knot of passion and knowledge has been referenced for ages, and not just by male teachers like Roethke. As feminist critic and humorist Regina Barreca wrote in her 1997 book, *The Erotics of Instruction*, "Sometimes we sublimate effectively, and become the beloved in our own classes, imitating, perhaps unconsciously, the mannerisms and habits of an influential professor. Sometimes we sleep with the teacher . . . Often we translate our desire into the love of the subject, or the text, or the way the light hits a four-o'clock window in a November classroom."

I myself have chosen all three of these paths at one time or another, but it is the first and the last that are of most interest for me here, as I am now a teacher at a university. I learned to "sublimate effectively" my desire for my own teachers by falling in love with the subject and, in my own teaching, taking on—maybe consciously, maybe not—their tics, their jokes, and the methods they used to make knowledge such a turn-on for me in the first place.

But it was men who engendered the allure of knowledge for me, and gender is key to making this kind of sublimation effective. An unspoken cultural consent backs Roethke's feelings for Jane. In many literary and pop cultural representations of teachers and students (not to mention in the minds of many male faculty themselves), the father/lover role is as natural as the moss clinging to the wet stone in "Elegy." Of course, this doesn't mean that as a culture we are entirely comfortable with teacher-student romance, let alone sex—only that for years it has been a tacitly, if not openly, accepted arrangement in higher education, and the student-teacher crush a hallmark of the heterosexual female high-school experience.

Still, the idea that male professors dote on the sweet, hopeful malleability of their students, and that female students in turn yield both intellectually and sexually to these male minds, doesn't exactly hold the same romantic frisson as it might have in Roethke's day. As we all know, many students have little to no appreciation of this behavior, and thanks in large part to the feminist movement, we can freely and publicly question the behavior of dirty old professors using the miracle of knowledge to get into the pants of their eighteen-year-old students. Though university sexual harassment policies have an annoying way of erasing female students' sexual agency—no matter how gender-neutral the official language is, it is female students with male professors that these laws are meant to "protect"—they have at least brought quid pro quo harassment out of the closet.

But the mutual desires of student and teacher still exist, even if they're not acted upon. In fact, such desires are frequently seen as an extension of charismatic classrooms and youthful self-discovery, part and parcel of the dynamics of instruction—and debates within academia and depictions in popular culture take as a given that what we talk about when we talk about teacher-student love is the love between male professors and female students. Movies like Woody Allen's 1992 *Husbands and Wives* (in which the Woodster makes time with his Columbia pupil Juliette Lewis) and the more recent and far less slapstick *Blue Car* (in which a young girl is wooed by a teacher she later discovers is less a brilliant, tortured writer than a sad guy with a midlife crisis), as well as David Mamet's vitriolic stage play *Oleanna*, only brush the surface of the pop culture canon of this pairing. (The disturbing-yet-hilarious 1999 film *Election*, in which a scheming twelfth-grade overachiever played by Reese Witherspoon has an affair with one of her teachers, paints a less idealized picture.)

And, with the exception of writers bell hooks and Jane Gallop (whose liberal stances on teacher-student relationships are routinely misunderstood), the age-old gendered assumptions (male professor = predator, female student = victim) are so taken for granted that popular culture rarely touches on their reversal. As Gallop wrote in her 1997 book, *Feminist Accused of Sexual Harassment*, "If we imagine a sexual harassment scenario where the victim is male or the culprit female, the abuse of power would not be reinforced by society's sexual expectations." That is, the expectation is that males are active and females passive, that men are the lookers and women the looked at. Only nowadays, with increasing numbers of female professors, it would seem as if such an equation would begin to falter.

So what do we do with a female professor whose classroom is a space, as hooks wrote in a 1996 article for *Z Magazine*, of "erotic energy" that "can be used in constructive ways both in individual relationships and in the classroom setting"? Is she merely Roethke in drag, or is she something else? In the female-run classroom, what happens to our tried-and-true perceptions of masculinity? Of femininity? Of power and desire?

For me, teaching does not reverse the gender of Roethke's father/lover figure to produce the mother-child/teacher-student dyad. When I began teaching undergraduates at twenty-three, I wasn't old enough to be my students' mother; more important, I have a built-in resistance to our culture's deification of the maternal role, knowing too well how it can be used to deflect female authority. Maternity simply does not get at my experience of university teaching, because while I know that my real job is to help my students by challenging them to think through complicated ideas and to avoid sound-bite writing, teaching—when it works—is deeply pleasurable for me, sometimes erotically so. Ten years into it, I still see teaching as at least partially seductive work, not entirely unlike flirting: It can involve the kind of witty banter where each party lobbies for interest from the other. It allows for the gratification of projecting one's best self outward and seeing it mirrored, however briefly, in the other.

But such seductions, with or without cultural consent, work differently for male and female students, for reasons beyond simple sexual desire. For instance, my experience and behavior as a female student in "love" with my male teachers differ sharply from what I have experienced in male students' attractions to me. Whereas smart girls like Regina Barreca (and myself) readily "translate[d] [our] desire into the love of the subject, or the text," in my own experience, and that of some of my female colleagues, this rarely seems to be the case with male students and their female professors. I've been surprised to hear (usually from other students) that former students have been hot for me, mainly because the students in question didn't work all that hard in class. This is alien to my own experience: When you have a crush on a teacher, isn't your first impulse (or at least the second) to work even harder to impress her or him? To, in the best of circumstances, see eros as the starter of wisdom and run with it? Doesn't getting turned on by the messenger get you turned on by the message?

As Gallop wrote of two of her professors, "These guys were brilliant: I wanted to do work that would impress them, and I wanted more than anything to be like them . . . And I did my utmost to seduce them." Why is this erotic-intellectual pairing so much more rare in our cultural mythology when the teacher is female and the student male?

I don't mean to imply that the sublimation of teacher for text never happens for male students. A friend of mine who has a graduate degree in French studies and scrimps his money to spend half of each year in Paris will tell you, without hesitation, that it all began because he was in love with his (female) high-school French teacher. Yet such relationships, due either to rarity or cultural discomfort (or both), fall under the radar of American literature and popular culture. Rarely do we see a female teacher as a figure of desire for her male students without violent or potentially violent repercussions. They are usually turned into maternal figures (as with Michelle Pfeiffer in the 1995 flick *Dangerous Minds*) or punished (attempted sexual assault in 1955's *Blackboard Jungle*, murder in 1977's *Looking for Mr. Goodbar*, rape in 1996's *The Substitute*).

I've been reflecting on this issue even more than usual this semester, because I'm teaching film theory, itself focused on answering questions of representation, knowledge, power, and desire. We began the class with an analysis of how classic Hollywood films reflect and affirm gender roles through the "gaze"—that is, who looks at whom, who is on display, and who is in charge of the story.

In reckoning with what film theorist Laura Mulvey termed, somewhat clunkily, "to-be-looked-at-ness" on an exam, one of my male students wrote, "When a woman walks into a room, she's a spectacle, even if she's an authority figure like a teacher." When I first read this, raving narcissism took over and I worried that it was about me: I always love marching into class that first day, because in my pink cowboy boots and short, dyed-platinum hair, I know I don't look like their idea of a "real teacher." Then common sense broke in and I realized he was probably referring to a clip from *Top Gun*, which I had screened as an example of the way a film can put even a potentially powerful female character in her place by overemphasizing her "to-be-looked-at-ness." When the class of flyboys is introduced to civilian flight-school instructor Charlie (Kelly McGillis), we follow the camera eye (back and forth with the eyes of the guys in the class) to her back-seamed black stockings and heels. She pivots and faces the class, expertly lit with the sun behind her. Maverick (Tom Cruise) quickly realizes she's the woman he tried, unsuccessfully, to pick up in a bar the night before. His response to this surprise is to challenge her authority, mocking her limited knowledge of aircraft capability. A few scenes later, of course, they're getting it on.

This scene brings into sharp relief the difficulties that ensue when the expected erotics of the teacher-student relationship are enacted with the genders reversed. To put it more bluntly, though we might accept a woman as sexual (as long as she is heterosexual) and we might accept a woman in a position of authority, the two together at the same time is threatening to masculine privilege.

Here's the problem: For a female student, identifying with the man at the front of the classroom means gaining power in the form of knowledge, authority, and sexual possibility. For a male student, however, identifying with a woman means losing it. So though the female teacher can be looked at as sexually desirable, looking up to her is problematic.

Take Van Halen's classic "Hot for Teacher" video, for instance, which works precisely because the sexy teacher has lost all control of the students before she strips down to an electric-blue bikini and shimmies on the desk. It's not about her desire (as if we could ever expect this from MTV); it's about their adolescence, their male prerogative to make an erotic spectacle of her.

Contrast "Hot for Teacher" with another MTV video staple of roughly the same era, the Police classic "Don't Stand So Close to Me." It's another song about teacher-student desire, this time centering on a male teacher tempted by a female student. The viewer is meant to lust after Sting, certainly, but he's not fetishized in the manner of either *Top Gun*'s Charlie or Van Halen's hot teacher. He's gorgeous, and appears more than aware of this fact, but he's covered up in black graduation robes and his looks at the camera/viewer are neither coy nor playfully come-hither. And despite the fact that he's in the typically feminine position of the gaze's object, as he stares down his classroom of off-screen admirers, his masculinity and professorial authority are never in question—even if, as the song implies, he's in danger of losing his job. It's next to impossible to imagine a gender reversal of this video, as a female teacher simply could not sing about the temptation to sleep with a male student with such assuredness and unspoken cultural consent.

None of this analysis is meant to imply that the female-run classroom must be either devoid of erotic energy or a free-for-all for male students who won't accept a female authority figure if they think she's sexy. I have had and continue to have thoughtful, invested, smart male students. But no matter how "hot" I might hear myself described as later on, I have only rarely experienced this kind of energy transformed into something else, like an intellectual passion for the subject.

Perhaps the division between a desire to be like and a desire for is not as tricky for the female student, not only with male teachers but with female ones as well. Female students who become enraptured by female teachers have more than one way to go with their desire, as they don't need to cross–gender identify. My experience as both a student with female teachers and a teacher of female students leads me to believe there's another layer to the erotics of instruction, one that does not necessarily replace sexual desire but complicates it, turning the passion for a person to a passion for the subject more easily and sometimes more intensely. When I was taking a class in modernist literature with Ms. Prosser in college, for instance, I would get nervous before I went to her office, trying on different outfits beforehand, and sitting there with shaking hands, not knowing what to do with myself once I sat down across from her. She was brilliant and funny, and sexy as hell. One time she complimented me on my earrings in class and I blushed dark red. I became obsessed with Virginia Woolf because this woman taught her. Female students, both straight and queer, look at female teachers as much as heterosexual male students do, but the gaze, and the intellectual inspiration that can arise out of it, is more complex.

Of course, there are few (if any) popular culture representations of nonpathological female-teacher/female-student desire. But what film theorist Jackie Stacey calls narratives of "intra-feminine fascinations" are another story. In her essay "Desperately Seeking Difference," Stacey takes on *Desperately Seeking Susan* as a means by which to theorize "homosexual pleasures of female spectatorship"—simply put, a particularly female desire, sometimes sexual but not necessarily so, yet always entangled with emulation. Stacey's point is that female-to-female desire is at its core delectably based on an identification with rather than a power over. She's not taking hot sex out of the picture, but she's expanding our definition of what might lie beyond as well.

And while Madonna's Susan is not an official teacher in that film, she has a pedagogical role, initiating Roberta (Rosanna Arquette) into the New York art scene, satisfying sex, adventure, and self-knowledge. A more recent, though far less compelling, movie sets us right down in the belly of the pedagogical beast: Wellesley College in the 1950s. Formidably banal, 2003's *Mona Lisa Smile*, despite its haphazard editing and Pretty Woman Professor stereotypes, does dramatize intrafeminine fascination between a teacher and her students. In shot after shot, Julia Roberts, as the bohemian art-history professor Katherine Watson, commands the looks of the girls as easily as she did those of men in her Erin Brockovich cut-offs. In Wellesley's amphitheaterlike classrooms, she's literally and metaphorically onstage: On her first day of teaching, when the lights are turned off and she shows her slides, she's lit against the darkness like an old-fashioned film star—her students spectators, just like the movie audience. Only in this case, her to-be-looked-at-ness has the added layer of a pedagogical directive to look, since she is seducing her students into art history. Yet she can't quite pull it off, at least not at first. It's not just that she's coded as dowdy in her neutral tones, pseudo-Indian jewelry, and peasant blouses; rather, she's reckoning with young women who assume they already know it all, and she must break down their defenses and get them to (cue the music) Think for Themselves.

And Katherine does break through to them. The more she cracks their shells, the more the camera constructs the audience's point of view as the girls'; we follow their eyes and see her as they do. They begin, one by one, to long for her—or for what she represents—and their creative, interpretive capacities grow. Maggie Gyllenhaal's character, Giselle Levy, is the first to be seduced. The most sexually active of the group, as well as the only Jew suffocating under the weight of WASP propriety, Giselle at one point peers intently into a mirror, asking, half to herself, half to her friends, if she looks "like her." Gazing at her own image and sucking in her breath, she whispers to her reflection, "I think she's fabulous."

We are treated to plenty of scenes like the one at a secret-society meeting in the girls' lounge, where the camera pulls back to a medium shot of Katherine, smack in the center of a cluster of adoring young women who are drinking in every word that comes out of her lipstick-liberated mouth. And despite the treacly final scene where Katherine's formerly most hostile student races after the teacher, tears in her eyes and graduation gown billowing behind her, the film does offer a window—however overidealized—into the process by which desire inspires learning, and vice versa.

This transformation, from desire for a person to desire for knowledge, keeps teaching rewarding and learning passionate. And while this transference of teacherly temptation onto text is most familiar in our cultural imagery when the father/lover role coalesces in the body of the male teacher, an erotic pedagogy—where sublimation leads to scholarship—between a female teacher and her students is not yet impossible. Perhaps in the best of student-centered classrooms, men and women together would pick apart the following lines from "Elegy for Jane" where Roethke describes his beloved's temper: "Oh, when she was sad, she cast herself down into such a pure depth, / Even a father could not find her." Maybe they'd conclude that she's not for fathers to find or a student/daughter to embody, but for all to study.

Holy Fratrimony

Male Bonding and the New Homosociality

Don Romesburg / SUMMER 2004

GAY MARRIAGE IS ALL OVER THE NEWS THESE DAYS, BUT YOU wouldn't know it in Middle-earth. There, Frodo and Sam, the youthful heroes of *Lord of the Rings*, enjoy a love story as big as an IMAX screen, declaring heartfelt devotions as loud as THX allows. But there's not necessarily anything gay about it.

All over the small screen, men are similarly affectionate, swapping commitments and even trying on pants together. On *Queer Eye for the Straight Guy*, straight men weep over the new intimacies they share with gay men (to say nothing of all the free products). On two seasons of *Average Joe*, the Joes share fierce loyalties and trade confessions of childhood traumas, even mourning the loss of their rejected fellow Joes as if they were comrades and not competitors. What's going on?

While it may seem brand-spanking-new, this growing trend in popular culture is a revived form of old-school romantic male homosociality. What I'll call the New Homosociality is a window opened within mainstream popular culture that shines light on male emotional relationships that place neither sexuality nor—more crucially—its disavowal at their center. The intimacies of *Lord of the Rings'* Frodo and Sam (or, for that matter, Merry and Pippin) represent a kind of high point of such representations to date: These hobbits clearly love one another, and they openly express it through tearful proclamations of fidelity, long-term commitment, and soulful support—and the occasional gleeful pillow fight. The depth of their affection circumvents the whole gay/not gay question by employing a transcendent romantic bond that makes asking whether they're having sex superfluous. It's not the Love That Dare Not Speak Its Name. It's the Love That Needn't Bother.

Male affection that hinges on emotional connection rather than sexual passion is not without precedent. About a hundred years divide the New Homosociality from the Old Homosociality. In the nineteenth century, it wasn't uncommon for American men—especially white, middle-class ones—to enjoy mutually tender, desiring, emotionally expressive relationships. They would write letters pledging their eternal love and snuggle together through long winter nights. (The correspondence of young Abraham Lincoln and his companion Joshua Fry Speed serves as a key example.) Numerous scholars, from the historian Jeffrey Richards to the literary critic Robert Martin, have found evidence of these male romances in everyday life and literary works. Such nineteenth-century men considered women marginal to this deep male bonding: Though marriage was a social duty to fulfill and an opportunity for heterosexual companionship and procreation, it often marked the end of a special period of men's lives in which they shared their greatest love with one another.

These affairs sometimes did and sometimes did not involve sex; the emotional style of the era placed not sex but love, in the most romantic and even transcendent sense, at the center of male emotional relationships. As Jonathan Ned Katz puts it in his 2001 book, *Love Stories: Sex Between Men Before Homosexuality*, "The universe of intimate friendship was, ostensibly, a world of spiritual feeling. The radical Christian distinction between mind and body located the spiritual and carnal in different spheres. So hardly anyone then asked, Where does friendship end and sodomy begin?"

In such a system of feeling and gender, Old Homosociality provided intimate shelter for all sorts of male relationships. Because sexuality in the twentieth-century sense—sexual desire, urges, anxieties—was not yet generally assumed to be at the heart of all emotional relationships, men could openly admire one another's physical beauty, express deep feeling and longing, and even be physically intimate without having to affirm or deny the "gayness" of such interactions.

You can see this kind of comfortable male-on-male emotional and physical proximity in hundred-year-old photographs (so popular on eBay these days) of strapping young men draped all over each other. To our present sensibilities, these photos provoke questions about the nature of such intimacy: Was it homosexual? Was it erotic? But our modern queries sort of miss the point. Whether or not the relationships were sexual, the emotional affection at their center existed entirely apart from the sinful, marginalizing concepts of sodomy, buggery, crimes against nature, and mutual onanism.

All that changed gradually during the late nineteenth and early twentieth centuries, as sexologists, psychologists, and popular culture redefined love in terms of its connection to concepts like sex drive and libido. Throughout the twentieth century, the modernization of sexuality has asserted that lust and love come from the same wellspring, with eros driving feeling. Consequently, over the past century, our culture has come to view practically all same-sex emotional expression as something that can be perceived to have some sexual basis. This has structured our interactions with one another and transformed the meanings of male relationships past and present by placing sexuality and/or its disavowal at their core.

Nowhere is this more obvious than in pop culture, where gay-baiting and sight gags have long been a staple of movies, TV shows, and music videos. Think of the nervous heterosexual resolution of *Rebel Without a Cause* (1955), which required Sal Mineo's character to die in order to bolster James Dean's heterosexual commitment to Natalie Wood; the incessant fag jokes in the 1980s *Porky's* franchise that reassured audiences that the intimacies of the main characters were just the palling around of ordinary guys; and the slapstick disgust and nausea experienced by Jim Carrey upon accidentally kissing a man in *Ace Ventura: Pet Detective* (1994), to name but a few. But of late, media representations in which intimacy between men can be pure and fierce without compulsively refusing sexual overtones are starting to look a lot more interesting.

Bravo's *Queer Eye for the Straight Guy* became a breakout hit in part because it presents same-sex affection that conforms simultaneously to ideas of both "gay" and "not gay." The Fab Five's desire for their straight male Eliza Doolittle can be articulated openly because it is assumed to be secondary to their more egalitarian relationship with the guy: Despite cheeky references to rimming and glory holes, they care about helping their charge achieve a very straight goal, such as a traditionally romantic marriage proposal, far more than they care about making out with him. The guy, in turn, comforted by the Five's openness, rarely feels compelled to qualify his affection toward them.

In a different way, the Joes of *Average Joe* I and II bond in the face of the pretty, popular boys who are their competition for the bachelorette's affection. Their nurturing closeness is freed from the burden of proving their heterosexuality—since they're all courting the same beautiful woman—and is distinctly New Homosocial. The Joes work together in competitions of tug-of-war and dodgeball against the hunks, vying not just for dates with the bachelorette but also, by extension, a chance to stay together longer. When Joes get kicked off, they frequently lament the end of their time cohabiting with the guys and often express that they'll miss not the girl but their fellow Joes. Some of the hunks use gay-baiting tactics to suggest that the Joes' mutual support, along with their already nerdy and thus compromised masculinity, marks them as sissies, not man enough to have the girl. The Joes, on the other hand, often embrace their fondness for one another without fretting (at least visibly) over any sexual implications.

Our Buddies, Ourselves?

In popular culture, male affection keenly aware of its possible sexual undercurrent plays out with some predictability in the forms of buddies, the father-son couple, and the brotherly couple. None of these can really be considered an exploration of the New Homosociality, which promises to be something quite different. Still, they are worth reviewing here to better display their contrast from the new style.

The buddy relationship plays out archetypally in the pairings of Mel Gibson and Danny Glover in the *Lethal Weapon* franchise and Will Smith and Martin Lawrence in the *Bad Boys* movies. It is aware of its own homoerotic overtones and so becomes a contest of sarcastic wit, masculine feats, and heterosexual side interests. Buddies flirt with their deeply felt affection and loyalty to each other even as they mock its seriousness.

The recent *Starsky & Hutch* movie attempts to satirize this genre, playing up the former adversaries' budding romance with a montage of couple-type activities: running on the beach together, wearing matching clothes, and tucking each other into bed. Once their partnership hits the skids, a postbreakup scene finds them trying unsuccessfully to find happiness alone doing things they used to do together. Ultimately, though, because the movie is so self-aware of its winking proximity to gayness—director Todd Phillips even described the film as "a love story between two straight men"—the joke undercuts its own attempt at subversion. Overly concerned with its hetero-sexuality, it ends up looking akin to frat boys who dress in drag and then spend the whole night groping their own fake boobs. Still, it's interesting how even predictable twentieth-century representations of male affection such as the buddy film now strive to accommodate some facet of New Ho-mosociality. *Starsky & Hutch*, like "metrosexuality," seeks to accessorize itself with only the surface aspects of queer male self-presentation as a means of shoring itself up against more radical implications. By expanding the depth of emotional ties while toning down—but retaining—sexual disavowals and buttressed masculinities, the buddy genre can feel fresh, rather than just being another helping of the same stale crap.

In paternalistic buddy relationships, any potential homoeroticism is re-fused (or at least downplayed) by the resemblance of the partnership to that of father and son. In *Lord of the Rings*, the white-bearded wizard Gandalf has this type of deep, protective love for just about all the fellows in the Fel-lowship, and the four young male hobbits in particular. The wizard never falters in the desexualization of his paternalism.

Another popular representation is fraternity. Brotherly love is a lot like buddy love: Both involve some degree of antagonism mixed in with affec-tion. Fraternity, however, often treads more closely to unironic sentimental-ity, because the presumed familial ties inoculate it from sexual desire. Slash fiction aside, the relationships between *Star Trek*'s Captain Kirk and Dr. Mc-Coy or *Star Wars*' Han Solo and Luke Skywalker seem fraternal; they are gentle, nurturing, and affectionate, as well as competitive and sarcastic.

Although some may disagree, the relationships of the men on *Friends* can be understood as a mixture of buddy and fraternal male affection rather than New Homosociality. Chandler and Joey's companionship in particular has al-ways flirted with gay undertones, and they've pushed the boundaries of straight male emotional expression, physical closeness, and cohabitation. Longtime roommates, they are tender, jealous of others' affections for their companions, and occasionally read as gay in their intentions and outcomes. Their anxiety about all this suggests their awareness of potential unconscious homosexuality as well as their need to police it. Their fixation on the sexual and on perceptions of an affiliation of their desires or actions with gayness indicates their cognizance of taboo and transgression. This places them just outside the New Homosociality—they spend too much time disavowing.

What's New About the New Homosociality?

Despite one hundred years of centering sexuality, traces of Old Homosociality have remained in popular culture. When they resurface in new contexts, however, they have different meanings and implications. So it was that J. R. R. Tolkien, writing about Frodo and Sam in the 1950s, could describe another world, one where old-school romantic homosociality could still exist without being pathologized as either conscious or latent homosexuality. In the early years of the twenty-first century, Peter Jackson's *Lord of the Rings* trilogy could, remarkably, do the same, despite a culture filled with gay this, straight that, and queer the other. Other glimmers of deep homosociality have, remarkably, appeared in pop culture over the years, despite gay anxieties: In the classic 1927 silent film *Wings*, for example, World War I pilot buddies Jack and David share a deeply affectionate relationship, complete with a tender kiss during David's tragic death scene. It is so loving that Vito Russo read it as subtextually gay in *The Celluloid Closet* (1981). More than five decades later, Francis Ford Coppola's 1983 film version of S. E. Hinton's *The Outsiders* has a truly tender and unapologetic scene in which Ponyboy recites poetry to Johnny without any self-conscious snickering or arm punching to temper the scene's almost gooey sentimentality.

These examples, as well as the televised reality spectacles mentioned above, aren't evidence of some postgay move beyond identity categories. Everyone in the New Homosociality can claim or be claimed by whatever labels there are. The queer eyes and their straight guys, for example, all have presumably fixed sexual identities—that's the show's gimmick. They are still able to hug, pat, confess, and emote without commentary about whether or not such expressions are "gay." This works because the main tie is a romantic rather than a sexual one. The open, breezy sexuality seems to free the interaction from sexual obsessions: How can there be gay subtext if it's all out in the open? This is what sets the New Homosociality apart from either twentieth- or nineteenth-century male affective forms.

There are any number of reasons why this new version of homosociality is emerging now. Over the last decade or so, the rapid mainstreaming of gay culture has, paradoxically, made male bonding less directly tied to sex. The brouhaha surrounding gay marriage has been profoundly desexualizing for gays: Despite being an ostensibly civic debate about rights, it has really been, of course, a cultural debate over how society imagines gay relationships. Although procreation and the protection of property and bloodlines have historically been the major reasons for marriage, the idea of romantic love and partnership has been the primary component of the cultural institution, particularly in the past hundred years. When the marriage model is open to homosexual couplings, same-sex intimacy in general seems less about gay sex and more about the emotional connections and responsibility that are assumed in straight marriages.

At the same time, popular representations of gay culture have been, like gay culture itself, teaching all kinds of men how to stop fixating on gay sex. Even *Queer As Folk*, which touts itself as sexually provocative, has any number of gay male relationships that don't have homosexual desire (or, clearly, its disavowal) at their core. The friendship of romantic, flamboyant Emmett and down-to-earth Michael, for example, is frequently loving and tender. While sexuality is certainly acknowledged—they know about each other's pickups, swap sex stories, and even recognize each other's attractiveness—their interaction is primarily about their emotional bond and its tensions. The sexual component is just, well, sex. It would seem that mainstream culture is also beginning to recognize, following the examples of gay men, that just because sex is part of a bond does not make it the obsessive center of that relationship. And the related implication of this realization is that all affection between men needn't be overly concerned with homosexual and feminizing inferences.

A more slapstick example of refusing the centrality of sex occurs, improbably enough, in the 2000 film *Dude, Where's My Car?* Take the scene in which the titular dudes, Jesse and Chester, sit in their car at a stoplight, while one car over is Fabio and his girlfriend. A brief competition ensues: Fabio revs his engine; Jesse revs his. Fabio puts his arm around his female companion; Jesse puts his arm around Chester. Fabio makes out with the woman; Jesse makes out with Chester. Clearly, Fabio cannot top this. Victorious in their one-upmanship, the dudes drive off to their next big adventure.

What's most remarkable about this scene is not its explicit homoeroticism—although that's well worth remarking upon. Rather, it's the difference between this exchange and the bond between previous dudes, like Bill and Ted of *Bill & Ted's Excellent Adventure* (1989) or Wayne and Garth of *Wayne's World* (1992), that suggests something new. Both buddy sets enact the aforementioned hug-then-back-awkwardly-away move—a moment of transgression that reveals perhaps too much about the homosexual undertones of their relationship. Like buddies and daddies and brothers everywhere, those dudes disclaim desire. Chester and Jesse, on the other hand, have every sign of a New Homosocial relationship. Their connection supersedes its potential sexuality; the dudes do not have to disavow their homosexual desire for each other, and not because they have girlfriends but because their desire for each other isn't sexual at all—it's romantic, sentimental, and playful.

The innovation of Jesse and Chester's emotional tie has provoked a number of cultural critics to explore its deeper social meaning. In recent conference talks, queer scholar Judith Halberstam has been exploring the fin de siècle position of the dude figure in pop culture. She argues persuasively that films like *Bill & Ted* and *Dude* mark the recent widespread popularity of the "dude," that is, the stupid white guy. He represents a particularly contemporary American sensibility, in which his identity remains stable in a universe of mixed time/space realities and racial, gender, and sexual slippages and blurrings, where, as Halberstam notes, "Anything goes (as long as everything stays the same)." The adventures of the dudes, she suggests, who can go anywhere, do anything, and yet claim accountability for nothing, are a powerful cultural trope in light of U.S. imperialism and, especially, the leadership of President George W. Bush.

Halberstam's analysis is important, because it's tempting to imagine that the New Homosociality is somehow more liberating or unencumbered than twentieth-century forms of male affection. Jesse and Chester's New Homosociality seems to spring organically from their white adolescent dudeness. As such, it privileges their style of romantic homosociality over other more labored or "unnatural" forms. (Gay men, for example, are caricatured in the film as overly styled and cartoonishly muscled Swedish homosexuals—who, as if to prove their inauthenticity, end up being aliens.)

Homo Saviors

Halberstam argues that because they never seem to get anywhere or do anything, dudes live in a time/space loop in which they never have to grow up and thus are freed from accountability. I'm suggesting a different reading: *Dude, Where's My Car?* implies that Chester and Jesse are on the cusp of responsibility and will eventually grow up and move on to primary relationships with women; with the burdens of maturity, their homosociality will gradually either drift away or transform into a more typical male friendship. The heteronormative logic of contemporary culture, in other words, overwhelms the internal logic of the film.

Situational homosociality like Jesse and Chester's is mirrored in reality television like *Queer Eye* and *Average Joe*. On *Average Joe*, the bonds between the men can't last forever; in the end, it's back to the boy and the girl. Moreover, in *Average Joe: Adam Returns*, former Joe Adam Mesh, the last one jilted in season one, becomes the bachelor choosing from female suitors. His old Joe companions are pressed into service to find a girlfriend for him in a variety of degrading settings, from ogling bikini models in Las Vegas to searching out his mate "scientifically," using database formulas for compatibility. Over on *Queer Eye*, most weeks the gays help the guy in order to get the girl. The boys' relationship can be affectionate in part because it is so temporary—the romance between the gay men and the straight guy ends when the episode does, replaced with good old heterosexuality. Nothing illustrates this better than the reunion shows, when the guys bring their female companions to visit the gays.

Back in Middle-earth, even Frodo and Sam can truly revel in their homosociality only while away from home. Distinct from the more fraternal, paternal, or buddy relationships of the other characters (like hunky would-be king Aragorn and dreamy elf Legolas), Frodo and Sam's affection while on the road is unabashedly loving, deep, physical, and emotive. Even so, in *Return of the King*, the trilogy's final film, lingering masculine sexual anxiety is pressing enough to demand forty cumbersome minutes of heterosexual resolution. All three times I saw the movie, the audience assumed that the end was going to be the Dorothy-back-in-Kansas moment in which Frodo awakes from his ring-weary exhaustion to find he is in his own bed back in the Shire with all his male companions surrounding him. Sam's entrance into the scene, followed by the soft-focus, slow-motion meaningful eye contact, hugging, and pillow fight, seems like the tale's conclusion. But that scene is almost directly followed by Sam's wedding to local barmaid Rosie. And of course, once Sam marries Rosie, Frodo is literally shipped off into the sunset.

An effect of this New Homosociality seems to be that women, pushed to the margins of these apparently progressive male relationships, find themselves represented in predictably boring ways—nag, supporter, sexy sidekick, mother, wife. In *Return of the King*, the men's romantic world only cursorily includes women. Poor Rosie seems to do little more than smile and reproduce. Even the powerful female elves, Arwen and Galadriel, are reduced to whispering cryptic messages and declarations of eternal heterosexual love. The women on *Queer Eye*, meanwhile, appear contained in a separate sphere as talking heads against a white, featureless backdrop.

So the question remains: How potentially progressive is this new (that is, old-as-new-again) form of male bonding in popular culture? Despite its current position either as dudelike global access to privilege without accountability or as situational and conditioned upon the marginalization of women, we should be enthusiastically cautious about the New Homosociality. Pushing sexuality away from the center of male relationships opens up different ways of defining and understanding sexuality and gender. If sex isn't the biggest game in town, it promises to become just one factor among others in appreciating the bonds we form and those that we reject. For all people, this holds some possibility for reducing the violence done in the name of sexuality and its refusals. Dare we dream of a New Heterosociality?

5

· · · · · · · · · · ·

Domestic
Arrangements

WOMEN HOLD UP HALF THE SKY, AS THE SLOGAN ONCE WENT,
but we also, historically, hold down the fort. Since the concept of an "angel
in the house" took hold in Victorian times, Western culture has elevated the
image of woman as domestic goddess while consistently undervaluing, if
not just plain denigrating, the actual content of domestic work—a contradiction that has often made, in the modern age, for major antagonism between the so-called female realm and the actual living, breathing women
who occupy it.

Okay, so you probably wouldn't know that from watching an average set
of television commercials on any given network in any given prime-time
slot. Check out this woman who's cheerfully scrubbing out the toilet while
her children and golden retriever look on. Man, she looks happy. Here's another woman practically speaking in tongues because she's so thrilled that
her dishwashing detergent doesn't leave spots on the glassware. Like Vanna
White on a letter-turning bender, she runs her fingers ecstatically down the
side of a glass in close-up. And sweet fancy Moses, here's a woman who is
apparently so taken by the new Swiffer duster that she's dancing, dancing
in her Mom Jeans, around a home that's not even hers. That's right—this
cleaning gadget is so incredibly unputdownable that this woman is fanati-
cally dusting a house where the dirt's not even her responsibility.

TV commercials have remained the one constant of angel-in-the-house propaganda through the years, staying bright-eyed and smiling even as more complicated truths about housework, "women's work," and happiness have been revealed through other cultural channels. The stereotype of the 1950s housewife as a satisfied homemaker cradled in the bosom of her shiny chrome appliances was stripped bare by *The Feminine Mystique*; the frantic underbelly of housewifery was exposed by movies (*Diary of a Mad Housewife, Pleasantville*), books (*Up the Sandbox, The Stepford Wives, The Ice Storm*), TV (*Desperate Housewives*), even music (the Rolling Stones' "Mother's Little Helper"). But the happy, fulfilled homemakers of commercials and print ads still remain as evidence that even though we've seen women rebelling, in real life and in pop culture, against domestic imperatives, the idea of home and hearth as an intrinsically female realm has never been sufficiently challenged by popular culture. (No, *Mr. Mom* does not count.)

There's an idea floating around out there that a revolution occurred sometime during the heyday of second-wave feminism, a moment of collective consciousness when women flung down their aprons and dustpans and, like *Network*'s Howard Beale, announced that they were mad as hell and weren't going to take it anymore. Then they streamed out of suburban houses en masse and, perhaps led by Gloria Steinem herself, flooded the wood-paneled hallways of corporate America, never to return to the drudgery of domesticity. This didn't actually happen—or at least it didn't happen that way. For one thing, the choice between working inside the home or outside of it is a fairly modern development enjoyed only by middle- and upper-class women; it's long been meaningless to women who never had the economic option not to work. For another, married or partnered women who worked outside the home invariably kept working when they got home, taking on what sociologist Arlie Hochschild called "the second shift" in her book of the same name—all the cooking, cleaning, and child care that was still expected of women even if it wasn't their paid work.

The idea has always been that women inherently *want* domesticity, and the media is quick to report facts and figures that support this notion. In 2000, for example, a study by the market-research firm Youth Intelligence found that of three thousand married and single women between the ages of eighteen and thirty-four, 68 percent said they would opt to live a domestic life if it were economically feasible; that same year, *Cosmopolitan* revealed that of eight hundred women polled by the magazine, two-thirds would choose to be a full-time housewife rather than a worker bee. More recently, *The New York Times* has been tireless in running "trend" stories trumpeting the desire of Ivy League–educated women for good old-fashioned house-wifery; though the stories themselves (Lisa Belkin's 2003 article "The Opt-Out Revolution" and Louise Story's 2005 "news" item "Many Women at Elite Colleges Set Career Path to Motherhood") have been widely criticized for overly anecdotal and sloppy methodology, the fact that the paper is so eager to make them front-page news says it all.

A slew of "new domesticity" coverage in the media accompanied Cheryl Mendelson's exhaustive 1999 homemaking guidebook *Home Comforts: The Art and Science of Keeping House* as it ascended bestseller lists alongside other happy-home tomes like Nigella Lawson's *How to Be a Domestic Goddess*. The shelter-magazine category has exploded all over the newsstand, with the high-end (*Wallpaper, Domino*) shoulder to shoulder with the slick but DIY (*ReadyMade*).

This is not to say that there's no interrogation of all this domesticity going on. Indeed, there's a ton of it. Motherhood in particular has been under the cultural microscope for the past several years, as the subject of media debates over gay mothers, stay-at-home vs. working mothers, public breast-feeding vs. putting those things away, and fertility treatments vs. adoption machinations. How we mother, how the media thinks we should mother, and how it's nobody's damn business how we mother have been the subjects of incisive and thoughtful books by the likes of Judith Warner (*Perfect Madness*), Susan J. Douglas and Meredith Michaels (*The Mommy Myth*), and many more. Still, for all the hand-wringing that goes on about mothering, one could argue that such attention just won't be as helpful as it could be until there's a correspondingly in-depth media look at equally crucial parenting topics—stories, for instance, on fathers' roles in the work/parenting balance, on foster parenting, on the effects of domestic violence on the children who live with it, and on gay and/or transgendered parents as more than just novelties. And a true conversation on the changing roles of women and domesticity—as opposed to the sensationalized woman-abandons-home! salvos launched by the likes of *Time* and *Newsweek*—would also require an acknowledgment of our corporate culture and its resoundingly unsupport-ive policies on child care, flextime, and other family-conscious necessities.

On the more generally domestic tip, feminist magazines like *Bust* and websites like GetCrafty and Not Martha have called for a new revolution on the home front, positing that the reclamation of domesticity is, in fact, a worthy feminist project. Jean Railla, editor of GetCrafty, writes in the introduction to her book of the same name, "I'm not suggesting that every woman should enjoy knitting and cooking and embroidery. But I am suggesting that we give women's work its props as something valuable, interesting, and important . . . Skill, love, and creativity go into creating a nice home, making things by hand, and raising children. It's not stupid and it's not easy; it's damn hard work that we need to respect. Moreover, it's our history, and dismissing it only doubles the injustice already done to women who didn't have any choice but to be domestic in the first place."

And then, of course, there's Martha. Fearsome, scandalous, contagiously domestic Martha Stewart, who has knocked the stereotype of the docile homemaker on its aproned rump even as her bruised-but-not-broken empire continues to make bank off its tenets. Martha, in fact, was one of the first domestic icons *Bitch* tackled back in the day (and you'll find our 1996 take on page 221): Back then, prescandal and before she accumulated quite as much powerful-woman baggage as her iconhood carries today, she was a quintessential example of pop culture's mixed messages about women, domesticity, and satisfaction. Her work and her public image played as much on fears that women who are too self-sufficient are doomed to remain alone as on women's anxieties about not being "good enough" at supposedly innate domestic tasks.

Whether you're a chicken-raising, wreath-making dynamo or a woman who can't boil an egg, the home front is endlessly evolving and endlessly complicated. We know that there are far more women struggling with how to reconcile their personal choices with domestic imperatives than there are shiny, happy detergent-commercial denizens, and it's always been *Bitch*'s pleasure to hear their stories.   —A.Z.

The Paradox of Martha Stewart

Goddess, Desperate Spouse-Seeker, or Feminist Role Model?

Jennifer Newens / FALL 1996

MARTHA STEWART: WHAT TO DO WITH HER?

Marry her off, says the mainstream media. Her single status is just too darn confusing. How can she be America's favorite housewife if she's not a wife at all? Perhaps people are so obsessed with Stewart's singlehood because she makes her fortune by performing the tasks that were once reserved for stay-at-home wives in conventional heterosexual marriages. No one can admit that her activities really aren't those of a housewife, because that would mean radically re-viewing what it means to be a housewife—and by extension, what it means to be feminine. But because her power stems directly from the feminized realm of homemaking and decoration, she can't be explained away as a masculinized female. So how does the mainstream media resolve this paradox? Not by questioning traditional notions of femininity or anything as potentially progressive as that, but by drawing attention away from how Martha Stewart has used housewifely duties to build an empire and instead focusing on her lack of a husband. From highbrow intellectualized fare like *60 Minutes* to trashy supermarket tabloids like the *Globe*, from the "male" perspective to the "female"—everyone wants to get her hitched. Not coincidentally, the two sides come to the same conclusions, but for different reasons.

60 Minutes represents the "masculine" viewpoint: Unless she is married, Stewart's power cannot be considered legitimate and must be denied.

She needs a man to make her less threatening—but she's a woman with too many masculine qualities, so men don't find her desirable. The *Globe*'s typically "feminine" perspective, on the other hand, portrays her as someone who cannot possibly be happy without a man by her side, but whose tendency to dominate sends men running to more feminine candidates. A photo gallery of possible Mr. Rights makes Stewart seem hysterical, searching desperately but fruitlessly for a meaningful relationship.

60 MINUTES' TAKE ON STEWART IS ESSENTIALLY CONTRADIC- tory. Interviewer Morley Safer acknowledges Stewart's power, describing her as a "multimedia corporation bringing in something like $200 million a year, probably the only one-woman, one-person conglomerate."

But simultaneously, he practically denies her very existence, repeatedly referring to her as an otherworldly icon. Rather than talk about who she actually is—a driven, committed woman who works hard and achieves big— he calls her a "goddess," an "image," a "symbol." He talks of her as if she were a queen, going "out to meet the multitudes." If we're not paying attention, we might mistake Safer's regal words for compliments. But symbols and images are not real people with real achievements and real power. Queens these days are merely figureheads, like the trophy wives of wealthy businessmen and politicians. Goddesses are passive objects of worship. Using a trope that's analogous to the treatment of many wives in traditional marriage relationships, Safer puts Stewart up on that pedestal of femininity, the place where women have historically been contained under the guise of admiration.

And even though he acknowledges her media power, he mocks her status and suggests that her business savvy is just something that makes it harder for her to find (or keep) a man. He says that "she neglects to mention the perfect husband, Andy Stewart, a publisher, who became imperfect and left her after twenty-nine years of marriage." Poor Martha! he implies. All alone. And she tried to hide it from us, too. (Oh, is there some rule in the Morley Safer universe that requires people to recount painful episodes in their lives during interviews?) Throughout the interview, Safer persistently refers to the negative facets of Stewart's personality, perhaps as a way of explaining why she couldn't keep her marriage together—and has been unable to remarry since. Some examples he cites are her "bossiness," "humorless[ness]," and "overpowering neatness." Also, the fact that she "doesn't abide frivolous activities" (read: doesn't like to have fun), observers are "driven up the wall" by her perfection, "there's no separation in her life," and "wherever Martha goes, Martha's agenda must be kept." (By the way, why does Morley insist on calling Stewart by her first name? In every other piece on that particular night's program, the male subjects are referred to by their surnames.)

So her power is both unreal and the root of all her problems. Because of her position she's a symbol, but the very concrete drive and skills that got her to the top send men scurrying to the hills. She may make a lot of money, but everyone hates her. She'd better refine her subservient-female act, says the subtext. But she seems to be doing just fine. She's happy with her life: with her career, with her single status, with her own perfectionism. But Morley Safer's not really paying attention to that little bit of info. It would interfere with his "reporting."

The final minutes of the piece only serve to cement the let's-get-Martha-married ethos. "Can such a woman find true happiness?" queries Safer, as if true happiness can be found only in a conventional male-female pairing. "Is there a George waiting for our Martha?" We couldn't be more battered by his point if he applied it with a sledgehammer, but just in case we missed it, Safer spells it out with his metaphor: If Martha Stewart is America's first lady, then she's quite literally nothing without a man by her side. (Bonus insult: throwing in a reference to the one job that women still can't have in this country.)

60 Minutes' masculine message: A woman without a man is somehow not a legitimate woman; a woman who takes traditional femininity and forges masculine power from it is scary and threatening. Martha Stewart is all of the above, so she must be lonely and bitter, without the "true happiness" that would come from a straight marriage.

A BANNER AT THE TOP OF THE TABLOID RAG THE *GLOBE* ADvertises what it thinks people standing in line at the grocery store want to read: "Martha Stewart's Desperate Search for Mr. Right." The tabloid concurs with *60 Minutes*' theory that Stewart needs to get married and fast, but for different reasons. Unlike Morley Safer, who reveals that others are uncomfortable with her single status, the *Globe*'s Candace Trunzo focuses much more on the emotional life of Stewart herself, rather than on an outside opinion of it. Also in contrast to the *60 Minutes* piece, there's no mention here of the self-made media force Stewart has become. Since the article focuses on her as a woman, not as a person, her accomplishments are rendered irrelevant. The reporter takes for granted that her readers worship Stewart and lures them into a discussion of why her life isn't happy and fulfilled. The reader, therefore, becomes concerned about Stewart and empathizes with her plight. Rather than seeing her power as a threat, the *Globe* sees it as an impediment to her own happiness. Trunzo insinuates that Stewart can't have a satisfactory life unless she has someone at home to nurture—and she won't find someone unless she stops being so ambitious and becomes more, well, womanly.

The *Globe* quotes Stewart on the breakup of her marriage: "I never thought this would happen to me . . . Maybe I didn't spend enough time polishing [my husband's] shoes." Trunzo uses this to validate her own thesis that Martha Stewart should strive to be more feminine (read: slavish and willing to coddle a man) in order to get remarried, but—hello in there—do you think Stewart was being sarcastic? Just maybe? I can see the headlines now: "Top Marriage Secrets Revealed! Shoe Polish! Turn to Page Three!"

Trunzo also depicts Stewart as an airheaded socialite who frequents trendy Manhattan restaurants with a never-ending stream of gentlemen. "Since her nasty divorce from Andy Stewart in 1991," explains the reporter, "Martha, 54, has been playing the field with a stable of men—and fielding the plays from prospective suitors to keep them at arm's length, say pals." The purposeful mention of her age here reinforces the urgency Stewart, and a reader who finds herself in the same circumstance, must feel at being single at such an advanced age. That "stable of men" must be made up of potential grooms, right?—because a fifty-four-year-old single woman could never just have some male friends.

The *Globe*, like *60 Minutes*, assumes that Stewart's career negatively affects her private life. Trunzo quotes a New York psychotherapist who claims to know why Stewart hasn't married again: "She's an ambitious woman who may only become involved with men who can further her career." The therapist implies either that Stewart is acting like a man might—seeking a trophy husband to make her look good in the public eye—and, since she's not a man, having no success, or she's looking for some guy in publishing or TV to help her out. The shrink conveniently ignores the fact that Stewart's career doesn't need any furthering—she's done just fine on her own. We're also treated to an oh-so-psychologically-sound theory about why men might not want to marry Stewart: She "may be a control freak who likes to do things her way. Publicly, she doesn't seem to exude that warmth and caring nature men enjoy."

The *Globe*'s feminine message: A woman cannot be happy without a man to validate her existence. Men don't marry women who display masculine characteristics and/or are more powerful than they are. (Here, the *Globe*'s perspective carries over into the assumption that no man wants an achieving wife.) Therefore, if you want to be married—and of course you do—try your damnedest not to make $200 million a year and try to be sweet, gracious, and meek. Otherwise, you'll end up lonely and bitter. Gee, what's a woman to do?

ISN'T THERE ANOTHER WAY TO LOOK AT THIS? DESPITE THE gripping analysis by these two media giants, it seems that Martha Stewart is a woman who's better off unmarried. Only after trying and "failing" at a traditional marriage was she able to successfully infiltrate traditional male power centers and become a prosperous and powerful media force. Even Morley Safer admits it; he notes that the breakup of her marriage "was just about the time Martha Stewart became Martha Stewart." Divorce, it seems, has been good to her. Yes, she's rumored to be a bitch: She's impulsive, insulting, and demanding, and she takes credit for other people's work. But even if we believe the buzz, it just means that she's doing the same things men have always done—and gotten away with.

Even though some see her as the ultimate feminine überwoman, a cook, decorator, and hostess-with-the-mostest, Martha Stewart may also be the ultimate feminist antihousewife. Why? She demonstrates that a woman's existence does not need to be justified, completed, or otherwise muddled by a conventional heterosexual marriage. The timing of her success even suggests that marriage is bad for women.

Furthermore, Stewart's empire brings a little refinement and allure to the chores previously deemed excruciating to the homemaker. Married women, as everyone knows, are not the only people who perform these tasks. She shows her fans—male, female, straight, gay, married, or single— that daily household tasks can be enjoyable, and maybe even a little glamorous. So why not let Martha Stewart be an example to all of us lured by the notion that marriage is a requirement for a happy and fulfilled life? If we're paying attention, we can all learn something other than the proper way to vacuum.

Double Life

Everyone Wants to See Your
Breasts—Until Your Baby Needs Them

Lisa Moricoli Latham / FALL 2002

FROM EARLIEST PUBERTY, A WOMAN MUST FACE THE PUBLIC nature of two of her most personal body parts. Trading in her cotton undershirt for a training bra is only the beginning: Between strap-snapping classmates, sadistic bra salesladies who insist on leaving the fitting-room door ajar, and relatives who chuckle over how she's grown, the first growing pain is the start of a lifelong push-and-pull between the public and the private appearance of a woman's breasts. From then on, cleavage depth, shirt transparency, bra-strap show-through, and nipple outlines are a daily concern—and that's not even getting into the unsolicited daily commentary a woman's breasts receive on the street, on the bus, and at the office.

But when the advent of motherhood transforms a woman's breasts once again, she is caught in an even deeper and more troubling conflict between the private and the public breast. From *Playboy* to the St. Pauli Girl, American culture declares that while breasts as a signifier of available sexuality should be flaunted, breasts doing the job nature assigned them are taboo. Right when a woman needs her breasts the most, she's told to cover up and move on.

The antagonism between the sexual and the working breast arises almost as soon as a woman discovers that she's pregnant. Publicly apparent changes such as substantial—even alarming—breast growth early in pregnancy increase the visual allure of breasts while, at the same time, private changes like tenderness and pain significantly decrease their actual potential to offer sexual pleasure to their owner.

In a culture where men on the street feel free to comment on the ta-tas of otherwise anonymous passersby, it follows that friends and relatives of a pregnant woman are unlikely to hold their peace when new developments occur on her chest. Nearly every mother I know has gotten a repeat dose of adolescent embarrassment early in her pregnancy with remarks like "My, how you've grown (again)!" which pretend to approve even as they seek to humiliate. Even more annoying are winking variations on "Your husband must be thrilled," which are not merely impolite but reinforce the idea that a woman's breasts are somehow not her own.

Once her baby is born, a mother's rack becomes even less private. Strangers are prone to asking whether she's bottle- or breastfeeding her newborn. Breastfeeding puts a mother's breasts out in public even more, because sooner or later, she'll need to feed her baby around other people. And while Americans gladly tolerate extensive sexual displays of cleavage, we demand that nursing breasts stay completely hidden—an impossible task, especially for the mother new to nursing, given the sometimes gymnastic efforts she must undertake to teach a newborn to latch on properly. Trying to cover herself while struggling with a squirming, wobbly-necked neonate can be like fighting a cat inside a tent: not pretty, and liable to cause injury.

In *A History of the Breast*, the definitive source on all things mammarian, the historian Marilyn Yalom points out that even in notoriously buttoned-up Victorian times, women could breastfeed in church without notice or comment; these days, the merest sliver of lactating nipple can be less welcome than a public nosepicking. A baby's fumble to latch on can inspire friends and relatives to leap up and shield a nursing mother with coats and tablecloths, like she's an adolescent changing clothes at the beach. That this comic spectacle is supposedly less embarrassing than the possibility that someone might glimpse a patch of flesh somewhere beneath the folds of a lifted blouse indicates that a normalized working breast is far, far off.

Even television, our great cultural leveler, has only recently begun to explore the conflict between the sexual and the working breast—and it always seems to be resolved in favor of the sexual. HBO's womancentric touchstone *Sex and the City* found itself in a position of judgment when lead character Miranda had a baby. In one episode, Carrie spies Miranda's breasts as she tries in vain to nurse her newborn son. Carrie is visibly disturbed and looks everywhere but at the offending appendages before blurting out, "Oh my God, your breasts are *huge!*" She then admits with more than a hint of disgust that she was "totally unprepared" for the size of Miranda's nursing nipples and adds that she'll "have to find some sort of trauma counseling" to deal with the impact. For a character who checks men out head-to-toe in the show's title sequence, Carrie's reaction to a good friend's breastfeeding is a powerful demonstration of the shock—and indeed, betrayal—many feel when confronted with a working breast instead of the sexual one we're expecting.

Carrie's seemingly disproportionate discomfort mirrors that of our culture at large: Because we are so used to thinking of breasts as sexual, we are unable to conceive of anything breast-related as truly free from sexual overtones. Thus, puritanical disapproval becomes extreme when we are confronted with breasts in what can be argued is their most natural, decidedly nonsexual state. Nursing mothers are routinely kicked out of public places, harassed into covering up, and generally looked upon as deviants bent on an exhibitionist thrill, rather than mothers simply trying to feed their offspring. Publicly nursing a toddler or a preschooler is likely to subject a mother to accusations of child abuse. Even women who joyfully nursed babies will admonish, "When he's old enough to ask for it by name, he's too old to nurse," as if the comfort value of suckling (not to mention its continued immunological benefits) were confined to the preverbal child. Because toddlers can be nourished by other food, the logic goes, they should be, because any use of the breast beyond what's absolutely necessary must have a dubious sexual element.

Indeed, exposing the public to a nursing mother has become tantamount to exposing the public to sex. Lawyer Nancy Solomon, of the California Women's Law Center (CWLC), has represented nursing mothers who were told to stop breastfeeding in parks because "children might see" (never mind that a child was the one doing the nursing). In 1999, a Los Angeles woman sued Borders when she was kicked out of the chain store for nursing her baby. In June 2002, seventy mothers gathered for a nurse-in at the Santa Monica Place mall after a woman was harassed by a security guard for nursing.

The 1999 Right to Breastfeed Act, which guarantees a woman's right to breastfeed on federal property, was precipitated by several complaints about the National Gallery of Art in Washington, D.C. Although the gallery reverently houses paintings of the Madonna nursing the Christ child, several women were kicked out for nursing actual babies—an appropriate illustration of America's simultaneous veneration of and contempt for mothers' roles.

States still have their own policies on breastfeeding in public places, though, and it can make for some bizarre demonstrations of the either/or nature of the sexual and working breast. In one of CWLC's particularly galling cases, a patron at a restaurant in Las Vegas—a city whose nude revues make it the undisputed champion of the visible breast—was informed by the management (incorrectly, by the way) that breastfeeding a baby at the table constituted a health-code violation.

The cognitive disjunction between the sexual breast and the working breast amounts to a vicious circle: Without more acceptance of nursing breasts as normal and necessary, acceptably decorative breasts are ever more divorced from the reality of their nonsexual functions, and working mammaries remain, in public perception, stubbornly sexual and therefore not fit for the literal public consumption babies demand. CWLC's Solomon, who makes regular media appearances on breastfeeding issues, recalls appearing on a Los Angeles radio station discussing a nurse-in she helped coordinate. Callers' reactions to nursing in public varied, but one man's opinion—"If she were hot, it'd be okay"—showed a loud-and-clear tolerance for nursing only as long as it also carries sexual gratification for the witness.

Motherhood itself, however, is considered beyond sex, if not actually antisex; mothers and breasts must not be associated if breasts are to retain their ability to arouse. Coincident with a new mother's sudden, purely practical need of her breasts, our culture desexualizes her. (Just try, for instance, to find a sexy nursing bra in a marketplace that only recently began offering them in the most opaque black cotton.)

With all the breasts used to sell out there, it's also notable how few belong to pregnant or nursing mothers. The fact that maternal breasts don't have the kind of immediately understood currency of, say, those of a teenage model means that Americans can go their entire lives without seeing pregnant, nursing, or postchildbearing breasts depicted as either beautiful or sexual (for adults, not children)—and that does a disservice to the full spectrum of meaning contained in women's roles.

The problem is not the dual nature of our breasts but a cultural unwillingness to understand or accept that this nature is fluid. Men who ogle breasts on the street and grandparents who object to public nursing represent two sides of the same coin: Both confine breasts in public to the realm of sexuality and tolerate no alternatives. If more American women face down these naysayers and adjust the exclusivity of that confinement, who knows where the social advantages might end. Nursing bras that acknowledge that mothers don't lose their libido when they gain an offspring are a step in the right direction; more widespread respect for the reduced cancer rates and lower incidence of childhood ear infections that result from increased breastfeeding would be even more so. But the understanding that working breasts and their bearer's sexuality are decidedly separate yet need not be mutually exclusive, and the understanding that a woman's breasts in public are nobody's business but her own—and sometimes her baby's—will benefit all women, from pubescent girls to mothers of five, whether they choose to keep their breasts public, private, or a little of both.

Queer and Pleasant Danger

What's Up with the Mainstreaming of Gay Parents?

Margaret Price / FALL 2003

FIVE YEARS AGO, I WROTE AN INDIGNANT LETTER TO *THE NEW York Times Magazine* because it had just published a special issue on motherhood and had failed to include any representations of queer moms. Surely, I argued, in an entire issue they could have found space for just one nonstraight mom. Well, be careful what you wish for.

Now queer parents are all over the media: Custody disputes in Florida. Adoption documentaries on PBS and Cinemax. Smiling, sweaty dykes giving birth on *Friends* and *Queer As Folk*. And with the recent progress toward the legalization of gay marriage, we can expect even more queering of the crib in the months and years to come.

This surge of attention to queer parents mirrors a rise in actual numbers. According to the nonprofit Adoption Family Center, in 1976 there were only about five hundred thousand biological children of gay and lesbian parents. But by 2002, as noted by Suzanne Johnson and Elizabeth O'Connor in *The Gay Baby Boom: The Psychology of Gay Parenthood*, as many as fourteen million kids (biological, foster, and adoptive) have at least one gay or lesbian parent. In a 2001 *Washington Post* article headlined "Lesbians Find Haven in Suburbs," David Elliott of the National Gay and Lesbian Task Force says proudly, "We are indeed everywhere."

But who is this "we," and how are we represented? If you refer to available media images of queer parents, what do you see? I've spent the last couple of months reading magazines, searching the web, and watching in-numerable episodes of *Queer As Folk* on DVD. And from where I sit, it seems that queer parents—in both fictional and nonfictional representations—are an awfully Brady-like bunch. They're predominantly white, middle- or upper-class, and partnered; moreover, they usually don't push boundaries of gender or sexuality. For example, a *Washington Post* article headlined "Lesbians Find Haven in Suburbs" eagerly documents the ways one pair of lesbians are discovering their inner soccer moms: "They're active in the PTA of their daughter's school. They drive a minivan and help at block par-ties. Neighborhood children flock to the huge trampoline in their back-yard." Now, there's nothing diabolical about helping at block parties or having a trampoline, but the real point of the article seems to be to under-score what these moms are *not* doing: namely, shaking things up.

Queer parents tend to be portrayed in ways that play up their normativ-ity. "We're just like you" is the rallying cry—or, depending upon who's pro-ducing the images, "They're just like us." Author and columnist Dan Savage, who adopted a son with his partner, Terry, has commented on the pressure that's placed on queer parents to seem as uncontroversial as pos-sible. "Some [gays and lesbians] felt that Terry and I—young, urban types—weren't the 'right' kind of gay couple to be adopting," he explained in an online interview with ABC News. "They felt that, due to the political con-troversy surrounding gay men and lesbians adopting, that older, 'safer,' co-zier gay couples should adopt." Although in that interview Savage didn't elaborate on what "safer" and "cozier" might mean, he does say more in his 1999 book, *The Kid*, which details his and Terry's experience. One objec-tion came from a queer activist who argued, in Savage's words, that gay adoptive parents should be "men in their forties, together at least eight years, monogamous, professional, irreproachable, and unassailable." Dan and Terry failed to meet the specs of this hypervirtuous profile on a number of counts, particularly given Savage's career as a sex columnist. Writing about bondage and anal fisting, apparently, does not mix with parenting. Or isn't supposed to.

This conflict is familiar to many groups battling for civil rights: Is the best strategy to assimilate with mainstream culture, or to try to radicalize it? Often, the urge is to downplay difference and therefore avoid conflict. But the fact is, queer parenting is itself a paradox. It's both conventional and radical, a gesture toward joining mainstream culture and a way to transform it. The 2002 documentary *Daddy & Papa* sums up this perspective in the voice of Johnny, a gay man who adopts two sons with his partner: "My most revolutionary act would be the most traditional thing in the world."

Most media representations of queer parents eschew this paradox and emphasize the seemliness of their subjects. It's almost as if, having decided to focus on one freak factor, those shaping the stories feel compelled to keep everything else (race, class, gender, family structure, sexual practices) as bland and unremarkable as possible.

The parents in the Lifetime movie *What Makes a Family*, HBO's dyke drama *If These Walls Could Talk 2*, Showtime's *Queer As Folk*, the ubiquitous *Friends*, and the Cinemax documentary *He's Having a Baby* are, for instance, overwhelmingly Caucasian. And the problem goes beyond quantity and into quality: Most portrayals of queer parents not only underrepresent parents of color, they downplay the ways that race can complicate the lives and choices of queer parents and their kids. This deficiency is unnervingly apparent throughout the documentary *He's Having a Baby*, which follows a white father, Jeff Danis, as he adopts a Vietnamese son. Danis decides early in the film that he wants to adopt a child from abroad but fails to make a peep about the issues inherent in cross-cultural and cross-racial adoption. Instead, his concerns are shown to be shallow to the point of absurdity. To wit: "The pictures of kids from China and Guatemala were very cute," Danis reports, "but the one from Cambodia, the kid wasn't that cute. So I'm like, Oh, God, what if I don't get a cute kid? He has to be a cute kid. Or at least kind of cute. He can't be ugly. I can't have an ugly kid."

Then there's the third segment of HBO's *If These Walls Could Talk 2*, which stars Ellen DeGeneres and Sharon Stone as Kal and Fran, two Southern California dykes with a pronounced case of baby fever. The most bizarre moment in this short film comes when Fran proposes to Kal, "Maybe we should think about having an ethnic baby. Ethnic babies are so beautiful." It's hard to discern the purpose of this racist comment. Is it meant unproblematically? Or perhaps to show that queer adoptive parents are susceptible to the same foibles as straight ones? Hard to say; the issue is not discussed any further.

Apart from being overwhelmingly white, most pop culture queer parents are extraordinarily well-off. Neither Fran nor Kal, for example, appears to be employed. However, they live in a large, well-appointed house, drive an SUV, and apparently have no concerns about undertaking a project whose dollar-suckage per month will run them somewhere between a car payment and a mortgage. Sitting in their kitchen next to a brushed-aluminum refrigerator, among yards of glowing blonde-wood cabinetry, they get on the phone with a sperm bank. Kal's end of the conversation goes like this: "We want it. Yes. We want it. All of it! All of it! How much is it? Wow. Okay, whatever." Just to put this dialogue in perspective, sperm banks charge between $150 and $300 for a single vial. Apparently, these dykes are in a position to order thousands of dollars' worth of jizz without thinking twice about it.

The narrative struggle of the film focuses solely upon whether Fran and Kal are able—biologically—to get pregnant. Although they're shown making multiple attempts, expressing frustration at their lack of success, and finally stepping up their efforts by visiting a fertility specialist, all of this is untrammeled by financial constraints. The audience can cheer wholeheartedly for them without having to consider difficult questions such as: Do Fran and Kal have health insurance? Can one of them cover the other through domestic partnership? Does their policy have implicit penalties for using donor sperm (for instance, a required twelve-month waiting period in which they must try to get pregnant before any coverage kicks in)? What options are open to the gals if they can't afford that nice fertility specialist—or the sperm from the sperm bank in the first place? How much does second-party adoption cost, and is it even legal in the state where they live? What safeguards can they put in place if Kal can't adopt Fran's baby, and how much would the legal fees for those safeguards run?

Admittedly, *Walls 2* would be as dull as dirt if it addressed every one of those questions. But the film avoids the topic of money to such an extreme that Fran and Kal seem to exist in a sunny, airbrushed paradise where tanks of frozen sperm, helpful medical professionals, and surgical procedures simply appear for the taking. And this omission, in turn, allows the heterosexist policies and laws that are built into our medical and legal systems to go unnoticed.

On the nonfiction side, *He's Having a Baby* once again disappoints. Potential dad Jeff Danis, who is "gay, nearing 50," is a Hollywood (do I sense a pattern?) talent agent who has discovered a sudden longing to have a child. The opening scenes of the film are taken up with luscious shots of his home, which includes an in-ground swimming pool, abstract sculptures, and enough square footage of hardwood floor to play roller hockey. Much of the film's action takes place in his BMW, from which he conducts impatient, agency conversations on the phone while driving from adoption interview to adoption interview. A later sequence shows his partner, Don, mulling over the idea of having a child. It's hard to tell whether the directors meant this montage cynically or not, but it's framed as a series of pensive shots of Don and Jeff on vacation, each with a subtitle to identify the posh locale: Saint Barts. Palm Springs. The Hamptons. Big Sur. When Jeff eventually gets on the telephone to inform the adoption agency which of two Vietnamese orphans he wants, the conversation sounds disturbingly as if he is purchasing a piece of real estate: "I'm going to go for Lam Xuan Chinh . . . Karen, thanks so much, I'll be back in touch with you real soon. Let's put a hold on Lam Xuan Chinh."

Child-as-property vibe aside, these representations of free-spending queer parents are problematic in that they simply don't mention the issue that is uppermost in so many would-be parents' minds: How the fuck am I going to afford this? When parents get pregnant for free (i.e., sperm meets egg without any further complications), money tends to become an issue after conception. But for queers, money is often a barrier to getting sperm near egg in the first place. Inseminating with sperm from a sperm bank costs— depending on where you live and what kind of specimens you want— between $300 and $1,000 a month. This might be manageable if one could count on getting pregnant immediately, but the average number of tries before conception, using frozen sperm, is between six and twelve. Adoption is still pricier, usually costing between $10,000 and $20,000. And surrogacy costs the most of all, generally coming in at more than $30,000. Even if you're lucky enough to go the cheap route—that is, your situation in some way allows you to conceive "naturally"—you're probably still looking at legal fees for items such as a donor agreement and/or second-party adoption.

Some representations include glancing references to the price of queer parenting; for example, in *Daddy & Papa* it's mentioned that adopting hard-to-place foster children is less expensive than private adoption or trying to adopt a more "desirable" (i.e., young, white, healthy) baby. But the most common approach is simply to ignore money as a factor. Asked by an *Ad-*

vocate interviewer why more gay men don't have children, actor and parent B. D. Wong responds, "I guess a lot of gay people have issues with their parents, and that must color their ideas about whether they want to be parents or not." Well, sure—but might it also be that they don't have $10,000 lying around?

Perhaps because the production of offspring by queers so rarely involves sexual intercourse, media representations of queer parents seem positively obsessed by the issue of where the baby comes from. The swell of media attention accompanying the gayby boom focuses not on queer parents who already have children, or queer stepparents joining existing families, but queer people who are making or obtaining children (usually babies). In other words, what you will see on television, in film, and in print is the procurement of babies by queer parents. If you're a thirty-seven-year-old mother of two, you've just left your husband, and you're trying to coordinate babysitting schedules with dating your first girlfriend, not to mention the issue of coming out to your kids—well, there are plenty of you out there, but your story's not going to show up on *Queer As Folk.*

In his *Advocate* interview, B. D. Wong delivers the apotheosis of this attitude: "There are no accidental kids of gay parents. Every single gay parent passionately wanted to be a parent." Oh, really? Did you ask the single dyke on food stamps who has three kids from a former marriage? Or the gay man who just came out to his two teenage kids? Wong's comment assumes that gay parenting involves a predetermined order of events: First, be gay; second, decide to parent; third, become a parent. Scenarios in which the order of these steps may be shuffled are erased.

Not that people who come out after having children didn't want their kids, but let's remember, not all children of queer parents sprout magically in a petri dish. Some of them are already hanging around the house, asking, "What's rimming?" However, most stories about queer parenting center on a single glimpse: the moment of becoming. It's as though the plot arc of TLC's *A Baby Story*—pregnancy, baby shower, birth, next episode—has taken over the queer-parenting narrative. Sometimes there are variations—in adoption stories, the peak moment is not birth but the first contact between parent and child—but the central focus remains the same: a money shot, with baby as climax.

This obsession with getting the goods, and the simultaneous downplaying of living with the result, again seems to stem from an impulse to make things as "normal" and as unqueer as possible. The parents in these portrayals mouth platitudes that align them with depressing heteronormative myths, such as the belief that a potential parent should feel empty and lonely without a child. "Without [parenthood]," mourns Danis in *He's Having a Baby*, "I feel very empty. Without it, I feel very incomplete." The next shot shows him walking sadly on his treadmill, while in the background we hear the opening bars of "You're Nobody 'Til Somebody Loves You."

But there's more going on. In this film, a baby seems to be merely another acquisition to go with Jeff's treadmill, artworks, and potted palms. Thus children become yet another means by which queers are folded into a larger consumption-oriented, and hence less radical, American culture. If queers have Subarus, house payments, even our very own "Rainbow" Visa card, how threatening can we be? I wish I could say that queers are resisting this consumer-driven image of parenthood, but the recent appearance of the glossy magazine *And Baby*, aimed at same-sex parents and laden with advertisements for products, does not seem to indicate that we are.

THE PUSH TOWARD NORMATIVITY ISN'T SIMPLY SOMETHING that is thrust upon queer parents by a homophobic media empire. In some cases, it's an impression that queer parents themselves seem eager to embrace. For instance, a 1996 *People* magazine article arguing that queer (excuse me, "gay or lesbian") families are "so different, so much the same" presents a gay father, Ron Frazier, whose description of his and his partner's decision to parent enthusiastically endorses *People*'s safety-in-sameness angle. "We weren't stereotypical gays," he explains. (He doesn't elaborate on what "stereotypical" might mean, but we can assume Frazier and his partner refrain from cranking "It's Raining Men" to earsplitting levels on school nights or wearing feather boas to the Stop-n-Shop.) "So when people saw that we were just two ordinary men, they realized there was no cause for alarm." *People* certainly isn't going to call our attention to the problems with this viewpoint; it's too busy assuring us that it "helped" (helped what?) that Heidi Frazier's dads "live their day-to-day lives in relative anonymity."

This issue is more complex than simple avoidance. The *People* article points to an ongoing problem faced by queer parents: Like oil and water, queerness and parenting seem to resist blending. "Becoming a parent was the straightest thing I ever did," a friend wrote me when she found out I was working on this article. As writer Mary Martone, a queer new mom, argues, "Babies make lesbians disappear." She describes herself as a "big, short-haired gal," but notes that the social stigma she usually encounters tends to evaporate when she's with her small daughter. At those times she's often placed into some acceptable social narrative—for example, that she has a husband who happens to be somewhere else. The usual view of parents tends to adhere to the logical syllogism "If parent, then straight," as well as its corollary, "If queer, then not a parent."

Although Frazier and his partner, Tom, have lost some of their gay friends because of their mutual commitment to fatherhood, parenting has trumped sexual preference as the governing social factor in their lives. "Now our friends are mostly heterosexual couples," says Frazier. Regardless of how common this phenomenon is (many areas have relatively few other queer families to befriend), it's outrageous that this loss is marked not as an isolation that Ron and Tom must live with but merely as something that "doesn't seem to have bothered them much."

Now, I'll be the first to say that hanging out with straight folks is not a horrible fate. The point is that queer parents are being forced to make an either/or choice. Without a doubt, we need more varied representations of queer parents in the future. But we should also pay attention to the grain of truth in the portrayals we have: that queer parents are simultaneously thrust inside and kept out of mainstream culture. The queer parents in TV shows, films, articles, and books whom I admire are those who can acknowledge the paradoxes they live with, those who give me some insight into what life is like when such paradoxes must be negotiated every day. I laugh when Johnny and William, the new dads profiled in *Daddy & Papa*, question the politics of acquiring a Volvo station wagon. I'm pleasantly surprised to find a portrayal of a disabled queer parent in the Lifetime Original Movie *What Makes a Family*. And I feel relief when folks like Patrick Califia and Matt Rice remind me that pervs are parents, too. These are the kinds of queer-parenting lives I want to see: messy, complicated, flawed. They don't simply announce that queers can be parents; they queer the institution of parenthood itself.

Mother Inferior

How Hollywood Keeps Single Moms
in Their Place

Monica Nolan / FALL 2003

AT THE SEVENTY-THIRD ACADEMY AWARDS IN MARCH 2002,
four out of five of the Best Actress nominees were honored for playing single moms: Unwed mother Juliette Binoche brought happiness to a small
town by making its residents candy in *Chocolat*; Ellen Burstyn went nuts as
the pill-popping mom of a heroin addict in *Requiem for a Dream*; Laura Lin-
ney struggled with child care, a bad love affair, and her fucked-up brother in
You Can Count on Me; and Julia Roberts triumphed (at the box office, at the
Oscars, and on the screen) as the eponymous heroine of *Erin Brockovich*.

Brockovich was sold to viewers as the true story of a feisty, trampy-dressing,
smack-talking, pink-collar single mom who brings corporate giant PG&E
to its knees for poisoning the environment—and, incidentally, picks up a
million-dollar bonus on the way. It was an inspirational, particularly American success story (do good and get paid for it) and presumably a vindica-
tion for single mothers everywhere, especially all those trashy-looking ones
with kids by more than one father.

Certainly Erin Brockovich was an improvement over early cinematic
single moms, who first existed as "fallen women" transgressing the moral
code by having extramarital sex and abandoning—or being forced "for their
own good" to abandon—their children. These films hinted at the mostly
unacknowledged economic realities of women, who had fewer chances to
be self-supporting outside marriage. Movies like *Madame X* (remade five

times between 1916 and 1966) and *Stella Dallas* (also remade multiple times, most recently as the 1990 Bette Midler vehicle *Stella*) focused on the unfitness of the single mom, emphasizing that her sacrifice in giving up her children resulted in the improvement of the kids' class status.

In the 1940s and '50s, when wartime taught women that they could be economically successful on their own, and as divorcées and widows became more common, Hollywood switched gears. Single moms, here transformed into the dreaded "career women," were now messing up not their kids' economic chances but their psyches. The most spectacular example was the 1945 classic *Mildred Pierce*, in which Mildred kicks out her deadbeat husband and builds a successful restaurant chain, only to have one daughter die and the other turn into an amoral murderess.

It wasn't until Ellen Burstyn hit the screen in 1974's *Alice Doesn't Live Here Anymore*, as an aspiring singer with her young son in tow, that single motherhood became a place of possibility rather than pathos. Other women's lib–influenced films like 1977's *The Goodbye Girl* and 1978's *An Unmarried Woman* followed; an upbeat ending to the single mom's story was now an option. Yet the evolution of the American family on film is more roundabout than it is a straight line of progress. After all, the flipped-out single mom in *Carrie* came between *Alice* and *An Unmarried Woman*; *Mommie Dearest* and *The World According to Garp* were made only a year apart; and single moms have sacrificed all for their children as recently as 2000's *Dancer in the Dark*. The recent plethora of single moms on celluloid is less a case of progress than an indication of the incredible amount of interest and anxiety centered on the rising number of female-headed households.

As we watch films grapple with the problems of working mothers, mothers having sex, and, most important, absent fathers and the implications for raising children, there are a number of surprises. Films that are hailed as showing the "real" single mom, surviving and triumphant, often conceal conflicted feelings about working moms and children raised without fathers. Romantic comedies aimed at a female audience are full of conservative subtexts as well as laughs, while in the genres typically thought to appeal to men—action, horror, sci-fi—there has been an explosion of single-mom heroines in stories that send a radical yet unmistakable message: We're better off without Dad.

IN THE PAST DECADE, SEVERAL SINGLE-MOTHER DRAMAS HAVE played the reality card, most notably *Erin Brockovich* and *Riding in Cars with Boys*, both based on true stories. As real as these stories purport to be, they are also the thematic heirs to the maternal melodramas of Hollywood's golden age. For better or worse, these movies foreground what are seen as "women's problems," all the while concealing the process by which they become both problems and exclusively women's territory.

The early scenes of *Brockovich* promise a film focused on the social difficulties of single motherhood: Erin's got no job and bills to pay, and her babysitter's moving away. Yet, quickly and unbelievably, these troubles are overcome. First, Erin blackmails her way into a job at a law office, then her child care problems are solved when George—a biker with a heart of gold and lots of free time—moves in next door and takes on babysitting duties with nary a discussion of payment.

The film defines Erin as a sacrificing mom on a grander scale than ever before, which justifies her "neglect" of her children and boyfriend; this is explicated in a late scene in which Erin's son picks up one of his mom's work files and reads about a girl his own age with cancer. "Why can't her mommy help her?" he asks. "Her mommy's sick, too," says Erin. The boy finally gets how important Erin's work is, that she's mothering a whole damn town (a justification that, alas, will not fly for most working mothers).

If *Brockovich* is about a supermom, 2001's *Riding in Cars with Boys* resides at the other end of the spectrum; it's a coming-of-age story about a girl who never gets to grow up. Though the film's publicity suggested we were going to see the story of a bad girl's triumph ("She did everything wrong, but got everything right," smarmed the poster), this film is a success story with all the good parts—the parts that actually show the heroine succeeding—missing.

Adapted from Beverly Donofrio's memoir about her tumultuous early adulthood—pregnant and married at fifteen, divorced a few years later—and her efforts to get a college education and make it as a writer, *Riding in Cars* is, it turns out, less about how Beverly triumphs over adversity than about how her son struggles with and resents her. As we move back and forth between the past and the present, the ongoing dilemma is not how Beverly's going to make it out of Wallingford, Connecticut, but whether her son, Jason, will be able to free himself from her domineering influence. In fact, we never do learn how Beverly made it out; we see only flashbacks to her miserable marriage and have to be content with the fait accompli of educated-writer Beverly in the contemporary scenes. What happens in between is a mystery.

The film's anxieties about single motherhood are obvious: At every turn, Beverly is surrounded by her father, husband, or son, all acting to control this immature woman. At the close of the film, Jason drives off, stranding his mom without a ride. She calls her dad to pick her up. In a film that takes as its metaphor the power and freedom that cars give, Beverly is still getting rides from boys until the very end.

In some respects, though, *Brockovich* and *Riding in Cars* have moved ahead of "realistic" forerunners like *Alice Doesn't Live Here Anymore* and *An Unmarried Woman*. In the latter two films, the perfect man was the reward for achieving self-realization, and the absence in *Brockovich* and *Riding in Cars* of male partners for their heroines allows for the possibility that self-realization can be a reward in and of itself. Yet this absence also strengthens the link to the maternal melodramas of the past; like the mothers in *Madame X* and *Stella Dallas*, Erin must sacrifice male companionship to become a more perfect mother, while Beverly is so carefully passed from son to father and back again that there's no room for a boyfriend.

Far more nuanced and complex portraits of single moms appear in the Cher vehicles *Mask* (1985) and *Mermaids* (1990), Allison Anders's *Gas Food Lodging* (1992), and, more recently, the film *You Can Count on Me* (2000). Part of their power is that they are not only about the "issue" of single motherhood. The resonant *You Can Count on Me*, for instance, focuses on the relationship between a ne'er-do-well brother and his normal-on-the-surface sister, Sammy, who despite their differences are grappling with many of the same problems. When single-mom concerns do come up, they often originate outside the family, not within it. (When Sammy's arrangements for picking up her son after school are disrupted by her narrow-minded boss, for instance, we're meant to blame him for being a tight-ass, not her for working.) The mothers in these films are imperfect, yet always adults: Motherhood hasn't swallowed them up, but we never think of them as bad parents.

Then there are the single-mom romantic comedies. They're meant to be a froth of fantasy, but what we usually get is Hollywood's idea of what our fantasies ought to be, rather than what they really are. And what women really fantasize about, according to height-of-the-backlash 1980s comedies like *Baby Boom* (1987) and *Look Who's Talking* (1989), is staying at home and raising their kids in cozy nuclear families. And if the films of the '90s finally, tentatively accepted working moms, the need to couple them with dads became proportionately greater. As cultural anxiety about the destruction of the nuclear family loomed, films like *Jerry Maguire* and *One Fine Day* (both 1996) argued that everyone—Dad as well as Mom and kids—needs a two-parent family.

In *Baby Boom*, Diane Keaton's J.C. is a high-powered Manhattan exec who suddenly inherits a baby. Initially, this looks like a radical twist on the *Three Men and a Baby* concept, as the film introduces the idea, in several comic sequences, that motherhood is no more instinctual for women than it is for men. But before the audience can grab another handful of popcorn, she's quit her job and fled to a farmhouse in Vermont, a move that the plot reassures us is all for the best: J.C. has always dreamed of a house in the country. In this movie, children don't entail real sacrifices, just changes that turn out to be redemptive. It's the baby's job to feminize Mom and, in the process, save her from the rat race.

The idea that a son—and in these movies, it's almost always a son—needs a dad is a timeless one, as we see a decade later in *Jerry Maguire*. Dorothy (Renée Zellweger) is even willing to marry a man who doesn't love her, simply because he's so great with her kid. When, at the end, she tells him that she can't be with him just for her son, it turns out he does love her—he just hadn't realized it yet. In a scene straight from a Harlequin romance, he returns to claim her from a group of embittered divorcées, who applaud as the couple embraces. Jerry (Tom Cruise) is the yuppie who must be humanized, and mother and son are the humanizing agents. Jerry loves Dorothy because she is a mother, because she represents the moral, family-centered values that he is traveling toward for the length of the picture, away from the self-centered business ethics he started with.

One Fine Day addresses the same work-vs.-family issue *Baby Boom* did, but also includes the "it's good for men, too!" angle. Architect Melanie (Michelle Pfeiffer) and her son are mirrored by reporter Jack (George Clooney) and his daughter. On a day that the kids miss their class field trip, the two parents (who loathe each other on sight, in true romantic-comedy fashion) must share child care in order to complete important job-related goals. But as their parallel stories play out, Melanie and Jack get very different treatment.

Although Jack is initially presented as the irresponsible parent, his turn at taking care of the children goes smoothly. When it's Melanie's turn, however, she loses Jack's daughter and ends up standing on cars screaming the girl's name as rain pours down and her mascara runs. Jack finds out, of course, and uses the incident to make Melanie admit her deficiencies, flaws, and need for help.

Similarly, when Jack is pulled in two directions by work and family, the crisis passes relatively painlessly: He soothes his unhappy daughter by buying her a kitten and makes it to his press conference on time. Melanie's moment of conflict, on the other hand, is very public. Trying to have a quick drink with some important clients, painfully aware that her son is waiting to be taken to his soccer game, Melanie must announce in a quavering, Julia Roberts–worthy speech that her son is more important then these clients' new business. *One Fine Day*'s magnetism consists of two broken halves irresistibly drawn together to form a whole, asserting that shared parenting can only take place within a nuclear family.

A SINGLE MOM AND HER KIDS ARE BY DEFINITION A FAMILY without a father, and the female-headed household is destruction of the patriarchy at its most basic level. Needless to say, in Hollywood, showing its unproblematic success is still a huge taboo. Contemporary single-mom films are truly reflective of our culture: A massive amount of energy is expended in a desperate attempt to prove that single parenthood is not good enough, even as an ever-increasing number of women parent on their own. (It's important to note that this anxiety manifests itself onscreen with an almost exclusive focus on white, middle-class single moms, despite the fact that more than one-third of American single moms are women of color. Though this is part and parcel of the overwhelming whiteness of Hollywood in general, it conveniently allows mainstream films to ignore the factors of class and race that are inextricably intertwined with single parenthood.)

Contemporary movies are always ready to give screen time to fathers and father figures, and whether they're heroin addicts (*Riding in Cars with*

Boys) or just your average immature screw-ups (*One Fine Day*), the films are as eager as a codependent girlfriend to forgive their flaws and give them credit for trying. If movies do manage to dispense with Dad, they do so by linking contemporary moms to the selfless single mothers of the past, who sacrificed love—and sometimes custody of their children—in the service of their all-powerful mother instinct. Interestingly, it's only in the male-dominated genres of action and horror that Hollywood dares to suggest that father figures are not all they're cracked up to be—movies from the 1987 horror classic *The Stepfather* to the *Terminator* series to more recent fare like *Domestic Disturbance* outline either the limits or the downright evil of controlling patriarchs.

These days, single-mom movies seem to occupy the space queer films did in the late '70s: A social reality is emerging onscreen, crawling out from under old stereotypes and not sure where to go next, wondering what a really positive image would look like. My ideal single-mom movie hasn't been made yet. But I know it won't be one in which Mom winds up with a man, or lets her kids boss her around, or has no other interest in life than being a mother. In the meantime, when I'm at the video store picking out something for the evening, it's *Terminator 2* over *Erin Brockovich* every time.

Hoovers and Shakers

The New Housework Workout

Sarah McCormic / WINTER 2005

THE OTHER DAY, MY NEIGHBOR KATHY STOPPED BY AND WIT-
nessed an unusual sight: me pushing a vacuum cleaner around my living
room. She nodded enthusiastically at my upright Hoover. "Did you know
that vacuuming burns almost two hundred calories an hour?"

I looked down at a week's worth of cat hair and dirt tracked in from the
yard. "No, I did not know that."

"You can also do lunges to burn even more calories," Kathy said, grabbing the handle away from me to demonstrate. Taking a giant step forward,
she bent her other knee almost to the ground while thrusting the vacuum
handle forward in a move worthy of one of the Three Musketeers. "It's a
killer thigh workout. You should really try it."

After she left, I did. But I felt ridiculous, and the lunges only prolonged
one of my least favorite activities. Despite the very real threat of flabby
thighs, I vowed to continue vacuuming as infrequently and as quickly as
possible.

A few days after Kathy's visit, I came across an article on the popular
women's site iVillage.com that called my decision into question. In order to
stay fit and trim, it suggested, women should "turn vacuuming into a race,
wash windows with plenty of elbow grease, or scrub floors until you work
up a sweat."

A quick web search turned up several similar articles in newspapers around the country, all touting this new housework-centric exercise regimen. In March 2004, a *Chicago Sun-Times* headline suggested that you "Scrub, mop your way to fitness." In April, the Louisville, Kentucky, *Courier-Journal* announced that "ordinary chores can promote health and burn calories."

From these and other articles, I learned that while making the bed burns a measly 136 calories an hour, washing windows takes care of a more respectable 204, and scrubbing floors knocks off a full 258. But if you really want to shed those pounds, you should consider rearranging the furniture (408 calories) or carrying a small child up and down stairs (578 calories per hour). An April 2004 *Atlanta Journal-Constitution* article recommended that you "intensify cleaning and outdoor tasks to improve fitness" and offered suggestions such as using shopping bags as weights for biceps curls or doing squats while dusting.

The Boston Globe went a step further in a March 2004 piece suggesting that in order to maximize the slimming benefits of housework, you should try to be less efficient when doing chores. It suggested "taking multiple trips upstairs with the laundry or other clutter instead of one trip" and ended with an ominous warning: "Hiring a cleaning service and gardener is attractive when you're too busy or can't be bothered to do it yourself, but it doesn't help your waistline one bit."

Since I can't afford to pay someone else to clean my house, I figured my figure was safe, but then I came across an article that implied cleaning just one house might not be enough to keep off the pounds. Under the headline "Grab a duster and lose some weight," a newspaper in England's Wiltshire County recounted the success story of Emma Langley, a young woman who shed her pregnancy weight by cleaning houses. After just a few months of scrubbing other people's floors, the article gushed, Ms. Langley "saw immediate health benefits."

I doubted that we were hearing Ms. Langley's whole story (perhaps a pressing need for money had something to do with her activities?). But it occurred to me that no matter where you find yourself on the socio-economic scale, the message is the same. On the upper end of the economic ladder, women in Boston are being told not to hire someone to clean their homes for the very same reasons that middle-class British women are being schooled in the benefits of scrubbing someone else's toilets: Doing housework is healthy for women.

And, apparently, only women. Not surprisingly, none of these articles profiled men who were taking advantage of the new domestic athleticism. Indeed, it's hard to imagine entreaties like "Wash windows for killer biceps!" or "Lose that gut with a little mopping!" appearing in the likes of *Men's Health*. The trend of housework-as-workout pairs two of the classic standards used to measure a woman's value. My own mother taught me from an early age that being a "good" woman meant steering clear of both extra flab and a messy house; combining these two sources of female shame in a self-help message is as ingenious as it is cruel.

Despite my annoyance with the retrograde messages of this new domestic weight-loss plan, when I thought about my neighbor Kathy—fit, upbeat, healthy Kathy—I realized that you can't argue with its basic premise: Staying active (whether by doing yoga or lugging loads of laundry) burns calories and builds muscles. And that can't be a bad thing in our couch-potato culture, right? But then I read something that upped the stakes considerably.

The March 29, 2004, BBC News headline read "Housework 'reduces cancer risk.'" The story that followed described how researchers at Vanderbilt University had found a decreased risk for a form of uterine cancer in women who do four or more hours of housework a day compared with women who do fewer than two. This study, picked up by Reuters, made headlines in newspapers from Chicago to London to New Delhi. At its most stark, the message was this: If women don't do enough housework, we're not just going to get fat—we're going to die. What those headlines didn't bother to mention, however, is that the study had also found that women who spent an hour walking each day were at lower risk for the same kind of cancer.

Although you probably don't need a study to tell you this, recent research shows that women are still doing much more housework than men. A 2002 study at the University of Michigan found that, on average, American men do sixteen hours a week of housework; women do twenty-seven. This eleven-hour gap actually represents some progress. Between 1965 and 1985, men's share of the housework increased by a whopping four hours. At the same time, women's share dropped from forty to thirty-one hours, reflecting the fact that more women were working outside the home. After 1985, women's weekly average dropped by another four hours, but after climbing slowly for two decades, men's share skidded to a halt in 1985 and hasn't budged since.

It's no coincidence that the 1980s also gave birth to Martha Stewart's homemaking empire. A rising nostalgia for domesticity has brought with it a slew of recent books and magazine articles promising women fulfillment through a return to the most time-consuming forms of homemaking. Cheryl Mendelson's bestselling *Home Comforts: The Art and Science of Keeping House* puts even Martha to shame in its painstaking attention to the most minute details of housekeeping, instructing readers in the proper method for folding socks and the correct distance between place settings. Nigella Lawson, bodacious TV chef and author of *How to Be a Domestic Goddess*, argues on her website that "many of us have become alienated from the domestic sphere, and . . . it can actually make us feel better to claim back some of that space," which she calls "reclaiming our lost Eden."

The new housework workout passes itself off as an ideal health plan for the busy modern woman, but it's another permutation of this resurgence in nostalgia for more traditional gender roles. It's a new and compelling justification to make the daily drudgery bearable: It's good for us. It will ward off a fat butt, flabby arms, and deadly disease. And it's man's best friend, too, allowing him to keep his housework hours minimal while women mop and scrub their way to tight abs and unmutated uterine cells.

But is the road to health really paved with dust rags? While some chores surely do burn calories and tone muscles, that's not the whole story. A 2002 study conducted by Nanette Mutrie, professor of exercise and sport psychology at the University of Strathclyde, looked at the effects of various forms of exercise—including housework—on depression in both women and men. As she told Scotland's *Sunday Herald*: "With vigorous exercise, the effect is clear: The more you do, the better it is for well-being. With housework, it is the opposite. The more you do, the more depression you report."

I made a mental note to share this information with Kathy next time I saw her. Maybe then she'd think twice about spreading the gospel of aerobic vacuuming. Then again, it might be hard to convince her that housework isn't healthy, since the depression study had barely registered in the media. I couldn't find it reported in a single American newspaper: While stories about housework's cancer-fighting qualities zipped around the globe, almost no one seemed interested in the inconvenient news that the unpaid, tedious, and necessary drudgery performed largely by the world's women might be making them depressed.

And it's not so hard to guess why. If we were to acknowledge that house-work, rather than constituting an all-purpose female health tonic, might actually be *harmful* to women, we might find ourselves faced with an uncom-fortably strong case for major social change: Men might be asked to take on a larger portion of the housework and child care. Companies might come under increased pressure to offer their employees—both male and female—more flexible, family-friendly schedules. Martha might even see sales go down for her Tuscan table linens and make-your-own-wrapping-paper kits.

The housework workout, on the other hand, asks nothing of men, em-ployers, the government, or corporate America—its message is for women alone. It knows you're tired, overworked, and overscheduled, and let's face it, the men in your life aren't likely to help out anytime soon. It's a tool to balance all the competing demands on your time without inconveniencing anyone else. Its time-tested advice? Adapt. Multitask. Try harder. And re-member what your mother (or popular culture) taught you: Keep up your body and your home, or risk everything.

6

. . . .

Beauty Myths and
Body Projects

SINCE 2002, WHEN *VOGUE* BEGAN AN ANNUAL TRADITION OF producing its "Shape" issue, I've looked forward with perverse pleasure to its appearance on the newsstand. *Vogue*, for eleven months out of the year content to ignore the existence of any bodies besides those of the razor-boned lovelies in its editorial pages, deigns to branch out in this special issue, celebrating—if I may quote from the cover of the April 2005 issue—"Every Body: Tall, Short, Thin, Curvy, or Pregnant."

Insert derisive snorting sounds here. A more accurate description would read: "Tall (and skinny); Short (and skinny); Thin (clinically anorexic); Curvy (breasts or booty, but probably not both); or Pregnant (horrifying yet temporary fat suit)." *Vogue* long ago perfected the process of erasing overweight folks from existence—even the all-powerful Oprah was tasked with losing twenty pounds before being allowed onto the cover in 1998—but their bizarre taxonomy of body types willfully insists not only that certain body types simply don't exist, but that you get to have only one to begin with. There's no mention, God forbid, of short and curvy ladies, nor any of the other odd proportions most of us possess.

It's pretty tempting to see this yearly conceit as parodic, as if the staff of *The Onion* had infiltrated Condé Nast for a month just to see if we were paying attention. Certainly nobody turns to *Vogue* for a realistic look at, as queenpin Anna Wintour put it in the 2005 Shape issue's editor's letter, "the beautiful variety of our female forms." But each year, it seems like the rest of pop culture is falling more and more in line with *Vogue*'s suspended reality, pushing inconvenient bodies out of the picture as it elevates one standard of beauty (with a few mild variations) above all.

Every facet of our popular culture reflects images of women, from preening starlet to big-screen action heroine to reality-show ugly duckling to yummy mummy, that regular gals are meant to emulate. A picture of Halle Berry, Jennifer Lopez, or Angelina Jolie in a magazine is no longer enough; the magazine is sure to tell us where Halle's stylist buys her clothes, where Jennifer goes for her electric-current facials, and how to duplicate Angelina's tantric-sex glow with makeup. Puzzling through these varied representations of idealized women is, for many, a lifelong obsession that begins when they first become aware of the power of image.

Girls learn from a young age that whatever soothing, self-esteem-building stuff their parents say about how it's what's inside that counts, their primary cultural value rests squarely on the physical. In the introduction to her 2004 play *The Good Body*, Eve Ensler writes of traveling the world and meeting with women everywhere who, no matter who they were or what they did, hated some part of themselves. "There was almost always one part that they longed to change, that they had a medicine cabinet full of products devoted to transforming or hiding or reducing or straightening or lightening. Just about every woman believed that if she could just get that part right, everything else would work out."

This is the crux of the body project, this belief that changing our bodies can make everything better, lighter, less problematic. It's been happening for as long as any woman can recall—check out Joan Jacobs Brumberg's book *The Body Project* for ample historical evidence—and it's been expressed in the most heartbreaking literature (Toni Morrison's *The Bluest Eye*), the trashiest television (*The Swan*), and the many outlets in between. These days, with such a cornucopia of problem-solving technology available to those who are inclined and can afford to nip, tuck, whiten, tan, straighten, melt, and mold themselves to perceived perfection, it's become increasingly hard to find cultural validation for just, you know, liking ourselves as we are. Witness the scene from an early season of *Sex and the City*, where our heroines sit in a circle, bemoaning their "problem" areas: "I hate my thighs," sighs Charlotte; "I'll take your thighs and raise you a chin," snarks

Miranda. When it's Samantha's turn, she admits the shocking truth: "I love the way I look." And though we're supposed to grudgingly admire Samantha's ease with her physical self, we're also supposed to acknowledge that she's blatantly broken the code of ladies' body talk: There is always, *always* a fault.

In 2004, Dove spearheaded its much-ballyhooed Campaign for Real Beauty with a study called "The Real Truth About Beauty: A Global Report," which was coauthored by Susie Orbach and Nancy Etcoff, professors and authors of *Fat Is a Feminist Issue* and *Survival of the Prettiest*, respectively. The study queried thousands of women in ten countries on their definition of beauty and on the impact its cultural imperatives have on their lives. Eighty-five percent of the women polled felt that every woman has at least one beautiful attribute, but only 2 percent described themselves as beautiful. There could hardly be a starker demonstration of our internalized struggles over bodies and beauty.

But thankfully, the subject is more than a locus of dissatisfaction and competition. For many girls and women, it's often the catalyst for a burgeoning feminist consciousness. When we're young, it takes hold as we listen to our mothers complain about their own graying hair or wobbly arm fat, or suffer teasing from classmates when we change for gym. Later on, it resurfaces when we look at magazines and find a whitewashed parade of size-0 stick figures who look nothing like us; when we see a fat or hairy woman who, contrary to everything we've been taught, is indisputably gorgeous; when we understand that the consumer-beauty machine gleefully fosters a climate of intense, looks-based competition between all women, all our lives. "Hips, lips, tits, power!" was a riot grrrl war cry that came up from the underground in the early '90s, and those who heeded it understood: The real—and really scary—revolution comes when women refuse to buy into the notion of our chronic imperfection and flaunt instead the confrontational bombast of our physical selves. All women know, deep down, that our crooked noses, big ol' badonkadonks, and nonwhitened teeth have little impact on the larger world; what's important is that we cease to be so thoroughly, literally sold on our potential to uphold a standard of improbable physical purity.

The culture has transformed—"mutated" might be a better word— since *Bitch* first ran stories, in the late '90s, about the growing normalization of cosmetic surgery that was starting to make new lips and calves seem like just your everyday consumer acquisitions. Our outrage then seems almost quaint now, in a time when head-to-toe surgical overhauls pass for heartwarming family entertainment on shows like *Extreme Makeover*. In another ten years, we'll probably look back on the current insanity and mumble about how we didn't know the half of it. The beauty myth that Naomi Wolf once described as a "violent backlash against feminism that uses images of female beauty as a political weapon against women's advancement" has changed only in its intensification and the increasing violence that surgery calls for. Even those of us who have long been aware of it still fall prey to its pervasive call—my lipstick collection alone can testify. But many women have themselves changed, becoming more media literate and quicker to see the marketing of cosmetics and weight loss as consumer shills engineered to take our stores of energy and turn them inward toward those "problem" areas.

The tricky thing about feminism, though, is that its rhetoric is these days so easily twisted to uphold the very things we wanted to change in the first place. To wit: Feminism is all about personal choices, and if breast implants or colored contact lenses are a choice, they must be feminist, right? Right? It's sometimes a chore to peel away the many layers of personal choice, cultural conditioning, ethnic imperative, and outside opinion that inform our spectrum of body projects. But such a task is eminently worthwhile, and as more women and girls learn to separate what they want from what they're told they need, we'll all get what's best for us.   —A.Z.

Plastic Passion

Tori Spelling's Breasts and Other
Results of Cosmetic Darwinism

Andi Zeisler / FALL 1998

IT SEEMS LIKE PEOPLE HAVE STARTED TALKING ABOUT HAVING cosmetic surgery the way they used to talk about having children—as an abstract inevitable, something that will occur at some unspecified time in the future. As a society, we've grown inured to the concept of cosmetic surgery and blasé about its presence in our daily lives. It's played for laughs in culture both high (a *New Yorker* cartoon) and low (your average sitcom). It's standard fodder for daytime talk shows, free weeklies and ads on public transportation hawk it aggressively, and the entertainment glossies make sure we know exactly what Demi Moore's breasts are up to. Its terms have invaded the vernacular—we're no more surprised to see a magazine with the cover line "Your Kitchen Needs a Face-Lift!" than we are to hear that Cher had another rib removed.

And we're not just hearing about other people's operations; where cosmetic surgery was once mainly the province of wealthy socialites, aging movie stars, and strippers, it's now an equal-opportunity proposition, complete with TV commercials and low-cost financing plans hawked on the Internet. The American Society of Plastic and Reconstructive Surgeons reports that, over the past five years, the rate of breast-augmentation surgeries has more than tripled, liposuctions have doubled, and liposuctions performed on men have tripled. Cosmetic surgeries in general have increased by more than half since 1992. In our society, it's no longer nature that determines who'll be the fittest—it's the surgeons, and the people with the money to pay their astronomical bills.

There's plenty that's disturbing about this kind of cosmetic Darwinism. There's the classism and racism inherent in the body-reshaping industry, for one, and the eugenic implications of a world full of people with bodies and faces that reflect a fashion-model ideal. Surgery and the fashion/beauty industries have informed each other from the start, and this union, along with long-standing Hollywood associations, has plenty to do with why lots of us deride cosmetic surgery as vain, shallow, and devoid of personal meaning, especially when compared to its hipper body-modification counterparts of tattooing and piercing. When a grown woman undergoes twenty-plus operations to transform herself into a giant Barbie doll (as frequent talk-show guest Cindy Jackson did) or compares cosmetic surgery to tuning up the car (as Loni Anderson has), is it any wonder?

The evolution of cosmetic surgery into pop culture touchstone ensures that there's now less stigma attached, but it also means that we're seeing a lot more media coverage of it that pushes a downright whimsical agenda. A recent issue of *Vogue* features "Calf Masters," a piece that asks, "Are you ready for spring's capri pants and pleated schoolgirl skirts? Are your legs?" and then swings right into a perky evaluation of surgical options (including calf implants and inner knee liposuction) for optimum capri-pant effect. Not that this kind of thing is unprecedented; most women's magazines start running their get-ready-for-summer exercise features around March, but those generally stop short of suggesting going under the knife in order to make the most of one's bikini. The ease with which *Vogue* proposes a spendy operation for the sake of a fleeting trend points to the classism implicit in cosmetic Darwinism, but also embodies a shift in the M.O. of the cosmetic surgery shill. Glossy magazines, despite their overstock of wafer-thin models, have generally shouldered the responsibility of urging their readers to think carefully and at length about what a big, expensive, and possibly dangerous undertaking surgery is. An article like "Calf Masters," by contrast, downplays the dangers of the gee-whiz fashion-forward thrill.

On the other hand, certain corners of culture seem ambivalent about participating in such lipo-for-everyone boosterism. This became apparent on a recent episode of *Beverly Hills, 90210*, which addressed, within one hour, a whole host of issues with an eye toward dramatically presenting the

Media Enslavement of Women. Pornography, sex toys, cutting, dieting, sizeism, and cosmetic surgery were trotted out one after another in neat five-minute segments. Cosmetic surgery's moment in the *90210* spotlight went a little something like this:

> KELLY'S MOM: I'm going to have a face-lift next week, and I won't be able to chew for a while. I'll be drinking lots of smoothies.
>
> KELLY: You're kidding me!
>
> KELLY'S MOM: Honey, this is Beverly Hills. We never joke about plastic surgery.
>
> KELLY: Mom, you look great! What are you thinking?
>
> KELLY'S MOM: Forty percent off for people in their forties got me started . . . and the thought of losing the bags under my eyes sealed the deal.

On its own, the skimpy exchange might have just been filler, but situated within the rest of the topic-heavy hour, it became a firmly antisurgery message (and a marvel of hypocrisy for a television show that sometimes seems to exist solely to display Tori Spelling's baseball-in-a-sock breast implants). The show's hastily assembled cosmetic surgery = oppression moral posturing indicates that someone within its chain of command is concerned that perhaps all these years of televised focus on bodily perfection might somehow poison the minds of impressionable viewers, and it's high time to start backpedaling.

The magazine *Living Fit*, meanwhile, published the results of a survey in which male and female baby boomers were questioned about their attitudes on cosmetic surgery. The piece, titled "The Unkindest Cut," aimed to counter the media buzz on a "cosmetic surgery boom" with an emphatic statement that people are really much happier with themselves than we'd all like to think. The main evidence of this, however, isn't that fewer people are choosing surgery, but that more people are having what *Living Fit* refers to as "lunch-hour surgery: non- or minimally invasive wrinkle-fighting procedures like laser skin resurfacing; Retin-A; chemical peels; and Botox, collagen, and fat injections." The intent seems to be to draw a line in the sand between what is and isn't cosmetic surgery, and the piece congratulates itself heartily for doing so, with a neat conclusion that the alleged boom is "really more of a boomlet."

But the distinction between boom and boomlet isn't the crucial point, is it? It's as though *Living Fit* thinks the fact that some folks are choosing to temporarily paralyze their faces with botulism toxin rather than go full-on with the face-lift is somehow indicative of a propaganda-free, antisurgery attitude. But the only thing it's indicative of is that vanity is still a huge issue when it comes to how people conceptualize/rationalize their body modification. Increasingly sophisticated technology has made cosmetic surgery less taxing and less embarrassing for the people who choose it, but in the process it's fueling the development of a bizarre moral hierarchy of cosmetic procedures.

Feminism these days is about defining our own terms, being able to adapt former definitions and shift them around to suit us. This is why we not only no longer have to shun lipstick but can actually turn the act of wearing it into a feminist statement (although, to the casual observer, the righteousness of this statement might go unnoticed and we might simply appear to be women in lipstick). And cheery testimony of how the face-lift or the breast implants were "for me"—and, by extension, for feminist self-realization—permeates many a first-person chronicle of surgery.

Elizabeth Haiken, author of *Venus Envy: A History of Cosmetic Surgery*, argues that, when it comes to current attitudes about surgery, the practice of dismissing the cultural context and rationalizing it as individual betterment "flattens the terrain of power relations." In other words, we can talk about doing it for us until our high-end lipstick flakes off, but we should also keep in mind that we probably wouldn't even be thinking about what life would be like with a new nose or perkier breasts or shapelier inner thighs if it weren't for a long-standing cultural ideal that rewards those who adhere to it with power that often doesn't speak its name, but is instantly recognizable to those who don't have it.

Sure, maybe pop cultural forces can help undo the history of body hatred foisted upon women and girls—but only if they avoid the kind of hypocritical pap peddled by the likes of *90210* and *Living Fit*. The blanket statement "Cosmetic surgery is bad for women!" ignores important subtleties. It's hard to condemn someone whose insecurity about having small breasts poisons the rest of her life; for her, that amounts to a feminist issue. The larger theoretical framework—the idea that by submitting to the knife, women capitulate to a pernicious social code that ranks female worth by adherence to the beauty ideal, etc.—is very real, but it isn't going to help someone whose day-to-day life has already been damaged by this code and just wants to get implants and get on with living. It's as hazardous to applaud only those who don't choose surgery as being worthy of feminist approbation as it is to roundly denigrate those who do.

Women are increasingly visible in forming culture and instituting change, but when we look at the rising cosmetic surgery statistics, the idea that there might be some sort of connection between the two is impossible to ignore. With visibility comes scrutiny, and we've all seen how the annals of pop culture treat the visible woman whose livelihood has nothing to do with her looks. It's the Hillary's Hair syndrome—show the world a potent woman and all they want to do is talk about how big her ass is or whether she should go blonder. One of the idealistic myths of feminism is that an increase in female power will somehow effect a momentous change wherein the multibillion-dollar fashion/beauty cabal will magically loosen its grip on women everywhere. It's the result of years of struggle within the constraints of our image-obsessed culture, but it isn't necessarily logical.

So even if nobody's strapping women to gurneys and rolling them down halls lined with scalpel-wielding men in green, cosmetic Darwinism is definitely greasing the wheels. The terrain of power relations, to cop Haiken's phrase, is only getting flatter with time. Whether we feel like we need to look a certain way to make up for cultural power that we don't have, or whether looks are still a major means by which we achieve power—or whether we refuse to give credence to either of these ideas—what we're born with is still going to be weighed against what surgery can give us. The occasional earnest media dispatch may suggest a minor, if not exactly emphatic, backlash against surgery as we've conceived it in the past, but it can't compete with the sexy media spectacle of safe and groovy space-age technology and a wrinkle-free future. So in spite of a queasy feeling and a temptation to dismiss the whole idea of cosmetic surgery as an antiwoman plot and anyone who "chooses" it as a sucker, we must admit that in a complicated time, our thinking has to evolve, even if our calves, chests, and cheekbones don't.

Vulva Goldmine

The New Culture of Vaginal Reconstruction

Julia Scheeres / WINTER 2000

Women: Have you ever found yourself behind closed doors, legs spread, mirror in hand, wondering if what you see is normal? Do those tiny wrinkles on your labia make you feel like less of a woman? Is that extra padding on your pudenda damaging your self-worth? Take a good look at yourself. What are your defects?

An abnormal vaginal appearance shouldn't keep you from living life to the fullest. Every woman deserves to feel beautiful. We understand your concerns and we're here to help. With a simple outpatient surgery,* you too can have a normal-looking vagina. Just call 1-800-BE-NORML for a free consultation.

*Warning: Patient could experience loss of sexual sensation or chronic pain.

SUCH ADVERTISEMENTS SOUND PREPOSTEROUS, BUT THEY EX-ist. And they don't carry a small-print warning. Welcome to the latest fad in plastic surgery: genital alterations for women. In what could be the final frontier of cosmetic cutting, women are paying beaucoup dinero to doctors who promise to make their goddess-given pudenda look younger, smoother, and smaller.

A sampling of the new genital surgeries includes procedures to liposuction and lift sagging pubes; inject fat into flat labia majora to give them

261

a plumper, more youthful look; tighten vaginas with lasers; prune long labia minora; and unhood clitorises for greater friction. And the doctors playing this market are no fools—at up to $10,000 a pop, they have struck cosmetic gold.

One of the most popular genital surgeries is labia minora reduction. When a similar procedure is performed on healthy girls in some African countries as a coming-of-age rite to control their sexuality, Westerners denounce it as genital mutilation; in the U.S. of A., it's called cosmetic enhancement. But both procedures are based on misogynist notions of female genitalia as ugly, dirty, and shameful. And though American procedures are generally performed under vastly better conditions (with the benefit of, say, anesthesia and antibiotics), the postsurgical results can be similarly horrific, involving loss of sensation, chronic pain, and infection.

Unless you've been reading the slave-to-beauty puffery of rags like *Cosmo*, chances are you've never heard of these cosmetic operations. That's why the doctors performing them—almost all of them men—have been raising public awareness with a hard sell, hawking their services in press releases, newspaper advertisements, and Internet ads. Typical of their marketing strategy is an ad that appeared in the Los Angeles press, appealing to women who "suffer from low self-esteem due to abnormal or enlarged vaginal appearance," whatever the hell that means. A spot for "vaginal tightening" features a bikini-clad broad on a satin sheet, her back and head arched as if in midorgasm. "You won't believe how good sex can be," moans the text. Another press release exhorts reporters to "take out [their] hand mirrors" and examine their vulvas for defects.

Until now, I had thought of my genitals only in terms of sexual fulfillment. The ads piqued my curiosity: Gee, what's normal? Don't plushies, like penises, come in a range of sizes, shapes, and colors? And why would a perfectly healthy woman choose to put herself under a scalpel, especially in this most delicate of areas?

Under the guise of obsequious-beauty-writer-awed-by-the-great-doctor, I ventured into the world of genital surgery. Not surprisingly, the trend's epicenter is Southern California, mecca of the forever young and all things silicone. Dr. Jane Norton, who hails from the geriatric oasis of Palm Desert, claims to have pioneered genital cosmetic surgery twenty years ago. According to Norton, she's snipped "about a thousand" lower lips, unmasked "a couple hundred" clitorises (purportedly for better stimulation), and laser-steamed "a couple hundred" vulvas, as well as lifted scads of sagging pubes. The aptly named Gary Alter, a Beverly Hills plastic surgeon and urologist whose résumé includes everything from facial implants to sex changes, says he's done about thirty labia reductions, including a pair of identical twins in their twenties whose obsession with sameness extended to their pudenda.

Gynecologist David Matlock promises women better orgasms with vaginal tightening. (The slogan for his Laser Vaginal Rejuvenation Institute of Los Angeles, the aforementioned "You won't believe how good sex can be," is trademarked.) His beaver-cleaving technique consists of using lasers to cut vaginal muscles and sew them tightly back together. A pamphlet distributed at his Sunset Boulevard office refers to vaginas that are no longer at their "physiologically optimum sexual functioning state" or "for whatever reason lack an overall optimum architectural integrity." But if that jargon confuses you, rest assured: All alterations are "performed electively only at the request of each individual woman." (Phew! We can all uncross our legs now.)

Are women really modifying their muffs for themselves? Or are they trying to meet the same standard of female beauty that compels them to stuff silicone bags into their chests, inject bacteria into their brows to paralyze wrinkles, and favor collagen-filled fish lips?

Matlock insists that his procedure is "specifically for female pleasure." But Alter says that men routinely tag along to consultations, leaning over his shoulder as he inspects their lover's crotch to suggest changes. Canadian twat-tweaker Dr. Robert Stubbs fully admits that most of the women who get tightened are doing it for their partners. In his opinion, these new techniques are no more than a twist on the postpartum "husband's knot," wherein the obstetrician throws in a few extra stitches after an episiotomy to create a snugger fit for a penis. In fact, when one couple came to his office concerned about the size of the hubby's bubby, he said, "I'll just tighten your wife." Directly contradicting Matlock, Stubbs explains that the vagina itself doesn't have much sensation. ("Otherwise the pain of childbearing would have decimated the human race long ago.")

Women also get labia reductions to please the capital-M Man, Stubbs says. Case in point: He performed his first labiaplasty on an exotic dancer whose labia "were sort of flapping during her dance routine." (Sounds like a unique talent to me—maybe she should have incorporated it into her act.) Stubbs glibly markets his lip snips as the "Toronto Trim" and allows as how most of his patients are plastic surgery junkies; for some, remodeling their bodies every few years is as routine as redecorating their homes: "If they redo the kitchen and see something in the basement they don't like, there's no reason they shouldn't get it fixed, too."

Queried about the wisdom of such unnecessary surgeries, Alter goes on the defensive. "This is legitimate, it's not bullshit!" he insists in an interview at his office. But as he riffles through a photo album of "before" and "after" snatch shots, he contradicts himself: "Most of these women aren't massively enlarged; it's basically a cosmetic thing. Most of them would fall within the norm." As a matter of fact, what was abnormal was the eerie similarity of all the cookie-cutter-cunt "after" shots.

Surgeons' opinions on why women are seeking out these expensive and risky operations also vary. Some point the finger at a heightened sexuality in our culture; Alter, for instance, ascribes it to a greater diffusion of crotch shots in magazines and film. "Videos and photos that people are seeing of pornographic images are making them become self-conscious." (Not surprisingly, photographic manipulation is a common practice in pornography. "We do all sorts of enhancements," says Gary Rohr, who retouches images for Flynt Publications, purveyors of such quality fare as *Hustler, Busty Beauties*, and *Barely Legal*. That means erasing stretch marks, banishing wrinkles and pimples, inflating tits, and narrowing hips—even eye color is faked. "The easiest thing to do is to replace genital shots," notes Rohr. "You take one you prefer and paste it over one you don't.")

Others say the labiaplasty demand was created by doctors trying to survive in an era of managed care. "People just want to do something to supplement their income," Norton says, without a trace of sarcasm—or self-awareness—in her voice.

And while these doctors claim they're boosting women's self-esteem by prodding pubes at minimal risk, some of their colleagues have raised concerns about the safety of the operations. "Anytime you make an incision, nerves are cut. For that reason, you can have decreased sensitivity," says Malcolm Lesavoy, who teaches plastic surgery at UCLA. "I would caution anyone against having genital surgeries for cosmetic reasons."

Mary Gatter, medical director of Planned Parenthood Los Angeles, is more direct. "These operations are completely bogus," she says, adding that after twenty years as a gynecologist, she's seen only three women whose labia were long enough to cause physical discomfort. "There is a large variation of what's normal."

In fact, such surgeries can have disastrous results. Nichole O'Neill, a thirty-one-year-old secretary from Bakersfield, California, first had misgivings about her genitalia in eighth grade when she stumbled upon a stash of *Hustler* magazines at a friend's house. "I thought I had enlarged labia," she explains. "They were more exposed than what I saw in porn magazines."

In 1993, she took several magazines to a gynecology appointment and told her doctor she wanted similar genitalia. According to O'Neill, the doctor said she'd never heard of a surgical procedure to reduce labia size but assured her that she could perform one in a simple, fifteen-minute operation.

When O'Neill woke up after surgery, she was shocked to discover that the gynecologist had simply excised the lower two-thirds of her nymphae. "She amputated my labia," said O'Neill. "There is just a gaping hole." A few days after the surgery, the skin turned grayish-green with infection. When the swelling and infection subsided, her clitoris was so exposed that it was too painful to wear underwear or tight pants. During sex, she felt either searing pain or numbness. The gynecologist ignored O'Neill's complaints, but she visited several other doctors who agreed that the surgery was botched. Finally, she decided to sue her gynecologist. Ten firms rejected her case as frivolous before she found a medical malpractice lawyer to go to bat for her. When the case went to trial in 1997, she endured the display of poster-size close-ups of her genitalia as well as an opposing attorney who characterized her as a slut.

During the lengthy trial, which she lost, O'Neill drank heavily and, in a moment of drunken desperation, slashed her wrists. She says the operation was sexual suicide. "It absolutely destroyed me. I would exchange all the money in the world just to have my sexuality back again."

The big question here is this: What is the beauty standard for vulvas and who sets it?

In some parts of Africa, long labia are desirable; girls tie weights to their nymphae to stretch them out. In Japan, big is also beautiful—a vulva with large labia is called "the winged butterfly." But according to UCLA psychology professor Paul Okami, in most cultures the ideal pussy looks a lot like that of a twelve-year-old girl. "Youth is a pancultural determinant of female attractiveness," he says. "These procedures are designed to approximate pubertal vulvae or vaginas." (The trend in shaved bushes and the proliferation of Internet sites featuring "teenage sluts" seem to corroborate his opinion.)

Obviously, no one is forcing women to undergo these surgeries. But those who decide to alter perfectly healthy pudenda should be aware of the risks and implications. It's too early in the game to know whether these surgeries will spawn medical tragedies on the scale of those wrought by silicone breast implants. The only sure thing is that as long as there's a quack hawking happiness in the form of snake oil, someone will buy it. Perhaps that someone should heed the classic piece of advice invoked by Planned Parenthood's Mary Gatter: "If it ain't broke, don't fix it."

Are Fat Suits the New Blackface?

Hollywood's Big New Minstrel Show

Marisa Meltzer / WINTER 2002

IN SAN FRANCISCO, MOVIE PREVIEWS ARE MORE THAN JUST ads—they're a chance for notoriously politically correct audiences to vent their disapproval of Hollywood, corporate America, and the powers that be. The standard mode of expression is hissing. I've witnessed *The Patriot*, *Rush Hour*, and several Freddie Prinze Jr. vehicles getting the San Francisco treatment. But over the summer, during a preview for *Shallow Hal*, no one in the audience saw fit to register sibilant protest against one of the most disturbing and offensive cinematic trends in recent memory: the fat suit. Gwyneth Paltrow stars in the Farrelly brothers comedy as Rosemary, the 350-pound love interest of womanizer Jack Black, who, because he can suddenly see only "inner beauty," falls in love with the Skinny Rosemary; the rest of the world sees Fat Rosemary waddling her way through the movie. Watch Fat Rosemary shop for clothes! Watch her do a cannonball into a pool! Watch her drink a really big milkshake—all by herself! The preview audience laughed uproariously. Not a single "ssss" was heard. I felt a little queasy.

Leaving aside the incongruity of "inner beauty" being taken so literally, the culturally tired but no less annoying assumption that thin = beautiful, and the fact that Black is no paragon of svelte pulchritude himself, *Shallow Hal* isn't an isolated case. Au contraire; Gwyneth has jumped on a veritable fat-suit bandwagon. A brief history of the fat suit would have to include

267

Goldie Hawn, living large and vengeful in *Death Becomes Her*; Robin Williams—annoying as ever—as the chubby, dowdy Mrs. Doubtfire; Martin Lawrence and a pair of really weird saggy boobs in *Big Momma's House*; Mike Myers as Fat Bastard in *Austin Powers: The Spy Who Shagged Me*; and Eddie Murphy playing an entire fat family in both *Nutty Professor* movies. More recently, there's Martin Short, unable to cross his legs in his new Comedy Central talk show *Primetime Glick*, and Julia Roberts scarfing down cookies as a (gasp!) size twelve in *America's Sweethearts*. Fat people are now America's favorite celluloid punch lines. Wanna make a funny movie? It's a pretty easy formula: Zip a skinny actor into a latex suit. Watch her/him eat, walk, and try to find love. Hilarity will ensue.

Of course, no conversation about the fat suit could be complete without a mention of Fat Monica, inhabitant of several flashback and alternate-reality episodes of *Friends*. While I will refrain from airing my personal theories about Courteney Cox Arquette's body image and eating habits here, I believe Fat Monica really takes the proverbial cake. She dresses badly, has no self-control, eats junk food, has poor hygiene, and is a virgin. She's the opposite of the control-freak Thin Monica, who has the husband, the job, and the adoring friends. Even worse than all that is the dance Courteney does in full fat drag to entertain the studio audience between takes. She calls it "the popcorn," and apparently folks watching find it quite comical. It involves her moving rhythmically in her latex suit. A fat person shaking her bod: mmmm, funny.

It's here that the true nature of fat-suit humor is revealed in all its glory. See, it's fairly acceptable to satirize a group of people we envy. Movies like *Legally Blonde* and *Clueless* work because we're laughing at rich white girls. Their problems are supposedly our fantasies—which boy to date, which pair of Manolos looks better with the Versace dress, which color SUV to drive—and these comedies treat them with the utmost affection. But when the punch line is a group euphemistically (and often erroneously) called a minority, things start to get dicey. Over the past several decades, comedy has gradually become less broad and more sensitive to overt racism (and to a lesser extent, to sexism and homophobia). Jackie Chan and Chris Tucker may trade black and Asian jokes in the *Rush Hour* series, but we've come a long way since Peter Sellers was cast as bucktoothed Chinese sleuth Sidney Wang in *Murder by Death*. By now, the cardinal rule of humor—you can make fun of a group only if you're part of it—is familiar enough to be a punch line itself. (Remember Jerry Seinfeld's outrage over his Catholic dentist's Jewish jokes?) But fat people are the last remaining exception.

In the spring and summer of 2001 alone, we were inundated with images of thin actors playing fat. It's not like there's a dearth of fat actresses out there, as if some casting director is saying, "We've been searching for a fat girl to star in the next Farrelly brothers film, but so far there are no takers." (Camryn Manheim and I aren't friends, but I'm pretty sure she wasn't offered Gwyneth's *Shallow Hal* part.) With a real fat woman in the lead, the movie wouldn't be funny—it would just be uncomfortable. Watching actual fat people on the big screen would be so authentically painful—because fat hatred is still deeply entrenched in American culture—that audiences would be unable to laugh. It's not just the exaggerated dimply thighs and man-boobs that keep us buying tickets; the crux of the joke is not the latex suit's physical fakeness but the ephemeral nature of the thin actor posing as fat. We all know that Julia, Goldie, and Gwyneth (and Martin, Mike, and Eddie) will return to their slender glory for the next part, and that's comforting—because otherwise we would have to confront the mean-spiritedness behind our giggles.

Such virulence makes all this faux fat seem very old-fashioned; it reeks of our country's less-than-perfect past. After all, it seems like a long time ago—although it was not—that great white actors of the twentieth century performed in blackface. The closing credits of Spike Lee's *Bamboozled* display a parade of them. There they are: Shirley Temple, Lucille Ball, Judy Garland, Mickey Rooney, and more, totally oblivious to the true meaning of their actions. Someday you'll see footage of Oscar winners Julia Roberts and Gwyneth Paltrow trundling along in their fat suits. It'll be depressing and pathetic, but it won't, in the end, be funny.

Busting the Beige Barrier

The Limits of "Ethnic" Cosmetics

Leah Lakshmi Piepzna-Samarasinha / FALL 2004

I HAVE ONE OF THE MOST COMMON SKIN TONES IN THE WORLD: dark olive, browning to café au lait in summer. Ginger bronze, honey almond, whatever you want to call it, I've seen it on thousands of women— on the subway, working in the next cubicle over, and onstage at poetry night. I also have vivid memories of standing with my best friend in a Shoppers Drug Mart as a salesgirl smeared beige crap from a jar onto her berry-brown hand and insisted, "Oh, don't worry, it'll blend right in." How come we had to wait 'til we were in our twenties to find foundation that actually matched our skin? And how come that involved a trip to the MAC counter and shelling out $20 for a bottle of StudioFix, not dropping $5.99 at the drugstore?

But damn, maybe there's hope. "Find your True Match!" exults L'Oréal's life-size cardboard display in my local megapharmacy. "At last, a formula that precisely matches your skin's texture and tone," coos text accompanied by a row of multicolored cuties, one of whom is even rocking baby dreads and all of whom are darker than usual. Every bit of the marketing is designed to appeal to me and other women of color—from the Asian, Latina, South Asian, and black women on their promo to their subtle acknowledgment that we're all stressed out from years of staring at a wall of products in "flesh tones" that ain't ours and never will be.

Visiting the L'Oréal website, however, bursts my bubble fast. I'm greeted by the same "Find your True Match!" spiel, but now it's coming from a very pale lady flanked by a row of different, lighter girls than those in the in-store display. Using L'Oréal's "shade and application advice" tool, I answer the "What is your skin tone?" query with a click on the "deepest" option, and select "cool" for undertone. And my match is . . . Tawny Beige? Oh, no no nooooo. Let's try that again. "Deep and warm" gets me Sun Beige, and "neutral and deep" gets me Honey Beige. Needless to say, there is no oak, copper, bronze, dark chocolate, or indigo shade listed in the results.

This isn't the first time a mainstream makeup company has made a half-assed attempt to capture the women-of-color market. From Maybelline's Shades of You line in the '80s to more recent efforts (and sometimes more successful ones—Revlon's ColorStay goes as deep as Mocha; the trick is finding a drugstore that actually stocks it), boy, have they tried. But either their shades don't go dark enough or they're just plain off. In this respect, True Match is nothing new.

The budget-conscious femme of color does have some options—if she's diligent. Black Opal, which debuted to much fanfare a few years ago, is the first line of cosmetics for women of color to be carried at national chains like Duane Reade and Walgreens. Unfortunately, distribution is patchy, and while their sixteen different shades of foundation are a godsend for darker-skinned women, lighter- and medium-skinned ladies may find them too deep to work. Real Cosmetics, founded by Pakistani former model Lubna Khalid, is still my favorite. She names her foundations after cities and offers colors for girls from San Juan to Harlem, Mumbai to Havana—but you can get her products only online, at some Sephora locations, or at smaller Afrocentric stores in New York. So until Real comes to my town, you'll probably find me back at the MAC counter . . . or at the drugstore, kicking over the True Match display.

Your Stomach's the Size of a Peanut, So Shut Up, Already

An Open Letter to Carnie Wilson

Beth Bernstein and Matilda St. John / FALL 2003

Dear Carnie,

As fat women, we were seized by morbid curiosity when we heard that you would be posing in the August issue of *Playboy*. We assumed that, like other celebrities-gone-nude, you were either attempting to maximize your bound-to-be-fleeting fame (see Jessica Hahn) or creating an airbrushed monument to your vanity (see Belinda Carlisle). Imagine how surprised we were to learn that you were doing it for us. In your second weight-loss chronicle, *I'm Still Hungry*, you wrote of the *Playboy* pictorial, "It would be my way of telling women out there that they could change their entire physical body, be the best they could be, and tell their detractors, Ha-ha!"

On behalf of ourselves and other women supposedly suffering from the "disease" of obesity, we beg you, please, stop trying to inspire, redeem, and instruct us by example. We kinda liked you in the early '90s—it was encouraging to see a fat woman on MTV, even if they did hide you behind a rock in all the Wilson Phillips videos. You made an attempt to address fat-phobia and promote size acceptance with appearances in fat-focused magazines such as *BBW* and *Radiance*.

Then you went away for a while, and we must confess we really didn't notice. In 1999 came the news that instead of being just a garden-variety fat person, you had become afflicted with the tragic disease of morbid obesity. Claiming that your size was threatening your health, you underwent a radical, complication-prone surgery that reduced your stomach to the size of your thumb and connected it directly to your lower intestine. As a public service to educate us about our shared disease, you let your surgery be broadcast on the Internet.

This wasn't a publicity stunt or a calculated marketing opportunity (even though it was sponsored by a clinic and a surgical-equipment maker). You told ABC News that you're "not the gastric-bypass girl." You don't like it that *People* refers to you as a "famous weight-loser." To help clear up the confusion, we suggest that you talk to Spotlight Health, the company that broadcast your surgery and cowrote your first book, *Gut Feelings: From Fear and Despair to Health and Hope,* about changing its website: It's hard not to think of you as the poster girl for weight-loss surgery when a keyword search for "morbid obesity" brings up your smiling face. Also, you might have considered keeping it to just one book about your surgically engineered transformation. Oh, and not releasing any creative work and focusing solely on your body in interviews may have further muddied the waters as to the reason for your fame.

But you must think it's worth it to be known more for what's not there than for what is. Or are you taking all the praise and pats on your newly slim back for us, too? As your latest book tells us, the *Playboy* feature is an "inspiration" for us fat gals; it's your "final redemption." And as you told ABC News, "This is for all the women who are ashamed . . . I'm saying, 'You can do it. You can let go and be free.'"

Let's get this straight. You have to strictly monitor your food intake forever to avoid pain, malnutrition, and "dumping syndrome" (cramps, nausea, diarrhea, and more). Your skin can't keep up with such a rapid and unnatural weight loss and starts hanging on you like a too-big suit, so you have to head over to the surgical tailor to get it taken in. But that's just the beginning. In addition to having seven pounds of excess skin removed, you also have to undergo a tummy tuck, a breast lift, liposuction, and a repositioning of your belly button. Then more dieting and that thrilling call from *Playboy*—which leads to yet more dieting, because they want you to lose another ten pounds before you pose.

At the shoot, you go through six hours of full-body makeup to cover your scars, then squeeze yourself into corset after corset, showing off your surgeon's supposed genius with your boobs. In a rare act of modesty, you don't display your much-operated-on abdomen. (What's up, not feeling so free?) Finally, your pictures are subjected to *Playboy*'s requisite heavy-handed airbrushing software.

So break it down for us: Exactly how does following in your footsteps allow us to "let go and be free"? Between the initial surgery, the stringent dieting, and more reconstruction than the post–Civil War South, it smells more like constriction than freedom to us. In *I'm Still Hungry*, you tell us about celebrating the close of this shoot: "Everyone clapped, and I rewarded myself in my favorite way: I ate exactly three peanut M&Ms." Girlfriend, no wonder you're still hungry.

The fawning response to your extreme physical transformation is an interesting contrast to, say, the public's incredulity at Michael Jackson's. While you've both subjected yourself to an alarming number of procedures, Michael seems to be striving for an ideal to which he alone subscribes. (Even those who argue that Jackson wants to look as white as possible would be hard-pressed to fully explain the cartoonish results.) In contrast, fatphobia makes your procedures and the results appear agreeable. So we can certainly understand why you're milking this approval for all it's worth. Americans have so many conflicts about fat—as a country, we hate our heft yet keep getting fatter—and you offer a tidy external resolution. In today's bizarre medicalized lexicon, "freedom" now means surgical installation of a radical behaviorist, one who responds with swift punishment when you eat more than your allotted two ounces.

You've presented your tale of transformation as something triumphant and radical, but its apparent denouement is the same tired image of the airbrushed blonde with her mouth hanging open. And your tragic attempt at rebellion through extreme conformity is even sadder considering you got bumped from the cover of *Playboy* by the younger women of *Survivor* ("Jenna and Heidi! Their clothes got voted off!"), not even meriting a cover line. Posing nude may give you the stamp of sexy approval, but as a thirty-five-year-old former fat woman, you're still marginalized.

Which leads us to the dilemma of people's need to see themselves reflected in celebrities so they're assured they have a place in the world. As fat women, our choices are getting slimmer all the time, as celebs from Oprah to Ricki Lake to Missy Elliott have trimmed down and renounced their former fat following. But if we find ourselves in need of inspiration, we would rather look to Kathy Bates, who has refused to make her body the cornerstone of her life's work or her fame. (And if we need to be redeemed by someone's nudity, we'll take Bates's hot-tub scene in *About Schmidt*, which showed her fleshy, fiftysomething body without comment.)

You could have used your new thin privilege to agitate for better treatment of fat people, but you elected instead to become an advocate for weight loss by any means, at any price. By spouting the company line that fat is unhealthy, ugly, and deadly, you've chosen to strengthen the forces that once made you so unhappy rather than work to disable them. So we release you, Carnie Wilson, from the burden of trying to save us fat women from ourselves. Perhaps you can find another group in need of your inspiration and leadership. We hear that Gunnar and Matthew Nelson have resigned as cochairs of the Los Angeles chapter of Narcissistic Children of '60s Rock Stars in Need of Attention but Unable to Produce Enduring Work of Their Own, leaving a void that surely you fit into at any size.

Love,
Beth and Matilda

Beyond the Bearded Lady

Outgrowing the Shame of Female Facial Hair

Aimée Dowl / SPRING 2005

IN JOHN CROWLEY'S 2003 IRISH ENSEMBLE FILM *INTERMIS-sion*, twentysomething Sally has an atrocity on her upper lip: a modest but noticeable mustache. The furry growth incites her mother's consternation and symbolizes the extent to which the brokenhearted character has allowed herself to fall apart. After enduring her mother's exhortations to remove the unsightly dark hair, Sally asks a bus driver if she has a "Ronnie," Irish slang for mustache. When he replies in the affirmative, but adds that she's no Tom Selleck, Sally retreats even further into her shell. It's not until Sally sees herself interviewed on television that she acknowledges the Ronnie. "I didn't see it," she explains as she weeps in her mother's arms.

Sally's facial hair is meant as a symbol of her character's emotional state, yet it also highlights the reality of many women who do not recognize their "excess" facial hair until it becomes glaringly apparent in a photograph or in the comments of others. For other women, the scene acknowledges an equally uncomfortable reality—that the removal of facial hair has become a bona fide female rite of passage.

According to a 1999 Bristol-Myers Squibb study, forty-one million American women between the ages of fifteen and seventy-four have removed unwanted facial hair within the past six months, and approximately twenty-two million American women remove facial hair at least once a week. Whether it's the translucent, downy hairs that appear on women's upper lips during adolescence or the darker, coarser hairs that ebb and flow with hormonal adjustments in their twenties and thirties, if it's there, it's "unsightly"; if it's unsightly, it's gone. But these numbers bring up another question: If so many women have facial hair, why is it considered abnormal? And if so many women are removing their facial hair, then isn't facial hair as genuine a part of the female experience as it is of the male experience?

When humans first walked across the plains in all our hairy glory, the fight for daily survival—to say nothing of the lack of reflective surfaces—presumably superseded the desire to present a soft, smooth countenance. Somewhere along the evolutionary way, women lost much more of their hair than men, and what some women didn't lose, they were eventually compelled to remove themselves. Since at least the time of the Egyptian pharaohs, women, beauticians, and doctors have devised methods to remedy the "problem" of facial hair: shaving, waxing, plucking, trimming, bleaching, and even scraping. It was in nineteenth-century France that a doctor first wrote about the procedure of cauterizing follicles with hot needles in order to remove unwanted hair—a procedure that may sound masochistic by current standards but was the antecedent to today's electrolysis.

Although many cultures across the ages have idealized hairlessness in women, modern American culture has perhaps more than others maniacally sought the hairless ideal through the relentless application of facial- and body-hair removal techniques. In the 1930s, upper-class women were so distraught about their "superfluous" facial hair that they fell victim to quacks who sometimes subjected them to carcinogenic X-rays that resulted in burns, scars, and death.

During this time, female hirsutes—defined as women with heavy hair growth on the face and body—removed their unwanted beards and mustaches; those who allowed their hair to grow often ended up in circuses, where they were displayed in sideshows as bearded ladies. These days, women sporting overt facial hair may not be confined to a tent, but they are still considered a freak show. The many ways women bleach, tweeze, and pluck their hair out of existence are more often than not played for either laughs or pity. In *Reality Bites*, we're treated to Winona Ryder's character Lelaina hurriedly bleaching her mustache before a date; Rosie O'Donnell, back in the days of her talk show, joked about stringing beads onto her chin hair. On the pity end of things, makeover subjects on *Extreme Makeover* and *The Swan* are shown in "before" montages staring morosely at their mustaches or wispy goatees in the mirror while a voice-over details their daily shame. Advertising for hair-removal methods both high-tech and old-school (laser hair removal has become increasingly widespread, while in some urban areas, the traditional Indian process of threading has come into vogue) urgently targets women, with occasionally brazen insults. (One recent advertisement for hair-removal services in a San Diego weekly newspaper used a photograph of a gorilla.)

Male-focused makeover shows like *Queer Eye* have brought the term "manscaping" into the pop lexicon with segments about back waxing and eyebrow plucking, suggesting that there's nothing strictly girly about men curbing their body and facial hair in order to enhance the overall package. But there's no female correlative, no suggestion that a little extra underbrush on the ladies is okay, too; if anything, the body-grooming imperative has intensified for women as it has been normalized for men. So it's hardly surprising that a masculine/feminine dichotomy still plagues the topic of facial hair, and for women this means a barrage of assumptions about power, sexuality, and—most of all—"normal" femininity.

During World War II, American women gave up their stockings to save silk material for the war effort, leading to a widespread appeal for bare, hairless legs. This look, which emphasized women's skin, and hence their femininity, also emerged at a time when women were entering the workplace and adopting traditionally male roles. These days, women's removal of their facial hair is just another concession in the militarized zones of masculine and feminine, where women must still conform or confront considerable judgment and ridicule.

A study conducted in 1998 by Susan A. Basow and Amie C. Braman asked 195 undergraduate men and women to watch two videos of a woman drying off after a swim. In one video, the woman's legs and armpits are hairy, and in the other, her body is shaved. The hairy woman was seen as significantly "less friendly, moral, and relaxed," and "more aggressive, unsociable, strong, nonconformist, dominant, assertive, independent, and in better physical condition." While the positive and negative meanings of these descriptors depends on individual perceptions, their gendered connotations cannot be mistaken.

But it doesn't take a social scientist to document the social disapproba-tion—from disgusted looks to job discrimination to outright violence—accorded to women who, by refusing the pressure to remove their body hair, dare to transgress into "masculine" territory. A small but growing subculture of lesbians and transgendered persons are proudly embracing facial hair as a marker of desired female masculinity, but homophobic con-fusion and ignorance in the larger culture have reinforced perceptions of this follicular reclamation as haplessly unfeminine rather than purpose-fully subversive. And in mainstream pop culture, especially as typified in shows like *The L Word*, lesbians are just as prone to normative femininity as straight girls.

Still, for some women, facial hair is simply a proudly revealed part of the female, even feminine, experience. Teresa Carr, a fifty-year-old consul-tant and poet, has not shaved since 1973, when she discovered hairs grow-ing on her chin. Strangers regularly inquire about her beard—which she describes as a Ho Chi Minh–style goatee—with questions that are gen-uinely inquisitive and sometimes rude. Jennifer Miller, forty-four, director of Circus Amok, a politically progressive circus that addresses current events through age-old acts, has reinvented the tradition of the bearded lady, developing the persona of the "bearded woman," which she wears proudly both in the circus and in her day job as an adjunct professor at sev-eral colleges and universities. The bearded woman doesn't wear hyperfem-inine clothing as former bearded ladies did, nor does she cloister herself within the circus sideshow tents; instead, she offers a positive, unapolo-getic image of bearded women in a world of the plucked, shaved, and waxed.

Miller recognizes the pressure women feel about facial hair growth—"women have fear of not being seen as women, fear of not being clean-skinned, fear of being a freak," she notes—but for both her and Carr, growing their substantial facial hair sends a message to others about the realities of women's bodies and personal freedom. "Socially," Carr states, "the discrimination is meant to proscribe the footsteps of women who choose to walk an alternative, self-determined path. I think that wearing your facial hair is an announcement of that self-determination."

Our culture sees too few women like Carr and Miller who choose to draw attention to their "abnormal" facial hair—and even when it recognizes them, does so in the service of further marginalization. An article on Miller that appeared in *The New York Times* almost a decade ago was titled "Step Right Up! See the Bearded Person!" and, though it quotes Miller as saying that she doesn't see her beard as a problem and doesn't care what caused it, the article makes no effort to position female facial hair growth as a common experience. We're even willing to revise history: Deeply carnal, famously mustachioed Frida Kahlo, for instance, was literally cleaned up for her transition to the big screen in 2002's biopic, the mustache she immortalized in so many self-portraits nowhere in sight.

If the recent normalization of cosmetic surgery has shown us anything, it's that people will go to great lengths and take big medical risks in order to conform to cultural beauty standards, and that women in particular seem sadly susceptible to the shame marketing that characterizes electrolysis, waxing, and laser hair-removal services. And though ideas of normative masculinity and femininity are questioned more consistently now than they were when doctors were scarring women with painful follicle cauterizations, the standard of hairlessness has a particularly tenacious hold on many cultures that, for lots of women, may never loosen.

But there are those who challenge it. Carr and Miller are joining women like Trish Morrissey, an artist whose photos of women with facial hair function as a direct confrontation with the idea of femininity, hair, and power. Her subjects stare unflinchingly into the camera; neither sideshow characters nor politically motivated facial-hair activists, they simply are—and by simply being, are a challenge.

Then there's *Intermission*'s Sally, who, after overcoming the denial of her Ronnie, tells a man to whom she is obviously attracted that she is going to have the mustache waxed at a spa. In this moment, when Sally is starting to recover her emotional strength, the fellow says, "What mustache?" Although he finally admits that he can see the facial hair, his kindness makes a big difference to the fragile woman. The audience doesn't get to see Sally remove the Ronnie—although she does—but, as for many women, knowing that some people accept her natural hair makes the plucking and prodding far less painful.

7

. . . .

Confronting the
Mainstream

AFTER A DECADE OF SURVEYING THE POP LANDSCAPE, WE'RE constantly reminded of what has changed since *Bitch* began. Pop culture critique, considered mere fluff journalism in the mid-'90s, has become commonplace in such formerly lofty organs as *The Wall Street Journal* and *The New Yorker*. The Internet, once a thrilling-yet-nebulous curiosity, has become an info mecca for culture junkies, a place where you can cross-reference actors on the Internet Movie Database, read blisteringly funny recaps of *The Apprentice* and *The Sopranos* on Television Without Pity, and suck hours out of each workday perusing thousands of political, artistic, and satiric web publications and blogs. Pop culture might even be making us smarter. Steven Johnson, in his 2005 book, *Everything Bad Is Good for You*, argues that increasingly sharp, complex writing in television, video games, and beyond challenges us to flex our problem-solving and abstract-reasoning skills—and in the process offers pop obsessives an ironclad rationalization for their avocation.

But if the critique of pop culture, as well as its perceived social value, has improved, why hasn't the culture itself evolved more? This is the question at the heart of *Bitch*. Over the past ten years, we've watched as women's soccer and basketball held young girls in their well-muscled thrall only to falter or even fold due to lack of funding, as weedy little Ally McBeal stamped her foot and pouted, as fashion mavens declared that Jennifer Lopez's keister made her "full-figured," and as the Spice Girls came and went on a sugary wave of girl power. We've puzzled over films like *Fat Girl* and book sensations like *He's Just Not That Into You*, survived an improbable number of dating-and-mating reality shows (*Married by America*, anyone?), and watched in bemusement as celebrity tabloids reproduced like especially trashy rabbits. But what we haven't seen is any meaningful, validating change in the mainstream perception and representation of women.

Loving pop culture comes at a price, and for many women that price is most often a deep sense of betrayal at being told the lives that we're shown onscreen, in books, and in advertising are accurate, important, and charmingly quirky reflections of our own. The stereotypes and limitations of popular representations of women haunt us everywhere from talk radio to chick lit, and the common language such products use when they discuss and define the world of women is often maddening. Though newspapers no longer feature condescendingly titled "women's pages," there's still a clear-cut separation between what's shaped for our cultural consumption and what isn't. We've got blocks of TV commercials that run during *Oprah* and *Desperate Housewives* (cleaning products, diapers, and tampons ahoy!); women's mags advertise "decadent" scented shaving gel, their language implying that each woman lives in a diet-obsessed *Cathy* comic; and news organs feel free to frame politics as a "women's issue" only when it involves abortion. The condescension may no longer be spelled out in twenty-four-point type, but it's loud and clear.

And it seems as though the more fantastical our would-be mass-market doppelgängers become, the more persistently they are held up as evidence of real women's selfishness, unrealistic expectations, or, hell, feminist failure. Never before have so many fictional women been asked to symbolize their generation: We thought it was bad back in 1992, when Dan Quayle got his Brooks Brothers shorts in a bunch over baby mama Murphy Brown. But who could predict the supposed role models that would slowly stack up? First there was Ally McBeal, fawned over in women's magazines as the working woman's alter ego but lambasted on the cover of *Time* as an emblem of feminism's failure. Hot on her bitsy heels was Bridget Jones, celebrated as the new voice of the man-crazed single woman. Then came Carrie Bradshaw and her potty-mouthed girl posse, anointed as the real new voice of the man-fatigued, shoe-crazed somewhat-single woman—empowered, we were told, by their shocking nondependence on men and the economic freedom they enjoyed. And then there were the Desperate Housewives, the *new* new voices of the crazed single and/or married woman—also empowered, we were reminded, by their independence and even their sneaky secrets. See a pattern?

It's really not fair to blame the people who created these characters for how they were snapped up by the mainstream as paragons of modern—and empowered, of course!—womanhood. It's not as if Helen Fielding ever represented Bridget Jones as anything other than the bumbling disaster she so cartoonishly is. The problem with Bridget is the problem with Ally is the problem with Carrie is the problem with the ladies of Wisteria Lane: As much as we'd like our most visible, quotable, merchandise-moving pop icons to be women we would want to be—rather than those we cross our fingers and hope we're not—the market seems to seize on endless variations on insecurity, incompetence, competition, and frivolity and then tries to pass them off to us as versions of feminism.

The pop culture world, as limited as it often seems, isn't lacking in multifaceted, thoughtful females—from smart-mouthed cops and doctors on prime-time procedural dramas to nuanced characters in contemporary fiction to real-life icons like Kate Winslet and Queen Latifah and Tina Fey. So seeing the women who pout over men, catfight with women, solve every ill with shopping, and perpetuate antifeminist cant heralded as those who, in fact, embody the modern female mind-set just won't work anymore.

That said, we know change is incremental. Ten years ago, for example, it was hard enough to find one lesbian character on TV; the fact that there's now a cable show like *The L Word* can't be dismissed as progress. But each step demands further steps: In this case, the next would be a show about lesbians where the characters look like they stepped out of somewhere other than the letters section of *Penthouse*. It doesn't mean that feminists, as so often rumored, just can't be happy with what the culture deigns to bestow upon us—what it means is that we have a right to lobby the culture (including the self-proclaimed feminists who are responsible for creating shows like *The L Word*, say) for more and better representations of who we know we are. The point is not to wipe all the bookstore shelves clean of those pastel-covered chick-lit novels, each with a shoe or martini glass on the cover, or to bully all the Kings of Queens off the TV networks, or to fill every single billboard and advertising page with models who look more like the actual girl next door than like wholesome fantasy neighbor Heidi Klum. What's important is to have a diversity of everything: people, viewpoints, races, classes, sexualities, religions, and ideals within pop culture and accessible to everyone.

People have often wondered why *Bitch* is so devoted to pop culture when pop culture has proved over and over again how completely nondevoted it is to giving feminism its props. (We love Maude like she's our own mother, but you just can't argue that she was created to make feminism look attractive to either women or men.) What we say in response is this: Mainstream pop culture can't be ignored, but, more important, it shouldn't be—that's where we all find our ideals and our cultural beliefs played out and reflected, and it's only going to continue. If politicians and the news media are going to treat fictional characters as stand-ins for real women, it's up to us to figure out how to make those stand-ins more lifelike. Women and girls need to arm themselves with media literacy like it's Wonder Woman's magic bracelets, because there are life-zapping consequences to letting mainstream dispatches about What Women Do go unchallenged. We might not be able to stop teenage girls from, say, taking their cues about personal worth from *America's Next Top Model* or *The Real World*, but we can ask them—loudly and repeatedly—to look at the machinations behind that "reality." Political idealism and activism are crucial, but pop culture has the juice to bring it to the people. We wouldn't believe in *Bitch* if we didn't believe in the power of pop to change minds, inspire lives, and put the need for action into words and images that last.   —A.Z.

Pratt-fall

Ten Things to Hate About *Jane*

Lisa Jervis and Andi Zeisler,
with special guest vitriol by Rita Hao / WINTER 1999

WHEN WE HEARD THAT JANE PRATT, THE FORMER EDITOR OF
Sassy—the sharp, celebrated teen mag that was staunchly unwilling to pull its
readers into the spiral of insecurity and product consumption so endemic to
the genre—was launching a new grown-up glossy, we, along with other feminist pop culture junkies nationwide, squealed with excitement. Then *Jane*
launched, and we weren't excited anymore. Here's why.

1. Its fake, sanctimonious, look-how-we-encourage-you-not-to-be-
obsessive-and-negative-about-your-body tone, combined with models even
skinnier than *Vogue's*, constant reminders of all the beauty tasks you absolutely must do, and plugs for an endless array of products to help you at it.
After August 1998's smug and self-satisfied proclamation that "We're so
against boot-camp tactics of body toning and the pressure to skinny up for
summer," the mag encourages you to "make a good thing better" with exer-
cises to get rid of your "Jell-O thighs," "Buddha belly," and other problem
spots. The editors think they're touting self-esteem, but they're really just reinforcing the idea that you can change the way you feel about yourself simply by changing the way you look: "We want you to be kissing that bathroom
mirror—even if your stomach makes it difficult to reach over the sink . . .
[But] if you're not that liberated yet, take baby steps and focus on your favorite peeve." Um, here's a better idea: Why not take a huge step and forget

285

your favorite peeve instead of letting some magazine writer sell you an exercise regimen under the guise of uncritical self-acceptance and distaste for exercise regimens?

Take *Jane*'s shot of the skinniest girl you ever saw. "A chubby tummy is sexy and an empty tummy is so not," gushes the accompanying hypocrisy . . . I mean, copy. Well, if you actually think so, then why not put your photo editor where your copywriter is and actually print a picture (gasp!) of a chubby, or even unemaciated, bod? I don't care if "[fashion director] Sciascia swears that Anne-Catherine, our model here, is a healthy eater with a healthy body." She could just as easily be illustrating a story about anorexia, so stop with the defensiveness and get new models already.

2. Never has a magazine been so self-obsessed as this one, under the auspices of reaching out to its audience. At first it's easy to believe that the *Jane* staff wants to be your friend. If they didn't, they wouldn't publish pictures of themselves in the editor's note—insouciantly titled "Jane's Diary"—so you're sure to notice how cute and stylish they all are, and so you won't overlook how wacky life around the office can be. And who else but your friends tell you when they get their periods and give themselves goofy little nicknames like "Granny Fanny"?

The fact that every page of the magazine has been injected with irrelevant personal tidbits is precisely what's supposed to make *Jane* more accessible than women's glossies like *Elle* or *Glamour*, ones in which you don't turn every page to discover that this editor was dumped badly or that writer was feeling bloated on the day of a big interview. This device was also much of what set *Sassy* apart from the teen magazines of its day, but the informative, girls'-room chattiness that permeated *Sassy* turns, in the context of *Jane*, into egregious narcissism. The difference can perhaps be attributed to the age gap between the writers and their audience; since the staff of *Jane* are ostensibly around the same age as its readers, their in-jokes and self-congratulatory tone aren't so much about reaching out to their audience in an effort to make them feel comfortable and understood as about holding themselves above said audience. To make a high-school analogy—which is the kind that seems most appropriate in this case—*Jane* is like the girl in your homeroom who chats with you pleasantly enough, but always manages to mention that her skirt cost more than yours.

3. The blithe unconcern with which the mag suggests spending huge amounts of money on items of debatable utility. Some of the items that are "affordable" and "guilt-free" in the *Jane* universe: $100 wooden thong sandals, $90 silver mesh slides, and a $195 miniskirt that's meant to be worn with a $158 bustier and a $98 sweatshirt. The presumably guilt-ridden stuff is, of course, more: A random sampling of fashion spreads yields a $490 Armani jacket (styled in a faux camping tableau, by the way), a $415 camisole, and one page featuring a selection of items that total more than many of us make in a month—a $590 skirt, a $365 sweater, a $720 coat, and more. The only thing that most of us could afford would be the socks from the Gap.

4. *Jane*'s emphasis on individuality is countered by fashion-forward dogma on a near-constant basis. Take the Jane Makeunder, in which a gal with some kind of individual look (big curly glam hair, funky eye makeup) is magically transformed to look hip, natural, and straight-tressed—conveniently, just like all the *Jane* girls. The magazine's encouragement to make your own decisions is hard to take seriously when placed beside such statements as "You'll be wearing violet shadow (oh yes you will!)" or "Haircolor used to be a bold move—now you feel almost naked without it." It's telling that the one beauty feature that actually realizes the magazine's credo of individuality wasn't written by any of the staff—it's the *Jane* beauty survey, in which readers write in to confess to a triple-digit lipstick collection and sing the praises of their favorite conditioner. Our suggestion to *Jane*—let your readers do more speaking for themselves, because if individuality is really what you're all about, why should we give a fuck that bright red eyeliner/orange lipstick/dead baby seal pelts/etc. were all over the runways in Milan?

5. Blatant advertorial. Isn't it convenient that a page singing the praises of impossible-to-walk-in stiletto heels is placed directly across from an advertisement for Gucci's, um, stiletto heels?

6. *Jane* thinks we're still supposed to give a tiny rat's ass how men want us to look and behave. The overweening focus on the superficial, ersatz do-it-for-you tone, and fake individualism (see item 4) add up to this: Your appearance and behavior are not about being attractive to men. Except when they

are, which is most of the time. Token staff boy Tony Romando, who functions as *Jane*'s voice of universal male opinion, graciously lets us in on scoops such as: Men don't like "granny panties" or "when action hair is excessive." The latter is "just too masculine for us and, besides, we were weaned on centerfolds in girlie magazines." (Maybe we girls would kinda like for you to learn the difference between the woman in your bed and the one in the magazine on the back of your toilet . . . but I digress.) The message is still that what men think matters more than what we think. Wouldn't it be better for us to eat (which, according to Tony, guys dig) and be opinionated (ditto) because we want to, not because some mag told us that boys like it?

7. When their lips are not actually attached to famous buttocks, the *Jane* staff keeps busy dropping names of close, personal celebrity friends. Each issue is stuffed to the brim with gratuitous celeb kissy-kissy: "Jane and I were unexpectedly whisked away to an intimate dinner hosted by Donatella Versace at the late Gianni Versace's town house. We ate lobster salad and drank champagne while Bono took a tour of the art collection." "By the way, Ethan Hawke called to say how much he liked Nicole Burdette's fiction story in our premiere issue. And Courteney Cox called to congratulate us." "Samantha Mathis is an amazing person and an amazing actress." The special Touched by a Celeb, Like We Care prize goes to Pratt herself: "I was going to say Michael [Stipe of R.E.M.] and I used to date, but he says, 'Let's just throw the euphemisms right out the window and say that we . . . were friends and lovers on and off for several years.'"

8. *Jane* is mean. And I don't mean mean like a mean martini. I mean just mean. In the June/July 1998 editor's note, for instance, Jane Pratt lashes out at an intern who thought that it might not be such a hot idea to put Pamela Anderson on the cover. (Said intern, and anyone else who isn't thrilled with the choice of cover model, are "so-called feminists" who are "elitist," "predictable," and "closed-minded." But certainly reasonable minds could differ on the appropriateness of putting a woman who arguably made her fame and fortune through her breast implants on the cover of a magazine that purports to speak to progressive women.) Writers also love to throw around choice phrases like "whiny coffeehouse wench" and use the magazine's letters column to insult their fans. Lovely.

9. When it comes to features, style over substance is definitely the order of the day. Granted, celebrity journalism is not known for its intrinsic depth, but *Jane*'s burning desire to be the Mag That Famous People Like (see item 7) ensures that the compelling stories they do run will always be outnumbered by those of the "Milla Jovovich is rilly cool and she invited me to her house, and by the way, she smokes Parliaments!" variety.

10. *Jane* made promises it couldn't keep. "I didn't want to create a magazine that would make women feel bad after reading it. I didn't want it to be a manual for all your flaws and all the things you need to fix," Pratt commented in a *New York Times* article that accompanied the magazine's release in September 1997. One of the standard criticisms of women's magazines is that they present their readers with a completely unrealistic idea of what a woman's life is/should be. Smart women know it's not all about curling irons and bikini waxes and dog-earing your copy of *The Rules*, and it's this knowledge that is supposedly the engine behind *Jane*.

But Pratt and her cohorts probably shouldn't strain their arms patting themselves on the back. It's true that you won't find diet plans, calorie breakdowns, or dopey self-discovery quizzes within *Jane*'s matte-finish pages. But much as *Jane* would like to believe that retro typefaces and bleeding-edge fashion styling make it the anti-*Cosmo*, it ain't so easy. In plenty of the ways that count, *Jane* is just like any other women's magazine (see items 1, 3, 4, 5, 6). There might not be an article on, say, how cellulite makes you a less valuable person, but *Jane*'s premiere issue's road test of cellulite creams featured Pratt herself remarking that she hid her tube of something called Chanel Multi-Hydroxy Cellulite Complex "so no one would think I cared about something so superficial."

MAYBE OUR EXPECTATIONS OF *JANE* WERE UNFAIR. MAYBE IT'S our own fault for forgetting that anything run by a major media conglomerate can hardly buck the ad-driven culture of women's magazines that literally depends on the product plug for its revenue stream. There was a reason, after all, why *Sassy* went down the tubes. But why insult intelligent women by instituting hypocrisy from the start? Sad as it is, we're used to women's magazines making us feel that we're not thin or pretty or rich or well-heeled enough, and that's why many of us choose not to read them. But it's far worse to be smugly informed that what we're getting from *Jane* is different, when in fact the only difference lies in the pitch itself. *Jane*'s snooty, preening reality is that much more painful for having the initial premise—and Pratt's own promises—dangled before us. Good design may allow *Jane* to assume the pose of an alternative to the usual crop of women's magazines, but the result is nothing more than, to cop a phrase from our high-school math teacher, an old friend in a new hat. An advertiser-smooching, beauty-product-hawking, celebrity-ass-kissing, skinny-model-filled old friend in a new, faux-iconoclastic, hypocritical, self-congratulatory hat.

Marketing Miss Right

Meet the Single Girl, Twenty-First-Century Style

Andi Zeisler / WINTER 2000

> "I'm single because I was born that way."   —Mae West, 1967
> "I am going to die. But I will die married."
> —Suzanne Finnamore, *Otherwise Engaged*, 1999

STANDING IN LINE AT THE MOVIES, I'M LISTENING TO A friend chat with an old acquaintance behind us. As they bemoan the state of San Francisco housing, the acquaintance mentions that her older sister just purchased a hunk of East Coast real estate. "She bought a six-room apartment," she says proudly. A dramatic pause, and then the kicker: "Without him."

Him? Who's him?

Oh, him. Right. I feel as though I've been transported into one of those General Foods International Coffee ads, where a knot of women sit around someone's living room with their Café Hazelnut Mochas, reinforcing female stereotypes for all they're worth. This woman is waiting for my friend to respond excitedly, but what is she supposed to say? "Gosh, it's great that your sister isn't afraid to look like a pathetic spinster, what with having her very own apartment and all"?

It's weird to hear women still mouthing the kind of stuff that even *Cosmo* seems to know better than to print these days. But then, it's kind of a weird time to be a single woman. On the one hand, the choice to be single is acknowledged and validated in ways that seemed unthinkable as little as a dozen years ago, when the famous you'll-have-a-better-chance-of-being-killed-by-terrorists-than-getting-married-in-your-thirties reports flowed in from every media venue around. Slowly, the ranks of the never-married are swelling, and with about forty million single women in America, it's a demographic that's getting noticed.

On the other hand, what's getting noticed about single women in 1999 can be summed up with two words: Bridget Jones. The current era of the single woman might as well be described as post-BJ, since it seems that no pop cultural mention of either women or singlehood can pass without trotting out her booze-swilling British ass as evidence that we're all thigh- and marriage-obsessed neurotics. Never mind that single women are owning their own businesses in record numbers, matching men dollar for dollar in spending, and remaking the arts in their own image. It's much easier to market to single women by dwelling on what they aren't—married, and by extension settled comfortably into society. Pick up a book, peruse a diamond ad, watch your television, eavesdrop on people at the movies: We're tapping a well of long-extant stereotypes, fears, and assumptions about single women and selling them back to ourselves at a bargain price.

Bridget Jones Superstar

The publication of 1995's *The Rules* may have set the wheels of pop culture's retro-cycle in motion, but the unprecedented success of *Bridget Jones's Diary* sent it into hyperdrive. Helen Fielding's *London Independent* column–turned-novel put a goofy, semi-ironic face on the same story women have been fed for years—the one about the single career woman who, rapidly approaching thirty, goes into what can only be called a marriage frenzy. But whether the million-plus women who bought and loved the book were responding to its gently satiric prodding of the beauty myth or letting its sarcasm fly right over their heads is beside the point— marketers everywhere saw a publishing zeitgeist waiting to happen and quickly positioned Bridget to be its patron saint. The newish crop of books featuring single female protagonists, all released in the spring and summer of 1999, testify.

Take Melissa Bank's *The Girls' Guide to Hunting and Fishing*, a book of interrelated short stories that, according to its promotional copy, "explores the life lessons of Jane, the contemporary American Everywoman who combines the charm of Bridget Jones [and] the vulnerability of Ally McBeal." Or Suzanne Finnamore's *Otherwise Engaged,* a comedy of prenuptial manners that replaces Bridget's now-famed fear of "dying alone and being found three weeks later half-eaten by an Alsatian" with the more prosaic "I'll die a spinster, a gaggle of cats sniffing my bloated corpse." Or Amy Sohn's *Run Catch Kiss,* the story of a sex columnist courting relationship disaster with her tell-all dispatches (the *Independent,* in a slice of praise that takes the fiction-as-reality thing to an unreasonable level, dubbed Sohn "the thinking person's Bridget Jones").

There are others: *In the Drink,* Kate Christensen's darker-than-dark-humored tale of a hapless, lovelorn, and unappreciated ghostwriter with an unbridled hankering for the sauce; and *A Certain Age,* Tama Janowitz's story of a woman whose ridiculously high standards preclude finding the Right Man. Finally, there's Melissa Roth, who, in the nonfiction book *On the Loose,* tracks three single women through one year in their lives in order to capture the "'real world' of single living."

If these books have any individual characteristics to separate them from one another, you wouldn't know it from their reviews and marketing. True, the characters share certain things: They're attractive women in their twenties or thirties; they're educated, self-aware, and quick with a wise aside; they live in New York, San Francisco, or London; they work in publishing or advertising; their families appear every few chapters, Greek chorus–style, to shake their heads in synchronized dismay. Within their pages, the characters are small-*s* single; with the exception of *On the Loose,* their singleness is simply part of a narrative life that doesn't itself purport to define the word. In a marketing context, however, they are Single Women—shameless, hapless, man-hunting single women—and their subtleties and differences are ignored in the spotlight's glare.

Where Are We Going and Why Am I in This Borders Handbasket?

Don't blame the authors. As long as women have been writing, they've been writing about young, single women searching for love, success, and happiness (though, please remember, not necessarily in that order). Still, it's hard to recall a time when so many female authors have been hyped so arduously and favorably all at once, and this Lilith Fair of literature would be wholly gratifying if not for one major thing: The books, marketed by their publishers as the spawn of Bridget Jones and addressed by reviewers as the direct result of Fielding's success, are made weaker on their own (in most cases considerable) merits.

New York magazine's rundown of the trend, titled "Success and the Single Girl," crowned *BJD* "The Gold Standard" before dismissing the new crop of books as no more than clones. (*The Girls' Guide to Hunting and Fishing* becomes "Intellectual Bridget"; *In the Drink* is "Dipso Bridget.") This easy categorization makes for snappy copy, but in doing so it dispenses with the literary context in which these books exist. It's as though everyone from Jane Austen to Alice Adams has been completely wiped from the cultural blackboard and the only ones left to represent in the single-gal arena are this year's girls.

"One reviewer called *Run Catch Kiss* 'A wobbly attempt to follow in Bridget Jones's Manolo Blahniks,'" says Amy Sohn, whose *New York Press* column, "Female Trouble," formed the basis for her cheerfully potty-mouthed debut novel. "She doesn't even wear Manolo Blahniks! What frustrates me is the idea that anyone who sits down to write a book is doing it to mimic someone else." It doesn't matter that *Run Catch Kiss* has more in common with *Portnoy's Complaint* than it does with *BJD*, or that Melissa Bank's subtle writing recalls the prose of Lorrie Moore far more than it channels Fielding's sugar-high stylings. The single-girl market is hot, and it behooves publishers to shoehorn as many books as possible into the demographic while the fire's lit.

It's worth noting that certain commercially undesirable factors disqualify a book for hard-core Bridgetized marketing. *My Year of Meats*, Ruth Ozeki's novel about a single Japanese-American television producer who unwittingly stumbles into a massive beef-ranching scandal—one of the smartest and most original books to come out in the past few years—hasn't found itself linking arms with BJ and her ilk. All the elements are there— the almost-thirty heroine, her noncommittal boyfriend, her neurotic mother, and her quirky coworkers have zeitgeist written all over them. But both its author and its main character are Asian American; add to that an explicitly political premise and you don't even have to start doing the math to know that *Meats* wouldn't reap the same caliber of PR booty as its single-girl sisters.

Slingin' Singles

What these books do have in common is that they center on single women, and, as such, provide ruminations on what it means to be single. Duh, right? Sure—the problem is that the marketing doesn't reflect the fact that characters like *In the Drink*'s Claudia and *The Girls' Guide*'s Jane don't, in fact, spend the entire narrative plotting to snag the honeymoon suite. Their version of singlehood doesn't necessarily treat the term "single" as a provisional tag, something to be endured until they find the person who lifts that semantic albatross from around their necks. *Otherwise Engaged*'s Eve, on the other hand, flaunts her equation of marriage = salvation on every page with ruminations like "The ring is my lump-sum payment for everything bad that has ever happened to me. I don't feel I can tell people this, or they will spoil it." Another entry in the genre, Kathy Lette's *Altar Ego*, presents us with a group of characters whose brain-free couplings and decouplings prop up every prejudice about both single women and marriage (women only marry rich; feminists discard their principles when Mr. Man comes calling; women concentrate on their careers only when they can't get a husband, etc.). And *On the Loose* compares and contrasts the lives of three single women in Los Angeles, New York, and San Francisco—or at least attempts to. For all the diversity that could be gleaned from both the premise and the locations, Roth gives us a trio of central-casting white girls, each working in the corporate world (two in entertainment, one in advertising), and all of similar socioeconomic backgrounds. The writing makes it almost impossible to tell whether these women have any characteristics that set them apart from each other, and in the course of following their interchangeable lives—a mélange of bad dates, film premieres, record-release parties, and expense-account vacations—it becomes difficult to care. If this was fiction, we'd simply write them off as caricatures. But *On the Loose* is a nonfiction work that claims to capture what it's like to be a single woman in the '90s, so the fact that its one-dimensionality is meant to resonate with actual women seriously rankles. You can't even get past the jacket blurb without stumbling onto a played-out cliché of singlehood:

"Jen . . . adopts kittens despite the old-maid stereotype." The upshot is that while some of these books do support the stereotypes that fuel the parade float of marketing, the ones that don't are swept up for the ride, smiling and waving in bewilderment.

Subtext and the Single Girl

What the marketing of these books shows shouldn't come as any surprise: Single women may be a blossoming demographic, but the industries courting our cash are the same ones whose doors still swing on the flimsy hinges of stereotypical gender difference. Advertising to women has only recently barely begun to address the idea that some women choose to stay single.

In a *Village Voice* article called "Women Are Easy: Why TV Ad Agencies Take Female Viewers for Granted," Susan Faludi mused on the gender bias that still rules advertising: "For all the talk about market research, when it comes to gender, people switch from the local part of the brain to creaky nostrums about what works for men and for women, and what doesn't."

Which is why, even when we see a lone woman in a car commercial, the car itself isn't being marketed to her. (That's to say nothing of the one that features a mother palming off her single daughter on a nearby man by fak-·ing her own car's brake failure.) The ads that are slowly popping up to address the single woman, in fact, fit right in with the same conception of singlehood advanced by the trend in single-girl lit—that is, they play on the twin specters of marriage and physical insecurity, reframing them to flatter the single woman. De Beers, the company that essentially invented the concept of the diamond engagement ring ("A diamond is forever"), is now wooing the women who may not be accepting an emerald-cut one-carat from Mr. Billfold, but who are sporting enough cash and pride to purchase their own rocks. In one ad, a semisilhouetted woman in a diamond solitaire necklace smirks opposite this copy: "It beckons me as I pass the store window. A flash of light in the corner of my eye. I stop. I turn. We look at each other. And though I'm usually not that kind of girl, I take it home."

The ad recasts diamond craving as something naughty; the single woman eyeing the stone isn't a demure bride-to-be but a coy, self-assured hussy. On the one hand, it's a nod to self-sufficiency and sexual agency: the *Sex and the City* of ads. On the other hand, De Beers knows full well that women associate the company with engagement rings, and this ad serves as a reminder of the buyer's marital status: She's defined against the company's bread-and-butter customers, and what's reinforced is her singleness.

Then there's an ad featuring a close-up of a smiling young woman and the message "Amber O'Brien, 25, is having the time of her life. Recently, she decided it was time to have breast augmentation." The ad, for Mentor breast implants, cloaks its hard sell in a contrived fact file ostensibly about Amber herself: It lists her "Pet Peeve" ("People who pressure you into doing things"), her "Proudest Achievement" ("Buying a condo"), and her "Life Mission" ("Always be open to new ideas"). The total effect is as subtle as sequined pasties on a pair of silicone double-Ds: Amber is successful and solvent, and buying fake hooters is simply another achievement in her life.

Like the recent glut of single-girl fiction, ads like these give unpartnered women the oh-so-generous gift of recognizing them as a viable consumer entity while simultaneously emphasizing their insecurities (or what are assumed to be their insecurities). Positioning diamonds and breast implants—things that are generally assumed to be done with or for a man—as choices made for their own sake, without the phantom "him" to influence the purchase, validates the single woman while still trying to exploit her fears. The ads apply positive signifiers of empowerment and well-being to products loaded with negative associations for the single woman (dangerous implants, rings that only "the lucky ones" get to wear), so that we think we're seeing a reexamination of single women in consumer culture. But the De Beers ad doesn't fundamentally change the line with which we connect its conceptual dots; it simply takes the familiar progression of relationship + diamonds = happiness and excises the first element.

On the other hand, almost all of the entries in the post BJ era of chick lit go where the ads can't afford to—revising assumptions of what it means to be single and coupled, recognizing societal strictures and how they affect our own ideas of what is or isn't "normal." Books like *The Girls' Guide* and *Run Catch Kiss* present us with relatable, smart heroines whose search for love is only one part of a larger need to find a comfortable place in a world they know full well rewards those who settle into the status quo. And only a very small number of their heroines ask us to believe that they're walking off into the sunset, ring on finger, in the last paragraph. But the marketing purposely masks this, ignoring the picture painted by the books themselves in favor of the single-girl shill proclaimed by Bridget-boosters as the Real Thing. Marketing hoodoo that relies on a conception of singleness that still translates to "looking for a man" rather than "alone and fine with it, thank you" will never offer the single woman a fair vision of herself—one that acknowledges that there's more than one route to happiness, and that the road there isn't always paved with empty bottles of gin and Slim-Fast.

The God of Big Trends

Book Publishing's Ethnic Cool Quotient

Noy Thrupkaew / SPRING 2002

"YOU KNOW, YOU REALLY SHOULD BE LOOKING FOR THE NEXT Arundhati Roy."

I plucked at the phone cord wrapped around my neck, sighed, and said, "Oh, absolutely."

It was 1998, and I was working at a publishing company that had just launched an imprint featuring "the writing of women of all colors." It was my internly task to call independent booksellers across the country to find out what and whom they thought we should publish. Their advice inevitably boiled down to variations on one response:

"That Indian subcontinent is really hot. Oh, oops, do you say 'South Asia' now?"

"Nah, our customers don't really like stuff in translation. But have you read that Jhumpa—"

Yes, yes, yes.

Literary brown ladies were the new new thing. Arundhati Roy's poetic, multilayered novel *The God of Small Things* had just garnered the Booker Prize. Jhumpa Lahiri would debut in 2000 with *Interpreter of Maladies*, her collection of elegantly written short stories that went on to win a Pulitzer. But Roy and Lahiri were just the beginning of what was to become a craze for South Asian and South Asian–American women's writing.

Of course, this wasn't the first time the publishing world had found its newest darlings in female writers of color. And it wasn't the first time book-stores would create pretty displays of books by authors of a "hot" ethnicity, or the first time readers would strip those displays as neatly as ants eating a sandwich at a picnic. The early '90s saw an explosion of Latina narratives—Laura Esquivel's *Like Water for Chocolate*, Sandra Cisneros's *The House on Mango Street*, Julia Alvarez's *How the García Girls Lost Their Accents*. And Terry McMillan's success with *Waiting to Exhale* in the mid-'90s ushered in a rash of books in which middle-class black women griped about their no-'count men, among them Connie Briscoe's *Sisters & Lovers*, Virginia DeBerry and Donna Grant's *Tryin' to Sleep in the Bed You Made*, and Eric Jerome Dickey's *Sister, Sister*.

Color had become a marketing boon. Interviewers probed into a writer's upbringing, seeking out ethnic factoids for a voracious public. De-tails about unusual foods, struggles with immigrant parents, and cultural oddities were all fair game. And in the case of attractive authors, whose im-ages were emblazoned all over magazines and poster-size publicity photos, one could hardly be sure what was for sale anymore—the "company" of a beautiful, exotic woman or the power of her words.

Looking back, the doyenne, the matriarch, the empress dowager of all women-of-color literary trends is Amy Tan. The 1989 release of Tan's *The Joy Luck Club* was accompanied by a hailstorm of publicity for both book and author. There had been other Chinese-American female authors to gain a measure of literary fame—Maxine Hong Kingston is probably the best known—but Tan's sales and crossover appeal far exceeded theirs; her book, with its interwoven stories of four Chinese mothers and their Chinese-American daughters, consumed the public's imagination.

What is it that makes a certain ethnic genre hot? If I could nail that one down for sure, I'd be rolling around in a room filled with nothing but money. But one can hazard some guesses. Many of the Asian-American and Latina books had lots of incense and spirits—"ancient Asian wisdom" and religious tidbits, or mystical realism in the form of pissed-off ghosts and fantastic vi-sions. They also featured nearly pornographic discussions of food; Isabel Allende's *Aphrodite: A Memoir of the Senses* even had recipes. The mystical stuff and the food seem to reflect the way that some white people come to dif-ferent cultures—through seeking religious or spiritual enlightenment, or by exhibiting their open-minded, adventuresome selves through eating our food. Our cultures are "better" somehow—closer to the earth, purer, more attuned to sensory pleasure—but in nice, nonthreatening ways, wrapped up neatly in fortune-cookie wisdom.

The Asian ladybook title game illustrates this point further. Asian-American women's fiction titles often fall into one of three categories: 1. they have some nature-related detail (Gail Tsukiyama's *The Samurai's Garden*, Mia Yun's *House of the Winds*), 2. they feature a familial relationship (Tan's *The Bonesetter's Daughter*, *The Kitchen God's Wife*), or 3. they contain a number (Mako Yoshikawa's *One Hundred and One Ways*, Tan's *The Hundred Secret Senses*). The nature aspect seems to show that we are in touch with the elements; the familial touch displays how wonderfully traditional we are in how we understand ourselves, especially women; and the numerical detail demonstrates that we are an ancient, wise people fond of the fairy-tale trick of enumerating knowledge. (Some titles even double up on these techniques, such as Mira Stout's *One Thousand Chestnut Trees*.)

But when we aren't better than the West in cute, quaint ways, we have to be a lot worse. A host of Asian historical memoirs seem based on a simple formula: Asia was hell; the United States is a hell of a lot better. Thank God I'm here! This is not to disparage the truly awful circumstances of many of the authors' lives or their bravery and resilience in writing of their suffering. Being abandoned, purged, "reeducated," jailed, tortured, chased, hunted, raped, and/or nearly murdered in Cambodia, Vietnam, or China would leave scars on anyone's soul. But that there is an entire genre so dominated by the Asian-hell-to-Western-heaven motif is disturbing, and Southeast Asian memoirs have an even more complicated twist, especially considering the lack of Southeast Asian women's fiction. There are many reasons for that dearth—years of war, relative unfamiliarity with English, a new and oft-traumatized or poverty-stricken refugee population. But Southeast Asian women writers also have a hard time overcoming U.S. narratives about the region. Movies about Southeast Asia are inevitably about the traumas of the Vietnam War or Pol Pot's regime in Cambodia: *Apocalypse Now*, *Platoon*, *The Deer Hunter*, *The Killing Fields*. The women in these movies aren't given a chance to speak for themselves; they spend their screen time undulating around poles, prattling in broken barroom English, or screaming without subtitles. Now that Southeast Asian and Southeast Asian–American women are finally armed with words, they are writing a crucial piece of history with the stories of their lives. But the emphasis on their war-torn experiences, to the exclusion of the imagined realms of fiction, is troubling. It's as if audiences are excused from being interested in worlds created or dreamed of by Southeast Asian women that are without bloodshed, or without Western involvement.

THERE'S A FLIP SIDE TO EVERYTHING, OF COURSE. DESPITE all the doom and gloom I've laid out so far, literary trends can be good for women writers of color. At least more voices are finding their way onto the store shelves; one can't protest the fact that Americans are expanding their reading horizons, or that female authors of color are receiving much-deserved attention. I'm not advocating a return to the color closet for authors—why shouldn't ethnicity be ripe for novelistic exploration? And even if the books are published as part of a trend, they are often far from formulaic.

Still, it's hard to balance those sweet and sour sensations each time the next ethnic girl wonder strikes it big with her book. Happiness over her success is often marred by the onslaught of exoticized marketing. After a while, ethnicity seems as much a commodity as anything else. And as such, it becomes subject to the fickle nature of the marketplace—ethnicities without a sexy hook, or without much media presence, lose out. Even though there are staggering talents among African women writers, for example—Bessie Head, Ama Ata Aidoo, and Buchi Emecheta come to mind—their day may be long in coming. A trend can also stymie the publication of books that fail to conform to a popular ethnic formula by being perhaps too radical, too unpleasant, or too accusatory.

Furthermore, there's the problem of the "one-nigger rule"—the one spot in an establishment set aside for "diversity." If the general public is filling its color quota with one flavor of the month, there usually isn't appetite for another. People of color wanting to get in run their eyes over a book catalog, a masthead, a table of contents, a list of personnel—checking for the SOB in the one POC slot. It's a shameful catfighting tendency, but one that cultural attention deficit disorder and tokenism foster. Trends may make the publishing world seem inclusive and diverse, but there is still a gatekeeper and the hordes in front of him, clamoring to get in.

When the South Asian–lit craze appeared in the late '90s, it became a juggernaut among ethnic trends, shaking the book world from top to bottom with the potent combination of crossover appeal and literary acclaim. The work of Indian women had been notably absent from our bookshelves (aside from a very few South Asian and South Asian–American women, like Anita Desai and Bharati Mukherjee, whose time came before the Tan-era mass marketing of ethnicity and authoress), and now stores were suddenly flooded with it—Kiran Desai's *Hullabaloo in the Guava Orchard*, Indira Ganesan's *Inheritance*, Lahiri's *Interpreter of Maladies*, and Chitra Banerjee Divakaruni's *Mistress of Spices*, among others. The books and the attention they brought with them were especially welcome, considering that even before the onslaught of what some U.S. publishers call "the *God of Small Things* effect," the modern Western literary realm of India was already a rich one for men: Vikram Seth earned one of the largest advances ever for *A Suitable Boy*; the cranky V. S. Naipaul snagged a Nobel; and the style of Salman Rushdie has so often been emulated by a new generation of South Asian writers that some literary critics even call them Midnight's Grandchildren, after Rushdie's *Midnight's Children*. Plus, India's literary past has also been forced to encompass the uncomfortably colonial narratives of Rudyard Kipling and E. M. Forster.

On the happy side, these new books were generally wide-ranging in style and topic, some drawing on Raymond Carver more than Rushdie or Seth, others exploring the complexity of a diasporic identity. As much as one can generalize, these authors were writing some wonderful literature. And although the texts were often seen as part of a single, monolithic publishing identity, their styles and subject matters varied greatly, with a broader range than was usually present in a given ethnic trend.

Inevitably, however, I started to feel an itch of irritation. It wasn't just the spread of the craze and the concurrent cultural obsession with all things Indian—something chafed beyond the sight of Madonna blotchy with mehndi and mangling Sanskrit, or the ubiquity of shitty boxed chai. There were many other dark reasons why this infatuation bugged as much as it pleased. For one, there was the distasteful fawning over the authors' beauty: Roy was gushingly named one of *People*'s "50 Most Beautiful People in the World" in 1998, and, after winning her Pulitzer, Lahiri was crowned a "Woman We Love" in *Esquire*. There was the awful sameness of booksellers' responses when asked about exciting female authors of color—all South Asian this, Indian that. And although many of the subsequent books avoided the kind of mystical realism that editor Pankaj Mishra—who signed Arundhati Roy and recently penned his own book, *The Romantics*—has disparagingly called "Rushdie-itis," a few do share a certain tinkling, quirky, food-based exoticism, a tired roundup of the angst of arranged marriages, bitchy squabbles over whose chutneys and pickles are better than whose, and slobbery details about saris.

Writing in the *Vancouver Sun*, Punjabi-Canadian critic Phinder Dulai offered up a biting criticism of what he termed the Indo–North American novel: "A kind of culinary alchemy dresses up what could be gritty reality and betrays an unfortunate middle-class romanticism about the country left behind . . . In the North American–style Indian novel, the focus is on domestic family prattle while larger themes of migration, racism, caste and generational conflict are barely touched. When things get too hot, the characters can slip away to the kitchen or the pickle factory to cool off." And here we come up against the other side of trendification's double-edged sword: Readers of color can place as many restrictions on "their" writers as mainstream expectations can. I agree with much of Dulai's argument, particularly his critique of the annoying food fetishes and the gloppy romanticism. But while his points about whitewashing are well articulated, not every author can write the great Indian treatise on injustice. Many do grapple with serious themes: Lahiri, for example, addresses the bloody creation and partition of Pakistan and India, poverty, harsh discrimination against women, and familial fractures. And Roy definitely takes on her share of political topics. But is the onus of political seriousness necessarily greater for writers with brown skin? Some would say so: When an author of color makes it big, he or she is sometimes viewed as the returned messiah, full of potential uplift but also heavy with the responsibility to take on all the experiences of the oppressed and relay them to the world in great tablets of wisdom. When the author reveals him- or herself to be a mere human telling a tale spun from one imagination, the crown of thorns is angrily snatched back, to be placed on the head of the next likely candidate. This sort of pressure is almost too much to bear: Who wants to be a sure-to-fail Jesus, dealing with the dashed expectations of a disappointed people? Those crushed hopes have more to do with the gatekeeping forces of literary cool than the power of any one author's pen. One must cast blame not at the feet of the authors, but at those who are deciding what and whom we might read.

Then there's the final pitfall of being the darling of a literary trend: Stray from the pigeonhole into which you've been placed, and you can kiss your darlinghood good-bye. Two years after her Beautiful Person crowning, Arundhati Roy cut off her long hair, telling *The New York Times* that she doesn't wish to be known as "some pretty woman who wrote a book." Instead of another work of fiction, she has produced two books of essays, *The Cost of Living* and *Power Politics*, and wholeheartedly thrown herself into activist work, protesting the influence of Western corporations in the developing world, the U.S. bombing of Afghanistan, and dam-construction projects that would make hundreds of thousands of Indian citizens homeless.

But the reception of Roy's radical activism has been far from supportive in both the United States and India—perhaps showing how bringing the implicit politics of fiction into explicitly and confrontationally political nonfiction can make critical acclaim waver. Instead of seeing Roy's lifelong commitment to the "small things"—poverty-stricken farmers, "the banks of the river that smelled of shit and pesticides bought with World Bank loans," as she writes in *The God of Small Things*—Roy's critics see her as an uppity lady biting the hand that feeds her. How could she write searing indictments of the Indian bourgeoisie that would garner electricity from the dams, decry the nationalism that lauded the nuclear tests—when she, as much as the "modern" dams and tests, has been hailed as part of India's success story? For Western critics, her intense scrutiny of the World Bank and globalization marked her as just another famous face touting the political cause du jour.

Just as being too politically ethnic can make one unpopular, not being culturally ethnic enough can also bump a writer from the in crowd. Aspiring authors attending November 2001's South Asian Literary Festival in Washington, D.C., told stories of dealing with editors who declined their manuscripts, asking why their work didn't deal with traditional Indian life. Their works were, in essence, too American.

The food metaphors that permeate literature by writers of color are useful here; the critic Amitava Kumar once wrote, "If immigrant realities in the U.S. were only about ethnic food, then my place of birth, for most Americans, would be an Indian restaurant." This language of cultural consumption is particularly apt—at the trend's worst, South Asian and South Asian–American writing is just so much tasty food to be chewed, digested, and excreted without a lot of thought. But hope springs eternal. Perhaps

Americans, having tasted something delicious, will seek out books that outrage and challenge as much as Roy's unflinching resistance to Western power and Indian complacency, narratives written from the diaspora or in translation that don't rely on bindi or kulfi to make their points.

I'm banking on those contrary writers. I'm banking on those readers who read with sensitive curiosity, who aren't afraid of pointed words about poverty, colonialism, and racism. I'm banking on publishers who are willing to take a risk on books that break the mold, works in translation (only 5 percent of India's one billion people speak English, after all), books that challenge as much as they entertain and uplift. This is a lot to bank on, certainly, but who would have thought that a first-time female novelist from India would have had such a strong impact on the American reading world in the first place? In the meantime, South Asian and South Asian–American writers are making themselves at home on the *New York Times* bestseller lists and within literary-prize committee sessions—but they have their eyes wide open. "I would be wary of the notion that South Asia is hip and can attract publishers," said Yale English professor Sara Suleri at the literary festival. "Those fashions come and die. Maybe in five years, we will be hunting for Tasmanian writers." Maybe so, but maybe some readers will demand more, and writers will be able to find success while defying trendiness. Perhaps we can all wedge the door open a little more firmly, making room for stories that will last longer than a peel-off mehndi tattoo.

The Black and the Beautiful

Searching for Signs of Black Life in Prime-Time Comedy

Lori L. Tharps / SUMMER 2002

ONCE UPON A TIME, TELEVISION BROUGHT ME GREAT JOY. Before there was cable, when a dish was something you served dinner on, our family's sixteen-inch RCA kept me entertained for hours on end. The love affair started early. At ages three and four, it was the commercials: I memorized every jingle and tagline and would perform them as a sort of one-woman show for anyone who cared to listen. When I was five, my mother and I bonded while watching *As the World Turns* and *Guiding Light* every weekday after my half-day kindergarten. When I turned seven, I started watching *Good Times*, *The Facts of Life*, and, later, *Punky Brewster*. I also liked *What's Happening!!*, *The Brady Bunch*, reruns of *Family Affair*, *Happy Days*, and *Laverne & Shirley*—the last two earned extra points because they took place in my hometown of Milwaukee, Wisconsin.

These days, however, I turn on the TV only to feel betrayed by my former friend. As a cable-deprived, thirty-year-old black female pop culture fanatic, I stare at the whitewashed screen, remote control in hand, wondering, Where am I? According to network prime-time sitcom lineups, I no longer exist.

Even though some of my beloved shows were all-white, while I was growing up I saw several versions of myself on network television. *The Facts of Life*'s Tootie was my preteen role model. She was the youngest of four roommates attending boarding school at Eastland, and even though she was "the black one," she wasn't also "the poor one" (that role was reserved for Jo, the tough scholarship student). Tootie was decidedly middle-class and dreamed of being an actress, just like me. I wanted to wear roller skates in the house like Tootie, curl my bangs like Tootie—I even begged my parents to send me to boarding school. (Thankfully, they refused.) But *The Facts of Life* wasn't the only show I could tune in to and see someone who looked and behaved like me. Punky Brewster's best friend, Cherie, could have been my city-mouse doppelgänger. There was Dee on *What's Happening!!*: a wisecracking, devious child always ready with a righteous tongue-lashing—too mean to emulate but so much fun to watch. And, of course, there was Penny on *Good Times*, who later turned out to be Charlene on *Diff'rent Strokes*, who later turned out to be Cleo on *Fame*, who later turned out to be Janet "Miss Jackson if you're nasty" Jackson—but I digress.

In my teenage years, I copied the hairstyles, fashions, even some of the mannerisms of the girls in *The Cosby Show*'s Huxtable clan and the coeds attending Hillman College on the *Cosby* spin-off *A Different World*. And I didn't mind when people on the street told me I looked just like Tempestt Bledsoe or "that girl from *Family Matters*," even though I didn't. I felt that my existence in the social fabric of American life was validated by these black pop culture icons. But then something changed. And now, even though a recent *TV Guide* article tells me that there are more African-American actors on television today than ever before, finding examples of black women on network sitcoms that in any way mirror my life (or the lives of any other black people I know) feels like an exercise in futility.

At this year's Black Arts Festival at Harvard University, New York University professor and author Tricia Rose broke it down like this: "While we have much more space to be visible in American popular culture than [at] any other moment in its history, [black women's] images are extraordinarily narrow." Narrow and, I would add, embarrassing. I'm looking for black characters I can identify with and respect; what I find instead are black comic actors who have been reinvented as homeboys and hoochie mamas ghettoized on inferior networks created just for colored folk. The number one show in black households, UPN's *The Parkers*, offers us a single mom raising a daughter who's as dumb as dirt. Mother and daughter attend community college together, where the mother spends most of her time chasing after a man who doesn't want her. Shows featuring black and white actors together on a regular basis—à la *Diff'rent Strokes* and *The Jeffersons*—have been eliminated. According to a recent survey conducted by child-advocacy group Children Now, white shows are getting whiter and black shows are getting blacker. During the spring 2002 season, only 7 percent of network sitcoms featured "more than one primary cast member of a different race than the show's stars." In essence, we have arrived at de facto Jim Crow television, with the networks adopting a practice of segregated programming. And, not surprisingly, separate is far from equal—making the outlook for black women in prime-time comedy particularly bleak.

In the mid- to late '70s, black sitcoms like *Sanford and Son*, *What's Happening!!*, and *Good Times* were applauded and watched by many black Americans and plenty of white ones. Although most of the characters were poor and struggling to get by, strong family values were emphasized and a lot of African Americans were just happy to see themselves included in prime time. The early '80s signaled the end of black welfare-family sitcoms, which were replaced with the scenario of pseudosubordinate black characters surrounded by a lot of well-meaning white people: Witness *Gimme a Break!*, *Diff'rent Strokes*, and *Benson*; and let's not forget *Webster*. In 1984, of course, came *The Cosby Show*, the first show with an all-black cast to become a hit with audiences across race lines. By the end of the '80s, buoyed by *Cosby*'s success, a flood of black shows had hit the airwaves. From *Amen* to *227* to *The Fresh Prince of Bel-Air*, an unprecedented swell of diverse characters and storylines for my kind of people was seen and supported by the major networks. Steve Urkel, *Family Matters*' nasal-voiced übergeek, gave cause to celebrate Hollywood's willingness to expand its view of the black male. *A Different World* showed the nation that young black women aspire to be doctors, museum curators, army sergeants, and mothers. In the early '90s, *Living Single* showcased twentysomething black women who were independent career gals instead of welfare recipients. I'd never argue that every black female character (or black male character, for that matter) in this period was an ideal depiction, but prime-time comedy was finally starting to touch on the real-life diversity of black Americans.

Today it feels like we've taken a giant step backward. Sitcom writers cannot seem to come up with a decent premise to bring black people into prime time besides the male-comic-with-a-family routine. Not that there's anything wrong with that premise—but the results are fairly limited. *The*

Bernie Mac Show and *My Wife and Kids*, driven by the talent of their I-was-a-comedian-in-a-former-life leads (Bernie Mac and Damon Wayans, respectively), have been well received by black and white audiences, but the actors playing these men's wives—Kellita Smith and Tisha Campbell-Martin—never rise above supporting-role status.

And integrated sitcoms have become rarer and rarer. The only consistently and thoroughly integrated sitcom of recent years has been *For Your Love*, which revolved around the lives of three suburban Illinois couples, two black and one white. Created and executive-produced by Yvette Lee Bowser, who did the same for *Living Single*, *For Your Love* premiered on NBC in 1998 and was quickly shuttled to the WB after a dispute with network execs. It lasted five seasons before being canceled this year due to low ratings. But were the ratings low because crossover audiences—audiences for shows where black people and white people are friends and neighbors—are hard to come by, or were the ratings low because the network did very little to promote and/or support the show?

I blame this state of televised segregation on *The Cosby Show*. The success of its warm and fuzzy spin on black domesticity spurred many advertisers and industry execs to realize the potential in black programming. Then, faster than you can say "bamboozled," more black-themed shows started finding their way onto the air, and, a decade after *Cosby*, the WB and UPN netlets sprang up and were soon catering to black audiences almost exclusively (though the WB has since moved on to blindingly white programming like *7th Heaven* and *Gilmore Girls*). The networks seemed to have no qualms about putting the most uninspired and offensive versions of African Americans on the air, indicating the TV industry's low opinion of black people's entertainment expectations. (Do I even have to mention *Homeboys in Outer Space?*) On these shows, black women had to be neck-rolling, finger-snapping, loudmouthed aggressors, while their men, for the most part, were clowns, ministers, or working-class clichés. In addition, these new sitcoms were more urban-focused and less mainstream-friendly. Shows like *Martin*, *Moesha*, and *The Jamie Foxx Show* were grounded in an all-black world that made no effort to be inclusive, and the effects were far-reaching. White people tuned out, taking their potential advertising dollars with them. In the meantime, industry insiders assumed blacks were happy watching the baby nets—so there was no longer a need to be inclusive with mainstream shows. Now the white shows are really white (see *Frasier*, which in nine sea-sons has featured approximately one black guest star and zero regulars) and the black shows are really black (see *The Parkers*, which has one regu-lar white character with no real purpose), and no one is bridging the gap.

What's worse, the so-called black shows, besides lagging at the bottom of the Nielsen ratings list, have inferior writing and content. Instead of offering clever dialogue or mining real-life situations for plots, these segre-gated sitcoms tend to derive all of their laughs from physical humor and trash-talking characters. *The Jamie Foxx Show* and *Martin* are prime exam-ples, relying on the crazy physical contortions and goofy facial gestures of their male leads, not unlike the days of minstrel-show shucking and jiving. I'm not surprised that such shows barely register on the ratings radar—but there are some equally tacky white shows that do garner more attention simply because they have network support on their side (see *Just Shoot Me*). Fledgling networks seem to be willing to air black programming but not to commit to its quality or support it through advertising. Whereas NBC promotes *Friends* with a billboard in New York City's Times Square, a few dozen bus signs, and dozens of prime-time teasers throughout the week, UPN advertises *The Parkers* only on Monday nights, when the all-black comedies air. No billboards. No city-bus signage.

It should not be too much to ask that Hollywood's sitcom writers come up with a way for white and black to share the small screen on equal terms. How about a black friend to hang out with the gang at Central Perk? Why not an ultrafierce black fag hag to spice up Will's life? The possibilities are endless. And audiences might even enjoy the variety if they were given the chance. White people seem eager to listen to black music, eat black food, co-opt black fashion and hairstyles; why wouldn't they take to a more inte-grated experience on the small screen as well? Not to mention the fact that very few people live the segregated life that's depicted in sitcomland, espe-cially in New York: Are we really supposed to believe that the *Friends* gang has never known or seen any black people except for Gabrielle Union that one time in 2001? Or that neither Will nor Grace knows one black guy?

I recognize that my feelings of being abandoned by the television in-dustry aren't exactly normal. The fact that Chandler, Joey, Monica, Phoebe, Rachel, and Ross don't have a black friend is not about me personally. Yet it still hurts—I feel left out of the lovefest because America cares so much about these six fictitious people, and not one of them looks like me. I'm sick of being the universal mother figure (from mammy to Oprah) or the ultimate sex goddess (from the Hottentot Venus to Lil' Kim) but not the businesswomen, teachers, chefs, journalists, and the like who populate white sitcoms. I miss the days of Tootie and Dee and Khadijah, Maxine, Regine, and Synclaire. I know if we were calling the shots in Hollywood, things would be different; *Girlfriends* creator Mara Brock Akil and *Living Single* and *For Your Love* creator Yvette Lee Bowser are working hard to make that happen. I wish them well—and in the meantime, I'm turning off the tube.

I Kissed a Girl

The Evolution of the Prime-Time Lesbian Clinch

Diane Anderson-Minshall / WINTER 2004

WHEN MADONNA AND BRITNEY SPEARS MADE OUT AT THE MTV Video Music Awards last September, some called it a brilliant marketing ploy (the pair duets on Spears's current release, *In the Zone*). Others dismissed it as a fading hipster's desperate homage to herself, Madonna anointing the next Madonna. Still more disdained it as a gratuitous display of vulgarity—for which conservatives immediately demanded, and in some situations received, an apology (from papers such as *The Atlanta Journal-Constitution*, which printed a photo of the event on its front page). The obsessively documented kiss could have served as an irreverent pop-art critique of America's concerns about same-sex unions; after all, anxiety about Supreme Court rulings and Canadian legislation had placed gay marriage in the headlines throughout the summer of 2003. The VMA routine had all the elements needed to make a statement: Christina Aguilera in hot pants, Missy Elliott as a butch groom, Madonna as a polygamous bride, and those ostentatious kisses.

But it wasn't a statement. Rather, the Madonna-Britney kiss was a choreographed moment of pure showmanship, the ultimate example of the lesbian kiss as sweeps ploy that prime-time producers have spent the last few years perfecting.

If you've turned on the TV during sweeps month in any recent year, you may well have wondered whether all the girls have gone gay. Jennifer

Aniston kisses Winona Ryder. Lisa Kudrow smooches Jennifer Aniston. Tiffani Thiessen snogs Jaime Pressly. Denise Richards lipsmacks Heather Locklear. There are so many girl-girl clinches during sweeps, in fact, that male pundits have started muscling in on the action: In 2003, David Letterman joked, "You know what Paul [Shaffer] and I are doing for our season finale? A lesbian kiss." Bada-bing!

Of course, network sweeps isn't the only time you can see girls snagging a kiss. From reality TV (*Big Brother*, *The Real World*) to movies (*The Real Cancun* and *Anger Management*), women are kissing each other like never before. Heck, even video games are getting in on it: Jada Pinkett Smith and Monica Bellucci's kissing scene in *Enter the Matrix* is the most talked-about gaming feature of the year. What are we to make of this? Are these public displays simply self-conscious, soft porn–style clichés of lesbians that feed boys' fantasies? Or do they signal a subversive seismic shift in the landscape of popular culture?

Television has offered up same-sex kisses longer than it has offered up portrayals of actual lesbians. That's because such kisses have come primarily in the guise of farce or satire. When Laverne locked lips with Shirley in 1978, they didn't have to worry about the sociopolitical context of the comedy: It was just about the yuks. In the '80s, lesbianism as a social issue made prime-time appearances on the chickcentric shows *Golden Girls* and *Designing Women*, with well-intentioned if formulaic plotlines concerned with the main characters overcoming their own homophobia when they discover a friend is a lesbian.

But it wasn't until 1992's *L.A. Law* that lesbianism as a sexual orientation was really explored. The show presented TV's inaugural lesbian kiss when bisexual attorney C.J. (Amanda Donohoe) romanced her bi-curious colleague Abby (Michele Greene) in a scene scripted without an ounce of nonsense and achieved in the absence of bombastic media attention.

This and other formative same-sex kisses proved controversial all around. Advertisers and religious groups hounded networks about moral decline, while gay-rights advocates and progressive media watchdogs found reasons to criticize the kisses, whether for not going far enough or for being handled awkwardly. (Of the smooch between Mariel Hemingway and Roseanne on *Roseanne*, lesbian comic Mary C. Matthews says, "Props to them for going there, [but] it wasn't very pretty to watch.")

But even more troubling to the moral-decline patrol was the specter of TV kisses that weren't one-off aberrations. These became more prevalent in the '90s and beyond, when ensemble casts with one or more lesbian characters—as opposed to the odd gay guest appearance or experimental auxiliary character—became commonplace. Shows like *ER*, the sadly short-lived *Relativity*, and *Buffy the Vampire Slayer* offered some characters who were already gay when they made the scene, so there were no coming-out dramas, no overplayed ratings ploys—and their kisses were treated no differently from those between hetero characters on the same shows.

But whatever evolution allowed for these thoughtful and realistic portrayals hasn't shouldered out the propensity for lesbian farce and the media-promoted kisses that go with it. A few years back, while Willow and Tara bickered and smooched unobtrusively on *Buffy the Vampire Slayer*, the sweeps-month kiss between *Ally McBeal*'s title character and her archrival Ling was hyped within an inch of its life. "More people heard about the kiss via the Fox publicity buzz than actually saw it," comments Scott Seomin, entertainment director for the Gay and Lesbian Alliance Against Defamation. For every natural, nuanced prime-time kiss—2002's slowly building romance between two teenage girls on *Once and Again* comes to mind—there's a nutty gambit like the Winona Ryder–Jennifer Aniston liplock on *Friends*.

These single-episode storylines and ratings ploys keep the subject firmly in novelty territory: A kiss, in these cases, is just a kiss. Yet the moralizing that has always dogged any televised portrayal of homosexuality hasn't evaporated just because TV has offered up a clutch of gay kisses, real or faux. This fact is amply illustrated by the fate of daytime TV's first lesbian character, *All My Children*'s Bianca. Though Bianca was already established as a lesbian, soap opera fans—widely presumed to be TV's most conservative audience—had begun to question just how long a young, pretty woman could go without getting some. After months of lobbying, in April 2003 *AMC* gave the people what they wanted, writing a storyline in which Bianca actually kissed a girl. Predictably enough, the smooch was a hit—ratings for the episode jumped 15 percent.

Then, nothing. Well, Bianca did get some action—in July, she was raped. Perhaps viewers should expect such drama from a soap opera, but it's hard not to conclude that having a girl raped after her first lesbian kiss reinforces society's negative attitudes about lesbianism. Historically, in Hollywood depictions—from *The Children's Hour* to *Basic Instinct*—same-sex desire has been followed by some sort of punishment meted out to the dyke. Tara's murder on *Buffy*, for instance, happened well after her first kiss with Willow—the couple had been shown seminaked in bed, even—but the fact that she was killed at all spoke to a concern, long argued by lesbian feminists, that authentic lesbian imagery arouses not just men's desire but also anxiety about their own sexual necessity.

No matter what you think about Tara's death—and *Buffy* fans both gay and straight are still furiously debating it—those of us who watch these things closely thought it might really shift the landscape of sexuality on television. But if it did, then why does it seem like there are more straight girls making out for prurient audiences than ever before?

This year, TV viewers have witnessed a proliferation of faux-lesbian kisses, especially on reality shows. The same kind of women who catfight sexily in beer commercials suck face with each other on programs like CBS's *Big Brother 3* and MTV's *Dismissed*. The Britney-Madonna stunt is an emblem of how far lesbian kisses have come since that milestone episode of *L.A. Law*: so far that they've ceased to be about lesbians at all. Though members of Spears's family were promptly interviewed regarding their thoughts on the kiss (a rebuttal by Spears's little sister Jamie Lynn in *US Weekly* was hilariously adamant: "I promise you, my sister is totally into boys"), the fact that Spears's sexual orientation even figured into the coverage seems almost quaint. Given today's prevalence of televised girl love, Madonna is—as usual—a lot farther behind the curve than she'd like to think.

Though the presentation of the lesbian liplock might have evolved from traditional farce to soft-core pornography, the intention is still the same: to titillate while avoiding trickier questions about sexuality. It's as if, subconsciously, producers are trying to minimize the political significance of realistically portrayed lesbians. These days, women who kiss women on TV aren't coded as gay; they're simply sexually adventurous, and their adventurousness is geared toward nothing so progressive as the advancement of lesbian visibility—it's simply meant to excite the men who are watching (and perhaps inspire their girlfriends and wives). While these fauxmos have become an indelible part of popular culture, there hasn't been a great deal of discernible change in how real, live lesbians are treated in society and how uncomfortable their presence still makes straight viewers.

Network producers offer no argument. Rather, wary of offending audiences in what they call the flyover states, they regularly issue "mature audience" warnings that serve to both arouse viewers and reinforce their negative stereotypes about women's sexuality. In an effort to capitalize on that arousal, they also exaggerate the kisses: After *Fastlane*'s ratings jumped 32 percent during an episode in which main character Billie (Tiffani Thiessen) kisses a woman, Fox reran it. Its print and web ad campaign, featuring close-ups of the two women, asked, "Did you miss the kiss?" By pulling the scene out of context, Fox essentially neutered the smooch of any sociopolitical meaning it might otherwise have held.

Still, some argue that even the most obvious of these male-targeted marketing ploys can be subversive ways to desensitize viewers. "Context definitely matters," says Sarah Warn, creator of the TV watchdog site AfterEllen.com. "A same-sex kiss designed specifically to titillate male viewers is clearly not as identifiable to lesbian and bi viewers as kisses between characters in an actual relationship. But that doesn't mean kisses promoted as 'hot girl-on-girl action' don't have some positive impact on desensitizing viewers. They're just not as powerful and as subversive as lesbian kisses in the context of a larger relationship would be."

If, as some media pundits claim, fewer television shows are issuing warnings, fewer TV stations are reporting complaints, and fewer advertisers are objecting to lesbian programming, it's still worth worrying that this new proliferation of girl-girl kisses on television imprints popular culture with a false sense of social—and political—acceptance. If straight audiences see lesbians leaping out from the TV each night, they may forget that we still don't have the same fundamental protections as they do in most parts of their lives. While it's wonderful to see yourself on TV, if TV is simply another realm in which cultural symbolism outpaces and overshadows real political progress, what's the point? Having more women kissing on TV might legitimize lesbians in real life—but, as Warn points out, only to the extent that it desensitizes and normalizes lesbian sexuality. "It's really the kiss as an expression of a deeper relationship . . . that legitimizes lesbians in real life," she continues. "Empty kisses don't have the same impact." And so far, what most television programs have offered are not only empty kisses but a host of empty promises about balanced and accurate depictions of lesbian lives.

XXX Offender

Reality Porn and the Rise of Humilitainment

Shauna Swartz / FALL 2004

IN MOST PLACES, PAYING FOR SEX IS ILLEGAL. THAT IS, UNLESS you document the transaction and sell the footage on the Internet. And if you show an attractive young woman, enticed by promises of cash, having sex with a complete stranger in a public setting—only to be kicked to the curb afterward with no pay and plenty of insults—chances are your porn site will be very, very popular. Unoriginal, but popular.

Gonzo. Porno *verité*. Reality porn. Whatever you call it, this particular variety of smut has flooded the Internet in much the same way that reality shows have taken over television. "Real" sex has always been valued in porn, but even the casual consumer can testify that realistic trappings—sets, plotlines, and especially dialogue—are usually an afterthought. The genre's latest offshoot has upped the ante, featuring scenes that appear to unfold unedited and in real time, with participants who directly acknowledge the camera. But what really distinguishes this new smut from its predecessors isn't whether the action is scripted, but whether it's portrayed as nonconsensual.

Reality porn features some of the most violent and demeaning scenes to hit the mainstream, what some call "humilitainment." Tagging these disturbing spectacles of deception and abuse with the "reality" label enhances their allure, as it claims to offer consumers unstaged and authentic action. Where reality TV panders to a collective schadenfreude, pornographic content sends already sleaze-bound reality entertainment into new and disquieting territory.

Take, for instance, the pithily named BangBus, which debuted in 2001 and features two men roaming the streets, trolling for young women they can lure into their van to have sex with them on camera in exchange for a little cash. The bang squad searches out "every girl's inner slut," testing how far she'll go to sexually satisfy a stranger. BangBus's popularity led to other reality sites popping up overnight like silicone implants: The throng of high-profile sexploitation offerings now includes websites like BangBoat, BaitBus, BackroomFacials, XratedGangBang, and Trunked ("It's simple. Throw the bitch in the Trunk. If she doesn't like it. She can get out. Oh yeah. We're goin' 55 mph . . .").

The guiding premise of these sites is that a woman must be coaxed into sex—but, once persuaded, she's soon begging for it upside down and sideways. "Under every skirt is a pussy that just wants to be fucked," proclaims BackseatBangers. Penetrability is simultaneously celebrated as a woman's most valuable quality and scorned as evidence of her indelible sluttiness. In the end, she always gets her due, with most episodes culminating in a facial (and not the spa-treatment kind), and many topped off by the guy spitting on her face. After the besmeared, duped woman musters a grin for the camera—sometimes, as on Trunked, with a sticker advertising the site plastered across her forehead—she is left stranded. While the money shot is the crown jewel of traditional hard-core porn—proving the action is genuine—reality porn derives its authenticity from a thornier crown: Someone has to be humiliated, and that humiliation has to look real.

While degradation in porn movies is certainly nothing new, the presentation of it as real rather than performed is a more recent innovation. The producers of these sites position their works as erotic documentaries that capture real encounters with eager women who are dumb or desperate enough to fall for their trickery. The people who have engineered these scenarios thereby downplay their own hand in the abuse in order to make viewers feel better about getting off on it. But behind the scenes, reality-porn producers must document the fictive nature of their productions in order for the operation to remain legal. They need to juggle the fantasy of authentic humiliation with the reality of staging in order to elude law enforcement's scrutiny—or even to maintain personal integrity.

"We do it where the girl has fun, not where she feels bad. I'm not into that," says Greggory Meyer, whose company, PhotoGregg, provides content for more than forty reality-porn sites. And though he provides site copy like "This little cum dumpster just has that look. The look that says, 'I suck dick!'" Meyer doesn't believe any of his creations are degrading.

It's worth wondering how many keyboard-noodling at-home viewers are taken in by the proclaimed reality. PhotoGregg's disclaimer—"The images and videos within this website depict real people and their behaviors when placed in fantasy situations. The behavior and actions within are intended only for the world of fantasy and it would be both irresponsible and dangerous to behave or act this way in the real world."—makes it clear (to fine-print readers, at least) that the smoke isn't confined to postcoital cliché or the mirrors to the ceiling. But fans do buy into the illusion, says Meyer, who receives more than a dozen e-mail messages each month from men touting themselves as excellent candidates for BikiniHookups, where average-looking beachgoers (really actors) score with young babes who'd otherwise shun them.

Faux reality has become the norm in pop culture, with far-reaching implications: Surrounded by convincing fakery, perhaps we're so hungry for something genuine that we're willing to suspend disbelief, ingesting even sham authenticity to sate our voyeuristic appetites. Reality porn lets consumers rebel against the tired old porn setups—the pizza man and the bored housewife, the take-charge nurse and her helpless patient—while enjoying the supposedly genuine degradation of women. If violence and debasement are presented as real—"human behavior brought to frightening lows," as Bang-Bus puts it—consumers can ignore their own complicity by believing they're merely witnessing a spectacle rather than perpetuating humiliation. While the desire to believe these scenarios are real rather than acted out is arguably more misogynistic, a viewer might justify initial interest by attributing it to curiosity or disbelief. But the fan who continues to be fascinated can lessen any shame by recognizing that the action is staged. "Ess2s2," a poster on an Ubersite.com porn forum, writes: "I get a kick out of it *because* I know it's fake. It appeals to my more meanspirited [sic] side. Do I debase real women because I enjoy watching bangbus? No. I respect women because I understand the difference between fantasy and reality." But fans don't necessarily acknowledge that their interest—along with a willingness to shell out cash in support of it—is precisely why this material exists in the first place.

As with most porn, humilitainment consumers and producers are mostly men, but many women are fans and some earn their living through it. Trunked acknowledges economic motivation for women's participation in the antics while calling their victimhood into question, featuring one performer saying, "I wasn't born fuckin' yesterday, ya know . . . The price was right so I let him have his horny little way with me." Candi, the twenty-one-year-old who has been fellating every guy in the virtual neighborhood for the past three years on CandiFromTheBlock, isn't in character when she bristles at the suggestion that her own work constitutes humilitainment: "What I do is have fun every single day. I get to fulfill some guy's fantasy in every single episode. I'm the girl who everyone jacks off to. I love that!"

The threat of criminal indecency charges is always hovering over humilitainment porn (one company, Extreme Associates, is facing federal obscenity charges for distributing its graphic, supposedly real rape-and-murder video over the Internet), revealing a double standard in public outcry over real violence against women vs. media depictions of it. The realest thing about humilitainment porn is the way it buttresses long-held assumptions of women's inherent inferiority, even if that's not foremost in the minds of those who get off on it. The question of authenticity overshadows the sexual politics of why a woman might be willing to play the dupe, and any law-enforcement fixation on its social demerit misses the point that pop culture reflects the popular imagination at least as much as it creates it.

Bias Cut

Old Racism as New Fashion

Rachel Fudge / FALL 2004

TWO YEARS AGO, THE PREPPY MALL STAPLE ABERCROMBIE & Fitch released a line of T-shirts that paired early 1900s–style caricatures of Chinese men (complete with coolie hats, big grins, and slanted eyes) with slogans like "Wong Brothers Laundry Service—Two Wongs Can Make It White" and "Wok-N-Bowl—Let the Good Times Roll—Chinese Food & Bowling." The clothing chain then professed great surprise when Asian-American activists cried foul; A&F's PR flack Hampton Carney told the *San Francisco Chronicle*, "We personally thought Asians would love this T-shirt . . . We are truly and deeply sorry we've offended people." The shirts were eventually pulled from stores.

Last year, Urban Outfitters played a similar game with a line of "Everybody Loves a [fill-in-the-blank] Girl/Boy" shirts; they had the poor taste and even poorer judgment to illustrate the "Everybody Loves a Jewish Girl" shirt with dollar signs. Absent those dollar signs, the Ts were little more than a retread of the silly "Kiss Me, I'm [an ethnic group]" T-shirts that have been around for decades. But unlike the shamrocks and rosaries that decorate the Irish and Catholic versions, respectively, the dollar signs evoke an especially nasty and persistent ethnic stereotype. In response to public protest, UO replaced the dollar signs with hearts but continues to sell the entire line, the range of which says some pretty interesting things about whom everyone loves: fat boys but not fat girls; Asian girls but not Asian boys.

It's no coincidence that UO and A&F are sticking these dubious slogans on shirts that look like they were picked up at Thrift Town. By emblazoning retro-racist words and imagery on shirts that are brand-new yet look well worn, these purveyors of lifestyle culture are trying to have it both ways: stirring up a whole mess of racially charged hoopla (which has made for bad-but-good PR for both chains) while attempting to deflate accusations of racism by making the shirts "ironic" (a misuse of the term in the first place, but that's another story). That is, A&F and UO are capitalizing on the vogue for retro kitsch by shilling not only faux-vintage T-shirts but faux-vintage bigotry as well. It's a clever attempt to claim distance from a literal reading of the shirts, because the companies can always argue that they were trying to make fun of the idea of racism, not of a particular race.

In the big picture of racism in America, offensive T-shirts are neither the biggest nor the most blatant problem. But their sellers' claims that these products are created with the intention of mocking, not encouraging, racism and bigotry rest on a false assumption that we are all beyond identity politics—and thus we are beyond any implications of hatefulness, so we can all have a good laugh at the very idea of, say, anti-Semitism or anti-Asian prejudice. In a sad sort of way, this post–politically correct "humor" is a measure of the success of the very identity politics it scorns.

It's also notably different from defiantly politically incorrect humor, which revels in its flirting with racism and sexism in the name of free speech, but doesn't argue or imply that we live in a postracist or postsexist world. All those knowingly crass "Bikini Inspector" and "Master Baiters Fly Fishing" T-shirts found at beach boardwalks and novelty shops across the country don't lay claim to any ironic distance. There's a difference between these cheesy souvenirs and the supposedly hip product being pushed by A&F and UO, and it's not just in the price point (A&F and UO charge upward of $20 for their shirts, while the novelty shirts can be had for half that). This distinction may be extremely subtle, but it's crucial: A&F and UO are shilling this stuff in a tongue-in-cheek manner to people they presume will get the joke.

Carney, A&F's aptly named PR rep, defended the "Two Wongs" shirt by assuring the *Chronicle* that "We poke fun at everybody, from women to flight attendants to baggage handlers to football coaches to Irish-Americans to snow skiers. There's really no group we haven't teased." Underlying

323

this equal-opportunity offensiveness is the notion that "teasing" an entire racial group by invoking some of its most pernicious stereotypes is no different from making fun of people who like to ski—a notion that willfully ignores the fact that racism and sexism are still very much a part of American culture. This line of defense—"We're all treated equally now, so we had no idea people would be offended!"—is in some ways more insulting than outright bigotry, which at least doesn't hide behind a pretense of equality. The companies can always dredge up an Asian-American or Jewish employee who "loved" the T-shirts, or point to the fact that some Asian Americans snatched up the "Wong" shirts for their kitsch factor, as proof that the gear isn't offensive. But unlike whatever making-fun-of-skiers Ts Carney referred to, the "Two Wongs" shirts don't intend to poke fun at the wearer—rather, they mock a population that is perceived to be the other.

The most recent entry in the pantheon of misguided egalitarian "teasing" came this spring, courtesy of *Details* magazine. For the past year, *Details* has been quietly running a one-page humor column, titled "Anthropology," that compares stereotypes of gay men with stereotypes of nongay but supposedly effeminate men: Gay or guido? Gay or British? Gay or magician? Gay or preppy? Even "Gay or Jesus?" managed to slip under the radar. But when writer Whitney McNally dropped "Asian" into the nongay slot in the April 2004 issue and accompanied it with a random assortment of Chinese and Japanese stereotypes, she really got people's attention. Straight and gay Asian-American activists staged protests outside the magazine's headquarters and demanded an apology from *Details* editor in chief Dan Peres. He complied and apologized in the following issue's editor's note. Of course, that mea culpa—which included the half apology "I apologize . . . to anyone who was offended"—didn't stop Peres from approving the "Gay or Country Singer?" bit that runs a mere five pages later. ("Whether you worship the Opry or wrestle to Oprah, a twangy set of tonsils will never be lonesome.")

Details, which has over the past fifteen years gone from being a very queer downtown rag to a self-consciously metrosexual style book, relies on its hipster legacy to deny that it's being homophobic or offensive in running this series that trades on vapid imagery. Gay men are hairless! They like to groom themselves with fancy products! They work out! They wear clean, well-fitting clothes! These stereotypes could well stand to be deflated, but *Details* doesn't pull it off. The setup promises a clever deconstruction of stereotypes—and I'll admit at first blush I found the concept funny—but the writing has a desperately grasping tone, the categories chosen are so dumb that they're meaningless, and in the end *Details* reinforces the very clichés it purports to send up.

This brand of satire is increasingly popular these days, thanks to the mass-market saturation of cool-kid lifestyle culture. At the risk of sounding like a conservative, Bill Bennett–esque postmodernism hater, I blame this phenomenon on the triumph of hipster-misidentified irony, which demands that nothing be taken seriously and lets people feel immune from criticism because they're being, you know, ironic. It's all made possible by the winking insiderness, the self-congratulatory illusion that the trend-driving hipsters are educated and informed enough to know better or rise above racism or sexism. In fact, these folks claim to be so beyond any sort of prejudice that they can wield ordinarily offensive terms and imagery with impunity: "I've got lots of friends who are gay—not that there's anything wrong with that!—so when I describe something stupid by calling it gay, you know I don't mean it in a bad way." But this style of usage—whether it's exercised by a schoolyard bully or an urban hipster—still relies on a general consensus that things that are gay are not good.

By now, the progression of name-calling from forbidden to fashionable should be familiar: Disempowered groups, from immigrants to gays and lesbians to people with disabilities, begin to advocate for their full rights as American citizens. In the process, radical activists reclaim derogatory terms—gay, queer, dyke, bitch, cunt, homo, slut, crip, heeb, and so on—and brandish them defiantly in an attempt to dilute their power to harm. The names and identity labels start to be picked up by enlightened friends and allies, who feel privileged to use the terms in the reclaimed manner because they are in on the politics. But inevitably, the terminology dissipates to the broader population, who re-reclaim the phrases in a not-at-all ironic or knowing way—thereby completing the cycle. Of course, most of the folks who toss around words like "queer" or "F.O.B." (fresh off the boat), or repopularized phrases like "that's so gay," are just as likely as activists and their allies to defend themselves from any accusation of hateful behavior.

And because, like everything else, the notion of "hip" is easily reducible to a commodity, this all-sarcasm-all-the-time lifestyle has become a mass-marketable trend, available at malls from coast to coast. But when so-called irony becomes a tool of marketing—just look at all those goddamned trucker hats!—it loses any claim to edginess and becomes merely a set of quotation marks and a smirk.

In its original sense—as subversive humor that adopts a mode of expression that is the opposite of what is intended—irony can be a politicizing force, deliberately playing up the most ridiculous of stereotypes or ideas in order to point out how dumb they are. *Details* had the opportunity to do this with the "Gay or . . ." series, but either lacked the political edge and depth of critique to make it happen, or simply didn't care to. In the current political climate, this kind of speech has enormous potential to upset the status quo: *The Onion* is one of few publications that has been quietly, consistently pulling off political critique through ironic humor for years. But it also has the potential to be widely misinterpreted or, worse, wielded as mere style devoid of content or context.

One of the most flamboyant exemplars of this irony-as-edgy-lifestyle product is *Vice*, which started out as a free paper catering to the punk/skater crowd in Montreal and has since expanded to become a glossy monthly available across the United States. It has also spawned a record label, several books, and a forthcoming TV show. A typical issue might include articles about what it's like to be a "jizz mopper" in an adult video store and fashion spreads featuring hookers, trannies, and runaway teens. It publishes trademark guides to all of the races, on how to be a whore, and on how to golddig. *Vice*'s editors and writers are infamous for freely tossing around in print and in interviews slurs like "nigger," "fag," and "Paki," claiming (as they did in one *New York Press* article) that because they rag on everyone—and because they are or are friends with blacks, gays, and Pakistanis—they can use these words with impunity. Given that *Vice*'s raison d'être is to push the edges of acceptability beyond any reasonable limit, it's not all that surprising to hear them spout off like this.

The same attitude is espoused by comedians like Sarah Silverman, who most notably got into trouble four years ago when she told a joke on *Late Night with Conan O'Brien* about trying to get out of jury duty: "My friend is like, 'Why don't you write something inappropriate on the form, like "I hate chinks"?' . . . I didn't want them to think I was a racist, but I did want to get out of jury duty, so I wrote 'I love chinks'—and who doesn't?" In a subsequent appearance on *Politically Incorrect*, after being chastised by watchdog groups like the Media Action Network for Asian Americans, she refused to apologize.

The difference between Silverman and, say, Abercrombie & Fitch is that Silverman's act is an extreme form of satire intended to expand her audience's comfort zones and to limn the very idea of racism, while *Vice*, A&F, UO, and their ilk are trying to sell us a range of products that add up to a lifestyle. One could argue that Silverman's racially charged humor rests upon a general understanding that ethnic stereotypes and labels still hold great power; there is at least a hint of political substance behind it, and in some ways her use of ethnic slurs attempts to foreground the racism that often operates in the shadows. The lifestyle shillers, by contrast, try to hang their T-shirt slogans on the myth that those stereotypes are so passé that the very idea of them is laughable. But what A&F and company either can't understand or willfully ignore is that if those stereotypes truly held no currency, the joke wouldn't be funny. Multiple interpretations are what allow for the possibility of humor—yet they also sabotage any attempt to control its reception.

The line between humor and offense is slippery, of course, and no one likes being told what he or she can and can't laugh at. That sense of transgression is a big part of "ironic" humor's appeal. You know it's wrong and maybe a bit mean, but you laugh anyway; that frisson of naughtiness can be addictive. But when that uncomfortable moment between laughter and outrage is sold as a hip lifestyle, it becomes impenetrable: What, exactly, are we laughing at here?

8

....

Talking Back

ACTIVISM AND POP CULTURE

RIGHT NOW WE'RE LIVING IN THE MOST INTENSELY MEDIATED world ever. Three decades ago there were four broadcast networks, just over a hundred women's magazines (including feminist publications), and no Internet. Now there are hundreds of cable channels, over five hundred women's magazines, and an online world teeming with publications and blogs. According to the book *Data Smog: Surviving the Information Glut*, in 1971 the average U.S. resident encountered 560 advertising messages a day; a 2000 *Advertising Age* article put the number at 5,000.

Content has shifted, too. Reagan-era deregulation and the resulting merger frenzy of the '90s increased pressure on news divisions and newspapers to turn hefty profits, shifting newsroom missions from informing the public to just getting us to stay tuned for the next segment. Ownership of those same news producers by multinational conglomerates has also greatly damaged their capacity to bring us important stories and hold governments and corporations accountable. It's only common sense that NBC will neglect to report on, say, parent company General Electric's refusal to clean up the million pounds of toxic chemicals it has dumped into the Hudson River, or that cable giant Comcast, dependent as it is on favorable treatment from federal appointees at the FCC, would stifle criticism of the executive branch (as it did when it refused to air antiwar ads on its Washington, D.C., system during Bush's 2003 State of the Union address).

Hand in hand with these changes have come others, most notably a rise in the embedding of commercial messages into narrative content. Sure, the ideas behind product placement have always been with us, from early broadcast-media sponsorships (how do you think daytime programming aimed at women in charge of the family laundry got to be called soap operas?) to the small type on *Glamallurelle*'s cover photo credit noting that Lindsay Lohan's lip gloss is Buy Me Now! by Maybelline. But the practices' meteoric rise and the nonstop extension of their reach are truly stunning. In 1982, *E.T.* made news by boosting sales of Reese's Pieces after M&M's declined to be featured; in 1991, the five top-grossing films of the year featured more than one hundred brand names. Another decade later, the entire genre of reality TV had sprung up around products to be placed: *Survivor* creator Mark Burnett told *Advertising Age*, "I've never understood why there has to be a separation between the advertising community and the creative television community." In late summer 2005, *Madison & Vine*, an online newsletter covering the product placement industry, trumpeted the release of fall's *Cry Wolf* with the headline "Chrysler's Feature-Length Film Hits Theaters: Jon Bon Jovi, AOL and Current Model Vehicles Play Starring Roles."

Political actions themselves can easily become commodified in this landscape—and because women are so often seen in terms of our consumer role, we're an easy target. Witness the bizarre efforts to get young women to the polls in 2004: An organization called 1000 Flowers printed slogans like "Shape the Oval Office: Vote Nov. 2" on nail files that were packaged with voter registration forms and given away at salons; they raised money by selling "Vote! It's a Beautiful Thing" lipsticks. Take, for example, the masses of pink-beribboned goodies that entice people to buy, buy, buy in the name of a paltry contribution to breast cancer research. (Meanwhile, corporations whose products and environmental practices may contribute to cancer—cars, bleached and dyed paper products, processed foods packaged in plastic—get good publicity, woman-friendly brownie points, and more profits.)

Given all this, responding to pop culture is an activist project vital to feminism, and responding through pop culture is a crucial tool. We need to ask: Whose interests are being served by—to name a few examples *Bitch* has consistently taken up over the years—the existence of an "ideal" female body, gender segregation from the toy store to the movie theater to the magazine rack, female sexuality as emotionally driven? Who's selling them, and why? Conversely, what are we *not* being told? How can we get our own views into the public debate?

Bitch was founded on this activist impulse. It was no longer enough for Andi and me to sit in our living room, throwing imaginary rocks at the TV and discussing Tori Spelling's fake boobs and *The Bridges of Madison County* (don't make fun—it was 1995). It was no longer enough to discover a fantastic feminist artist, writer, or filmmaker and have only a few people to share her work with. We had to find people who shared our frustration and who wanted to add their own voices of dissent. We needed to take it outside.

As the media landscape becomes both increasingly corporatized and more chaotic—with more grassroots potential through phenomena like blogs, low-power radio, digital video, and podcasting but also more risk that those venues will be used to sideline our voices in favor of more and more advertising messages—we need to take it further still.   —L.J.

Please Don't Feed the Models

A Day in the Life of an Urban Guerrilla

Kathy Bruin / FALL 1998

FEBRUARY 19, 1998.

8:00 a.m. We're postering the city tonight and it's raining like a son of a bitch. The forecast says we're in the middle of a big storm with rain all day and seventy-mile-per-hour winds. One hundred percent chance of rain in all areas. Great.

The postering is a guerrilla effort on the part of About-Face, a San Francisco group dedicated to combating negative images of women through education, action, and humor. About-Face started a few years ago, when I was standing in line next to a family with several girls ranging from twelve to fifteen years of age. Their mother offered them some cookies and the girls took them, laughing, "Oh, I'll have a cookie. I can start my diet tomorrow." A few months later, I became obsessed with Calvin Klein's Obsession perfume campaign. The ads had been around for a few years, but a particularly annoying new one put me over the edge. On the buses of San Francisco and huge billboards towering over the city were pictures of Kate Moss reclining nude, her bones so accentuated and her face so sunken and gray that she looked like she was starving.

I wanted to do something louder than just writing Calvin Klein a letter. I took a picture of the ad and changed the text to read, "Emaciation Stinks—Stop Starvation Imagery." I made posters and conned friends and family into helping me plaster the city with them. About-Face's goal in postering is to use public space as a forum to challenge our culture's messages and remind people that they too can make a stink.

Our new poster has a brightly colored circus cage and in it are fashion models lounging about in various poses. It says, "Please don't feed the models."

11:00 A.M. DROVE TO WORK IN A TORRENTIAL DOWNPOUR TO check my e-mail. Coworkers are giving me the ol' "guess you can't do it tonight, huh?" looks, with concerned eyebrows and squinched-up mouths. "Scattered showers by evening," I tell them. I am in a total panic. If we cancel, we won't have the number of people we need to really cover the city when we reschedule. If we don't cancel, we risk people coming out and being sent home if it's still too wet.

I think it's illegal to poster the streets. I am not absolutely positive about this because I didn't come right out and ask the police department about it. ("Excuse me, officer, I wonder if you would help me with something. If someone were to, hypothetically, hang posters in city streets with wallpaper paste . . .") If you live in a city, it's normal to see posters plastered all over pedestrian walkways. Everything from B movies to antiwar rallies is advertised through posters pasted to construction sites. We have postered San Francisco twice before and I have been tracked down and screamed at by construction managers both times. "We have seventeen posters on our brand-new pedestrian walkway," one man rightfully yelled. "Ugh," I thought as a knot formed in my stomach. I am a hyperresponsible person, the classic "good girl." Do I do what I think in my gut is right even if I might get in trouble or piss someone off? I believe every individual ought to have the right to create imagery and put her ideas out in the public sphere, but without the resources to do it, you can't reach many people. Without a lot of money to buy your own billboards, your ideas and images are relegated to photocopies stuck under windshield wipers and passed out at parades—hardly the great societal impact you were hoping for. We don't set out to anger construction managers or create more work for them, but guerrilla tactics are a perfect way to reach people on the same level that billboards do.

1:00 P.M. SAN FRANCISCO BROKE THE RECORD FOR FEBRUARY rainfall: 12.7 inches. I fear that volunteers are already psychologically jumping ship and making other plans.

4:30 P.M. I CALL KT, OUR WEBMISTRESS, FOR A PEP TALK AND she thinks we should do it. So does my fiancé, Frank, who's a weather fanatic. We figure we'll just do as much as we can.

6:00 P.M. I GET A MILKSHAKE FOR MY NERVOUS STOMACH ON the way to the warehouse. Miftah and Marcella, two About-Face members, arrive first. We stand aghast as hail roars down. A few other volunteers arrive. We are all feeling excited and determined to go, regardless of the weather.

Postering is thrilling. It's a rare event that can bring such kidlike excitement to a bunch of cynical city dwellers, but the combination of doing something that is potentially illegal and that we feel so strongly about is too compelling to resist. It makes you feel powerful and righteous and brave; it makes you think you can effect real change in the world if you just decide to do it.

7:00 P.M. TWENTY-THREE PEOPLE SHOW UP. WE DIVIDE INTO nine teams. Each team gets a map with a specific section of the city, a can of paste, two rollers, and a damp rag. It is lightly drizzling as we set out.

9:00 P.M. THE TEAMS COME BACK WITH PASTE IN THEIR HAIR and on their clothes, and stories to tell. "We totally plastered this site near the park." "People were stopping and asking about the posters, so we gave them some." "We ran out of paste and bought some flour to make more." (To make your own wheat paste, mix three tablespoons of wheat flour with a small amount of cold water. Stir into one cup of very hot water. Bring to a boil, stirring constantly, until mixture thickens.) Frank and I collect the goopy rollers, rags, and cans and load up the cars. By tomorrow, many of the posters will already be torn down by annoyed construction workers, but some will stay up for months. In total, we hung about four hundred posters throughout the city. While they won't be as noticed as a Calvin Klein billboard, they will still produce a reaction in people. For those of us who went out postering tonight, there is an amazing experience still to come. In a month or so, you may find yourself on a crosstown bus. You'll look out the window and see some of the posters hanging on a plywood wall. A sense of pride will well up in you. You participated in something big. You took a stand instead of being complacent. Thousands of other people will have seen the posters. Maybe someone will be inspired to make a loud statement of her own.

Refuse and Resist with Jean Kilbourne

How to Counteract Ad Messages

Laura Barcella / WINTER 2001

JEAN KILBOURNE KNOWS ACTIVISM ALMOST AS WELL AS SHE knows advertising. Best known for the documentary *Killing Us Softly* (now in its third edition), Kilbourne is an expert in analyzing advertisers' exploitation of female desires and insecurities for profit, and the ways corporate power has come to dominate our lives through marketing. "In this culture, the real authorities are huge corporations—the tobacco industry, the alcohol industry—and we tend to be unaware of that," she says. "We have a great deal more to fear from corporate power than from the government, yet it's kind of invisible because they're so smooth. We have a lot of kids these days who are drinking and smoking because they think they're rebelling, but what they're really doing is following orders from these corporations."

Her most recent book, *Can't Buy My Love*, takes this analysis a step further, exploring the advertising industry's inculcation of an addictive mentality—one that persuades us that low-fat cookies are a perfect substitute for self-love and that even if men don't respect us, our ultraslim cigarettes always will. Kilbourne's extensive experience with advertising's psyche-invading images makes her the perfect woman to dole out a few handy antiadvertising tips to you. Here's what she has to say:

- The first thing is to pay attention. We all believe we're not influenced by advertising. The longer we believe we're not influenced, the more likely we are to be influenced, because we don't pay conscious attention. We need to really focus and look at the TV commercials and the print ads, and ask ourselves, "What's really being sold here?"

• We [must] get advertising out of our schools. There is no excuse for allowing corporations to control our kids' attention and time at school. That means getting rid of Channel One and other media that encroach on education. Young kids don't have the cognitive abilities to process advertising, so they're sitting ducks. [We need] to have a comprehensive media-literacy program in our schools, to help kids become critical viewers starting in kindergarten. The United States is one of the few developed nations in the world that doesn't do this.

• When you're reading a magazine and those irritating subscription cards fall into your lap, write on the card something like "stop exploiting women" or "feed your models" and mail it. It costs them something like 30 cents for every one that's sent back. It takes about 10 seconds, and it cleans up litter.

• Try not to buy products that are advertised in ways you find offensive. I try not to buy products from the tobacco industry, which doesn't just include cigarettes (for example, Philip Morris owns Kraft). [Research the business practices of the companies you're buying from] and you can put your money where your values are.

• Work for political measures. For example, the European Union will be debating a bill to ban all advertising directed at children—wouldn't that be wonderful? Write to congressional representatives and take part in such activities as a protest of the Golden Marble Awards, which is what the advertisers give to each other for their success in targeting children.

• Counter-advertising can be extraordinarily effective, whether it's an individual writing something on an ad, or a group such as the ones in Massachusetts, Florida, and California that have come out with phenomenally effective antitobacco advertising. The smoking rates in those states are way below the national average, and part of the reason is the counter-advertising. That's very effective because it's a way of getting us to look at advertising with new eyes.

Full Frontal Offense

Bringing Abortion Rights to the Ts

Rebecca Hyman / WINTER 2005

THERE'S A NEW FRONT IN THE BATTLE FOR ABORTION RIGHTS—
the literal front, that is, of a T-shirt designed by writer and feminist activist
Jennifer Baumgardner. It proclaims, "I had an abortion." The shirt, initially
for sale on Planned Parenthood's national website and now available on
Clamor magazine's website, has generated controversy among antiabortion
folks and pro-choice feminists alike.

Inspired in part by the bold irreverence of second-wave feminists,
who circulated a petition proclaiming the fact of their own abortions and
published it in the first issue of *Ms.*, Baumgardner created the T-shirt to
combat the stigma that still shames and silences those who have had an
abortion. The shirt is one component of a multipart project she conceived
to document the history of abortion through personal stories, including a
film featuring interviews with women who have had abortions, a guidebook to busting through the gridlock on the abortion debate, and resource
cards to help women locate abortion services and obtain postabortion counseling.

The shirt has certainly fulfilled Baumgardner's hope that it would start
a conversation about abortion, but the very brevity of its message has had
an unanticipated consequence. Although it's no surprise that individuals
such as Jim Sedlak, executive director of the American Life League's
STOPP International, think the shirt "celebrates an act of violence" and

337

demonstrates that Planned Parenthood "lacks any sense of integrity, tact, and compassion," it's interesting to note that many pro-choice feminists are ambivalent about—or even angered by—the shirt's message. Why, they ask, is the abortion fight taking place on something as public and casual as a T-shirt?

In one respect, using a T-shirt to proclaim the reality of abortion in plain language is the perfect antidote to the climate of fear that informs the ongoing battle for women's reproductive rights. The Bush administration's attack on sex education and prenatal care, as well as abortion, is taking place in multiple arenas: the gag rule, limits on stem-cell research funds, the Partial Birth Abortion Ban's vague and overbroad language, and the Unborn Victims of Violence Act (which creates a precedent in which the fetus is granted the legal status of a person).

In the face of such a far-reaching anti-choice agenda, T-shirts proclaiming abortion histories would seem a forceful response. As Barbara Ehrenreich recently reminded readers in a *New York Times* editorial, "Abortion is legal—it's just not supposed to be mentioned or acknowledged as an acceptable option." Since *Roe v. Wade*, she writes, "at least 30 million American women" have had abortions, "a number that amounts to about 40 percent of American women." Yet according to a 2003 survey conducted by a pro-choice organization, "only 30 percent of women were unambivalently pro-choice." Ehrenreich logically surmises that many women who refuse to state publicly that they are pro-choice have nevertheless obtained safe, legal abortions. To be vocal about abortion—not by supporting an abstract "freedom of choice" but instead by naming abortion as a fact of women's experience—is thus to break the dual threat of political and private shaming that keeps women silent.

Like Ehrenreich, who called for women to "take your thumbs out of your mouths, ladies, and speak up for your rights," Baumgardner sees a direct correlation between the increase in women's speech and the increase in their rights. "When women were most vocal about their experiences of abortion," she says, "*Roe v. Wade* was enacted. Now that women are silent about their experiences of abortion, we are seeing a decline in their reproductive rights." Given this history, it's no surprise that Planned Parenthood, which initially agreed to sell two hundred shirts on its website, sold out so quickly that it had to refer potential customers to Baumgardner's site to meet the demand. Ehrenreich wears her shirt to the gym; Ani DiFranco wore hers to an interview with *Inc.*, an apolitical business magazine. When the photograph of DiFranco sporting the shirt and holding her guitar appeared, readers wrote to the editors to protest, sparking an extended dialogue about abortion rights on Fresh Inc., the magazine's blog.

I spoke with many women in the Atlanta area about the shirt, most of whom were pro-choice feminists, and heard it called tacky, cavalier, simplistic, arrogant, cool, shameful, and brave. One twenty-four-year-old woman found the shirt offensive because it returns the abortion debate to the public realm. "The whole purpose of abortion rights," she told me, "is to ensure that a woman can make her own decision about her body, in private, without having to seek permission from anyone else—not even her partner." A woman wearing the T-shirt, she explained, is asking for comments of approval or disapproval from men and women. "My body is mine," she said, "and I shouldn't have to justify or announce my decisions to anyone else."

Another woman told me that, though she's pro-choice herself, she couldn't understand why a woman would announce her abortion unless she was doing so as a matter of pride. "Does she want me to think about the fact that she had an abortion every time I see her?" she wondered. "Because if I saw her wearing the shirt, that is what would stay with me, even if she never wore it again." I asked why she was associating a factual statement with the sentiment of boastfulness. "Because it's on a T-shirt," her friend chimed in. "Like the one I have that says, 'No One Knows I'm a Lesbian.'" Her statement was greeted by nods of approval from the other women who were listening to our conversation.

And what about the shirt as a fashion statement? If a woman wears the shirt because she likes it but hasn't had an abortion herself, she could be seen as an ally in the struggle, or she could be faulted for appropriating another woman's experience—or, worse, disregarding it altogether. It all depends on the way others perceive her. An activist from California told me that she wants to see as many women as possible wearing the shirt, regardless of whether they've had an abortion, to "participate in the collective destigmatizing of the procedure." To represent the fact of abortion, as the shirt certainly does, is not equivalent to representing experience. It's only an opening line.

The negative reaction many feminists have to the shirt reveals a fundamental contradiction in the current state of pro-choice politics—or, more precisely, the extent to which those who are pro-choice feel ashamed, at some level, to support abortion. The fact that so many women read a simple statement as a "celebration" of the procedure speaks volumes about the feelings women have internalized as a consequence of the conservative assault on women's rights. Although most of the women I spoke with were uneasy about their response to the shirt, repeatedly insisting that they were pro-choice even as they told me they would never wear it, some reacted to a photograph of the shirt with anger.

"The only reason anyone would wear such a shirt would be to piss people off," one nineteen-year-old woman snorted. "No one who was serious about supporting abortion rights would wear it." Those who saw the shirt as an aggressive tactic also thought it was perfect ammunition for the antiabortion movement, playing into the propaganda that paints pro-choice women as glorying in the selfish taking of a life. And judging from the comments on conservative blogs like Outside the Beltway and Baby Center, this argument has some merit. Amid the usual vitriol and sardonic humor (one person wrote that the back of the shirt should say *"Roe v. Wade*—Eliminating Future Democrats One Choice at a Time") is a sense that, by creating a T-shirt so many would see as offensive, the pro-choice movement had intentionally sought to outrage the Christian right.

In fact, the fear that the shirt could inflame the existing passions of the anti-choice movement has led some Planned Parenthood affiliates to condemn it. Leola Reis, Planned Parenthood of Georgia's vice president of communications, education, and outreach, told me the chapter had not been consulted about the national organization's decision to sell the shirts. "Women have enough trouble trying to secure safe and legal abortions without having to become the unwitting victims of pro-life wrath," she says. Though she understands the intention behind the shirt, she's not sure it will have a positive effect on the actual experience of women trying to attain abortions in such a conservative time. Chapters of Planned Parenthood in Idaho, North Carolina, and South Carolina have criticized the shirt outright, and Planned Parenthood Canada distanced itself from the controversy by saying, via its website, that it "cannot comment on the approach" taken by Planned Parenthood of America.

It's important to recognize the extent to which the attention of the pro-choice movement has shifted away from the bodies and lives of women who need abortions and toward those who aim to strip women of the right to control their reproductive lives. So it's not surprising that a large part of the movement is plagued by the notion that anti-choicers riled up by the sight of women proclaiming their abortions on their chests will want to step up their efforts to deny them this power. Given this fear, it would seem a smart strategy to keep quiet, stay under the radar, and hope that women will vote anti-choice legislators out of office. Such a focus, however, ignores the effect pro-choice speech, including the shirt, might have on a woman feeling isolated and ashamed because she had an abortion or is considering it. A public sisterhood of those who have chosen abortion, for a variety of personal reasons, could do a lot to counteract the hateful rhetoric of the anti-choice movement.

Baumgardner's T-shirt is a lightning rod for the emotions that surround the abortion issue—especially among feminists—because it forces the current unspoken contradiction of the pro-choice movement into public speech. Keeping quiet might seem like a smart political tactic, but when women muzzle themselves because they are afraid, their silence can masquerade as the appearance of support for an anti-choice agenda. If we don't break the silence about abortion, our right to control our reproductive destiny will never seem as natural as the right to wear our political opinions on a shirt.

Meet Anne

A Spunky, Adventurous American Girl

Anne Elizabeth Moore / SPRING 2005

JUST OFF MICHIGAN AVENUE IN CHICAGO EXISTS A PLACE where girls shop in special boutiques, dine in specially constructed chairs, and beautify themselves at the hands of trained experts. There's even an on-site hospital in case of a medical emergency such as decapitation, a plight suffered tragically often by this community. For here, American Girls are given everything they desire. At least the dolls are: I was hassled for two hours, escorted out of the store by the cops, and told never to return upon penalty of immediate arrest.

A three-floor worship center for the female consumer, American Girl Place exists to hone a sense of class and race privilege, and to foster in youth the ability to locate, and financially capitalize on, difference and tragedy. Shoppers grab small cards printed with pictures of the American Girl dolls—like Addy, who was born into slavery in 1864 and escapes with her mother to the North, or Kit, who lives during the Great Depression—as well as a brief description and a price. The cards are meant to be contained in small maroon folders imprinted with the phrase "Pocket full of wishes." It's a brilliant scheme: These can be brought to the nearest cash register or, as the folders brightly suggest, brought home as souvenirs, whereupon the cards can be flipped over and the pictured item ordered via the handy toll-free number.

I like American Girl Place, especially compared to the other screwy options offered to young girls in our culture. Parent company Mattel uses the American Girl products to teach history and instill an early sense of self-worth into a diverse array of young lives. In teaching consumers about the lives of past girls, however, Mattel conveniently avoids showing them the reality of female futures. So I planned American Girl Project: Operation Pocket Full of Wishes, and created a batch of cards that mimicked American Girl shopping aids and included the following actual wishes of actual girls: Equal Pay for Equal Work, Self-Confidence, Healthy Body Images, Safe and Effective Birth Control, Ample Career Opportunities, Safe and Legal Abortion Access, and Free Tampons. These were described by the phrase "not pictured" and priced at $0. I took the "Pocket full of wishes" folders home, placed the cards inside, and returned them to the slots whence they had originated at American Girl Place. (Since the inside of the sleeves does offer the option of taking them home, it is completely acceptable to have removed them from the premises.)

No crimes were committed, no acts of civil disobedience were undertaken. In fact, two hours of intimidation and interrogation by security guards succeeded only in acknowledging that the messages I had planted were consistent with American Girl Place's stated values. (One guard flipped through the cards mumbling comments like "Well, everyone agrees with *that*," while the other, I am convinced, kept a set for herself.) And still: a frisking and between eight and ten on-duty Chicago police officers—fully armed and wearing protective body armor—were apparently required to keep the girls safe from such notions as Domestic Partnership Benefits.

Outside on the street, one of the officers tried to bad-cop me. "Next time you wanna commit your freedom-of-speech thing, you're going to have to do it out here on the street. And only to adults!"

"So, American Girl Place doesn't allow freedom of speech on its premises?" I asked him. I knew I was provoking him, but—like Kaya, a Nez Percé Indian girl from 1764—I just can't keep my mouth shut when there's a point to be made.

How to Reclaim, Reframe, and Reform the Media

A Feminist Advocacy Guide

Jennifer L. Pozner / BITCHfest 2006

YOU FLIP TO YOUR LOCAL CLEAR CHANNEL STATION TO FIND A shock jock "joking" about where kidnappers can most easily buy nylon rope, tarps, and lye for tying up, hiding, and dissolving the bodies of little girls. Reuters runs an important international news brief about a Nigerian woman sentenced to death by stoning for an alleged sexual infraction—in its "Oddly Enough" section, where typical headlines include "Drunk Elk Shot Dead After Attacking Boy" and "Unruly Taxi Drivers Sent to Charm School." When California Democrats Loretta and Linda Sánchez become the first sisters ever to serve together in Congress, *The Washington Post* devotes 1,766 words in its style section to inform readers about the representatives' preferences regarding housekeeping, hairstyles, and "hootchy shoes." (Number of paragraphs focusing on the congresswomen's political viewpoints: one.)

After more than a million women and their allies storm Washington, D.C., for the March for Women's Lives in April 2004, typical headlines refer only to "thousands" of protestors, downplaying its political importance, and most stories fail to mention that this feminist demonstration was the largest single political protest in the capital's history. In summer 2005, when thousands protest in solidarity with Cindy Sheehan—an activist demanding answers from President Bush after her soldier son was killed in Iraq—the Selective-Memory Bureau at ABC's *World News Tonight* relies on misleading poll numbers to report a so-called reality check that "public protests thus far have been relatively small" and that Sheehan is not likely representative of a real antiwar movement in this country. Never mind that nearly a million demonstrators gathered in cities across America—and many more internationally—on February 15, 2003, to protest the war before it started. And pay no attention to the numerous polls showing that 60 percent or more of Americans do not approve of our government's handling of the war.

We rely on news media to provide the information we need to function as active members of a democracy. But, as the above examples show, coverage often reveals a dire need for institutional optometry. The systemic underrepresentation of women's and, in particular, feminist and other progressive perspectives in American media is the result of a variety of institutional factors, including the financial and political agendas of corporate media owners, and the pandering of news networks and entertainment studios to the whims of advertisers. Furthermore, right-wing organizations have spent decades training student journalists, funding think tanks, pumping out pundits, buying up media outlets, and doing everything in their power to frame discussions about American politics in their own terms (all the while railing against the mythical "liberal media").

Feminists and progressives need to learn from those strategies. If we want to move public opinion, defend our rights, and advocate for our future, we have to decide, today, that we're going to compete on the media battlefield. This means critiquing negative media and, more important, actively working to create positive media coverage and advocating for structural reform. The following tips, adapted from the media trainings WIMN conducts for women's social justice groups, will help you make the leap from righteous indignation to effective agitation.

• READ (AND WATCH) BROADLY. Familiarize yourself with the ways various outlets cover the issues that you care about. Read—or at minimum, scan the headlines of—at least one major national daily newspaper, one national weekly newsmagazine, one independent online outlet, and one or more independent magazines, paying special attention to the issues most urgent to you. Watch nightly news reports and network and cable debate shows to get a clear insight into the way that the majority of the U.S. public gets their news, and don't forget that popular TV shows are often as influential as news media when it comes to perpetuating stereotypes about women. Over time, you'll start to recognize which outlets offer a reasonable sense of balance or do an especially good job exploring important issues. You'll also see which ones virtually ignore women's issues, and which ones regularly publish inaccuracies and overrely on the perspectives of "official" (read: governmental and/or corporate) or right-wing sources without quoting public interest voices.

• COUNT THE "EXPERTS." Despite years of right-wing attacks on the "liberal media," decades of studies reveal a few salient facts: The range of debate in news media is skewed heavily toward the right, the perspectives of anyone who's not a white man are systemically marginalized, and corporate representatives and political officials are regularly tapped as experts while public voices are virtually invisible. The media watchdog organization Fairness & Accuracy In Reporting found that in 2001, network nightly news sources were 85 percent male, 92 percent white, and, where party affiliation was identifiable, 75 percent Republican. In 2004, a Project for Excellence in Journalism study of more than seventeen thousand news reports showed that women are underrepresented as news sources across all outlets, faring worst on PBS's *NewsHour with Jim Lehrer* and cable news (where 83 and 81 percent of stories, respectively, had no female sources at all) and better in newspapers (where "only" 59 percent of stories used all-male sources). Women were least likely to be cited as experts on foreign affairs—and the only place where female sources appeared in more than half of the stories was lifestyle stories.

• PHOTOS COUNT, TOO. If you're particularly peeved by a certain outlet's habit of publishing photos of women who are either victims of sexual assault or provocatively dressed celebrities, or running captions that trivialize or disparage women, evaluate all images that appear there over a significant period of time and assess your findings. Such studies can yield powerful evidence: Yearbook or suit-and-tie photos tend to accompany stories about white youth accused of crimes, while black and Latino youth accused of similar crimes are often photographed in handcuffs or during "perp walks," as reported in "In Between the Lines: How *The New York Times* Frames Youth," a study by advocacy groups We Interrupt This Message and Youth Force.

• CHALLENGE DOUBLE STANDARDS. *The New York Times* has referenced Condoleezza Rice's dress size and "girlish laugh" on the front page, while *The Washington Post* described her as a "dominatrix" after she happened to wear a black coat and leather boots together; a CNN *Larry King Live* panel once convened to discuss Hillary Clinton's electoral disadvantage of being "fat," "bottom-heavy," and "bitchy." Needless to say, Donald Rumsfeld's inseam measurements and Rudy Giuliani's comb-over have never been considered newsworthy. And we all recall the widely circulated wire-service photos of Hurricane Katrina victims whose captions noted that a black man wading through chest-deep water was "looting" the food he was carrying, while white people in a similar photo were described as "finding" groceries.

• CORRECT THE RECORD. Provide accurate, corrective follow-up information when media uncritically report misinformation that has already been debunked—even in their own newspapers, magazines, and broadcasts. For example, when George W. Bush reinstated the Global Gag Rule on family planning, the administration claimed, and the majority of news outlets dutifully repeated, that the act would prevent U.S. dollars from funding abortions overseas—despite the fact that, as had been widely reported in these same outlets years before, the United States had not funded foreign abortions for decades. Just make sure you check your own facts thoroughly when you're making a stink about someone else's inaccuracy.

• ILLUMINATE BIASED OR DISTORTED FRAMING. Ask whose viewpoint is shaping the story—is the public interest subjugated to the perspectives of the powerful? In light of the Bush administration's assault on affirmative action, for example, Peter Jennings once framed a *World News Tonight* Martin Luther King Day segment this way: "President Bush and race: Does he have a strategy to win black support?" Responsible journalism would have investigated the economic, academic, and political implications of the president's agenda for African Americans rather than the effects of race policy on Bush's approval rating. When filmmaker Roman Polanski was unable to return to Hollywood to accept an Oscar for *The Pianist* in 2003, a *Los Angeles Times* writer explained that "controversy" surrounded the director because he "became swept up in a sex scandal" of "cloudy circumstances" decades prior; a fully accurate story would have reported that Polanski fled the United States to escape sentencing after a conviction for drugging and raping a thirteen-year-old girl.

• HIGHLIGHT HEADLINE MISREPRESENTATION. Call attention to inflammatory or misrepresentative headlines that contradict the actual facts reported. After 9/11, for instance, *The Washington Post* headline "Public Unyielding in War Against Terror; 9 in 10 Back Robust Military Response" misleadingly implied that 90 percent of the public at large favored a full-scale war in Afghanistan. Yet the end of the story noted that women "were significantly less likely to support a long and costly war" than were men, that their hesitancy might develop into "hardened opposition" over time, and that while 44 percent of women said they'd favor a broad military effort, "48 percent said they want *a limited strike or no military action at all*" (emphasis added).

• SHED LIGHT ON SELECTIVE SOURCING AND CREATIVE USE OF ELLIPSES. Are ideologically motivated studies from right-wing-funded groups like the Independent Women's Forum being presented uncritically as neutral? If so, demand full disclosure and critical follow-up. Have reporters fairly assessed that original material? If not, suggest that the outlet publish or broadcast corrective data and analysis. And don't forget that movie marketers aren't the only ones who can use partial quotes in service of something less than the full picture: Someone could quote me as saying, "I . . . trust the corporate media," and it wouldn't technically be a misquote—but selectively omitting the word "don't" between "I" and "trust" would still be wildly inaccurate.

• HELP PROVIDE THE DIVERSITY YOU WANT. When reminding news outlets that they cannot present an accurate or comprehensive picture of news and public affairs without a broad, diverse, proportionally representative range of experts including women, people of color, queer folks, workers' advocates, and other public interest voices, turn them on to all the articulate, media-savvy experts and activists you know and point out organizations doing relevant work that they may not know about.

• BE FIRM BUT POLITE. Make your case sans insults, rants, and vulgarity. Nothing makes it easier for editors and producers to dismiss your argument than name-calling. Good idea: "Your discussion of the rape survivor's clothing and makeup was irrelevant, irresponsible, and inappropriate. Including those details blames the victim and reinforces dangerous myths about sexual assault." Bad idea: "Your reporter is a woman-hating incarnation of Satan!"

• CHOOSE YOUR BATTLES. Avoid utopian demands; calling for *The New York Times* to transform itself into a socialist newspaper will get you nowhere. Specific suggestions for improvement, such as requests that quotes from industry executives be balanced by input from feminist economists, and labor and public-interest groups, are more likely to be taken seriously. Don't complain to Clear Channel that its shock jocks are "insensitive" or "impolite"; do advocate for the radio conglomerate to adopt and adhere to a no-tolerance policy against hosts spouting hate speech or advocating violence.

• TARGET THE RIGHT PEOPLE. Familiarize yourself with news beats and who covers them. If you send a complaint about a paper's lack of reportorial objectivity to the opinion-page editor, it'll just get tossed. Also, while we'd all like to see fewer female bods used to sell beer, asking the networks to reject such ads is a waste of time. Instead, aim your ire at the companies producing the ads that offend.

• ADAPT YOUR APPROACH TO YOUR GOAL. If you want your letter printed on the letters page, keep it concise and informative; a couple of well-documented paragraphs will always be better received than an emotional three-page manifesto. However, if your goal is to raise concerns within a news outlet, you can send a more detailed, researched letter directly to a specific reporter or columnist and his or her editor or news manager, offering data to correct inaccuracies, a brief critique of problematic rhetoric, and/or further information for follow-up stories. Tailor your language, rhetoric, and angles to match the tone of the outlet you want to reach—what works in *Glamour* wouldn't fly in *The Wall Street Journal*. No matter what, though, be sure to proofread—nothing peeves an editor more than typos or bad grammar. Plus, know that notes on organizational or personal letterhead faxed or sent in the mail are often taken more seriously than e-mails, especially those that seem to be mass-generated.

• COMMEND GOOD COVERAGE. Positive reinforcement can be as effective as protest. Speak up to both reporters and their editors or producers in support of news stories that you consider fair and accurate, journalism that exposes governmental or corporate corruption, and articles that offer a variety of perspectives and allow women, people of color, and others to comment on the issues that affect their lives. Likewise, applaud TV networks and movie studios when they offer entertainment options that are enriching, enlightening, and challenging. Ask for more of the same.

• PRIORITIZE MEDIA MESSAGING. Resolve to devote a certain amount of time, thought, and practical work every week to the goal of generating positive media coverage of the issues you care about. You could decide to send three letters to the editor, thank at least one reporter or producer by phone, and pitch at least one story idea to a booker or editor every week; if you're a member of an activist group, you could initiate a weekly media messaging session to collectively discuss breaking news, deconstruct sexist framing, develop talking points, and generate story ideas.

• INITIATE AND BUILD RELATIONSHIPS. Get in touch with reporters, editors, and producers by sending information-rich letters, press releases, and media advisories (with enough lead time to respect mediamakers' deadlines). Communicate regularly with reporters about issues of concern to you that fall within their beat. Provide study/report data, compelling human-interest stories relevant to their audience, and connections to expert sources and new research in your area of expertise. If you work with an organization, request editorial board meetings to discuss your issues with your local news outlets. Develop catchy, persuasive, and understandable sound bites for the messages you want to convey.

• GET CREATIVE. Organize a public informational or protest event and invite C-SPAN to cover it; use satire (à la Billionaires for More Media Mergers and the Guerrilla Girls) and action ripe for photo ops (à la Code Pink or ACT UP).

• DON'T LIKE THE MEDIA? BE THE MEDIA. Attend or organize media skills–building training in your community. Do your own reporting on Indymedia.org websites, make your own films with PaperTiger.org, DykeTV.org, or the Media Education Foundation, and host your own college, community, or cable access TV or radio show.

• DEFEND THE PUBLIC INTEREST IN TELECOMMUNICATIONS POLICY. The Telecommunications Act of 1996, passed under President Clinton, heralded the biggest wave of media mergers ever seen in the United States. Today, a tiny handful of multinational corporations owns the vast majority of American newspapers, magazines, TV networks, cable and online news and entertainment outlets, record labels, radio stations, TV and movie production companies, publishing houses, Internet and cable distribution chains, and billboards—not to mention sports teams, stadiums, theme parks, nuclear and weapons-manufacturing businesses, and lots more. The Federal Communications Commission has all but abdicated its responsibility to regulate the U.S. media industry in the public interest. Urge senators and representatives to fight against media concentration and support legislation for diverse, local, independent, and uncensored media. Corporate broadcasters who get to use the public airwaves for free should be required to provide news and entertainment programming that is diverse, informative, educational, and produced by a range of independent creative sources.

• DEMAND FAIR HIRING AND PROMOTION PRACTICES AMONG MEDIA COMPANIES. Media conglomerates are not magnanimous; they will not change their priorities without major incentives. In the 1930s, Eleanor Roosevelt would speak only to female reporters at her press conferences, forcing newspapers to employ women journalists. In the 1970s, newspapers and TV networks had to be sued by women journalists before they'd stop discriminating against women in hiring and promotion. It's time to reprioritize gender equity in the media industry as a major feminist issue and pressure media companies to address not only the glass ceiling but also the corporate climate that pushes many women and people of color to leave the field. Though biology certainly doesn't determine politics— right-wing women like Ann Coulter, Peggy Noonan, and Laura Ingraham do maintain a high profile in the mainstream media, but they generally use that platform to bash feminist concerns and lobby against women's rights protections—newsroom and media-boardroom populations that more closely reflect the general population are a necessary first step.

• CLAIM THE AIRWAVES AND CABLE SYSTEMS FOR YOUR COMMUNITY. A variety of grassroots groups are organizing in local communities across the country to help set up low-power microradio stations, advocate fairer radio spectrum regulations that support diversity and access, offer legal and technical assistance, demand better programming and public accountability from radio and cable conglomerates, challenge cable license renewals, ensure equitable and affordable access to broadband networks, and more.

• EDUCATE YOURSELF AND OTHERS ABOUT TECHNOLOGY POLICY'S EFFECTS ON ACCESS TO INFORMATION. Profit-hungry corporations are gunning to privatize and commercialize emerging technologies, which would restrict public access to means of communication and information, expanding the digital divide between wealthy white Americans and low-income people and people of color. Understanding how these forces affect your own community and our culture as a whole is key to standing up to Internet censorship and control, protecting bloggers' rights, advocating privacy protections, and working to keep existing and emerging Internet, cable, and radio communications technologies broadly, affordably accessible as a public good.

• FIGHT THE INFLUENCE OF ADVERTISING, COMMERCIALISM, AND GOVERNMENTAL PROPAGANDA. Combat the widespread use by media companies of misleading video news releases (VNRs), which appear indistinguishable from average news broadcasts but are actually propaganda pieces paid for, packaged, and promoted by corporations and the government. The Federal Communications Commission, the Federal Trade Commission, and the Food and Drug Administration (in the case of pharmaceutical VNRs) have the power to force media companies to disclose product placements that masquerade as media content on reality TV, news programming, music, and more—but they have thus far refused to use this power in the public interest.

• THINK LONG-TERM. Finally, remember that your efforts won't instantly reverse the tide of decades of right-wing media organizing, corporate consolidation, and commercialism run amok—but every action you take is important. Don't get discouraged if your letters to the editor don't see newsprint very often: Not only do outlets read and discuss critical communications from their audience, they count on multiple letters to measure public perception of key topics. If you read a letter similar to one you sent, yours may have helped it get published. And even with the perfect set of talking points, a well-tailored message, and many conversations with reporters, there will be times when your messages still get marginalized, misrepresented, or ignored. But your and others' media outreach and advocacy efforts will still help generate informative, critical, accurate, authentic, positive, and influential coverage of women and the issues that most affect us—and our collective efforts can and will result in structural change. Learn from your mistakes, replicate your successes, and never give up. The fight for media and gender justice needs you.

the *BITCHfest* resource list

AS MUCH AS WE TRIED TO PACK INTO THIS BOOK, THERE'S always more to say. So here's a wholly incomplete, purposely nonexhaustive, and all-too-brief guide to some of our favorite writers, thinkers, organizations, and more who shed further light on topics addressed throughout the book.

Chapter 1. Hitting Puberty

Amelia Bloomer Project (www.libr.org/FTF/bloomer.html) Every year, the Feminist Task Force of the Social Responsibilities Round Table of the American Library Association (say that three times fast!) puts together a list of the latest and greatest feminist books for kids and teens.

Children's Media Project (www.childrensmediaproject.org) An arts and educational organization that teaches "children and youth . . . to interact with the media arts as both creators and critical viewers," the CMP features summer workshops, after-school programs, and DROP TV, an entirely youth-produced magazine-style show.

Deal With It! A Whole New Approach to Your Body, Brain, and Life as a Gurl by Esther Drill, Heather McDonald, and Rebecca Odes (Pocket Books, 1999) By the creator of the cool-ass website gURL, this book tackles the perennial concerns of young womanhood—zits, sex, unexpected body hair—with frank advice that never talks down.

GirlsFilmSchool (www.girlsfilmschool.csf.edu) This two-week summer program held at the College of Santa Fe gives high-school girls the opportunity to learn the basics of writing, producing, documentary techniques, editing, sound, cinematography, and more. The program prioritizes low-income and at-risk students, and more than two-thirds attend on scholarship.

Scarleteen (www.scarleteen.com) All the more important in an age of abstinence-only "education," Scarleteen provides info on everything from pregnancy and STDs to negotiations within relationships, all with the mission of "furnishing [teens] with the facts they need to know [in order to] develop their own systems of ethics and values."

Teen Voices (www.teenvoices.com) "Because you're more than just a pretty face" is the tagline of this magazine by, for, and about teen girls. The contributors to *Teen Voices* cover everything from censorship to acne to birth control to same-sex marriage to girls in sports, with the help of a few adult editors.

Chapter 2. Ladies and Gentlemen: Femininity, Masculinity, and Identity

Dyke TV (www.dyketv.org) The first (and so far, only) cable-access program by and for the ladies who love ladies, Dyke TV offers vital documentation of lesbian culture and activism.

GenderQueer: Voices from Beyond the Sexual Binary, edited by Joan Nestle, Clare Howell, and Riki Wilchins (Alyson Publications, 2002) An overview of radical gender theory and politics, plus a multitude of first-person narratives. This is a valuable collection that bridges the personal and political and doesn't presume to define what a genderqueer looks like.

Girls Will Be Boys Will Be Girls Will Be . . . , by Jacinta Bunnell and Irit Reinheimer (Soft Skull Press, 2004) This whimsical coloring book/zine offers sweet clip-art-inspired illustrations of, among others, crying boys and angry girls. Accompanying commentary says things like "Don't let gender box you in."

My Gender Workbook, by Kate Bornstein (Routledge, 1997) A playful, accessible, and interactive exploration of what makes us "masculine," "feminine," both, and neither.

Chapter 3. The *F* Word

Angry Women, edited by V. Vale and Andrea Juno (RE/Search, 1991) A collection of some of the most radical female voices in art circa 1991, *Angry Women*'s interviews—with the none-too-shy likes of Annie Sprinkle, Karen Finley, sapphire, Holly Hughes, and Susie Bright—proffer performance and provocation as a heady refutation of everything women are "supposed" to be.

Black Feminist Thought: Knowledge, Consciousness, and the Politics of Empowerment, by Patricia Hill Collins (Routledge, 2000) Originally published in 1990, this instant classic draws on history, literature, and cultural movements to highlight previously sidelined African-American feminist intellectual traditions and provide a much-needed corrective to exclusive white feminist movements.

Colonize This! Young Women of Color on Today's Feminism, edited by Daisy Hernández and Bushra Rehman (Seal Press, 2002) Feminist writers of color on how their backgrounds, cultures, and families have shaped their interest in and understanding of feminism and identity.

Feminist International Radio Endeavor (www.radiofeminista.net) The first ever women's Internet radio station, FIRE is where to go for English and Spanish coverage of feminist issues and events.

hooks, bell She is one of the most insightful thinkers ever on the interlocking forces of race, class, gender, and how we can dismantle "the white supremacist capitalist patriarchy," and her emphasis on coalition building, decolonization of the mind, and the power of love is always inspiring—yet she never lets anyone (including herself) evade her keen analytical eye.

Listen Up: Voices from the Next Feminist Generation, edited by Barbara Findlen (Seal Press, 2001) Now in its second edition, this vibrant collection was one of the first to give the lie to the greatly exaggerated reports of feminism's death among the post-'70s crowd. Now it's a third-wave classic.

Pollitt, Katha Her biweekly column for *The Nation* is always intelligent, progressive, and provocative; it's also often hilarious. She's a consistent voice of feminist reason, backing up her articulate analysis with carefully researched facts that would otherwise be ignored.

The Scholar and Feminist Online (www.barnard.edu/sfonline) This web-based journal of Barnard College's Center for Research on Women includes contemporary scholarship, art, audio clips, and activist resources.

Sisters of '77 (www.pbs.org/independentlens/sistersof77) In November 1977, twenty thousand delegates converged on Houston for the National Women's Conference, a federally funded gathering to hash out a platform for women's rights that was then presented to President Jimmy Carter. *Sisters*, produced by Media Projects, Inc. (www.mediaprojects.org) and originally aired on PBS, is not just a valuable history of the event but also a vibrant reminder of the continuity of the feminist movement.

Chapter 4. Desire: Love, Sex, and Marketing

Alan Guttmacher Institute (www.agi-usa.org) This national non-profit devoted to advancing reproductive choice and comprehensive sex education is a powerhouse of information on everything from public-policy analysis to social-science research.

Bisexual Resource Center (www.biresource.org) The online presence of this Boston-based organization features articles, online resources, a bi bookstore, and more. It's an organizing tool, a force for change, and a source of affirmation.

The Girl Wants To: Women's Representations of Sex and the Body, edited by Lynn Crosbie (Coach House, 1993) Fiction, poetry, drama, drawings, and everything in between, brought together to explore the female sex drive from a million and one angles.

Mary Jane's Not a Virgin Anymore The celluloid story of suburban teen misfit Jane finding her clit for the first time would be a cult classic if only it were more widely available. Screenings and copies are hard to come by but worth seeking out if at all possible.

No Fauxxx (www.nofauxxx.com) This alternaporn site truly lives up to the promise of breaking the boring, narrowly constructed molds of bodies and genders that mainstream porn has made. It's hot, it doesn't categorize content by gender or sexuality, it features genderqueer models aplenty, and its creators openly address their own conflicts and shortcomings (check out their notes about gender and cultural appropriation).

Pleasure and Danger: Exploring Female Sexuality, edited by Carole S. Vance (Routledge, 1984) Taking as its starting point "the notion that women cannot explore sexuality until danger is first eliminated is a strategic dead-end," the questions this collection speaks to are as relevant today as they were when it was first published.

Chapter 5. Domestic Arrangements

Alternatives to Marriage Project (www.unmarried.org) The AtMP advocates for folks who, like Joni Mitchell, don't need no piece of paper from the city hall keeping them tied and true. The organization believes in the diversity of unmarried relationships and is committed to fighting all forms of discrimination—from family disapproval to workplace stigma—faced by the nonhitched.

East Village Inky (www.ayunhalliday.com/inky) This profoundly hilarious, 100 percent done-by-hand zine chronicling author Ayun Halliday's life as an urban-dwelling, video-reviewing mother of two is indescribably brilliant. Get yourself some copies.

Hip Mama and its sister websites (www.hipmama.com) The print version of *Hip Mama* is the parenting magazine for anyone insulted by most parenting magazines: It's fiercely political, bitingly funny, and radically inclusive, and it never tries to sell you on the latest diaper genie. Its online incarnation is a thriving community that has spawned teen-mom site Girl-Mom.com, artist/writer/musician mom site Mamaphonic.com, and politics site YoMamaSays.org. Whether or not you're a parent, they are not to be missed.

The Mommy Myth: The Idealization of Motherhood and How It Has Undermined Women, by Susan J. Douglas and Meredith W. Michaels (Free Press, 2004) A pointed and resonant analysis of our culture's Jekyll-and-Hyde relationship with mothers and mothering, and its effects on politics, pop product, and all women—breeders or not.

Single Mothers by Choice (www.singlemothersbychoice.org) A membership organization that provides support and information for women who are either tired of waiting for Mr./Ms. Right or prefer to go it solo.

Welfare Warrior's Voice (http://my.execpc.com/~wmvoice) This quarterly newspaper by, for, and about mothers in poverty provides the perspective sorely missing from all the punditry, reportage, and politicking about welfare we've all heard so much of. Get the real story here.

Chapter 6. Beauty Myths and Body Projects

About-Face (www.about-face.org) Founded by contributor Kathy Bruin (see "Please Don't Feed the Models," page 331), this San Francisco–based organization combats negative media images of women through media literacy workshops in schools, actions like its "I don't need a makeover because . . ." letter-writing campaign in response to Fox's *The Swan,* and a web-based gallery of offenders, complete with contact info for your complaints.

Adiosbarbie.com This vibrantly designed and sharply written site from Ophira Edut, the editor of the excellent *Body Outlaws: Young Women Write About Body Image and Identity* (Seal Press, 2000), features articles, book recommendations, rant opportunities, and resource links aplenty.

Fat!So? Because You Don't Have to Apologize for Your Size!, by Marilyn Wann (Ten Speed Press, 1998) A book from the long-dormant zine of the same name, *Fat!So?* is a big fleshy antidote to antifat messages, skinny-folks-only images, and dieting propaganda, all done up with personal stories, sharp analysis, and health-myth debunking.

Hope in a Jar: The Making of America's Beauty Culture, by Kathy Peiss (Owl Press, 1998) An engaging, enlightening history of the billion-dollar-and-growing U.S. beauty industry that will shed some light on your susceptibility to perfume ads.

Our Bodies, Ourselves, by the Boston Women's Health Collective (Touchstone, 2005) This überbook of women's health information came out in 2005 with a spankin'-new, totally revised and redesigned thirty-fifth-anniversary edition and a frequently updated web companion (www.ourbodiesourselves.org).

Phat Camp (www.morethanjustphat.com) This Chicago-based organization "provides safe, non-judgemental space for youth to foster positive relationships with their bodies and debunk beauty myths" through discussion groups, trainings, activist retreats, and more. Issues like racism and trans discrimination are as much a part of their programs as fat—their mission is to "link beauty, bodies, and self-esteem through an anti-oppression lens."

Chapter 7. Confronting the Mainstream

The Media Project (www.themediaproject.com) A kick-ass non-profit that encourages TV networks to use their power for good and promote healthy, realistic attitudes about teen sexuality. The group honors two shows per month for honest depictions and accurate information about teens and sex.

Rock She Wrote: Women Write About Rock, Pop, and Rap, edited by Evelyn McDonnell and Ann Powers (Cooper Square Press, 1999) The first—and we hope not the last—collection of women-penned music criticism.

Turn Beauty Inside Out (www.mindonthemedia.org) A campaign to "promote healthy body image and expand the definition of what makes people beautiful," TBIO is a girlcentric program of leadership training, media literacy, and media protest that focuses on a different media sector (e.g., advertising or the music industry) each year.

Where the Girls Are: Growing Up Female with the Mass Media, by Susan J. Douglas (Three Rivers Press, 1995) One insightful woman's story of growing up amid contradictory pop cultural influences from *I Dream of Genie* to the Shirelles.

Chapter 8. Talking Back: Activism and Pop Culture

Center for International Media Action (www.mediaactioncenter .org) A powerful movement-building force in the media justice world, CIMA offers robust research, organizational development resources, activist manuals, and a much-needed forum for networking and information sharing.

Downhill Battle (www.downhillbattle.org) A collaboration among musicians, fans, and others working on assorted copyright issues and other aspects of major-label music-business monopolies.

The Fire This Time: Young Activists and the New Feminism, edited by Vivien Labaton and Dawn Lundy Martin (Anchor, 2004) This diverse anthology is incredibly valuable for how it enlarges the definition of feminist activism to include vital work on issues— prison abolition, foreign policy, and immigration are just a few—that are too often left out when feminism is assumed to be only about traditional "women's issues."

Free Speech TV (www.freespeech.org) Available through satellite networks and public access channels, FSTV is the nation's first and only progressive TV station. It airs documentaries, underreported news stories, video zines, and much more that you won't see anywhere else.

Isis International (www.isiswomen.org) Founded in 1974 to "create opportunities for women's voices to be heard, strengthen feminist analyses through information exchange, promote solidarity and support feminist movements across the globe," the Manila-based Isis works with activists in more than 150 countries to promote feminist and social justice viewpoints in all channels of communication.

Media Report to Women (www.mediareporttowomen.com) A quarterly news journal monitoring industry trends and conducting in-depth research, *MRTW* takes on such topics as whether female reporters covering the White House are overlooked at press conferences, how girls are positioned in ads in *Seventeen*, and more.

PR Watch (www.prwatch.org) In October 2005, the Government Accountability Office found that the Bush administration had illegally used public funds to promote its agenda via "covert propaganda"; instead of a national citizen/media outcry, the company that masterminded the whole thing got another fat government contract. These are the kinds of stories covered by the more-essential-than-ever *PR Watch*, a quarterly journal on the public relations industry published by the Center for Media and Democracy.

Well Connected (www.openairwaves.org) A project of the Center for Public Integrity, a nonprofit organization that conducts investigative journalism in the public interest, Well Connected is an ongoing investigation of the corporations and government agencies that control the information industry. Find out who owns which media outlets in your area, which companies spent how much on campaign contributions or lobbyists, and much, much more.

Women in Media & News (www.wimnonline.org) A feminist media analysis, education, and advocacy organization that gives public education presentations, trains social-justice organizations on media outreach, and works to expand the range of public debate by connecting working media producers with female sources.

Youth Media Council (www.youthmediacouncil.org) An organizing, leadership development, media capacity–building, and watchdog project aimed at developing youth-led strategies for media justice.

about the contributors

DIANE ANDERSON-MINSHALL ("What Happens to a Dyke Deferred?"; "I Kissed a Girl") was the founder and former editor of the magazines *Girl-friends* and *Alice*, and her work has appeared in dozens of magazines, news-papers, and anthologies. She edited the critically acclaimed but poorly selling anthology *Becoming: Young Ideas on Gender, Identity and Sexuality*. At thirty-eight, she's been in publishing for a full twenty-five years (yeah, you do the math) and is very, very tired. Check out her new venture, www .quirkygirls.com.

GUS ANDREWS ("The, Like, Downfall of the English Language") is work-ing on a doctorate in literacies, video games, and education at Teachers College of Columbia University. This article arose from research she did on the subject at Hampshire College, where she completed a BA in pub-lic screaming. Her freelance writing has been published in *Salon*, *City Limits*, and *The Village Voice*. She maintains an online journal at www .dancingsausage.net and entertains herself by code-switching in the streets of New York City.

LAURA BARCELLA ("Refuse and Resist with Jean Kilbourne") is a writer living in San Francisco. Her work has appeared in *Salon*, *The Village Voice*, *Bust*, and *Time Out New York*.

BETH BERNSTEIN and MATILDA ST. JOHN ("Your Stomach's the Size of a Peanut, So Shut Up Already") live in the San Francisco Bay Area. They're not as cranky as you might think. They believe everyone, regardless of size, has the right to feel good about herself.

AUDREY BILGER ("On Language: You Guys") teaches literature, gender studies, and yoga at Claremont McKenna College in California. She is the author of *Laughing Feminism: Subversive Comedy in Frances Burney, Maria Edgeworth, and Jane Austen* (Wayne State University Press, 1998) and the editor of Jane Collier's 1753 work *An Essay on the Art of Ingeniously Tormenting* for Broadview Literary Texts (2003). Her work has appeared in, among other places, *Rockrgrl,* the *Los Angeles Times,* and *The Paris Review.* She and co-writer Eberle Umbach are currently working on a cookbook based on excerpts from novels by eighteenth- and nineteenth-century women writers, to be titled "Jane Austen's Muffins and Louisa May Alcott's Buns." She lives near Los Angeles with her partner, record producer Cheryl Pawelski. They're probably backstage at a show right now.

CARSON BROWN ("The New Sexual Deviant") runs a small editing company and works at an integrative health clinic in San Francisco. After years of freelancing and freewheeling, she surprised herself by applying to medical school. Her hobbies include sleeping, karaoke, and brewing beer.

KATHY BRUIN ("Please Don't Feed the Models") has two unpaid jobs: one as founder of About-Face, a campaign educating about the ways media impacts female body image while promoting alternatives through education and action, and the other as a mom. About-Face was launched in 1995, the kid in 2001. For an occasional paycheck and getaway, Bruin works as a trade-show manager and gets to go stay in hotels far from home.

KEIDRA CHANEY ("Sister Outsider Headbanger") lives and works in Chicago. When not working at her day job at a small nonprofit arts organization or attempting to fulfill her life's dream of starting a Faith No More cover band, she's a freelance writer and editor. Her publication credits include *Bitch, Clamor, Colorlines,* africana.com, notfortourists.com, thirdcoast press.com, and a whole slew of independent/alternative publications that, sadly, no longer exist. She whines and waxes poetic on pop culture, music, and politics daily at enjoyandexciting.blogspot.com.

JULIE CRAIG ("I Can't Believe It's Not Feminism!") is a graduate student with roots in San Francisco and Portland, Oregon. Her hobbies include rocking out to alt-country music, mulling over the implications of bacterial genomics, and nitpicking George W. Bush's grammar. She is a frequent contributor to *Bitch*.

ATHENA DOURIS ("What Happens to a Dyke Deferred?") has an MA in feminist psychology and is currently collecting hours toward licensure as a marriage and family therapist. She lives in the Bay Area with her partner and their furry, four-legged son.

AIMÉE DOWL ("Beyond the Bearded Lady") is a former film editor who has worked on several award-winning features and documentaries about gay, feminist, and teen issues, and, when she needed more money, on an animated television series for the WB. More recently, she became a high-school teacher at an international school in Ecuador and a student of women's medical history. Someday she hopes to bring all her skills together by producing a cartoon melodrama about a goateed teenage lesbian called *Duh, It's a Beard!*

KAREN ENG ("The Princess and the Prankster") is a freelance writer and editor who has worked in the magazine industry since 1991. She has published a wide range of articles, mainly about independent arts and culture, in a variety of publications, among them *Wired* and *Publishers Weekly*. She is the editor of the 2004 Seal Press anthology *Secrets and Confidences: The Complicated Truth About Women's Friendships*, and her essays are included in the Seal Press anthologies *Women Who Eat: A New Generation on the Glory of Food* and *Young Wives' Tales: New Adventures in Love and Partnership*. In 2002, she received a George Washington Williams journalism fellowship sponsored by the Independent Press Association. She lives in Cambridge, England.

RACHEL FUDGE ("Celebrity Jeopardy"; "Girl, Unreconstructed"; "Bias Cut") is the senior editor of *Bitch*. She has been involved with the magazine since its early days as a volunteer, board member, and frequent contributor. Her writing has also appeared in *Clamor*, *AlterNet*, the *San Francisco Chronicle*, *PekoPeko*, and the Seal Press anthologies *Young Wives' Tales* and *Women Who Eat*. She was a contributing editor to the 2005 edition of *Our Bodies, Ourselves* and is the cocreator of the zine *Nebulosi*.

RITA HAO ("And Now a Word from Our Sponsors"; "Pratt-fall") is *Bitch*'s attorney. She lives and writes in San Francisco.

AMY HARTER ("In Re-Mission") is a writer, editor, and gardener living in San Francisco.

REBECCA HYMAN ("Full Frontal Offense") is director of Women's and Gender Studies and assistant professor of English at Oglethorpe University. She has written for publications such as *Women's Studies Quarterly*, *Women in Performance*, and *Clamor*. She is at work on a book about conservative political strategy and the left's renewal. She lives in Atlanta, Georgia. She can be reached at rebecca.hyman@gmail.com.

LISA MORICOLI LATHAM ("Double Life") has written humor and/or journalism for *The New York Times*, the *Los Angeles Times*, *Salon*, *Playboy*, *Men's Health*, *Cooking Light*, *The Seattle Times*, *America West*, *Babytalk*, Babycenter.com, and many other publications. She is a produced sitcom and film writer, as well as an etiquette columnist.

JENNIFER MAHER ("Hot for Teacher") teaches in the Department of Gender Studies at Indiana University, Bloomington. Her classes focus on popular culture, American women's literature, third-wave feminism, and gender and the body. She was published most recently in the NYU Press anthology *Reality TV: Remaking Television Culture* and in Seal Press's *Secrets and Confidences: The Complicated Truth About Women's Friendships*. She is currently at work on a larger project focused on gender and the representation of teachers in popular culture, inspired by the drafting of the article in this anthology.

SARAH MCCORMIC ("Hoovers and Shakers") grew up on an island in the Pacific Northwest. She lives in Seattle, where she works as a website editor at the University of Washington. Highlights of her varied writing and editing career include encyclopedia entries about Chinese despots, a book about Elvis, and articles celebrating the highly underrated sport of dogsledding. She is grateful to the three men in her life, Ralph (cat), Wally (cat), and Ben (human), all of whom agree that vacuum cleaners are too loud for regular use and that the best laps have some extra padding.

MARISA MELTZER ("Are Fat Suits the New Blackface?") is a freelance writer based in New York. She has contributed to *The New York Times*, *Entertainment Weekly*, *Elle*, and *Teen Vogue*, and is the coauthor of the forthcoming book *How Sassy Changed My Life: A Love Letter to the Greatest Teen Magazine of All Time*.

ANNA MILLS ("Envy, a Love Story") writes essays and poems on sex, gender, nature, and capitalism that have appeared in *Lodestar Quarterly*, *Identity Theory*, *SoMa Literary Review*, *Three Candles*, *Clamor*, and *Moxie*. She teaches English at City College of San Francisco.

ANNE ELIZABETH MOORE ("Meet Anne: A Spunky, Adventurous American Girl") is the author of *Hey Kidz! Buy This Book: A Radical Primer on Corporate and Governmental Propaganda and Artistic Activism for Short People* (Soft Skull Press, 2004), the associate publisher of *Punk Planet*, and the series editor for Houghton Mifflin's Best American Graphic Narratives.

GABRIELLE MOSS ("Teen Mean Fighting Machine") studied the history of American popular culture at Hampshire College in Amherst, Massachusetts; this essay is based on her senior thesis. She is currently a freelance writer and indie-rock nanny in New York City.

JENNIFER NEWENS ("The Paradox of Martha Stewart") has worked as a restaurant cook, caterer, recipe developer, and food writer. She currently works as a senior editor specializing in cookbooks for a San Francisco–based publisher. She coauthored the cookbooks *Basic Cooking* and *Basic Baking*. She continues to follow the story of Martha Stewart.

MONICA NOLAN ("Mother Inferior") is a writer and filmmaker based in San Francisco. In addition to her work for *Bitch*, she has written about film for *Release Print* and coauthored *The Big Book of Lesbian Horse Stories*. Her first novel, *Lois Lenz, Lesbian Secretary*, will be published by Kensington. She worked as an editor and writer on Kara Herold's documentaries *Grrlyshow* and *Bachelorette, 34*. She has one of the most extensive collections of 1950s teen-girl literature west of the Sierras.

TAMMY OLER ("Bloodletting") is a writer, editor, and rollergirl living in Denver, Colorado. Her work has appeared in local alternative newspapers and magazines and several online literary journals. She is currently at work on a memoir about science-fiction fandom.

BRENDAN O'SULLIVAN ("Dead Man Walking") lives in Oakland, California, and likes reading theory a little too much. Though, all things being equal, he would rather just eat semisweet chocolate and dance. He has actually seen *Weekend at Bernie's II* in its entirety. He can be reached at bosullivan@riseup.net.

LEAH LAKSHMI PIEPZNA-SAMARASINHA ("Busting the Beige Barrier") is a U.S.-raised, Toronto-based queer Sri Lankan writer, spoken-word artist, and arts educator. The author of *Consensual Genocide* (Toronto South Asian Review Press, 2006), she has been published in the anthologies *Colonize This!*; *Dangerous Families*; *With a Rough Tongue: Femmes Write Porn*; the Lambda Award–nominated *Brazen Femme*; *Without a Net*; *Geeks, Misfits and Outlaws*; and *A Girl's Guide to Taking Over the World*, as well as in the periodicals *Lodestar Quarterly*, *Mizna*, *SAMAR*, *Bamboo Girl*, *Bitch*, *Broken Pencil*, *Colorlines*, *Fireweed*, and *Anything That Moves*. She has performed her work throughout the United States and Canada, teaches writing to GLBT youth at Supporting Our Youth Toronto, and is one of the organizers of the Asian Arts Freedom School, a writing, performance, and activist education program for Asian/Pacific Islander youth.

JENNIFER L. POZNER ("How to Reclaim, Reframe, and Reform the Media") is the executive director of Women in Media & News (WIMN). She conducts media trainings for women's groups and is a regular speaker on college campuses with multimedia presentations such as "Bachelor Babes, Bridezillas & Husband-Hunting Harems: Decoding Reality TV's Twisted Fairy Tales" and "Condoleezza Rice is a Size 6, and Other Useless Things I Learned from the News." She can be reached at director@WIMNonline.org.

MARGARET PRICE ("Queer and Pleasant Danger") lives in Atlanta and teaches writing at Spelman College. Her essays, poetry, and short fiction have been published in *Ms.*, the *Michigan Quarterly Review*, *Creative Nonfiction*, and *The Gay and Lesbian Review*. She is at work on a scholarly tome titled "Writing from Normal" and a novel titled "Knocking Alex Up." She satisfies her parenting urges by adopting another cat every time she drives past the shelter, and watches *The L Word* with equal parts enjoyment and horror.

DON ROMESBURG ("Holy Fratrimony"), a freelance writer and PhD candidate in U.S. history at the University of California, Berkeley, lives in San Francisco with his boyfriend, dog, and TiVo.

DANYA RUTTENBERG ("Fringe Me Up, Fringe Me Down") is the editor of *Yentl's Revenge: The Next Wave of Jewish Feminism* (Seal Press). She serves as a contributing editor to both *Lilith* and *Women in Judaism: A Multidisciplinary Journal*, and is a contributing writer for Jewschool.com. Her writing has appeared in numerous anthologies and magazines, including the *San Francisco Chronicle, Tikkun, Bitch, Heeb, Salon, The Best Jewish Writing 2002, The Unsavvy Traveler, The Women's Seder Sourcebook, The Women's Movement Today: An Encyclopedia of Third-Wave Feminism*, and the forthcoming edition of *Encyclopedia Judaica*. She is currently studying for rabbinic ordination at the University of Judaism in Los Angeles and speaks widely about religion and culture.

KEELY SAVOIE ("Screen Butch Blues"; "Unnatural Selection") is a freelance writer based in Brooklyn, New York. She writes on science, politics, and feminism separately, but enjoys it most when they all collide. She is a frequent contributor to *Bitch* and a featured writer for Women in Media & News' blog. She also writes regularly for *Choice!*, Planned Parenthood's online magazine; *In The Fray*, an online magazine; as well as for a politician whose views she generally respects. One of her recent essays appears in *50 Ways to Support Lesbian and Gay Equality* (Inner Ocean, 2005).

JULIA SCHEERES ("Vulva Goldmine") is a San Francisco–based journalist and the author of the memoir *Jesus Land* (Counterpoint, 2005).

HEATHER SEGGEL ("I Heard It Through the Loveline") is a freelance journalist and frequent contributor to *Bitch*. Her work has appeared in the *North Bay Bohemian*, the *San Francisco Bay Times*, and throughout the zine world. It makes her teeth ache to know that Adam Carolla continues to find gainful employment on the air.

JULIA SERANO ("Skirt Chasers") is a writer, spoken word artist, scientist, and gender activist. She has presented and performed her work at universities, high schools, cafés, clubs, libraries, poetry slams, and queer and women's events across the United States. She is currently working on a collection of personal essays, tentatively titled *Feminine Wiles: On Transsexual Women, Gender, and the Future of Feminism* (forthcoming from Seal Press in 2007). For more info about Julia's various creative endeavors, visit her website at www.juliaserano.com.

LEIGH SHOEMAKER ("Urinalysis") notes that when this piece was originally published in *Bitch* in 1997, her bio read as follows: "Solipsistic Leigh Shoemaker will not rest until she has brought the transcendent stream down to earth with her incredible powers of concentration." Nine years later, she still considers the attempt to ground the transcendent to be a worthwhile task. These days, however, she's more inclined to get some rest between attempts.

SHAUNA SWARTZ ("XXX Offender") is a freelance writer who spent her first thirty-two years in Los Angeles and moved to Philadelphia in 2004. After enjoying a stint copyediting gay male porn (after all, there's no bigger turnoff than typos), she turned to the seedier world of technical writing. She is also a regular contributor to AfterEllen.com. She can be contacted at shauna.swartz@avantguild.com.

LORI L. THARPS ("The Black and the Beautiful") is a freelance journalist, author, and teacher. Originally from Milwaukee, Wisconsin, she attended Smith College and received a master's degree from Columbia University's Graduate School of Journalism. She has written for *Ms.*, *Savoy*, *Suede*, *American Legacy*, *Odyssey Couleur*, and *Essence* magazines. She was a staff reporter at *Vibe* magazine and then a correspondent for *Entertainment Weekly*. She is the coauthor of the award-winning book *Hair Story: Untangling the Roots of Black Hair in America* (St. Martin's Press, 2001). Her work can also be read in the Seal Press anthology *Young Wives' Tales: New Adventures in Love and Partnership* and *Naked: Black Women Bare All About Their Skin, Hair, Hips, Lips and Other Parts* (Perigee). Tharps recently relocated to Philadelphia after living in New York City for over a decade. She has yet to unpack her television.

NOY THRUPKAEW ("Fan/Tastic Voyage"; "The God of Big Trends") writes frequently on international affairs and culture as a freelance journalist and senior correspondent for *The American Prospect*. A former Fulbright scholar and Pew fellow in international journalism, she has reported from Cuba, Iran, Cambodia, and Morocco, and worked as a discussion panelist for Japan's largest English-language radio station. She has written for *The Guardian* (U.K.), *Marie Claire*, *Nerve*, *Ms.*, *The Nation*, and *Kyoto Journal*, and was an Online Journalism Award finalist for cultural commentary.

VANESSA VESELKA ("The Collapsible Woman") is a writer and musician. Her work has appeared in many publications, including *Bitch*, *Bust*, *Ms.*, *Jane*, *The Seattle Weekly*, and *MaximumRocknRoll*. As a musician, she tours and plays with her band, Vanessa Veselka and the Godless Moravians, as well as with the political punk duo The Pinkos. She lives in Portland, Oregon, with her daughter, Violet, and is now delving into the messy waters of fiction.

SUMMER WOOD ("On Language: Choice") is a student in the PhD program in anthropology at New York University, where her research focuses on the intersections among health, gender, culture, and human rights. She holds a master's degree in public health and women's studies from the University of Michigan, and has worked as a journalist covering issues of science and health, economics, and women's rights.

acknowledgments

FIRST AND FOREMOST, WE OWE SO MANY GINORMOUS THANKS to the staff and board of *Bitch*, without whom this book (and the magazine itself) would not exist. It's often said that no book is solely the work of its author, and in this case it's more true than usual. Over the course of *Bitch*'s life, we've been lucky to work with way too many talented folks to name here, each of whom helped make this all happen. Extra-special, all-inclusive thank-yous go to our longtime stand-up bitches: Rachel Fudge, Debbie Rasmussen, Cheryl Taruc, Juliana Tringali, Rita Hao, and Jeffery Walls.

We first discussed the possibility of an anthology more than six years ago with founding art director Ben Shaykin. Four art directors and one cross-country move later, we are pants-peeingly happy that Ben was able to design the book and bring this whole megillah full circle.

Denise Oswald, our fine editor at Farrar, Straus and Giroux, has been awesome in every way; ditto her assistant, Sara Jane Stoner, whom we plagued with our every pesky detail.

Jill Grinberg, our agent, was excited about this project from the start; we're lucky to have her enthusiasm and hard work in helping us make an abstract concept into a still-somewhat-abstract reality. Thanks also to Jill's assistant, Kirsten Wolf, who handled our many, many questions with unfailing graciousness.

Margaret Cho is a longtime inspiration and a formidable loudmouth.

We're thrilled that she wrote our foreword; thanks also to Keri Smith for helping make it happen.

We're so very grateful to our families, who have been tireless supporters of and cheerleaders for the magazine even when they weren't sure if the name was such a hot idea. Their words of wisdom, unsolicited PR and networking efforts, and occasional tough love have helped keep us going for ten years and counting. Colossal gratitude (and apologies) to the friends who have put up with our crankiness amid the deadlines for this book and, over the years, the magazine. You know who you are.

Tremendous thanks also go to the many contributors to *Bitch*, whose insight, smarts, and wit have been the reasons for the magazine's success.

Most of all, we thank our readers, who have kept us going with praise, crucial financial support, and the occasional photos of their pets reading the magazine; they've kept us sharp with constructive criticism, difficult questions, and constant reminders of all that remains to be done.